STRUCTURAL CHANGES
IN
JAPAN'S ECONOMIC DEVELOPMENT

STRUCTURAL CHANGES
IN
JAPAN'S ECONOMIC DEVELOPMENT

BY

MIYOHEI SHINOHARA

ECONOMIC RESEARCH SERIES
No. 11
THE INSTITUTE OF ECONOMIC RESEARCH
HITOTSUBASHI UNIVERSITY

KINOKUNIYA BOOKSTORE CO., LTD.
Tokyo, Japan

Copyright © 1970 by MIYOHEI SHINOHARA

Reprinted in 1974

Printed by
Kato Bummeisha Printing Co., Ltd.
Tokyo, Japan

PREFACE

This book is a companion volume to my earlier work *Growth and Cycles in the Japanese Economy*, Tokyo, Kinokuniya, 1962 (Economic Research Series 5, Hitotsubashi Institute of Economic Research). While the objective of the earlier volume was primarily to 'ascertain various features of Japanese economic growth statistically,' the present volume is more ambitious in its scope in that it also attempts, as far as possible, to delineate in quantitative terms the structural changes which accompanied Japan's rapid economic growth during the pre and post World War II periods. Such an attempt necessarily involves extension of my earlier analysis, preparation of original (long-term as well as cross-section) estimates for certain economic variables and advancement of certain new yet controversial hypothesis on the basis of these estimates.

Part I of this volume deals with the causes and consequences of the extremely high rate of economic growth by international standards which Japan experienced, while Part II specifically examines structural changes which occurred during the process of growth.

Part I begins with an analysis of two different set of factors (Chapter 1) which were responsible for the high growth rate. These consist of the essentially postwar factors as well as others whose origins can be traced to the pre World War II period. In the former are included such factors as the influence of the war dislocation and the subsequent rehabilitation as well as sharp decline in defense expenditures. The latter consists of, among other factors, the influence of financial structure on investment behavior, the dual structure and its impact on exports and the role of education.

It is often argued by many scholars that Japan's late entry into the international economy meant a greater backlog of unexloited technology. Her high rate of growth is, consequently, termed by these scholars as a process of 'catching up' with the advanced nations. While one may agree with such a viewpoint, one has to bear in mind that the imitative process of the Western mode of consumption started rather late in the case of Japan due to the firm establishment of an 'indigenous' or 'traditional' consumption pattern. This meant a higher rate of savings which was crucial for economic growth. An analysis of the role of savings in the process of economic growth is attempted (Chapters 2 & 3). In our earlier work our attention was devoted primarily to a statistical analysis of the savings function, while in the present volume we go into a detailed analysis of the savings ratio and its composition and an examination of these variables in international perspective. Using the tools of econometric analysis we also try to measure the impact on farm household savings behavior of the increasing proportion of non-agricultural income in farm household income. Such an attempt is particularly important because during the process of economic growth an increasingly higher proportion of farm household income came from sources outside agriculture.

It is very well known that investment is one of the basic determinants of cyclical fluctuations in an economy. Japan was no exception to this historical pattern, and the Japanese data also shows the Kitchin cycle for inventory investment and the Juglar cycle (the duration of which is about ten years) for fixed investment. While we concentrated most of our attention in our earlier volume on the behavior of inventory investment over time, we try in the present volume (Chapter 4) to delineate the Juglar cycle in fixed investment-GNP ratio for postwar Japan. Such a phenomenon is not clearly found after the war in case of other countries. It is interesting to note that the upswings and downswings of the cycle correspond to the alternation of the capacity-shortage and excess-capacity phases in accordance with the capital stock adjustment principle. This finding is substantiated by a detailed analysis of the "Investment Superboom" for 1956–1965 which saw an extraordinarily high rate of increase in fixed investment and the subsequent fixed investment stagnation of 1962–65.

In the last chapter of Part I (Chapter 5) we construct an international cross-section index of industrial production. While such an attempt was made earlier and the results presented in the previous volume, the present effort is more ambitious. In contrast to the earlier index which was estimated for only 7 countries for the year 1956 the present index covers 89 nations and is estimated for the year 1958 and 1967. Our finding: In 1958 Japan ranked 6th in the level of industrial production, but by 1967 she had risen to occupy 3rd place following U.S. and U.S.S.R.

One interesting fact that came to light after the completion of this index was the existence of a considerable gap between the physical volume of industrial production and the dollar values of industrial incomes, the former being consistently higher than the latter in the case of Japan. Two hypothesis are advanced to explain the existence of this discrepancy. One is the undervaluation of exchange rate which is manifested by the conspicuously high growth rate of exports. The other is the greater degree of 'fabrication' in the evolution of industrial structure indicated by the increasing ratio of the more fabricated commodities to the relatively more primary or 'basic' commodities in manufacturing production. Since Japan has developed rapidly in the postwar period placing strong emphasis on expansion of basic commodities like iron and steel, there is a possibility that the production of fabricated commodities may be delayed in comparison with advanced nations. Consequently, Japan's industrial level may have been somewhat overstated in our index. If so, our findings should be interpreted by the reader with some caution.

Part II begins with the presentation and analysis of my long-term estimates (1874–1940) relating to personal consumption expenditure in Chapter 6 followed by my work on mining and manufacturing production in Chapter 7 (see, Estimates of Long-Term Economic Statistics of Japan Since 1868, Vol. 6, Miyohei Shinohara, *Personal Consumption Expenditure*, Tokyo, Tôyô Keizai Shimpôsha, 1967) and Vol. 10, Miyohei Shinohara, *Mining and Manufacturing* (forthcoming).

Our estimates for trends and structure of personal consumption expenditure, calculated by the commodity flow method, have been compared with both the existing official national income data and the scattered family budget surveys and found to be highly reliable. The long swing framework has been used to clarify the trends and swings in industrial output. Regarding the structure of industrial output we also find an inverse relation between the evolution of industrial structure and that of price structure. This finding may help explain the process of Japan's unique success in 'export promotion' as well as 'import substitution'.

One of the basic structural changes which accompanied Japan's economic growth was the oft-quoted emergence of the 'dual economy'. In the case of Japan, such a duality within the industrial sector can be seen from the coexistence of big business on the one hand and small enterprises on the other. We had, in the earlier volume, presented a hypothesis which connected these extremes of the duality via capital concentration in big corporations. Our hypothesis has since caused considerable controversy among scholars, and I have taken this oppurtunity to present the main criticisms offered to date together with my rejoinders (Chapter 8). Also, an analysis involving capital concentration and the phenomenon of duality in the product and labor markets is made to explain the 'formation' of dual structure. During the 'transition' process of the dual economy, we also find a clear inverse relationship between productivity increase and changes in the relative prices of different industries. For example,

PREFACE

prices go up in such low productivity sectors as food and services while prices of manufacturing commodities remain relatively stable.

Part II ends with an examination of the effects of high growth rate on different regions of the economy (Chapter 9). Thus, effects of growth on both changes in regional output and employment structure as well as changes in income and productivity differentials are analysed in detail. To mention one of the many important findings of this analysis, we find that there exists an apparent stability in the coefficient of variation of per capita income of all the 46 prefectures. On closer examination, however, it becomes clear that such a finding conceals within it two diverse tendencies, namely, a widening gap in the per capita income between industrialized and non-industrialized prefectures (or aggravation of inter-group income differentials) and an equalization of per capita income within each group (or intragroup equalization). The chapter ends with an analysis of the factors responsible for productivity differentials among prefectures.

Chapters 1, 8 and 9 originally appeared in the *Hitotsubashi Journal of Economics*, and chapter 3 and 6 were published in the *Riron-keizaigaku* (Economic Studies Quarterly) and the *Developing Economies*, respectively. I am grateful to the editors of the above journals for their generous permission to include these articles in the present volume. However, considerable revisions had to be made prior to their inclusion here. Most of the contents of the book originally appeared in different Japanese language publications. The task of translating them into English was made possible thanks to a generous grant from the East West Center, University of Hawaii, where I stayed as a Senior Specialist from September 1965 to June 1966; a major part of the job of translation was done during my stay at the Center. Finally, I must also express my thanks to Messers Bernard Key and A. Randha Krishnan for their painstaking efforts in the editing of my English and to Messers Takehiko Musashi

v

PREFACE

and Katsuyoshi Watarai for preparing the manuscripst for
publication.

December, 1969
Kunitachi, Tokyo   MIYOHEI SHINOHARA

CONTENTS

CONTENTS

CONTENTS

CONTENTS

CHAPTER 1

FACTORS IN ECONOMIC GROWTH

1. Facts about the Rapid Economic Growth

Miraculous as the postwar economic rehabilitation of West Germany in 1950's was, the pace of Japanese economic growth has been no less outstanding.

Industrial production, which fell in 1946 to 27.8 percent of the 1934–36 figure, regained the prewar level in 1951, reaching 153.6 percent in 1955, 570.3 percent in 1965, and 802.9 percent in 1967.

In this chapter we are mainly concerned with the study of the factors that contributed to the nation's swift economic rehabilitation and growth in the postwar years. But it may be useful, before proceeding to this question, to obtain a general idea of the economic growth after the war.

Table 1 shows the average annual rate of real gross national product for 1950–60, and 1960–66. What we realize from this table is that the rate of increase in real gross national product is one of the highest among the capitalist industrial countries. The rate of increase in industrial production has likewise been one of the highest and comparable to that of the socialist countries. It was 14.4 percent in 1953–61, being higher than 8.3 percent for West Germany, 7.6 percent for France, 9.2 percent for Italy and 3.3 percent for the United Kingdom. Also, it was comparable to 11.2 percent for Yugoslavia, 10.6 percent for the Soviet Union and 11.8 percent for Rumania, thus attaining the growth on a level with the socialist countries. In the sixties, however, we see a considerable retardation of industrial growth not only in West Germany and Italy, but also in the socialist countries. Thus, Japans relatively high rate of industrial growth became much more conspicuous.

The motive power for this rapid growth was the private investment in plant and equipment. The ratio of the private fixed investment to the gross national product stood at 7.8 percent in 1946. It continued to rise steadily and reached 21.9 percent in 1961. Noteworthy has been the fixed investment boom since 1956. The private fixed investment amounted to ¥ 944.1 billion in 1955, but it rose up to ¥ 4231.7 billion in 1961, a 4.5 fold increase during the six-year period. The National Income Doubling Plan contemplates to double the real gross national product during the ten years ending 1970. However, the private fixed investment as a component of gross national expenditure rose 4.5 fold during the past six years, the rate being unparalleled even in the socialist countries. Moreover, the amount of

Table 1. Increase in Real Gross National Product, 1950–60 and 1960–66

| | Annual rates of growth | |
	1950–60	1960–66
Japan	9.5%	9.9%
West Germany	7.6	4.6
Austria	5.9	4.2
Italy	5.9	5.3
Netherlands	4.7	4.8
France	4.3	5.2
Canada	3.8	5.6
Norway	3.5	5.5
Denmark	3.4	4.9
United States	3.3	5.0
Sweden	3.2	5.0
Belgium	2.9	4.7
United Kingdom	2.7	3.1

Sources: United Nations, *Yearbook of National Accounts Statistics*, and Bank of Japan, *Nihon-keizai o chûshinto suru Kokusai Hikaku Tôkei (Japan and the World: A Comparison by Economic and Financial Statistics).*

the ¥ 4,232 billion fixed investment in 1961 surpassed the outlays set for the closing year under the National Income Doubling
Plan. This explains how sharply the growth has concentrated
on fixed investment.

Nevertheless, the course of development has never been even.
It would therefore be appropriate to analyze the postwar period
by dividing it into four phases, namely 1946–51, 1951–55, 1955–
61, and 1961–65. Table 2 shows the rate of increase in real
gross national product computed for every phase and the marginal fixed capital coefficient estimated from the ratio of fixed
investment to gross national product and GNP growth rate.

I_f stands for private fixed investment, and hence,

$$a/b = \frac{I_f}{GNP} \Big/ \frac{\Delta GNP}{GNP} = I_f \Big/ \Delta GNP$$

Table 2. Marginal Fixed Capital Coefficient and the Rate of
Growth in Gross National Product

	$\left(\dfrac{\text{Private fixed investment}}{\text{GNP}} \right)$ (a)	Growth rate in GNP (b)	Marginal fixed capital coefficient a/b (c)
1946—51	8.8%	11.2%	0.79
1951—55	11.2	8.6	1.30
1955—61	16.6	10.6	1.56
1961—65	18.4	8.1	2.27

What we learn from this table is that, while the rate of increase in the gross national product declined from 11.2 percent
in the first phase to 8.6 percent in the second phase, it rose to
10.6 percent in the third phase. One tends to think that as we
pass through the rehabilitation period, the rate of growth will
naturally slow down. In Japan's case, however, it has gained
momentum since 1956 through the technological innovation
boom. The share of the private fixed investment in the gross
national product rose gradually from 8.8 percent to 11.2 percent
and then to 16.6 percent during the three phases. In response

to this, the estimated marginal fixed capital coefficient (that is, the amount of real fixed investment necessary to increase a unit of real gross national product) rose sharply from 0.79 to 1.30 and to 1.56. The rise in the marginal fixed capital coefficient from the first to the second phase indicates that the increase in production in the first phase was due to a rising utilization rate of production facilities, but that in the second phase it was attributable to the increase in fixed investment. The rise in the marginal fixed capital coefficient from 1.30 to 1.56 in the third phase seems to reflect, for example, that, with the technological innovation, there was an introduction of large efficient equipments, such as strip mills in steel making, an expansion of harbor facilities, etc.

In the fourth phase (1961–65), when the rise in the private fixed investment showed some stagnation, the growth rate decreased to 8.1% but the fixed investment ratio did not indicate any decline and the marginal fixed capital coefficient increased from 1.56 to 2.27. Probably, this may be to a great extent due to the fact that, in contrast to the stagnation of fixed investment

Table 3. Average Annual Rates of Growth in Industrial Production (%)

	1946—51	1951—55	1955—61	1961—65
Manufacturing and mining	29.3	11.2	16.8	9.9
Iron and steel	48.4	9.2	19.3	9.0
Machinery	30.8	10.3	28.6	11.4
General	37.2	4.3	24.2	7.9
Electrical	23.3	13.0	40.9	7.5
Transportation	25.3	13.2	25.3	17.3
Ceramics	32.1	9.0	14.3	8.9
Chemicals	35.6	15.3	14.9	16.8
Textiles	32.7	13.5	9.0	8.0
Public utilities	9.8	7.0	13.3	9.3
Mining	17.5	1.7	5.4	—0.2
Capital goods	31.4	7.8	24.9	12.9
Construction materials	26.7	5.6	13.8	8.4
Consumer durables	29.2	22.9	37.2	5.7
Non-consumer durables	23.1	15.0	7.9	8.3
Producer's goods	31.2	10.3	10.2	10.0

in manufacturing sector, a tremendous increase was seen in the sphere of the service industry, in which the fixed investment does not necessarily bring about an increase of physical capacity of the economy.

Meanwhile, the annual rates of growth in the principal fields of the manufacturing industry are given for the respective phases in Table 3. There was a decline in growth rate in almost every field from the first to the second phase. However, there occurred a change in this tendency in the third phase, and notable development was that the machinery output showed a rapid rise from 10.3 percent in the second phase to 28.6 percent in the third phase. Most striking performance was that of electrical machinery output which rose from 13.0 percent to 40.9 percent, and was much higher than the rise in general machinery output from 4.3 percent to 24.2 percent. A similar trend is observed in the case of the capital goods output which rose from 7.8 percent to 24.9 percent, while consumer durable goods output grew from 22.9 percent to 37.2 percent. This was the result of the widespread use of consumer durables in recent years. According to the *Survey of Consumer Behaviors and Expectations*, 15.9 percent of the 4,132 urban families under survey owned television sets in September, 1958 but by August, 1961 this percentage had risen to 71.9 percent. In case of the 2,169 farmers' families, this percentage rose from 2.6 percent in September, 1958 to 28.5 percent in February, 1961. The spread of the consumer durables, such as television sets, electrical washing machines and refrigerators, was very sharp during the period, and this was distinctly reflected in the increase in production.

It is true that the growth of general machinery output was below that of the electrical machinery output until 1959, but in 1960, in contrast to the rate of increase for general machinery, which rose from 24.3 percent in the previous year to 43.9 percent, that of the electrical machinery output fell from 62.3 percent to 37.6 percent. Thus, with the implementation of the "trade liberalization schedule," the fixed investment boom seems to

5

have outstripped that of the consumer durables boom in early 1960.

As a reaction to the 1955–61 investment boom, the 1961–65 phase turned out to be one of investment stagnation. As a result, the growth rate of industrial production dropped to 9.9% from 16.8% in 1955–61. That of machinery production decreased from 28.6% to 11.4%. Such a growth cycle seems to typically represent a pattern of the fixed investment cycle, the duration of which is almost ten years. However, in the fourth phase of investment stagnation, it is to be noted that the growth rate of transportation equipments maintained a high level of 17.3%.

During this process of dynamic growth, many industries, such as iron and steel, automobile, petro-chemicals and so on, strengthened their competitive power in the world market. Those industries which were "infant industries" about fifteen years ago now converted themselves to powerful export industries.

It may well be said that the disproportionate growth concentrating on plant and equipment has greatly changed the nation's industrial structure in recent years. As indicated in Table 4, the percentage of the value added (1961) in the case of Japanese chemical, metal and machinery industries accounted for 61.2 percent, which was higher than that of West Germany and the United States and surpassed that of Denmark and Norway. The United Kingdom was the only country showing a com-

Table 4. Percentage Composition of Gross Value Added in Manufacturing

	Japan (1961)	West Germany (1954)	United States (1958)	United Kingdom (1958)	Denmark (1959)	Norway (1958)
Chemicals	11.8	11.7	10.5	9.4	8.5	10.6
Metals	17.1	18.1	14.9	14.4	7.7	17.0
Machinery	32.3	24.8	29.0	35.5	28.8	21.5
Total	61.2	54.6	54.4	59.3	45.0	49.1

parable ratio of 59.3 percent, thereby reflecting the magnitude of machinery exports to the Commonwealth countries.

It may justly be said that the rapid shift in the industrial structure of Japan towards the heavy and chemical industries reflects the rapid economic growth and the fixed investment boom. The cessation of the fixed investment boom in 1962 is estimated to have decreased the relative weight of the value added for the three industries in manufacturing from 61.2 percent in 1961 to some 57–58 percent in 1962–66. The reason is that, according to the *Census of Manufactures*, the relative weight of the net value added in establishments employing 20 workers and above in the chemical, metal and machinery industries was 62.2–61.9 percent in 1962–66. Considering that it was 64.3 percent in 1961, the percentage for the establishments employing four workers and above must have declined to 57.1–58.8 percent in 1962–66.

Then, the United Kingdom is possibly the only industrial country that has maintained a high heavy industry ratio of about 60 percent in terms of the value added. However, Japan's rapid growth has thus changed the industrial structure oriented to light industries in the prewar period to that oriented to heavy and chemical industries and has recently raised the heavy industry ratio up to some 60%, thereby placing her ratio the first or second among the capitalist countries. It must be a phenomenon exceptional in the world economic development that Japan with a low per capita income has been shifting to the heavy and chemical industries at much faster rate than in the other industrial countries. Thus, the question of what the shift will bring about to the nation's economy in the future will need our careful study. Anyway, it will be more interesting to inquire into the motive power behind the rapid growth. Now we shall trace the factors that have contributed to such phenomenal growth.

2. Factors behind the High Rate of Growth

The high rate of Japan's economic growth is not a mere post-war phenomenon, but can be traced to the prewar period, possibly from the late 1800's. Thus, in some cases the growth may be ascribed to factors in operation from before the war, while in other cases the factors may have been unique to the postwar period.

A. POSTWAR FACTORS

1. Rehabilitation Factors

By and large, every country has experienced a high rate of industrial growth in the postwar period. Above all, those countries that experienced a heavy drop in industrial output due to war damages, such as Japan, West Germany and Italy, have achieved a rapid recovery. This is illustrated in Fig. 1. Almost all countries followed the law of reciprocity under which industrial decline and recovery were inversely correlated with the exception of the socialist countries, such as Rumania, Poland and the Soviet Union, and the United States and Canada, which were free from war damage and served as an ordnance depot for the Allied Forces during the war, and converted their industries smoothly to the production of civilian goods after the war. Thus, while certain countries enjoyed an extraordinarily high rate of growth in the postwar period, the reasons must lie partly in the rehabilitation factors. Given that idle capacity existed and the labor force, technological level and entrepreneurial ability remained unchanged, it is natural that these countries should achieve a rapid recovery, when normal conditions are restored.

The same relationship can be found in the decline and recovery of real national income and exports, but this point will not be discussed here. At any rate, if we view the matter solely from this standpoint, we shall reach a conclusion that the extraordinarily quick pace of the postwar rehabilitation will be slowed

Fig. 1. Industrial Decline and Recovery Inversely Correlated

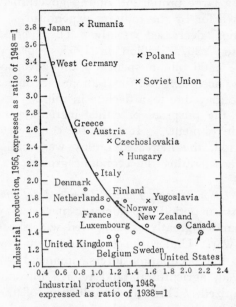

Industrial production, 1948,
expressed as ratio of 1938=1

down as the economy passes through the postwar period. However, in understanding the rate of growth of Japanese economy, which still continues to be high in defiance of the popular phrase, "we are no longer in the postwar period", we must necessarily take into account other factors.

2. *Sharp Decrease of Military Expenditures*

Under the postwar peace Constitution, the Japanese are not authorized to have any armed forces. Of course, we have the Self-defence Forces, but the expenditures are far less than the former military expenditures. In 1940, combined spending on goods and services by the central and local goverments amounted to ¥10,458 million, of which ¥6,667 million, a high rate of 63.8 percent, was accounted for by military expenditures.

9

The weight of military expenditures, of course, may have been generally lower as we go farther back to the past, but it cannot be denied that a large proportion of the government expenditures was accounted for by the military expenditures. After the war, the proportion decreased greatly. The defense expenditures amounted to ¥307.2 billion in 1965, representing only 4.8 percent of ¥6,406 billion spent by the government on goods and services, according to the national income statistics. The increase in outlay due to a decline in military expenditure may be used for the purposes of either increasing consumption or expanding investment. It may be considered that, in the postwar period, the increased outlay was employed for investment, thus accelerating the economic growth.

3. Roles of Labor Unions, Land Reform and Inflation

In the postwar period, the domestic market may be considered to have expanded greatly as compared with the 1926–35 period before the war. Under the economic democratization policy pursued by the occupation forces, financial groups (*zaibatsu*) were dissolved, agricultural land reform introduced and labor unions organized. Through introduction of the land reform, some 5 million acres of tenant land was released to farmers, and absentee landlords ceased to exist. Some three-fourths of agricultural land owned by landlords were transfered to tenants. The share of farmers' income increased and that of landlords, which had been remarkably large before the war, declined sharply. Moreover, upon the request of the occupation forces, war time labor regulations were abolished, while organization of labor unions was encouraged. As a result, the distributive share of labor income in the value added for manufacturing, which had been at a low level of approximately 30 percent before the war, increased to 50 percent by around 1950.

The prewar Japanese economy was characterized by the holding down of the domestic market through low wages, and by the expansion of overseas markets particularly in the decade of the

10

1930's. However, in the postwar period, by around 1950, it was marked by the expansion of the domestic market and by the enlarged share of laborers' and farmers' incomes, and this constituted an important factor for the recovery of the economy. Of course, the market expansion took place within the context of acute commodity shortage and inflation. Consequently there was a decline in the real value of loans from the state funds (Reconstruction Finance Bank and U.S. Aid Counterpart Fund) and from private financial institutions, which were made for the recovery of war damages and industrial rehabilitation, so that the borrowers felt it profitable to borrow in large sums. This resulted in the development of capital formation by means of *forced savings* through inflation. In this sense, inflation played an important role in accelerating capital accumulation as well as in causing various evils. Such a pattern of inflationary and domestic-market-expanding economic growth could only be successful in a situation where the multiple exchange rate was in effect and the nation's economy was isolated from the world economy by receiving aid materials from abroad. However, under the economic stabilization policy proposed by Mr. J.M. Dodge, then financial advisor to SCAP, the exchange rate was fixed at ¥360 against the dollar in 1949, and the deflationary policy was introduced during 1949–50. Soon after that, the Korean war broke out, and so the Japanese economy continued to be inflationary until 1951. The roles that the progress of inflation and the domestic-market-expanding rehabilitation had played must have been effective in so far as they caused no balance of payments difficulty. In this sense the effectiveness can be better understood possibly by confining the period to the immediate postwar years.

4. *Technological Innovation*

The technological development in Japan may be considered to have come to a standstill during and immediately after the war. This situation may have caused a substantial technological gap

11

vis-a-vis other advanced countries. However, circumstances became favorable to make up for the gap. Japan had excellent internal conditions to introduce technology—superior educational background, intelligence as well as entrepreneurial ability. Moreover, even small and medium enterprisers were enabled to introduce technology competitively from abroad, thanks to the enactment of the Anti-Monopoly Law and the dissolution of financial groups. Democratization which had been initiated by the occupation forces promoted the modernization of the nation's mode of living and the consumption pattern and helped in the application of the technological innovation of production Thus, the third phase, 1956–1961, was an age of unprecedented technological innovation. The introduction of large size efficient equipment, for example, in steel making, has facilitated the expansion of the machinery industry. Thus, the introduction of new technology has been made at an unprecedented rate as is seen in the developments of synthetic textiles, synthetic resins, petrochemicals and electronics, and the undertakings for combinations has proceeded among related industries. Especially, the share of the heavy and chemical industries, centering on machinery, has risen at a faster pace than in the United States and West Germany, as already stated.

In assessing the period since 1956, it may be useful to refer to the prewar long swings. The first prewar long swing or growth cycle, extending over 20–25 years, continued from the first trough during the so-called "Matsukata deflation", 1881–86, until the second trough in the early decade of 1900's. In this case, about ten years since 1890 was, so to speak, a period of take-off. The receipt of reparations for the Sino-Japanese war, equivalent to one-fourth of the national income of that time, proved to be a great impetus. It was used to finance the construction of iron mills and the establishment of railways and communications enterprises. It may thus be considered to have contributed to the raising of the balance of payments ceiling, and played an important role in quickening the pace of economic growth. The second long swing lasted from around 1914 until 1920's. In some sense, this may be said to have been caused by the tremendous accumulation of foreign exchange earned during World War I. The two long swings had this in common that some great shocks from outside the national economy created within it the long swing each extending over 20 years.

There may be a divergence of opinion as to whether or not the postwar economy is riding on the rising segment of the long swing. However, there would be no gainsaying the fact that the massive introduction in a short period of technology from abroad has contributed to the faster growth since 1956 than in the 1951–55 period, and that Japanese economy is now on the upswing of the long swing. The factors responsible are different from prewar factors which had given rise to long-term waves. Nevertheless, there may be a resemblance between pre- and post-war factors in that external shocks accelerated the growth of the economy.

When this long-term wave will enter on a downward course is another problem, but the role of the technological innovation cannot be ignored in understanding the postwar growth. While the demonstration effect operated upon production and technology greatly quickened the pace of innovation, the same effect operated on the consumption pattern manifested itself in the rate of increase in the output of electrical machinery and other consumer durables.

5. Labor Force

Generally speaking, an economy with an excess labor force has a strong possibility of realizing a higher rate of growth than one lacking such condition, if other circumstances are equal. It is not only because the labor force will constitute no bottleneck there but because the relatively low wage combined with the high level of technology introduced from abroad will result in lower prices and the expansion of exports. By contrast, the

Fig. 2. Growth Rates of GNP and Labor Force, 1950–55

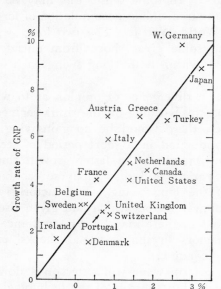

Source: M. Umemura, "Trends of Labor Force and Employment" (*in Japanese*), *Keizai Kenkyū,* April 1960.

growth of an economy with an acute labor shortage is likely to be retarded by cost inflation coupled with the aggravation of the balance of payments.

Fig. 2 illustrates the international comparison of annual rates of increase in labor force and gross national product for the period 1950–55. It suggests how closely the rate of increase in labor force is related to that of gross national product. Of course, as a result of the progress of automation, certain industries may not see bottlenecks in the shortage of labor force. However, since the development of an economy may be accompanied by an expansion of the relatively labor intensive machinery industry, as well as the tertiary industry, the implication of the figure may be evident. The high rate of Japanese economic growth is closely associated with the high rate of increase in the labor force.

The postwar Japanese economy has grown at a far quicker pace than before the war. However, it should be noted that the labor supply needed to expand manufacturing and service industries has been provided by the agricultural sector more abundantly than before the war. For many years before the war, the absolute number of the farm population remained constant. This was because a high birth rate sustained the roughly constant agricultural population in spite of the incessant exodus of labor force into urban areas.

However, the agricultural labor force, which had been almost constant at a level of 14–15 million before the war, began to experience an absolute decline after the war. According to the *Census*, the number of farm labor force fell from 16.1 million in 1950 to 14.8 million in 1955, to 13.2 million in 1960 and 10.85 million in 1965. Before the war, only the second and third sons of a farm household would resort to jobs in some other industry, whereas, after the war, even the eldest son, who is normally expected to succeed his father's job, wishes to leave his village. This tendency is an important factor supporting the rapid expansion of our economy centering on the manufacturing industry.

6. *Government's Role*

The role of the government in the postwar economy was multifarious and is still very important. The present study, however, will be confined to the role that the government has played in capital accumulation.

First, we shall explain the expenditure side of the government's role. When there was an extreme shortage of goods in the period immediately after the war, the expansion of production was absolutely essential. Consequently the *"tilting or priority production system"* was introduced, with main emphasis on key industries, such as coal mining, iron and steel industries, and raw materials were allocated to these industries by priority. Regarding finance, as the resources of financial institutions were limited, state funds were in great demand. It was the Reconstruction Finance Bank and the U.S. Aid Counterpart Fund that played an important role during the period of rehabilitation.

The Reconstruction Finance Bank started its operation in Januray, 1947, but suspended functioning in 1949 under the economic stabilization policy proposed by Mr. J. M.Dodge. The importance of the Reconstruction Finance Bank as a financing channel may be readily understood by its large share accounting for 72.1 percent and 68.9 percent of the total funds for corporate fixed investment in 1947 and 1948, respectively. It granted loans amounting to ¥132 billion during the two years, the main borrowers being coal mining (36%), electric power (17%) and shipping (9.6%). These industries looked almost entirely to this Bank for funds.

The U.S. Aid Counterpart Fund also contributed to the growth. It continued to play an important role until June, 1951. During that period when the total U.S. aid was estimated at around $2 billion, it performed the function of 'invisible' export and import subsidies under the Foreign Trade Special Account until April, 1949. However, with the establishment of the single exchange rate and with the enforcement of the Dodge policy, the proceeds from the U.S. aid materials were deposited in the Counterpart Fund Special Account. Of the total funds accommodated for financing private fixed investment, the counterpart fund accounted for 19.4 percent in 1949 and 17.3 percent in 1950. In this particular respect, the U.S. aid may be said to have contributed more to the rehabilitation than the state funds.

Later, with the abolition of the Counterpart Fund Account, the Special Account was replaced by the Industrial Investment Account. The former Account's business, together with the remaining business of the Reconstruction Finance Bank, was taken over by the Japan Development Bank. Of course, the

16

importance of the financing by the state funds through the Japan Development Bank and various special accounts declined gradually with the replenishment of private financial sources. The share of the state funds in the total funds advanced for corporate fixed investment accounted for 25.3 percent in 1952, but declined to 18.2 percent in 1956 and 13.5 percent in 1960. Instead, the share of investment in public works in the total amount of the Fiscal Loans and Investment Program will become greater in the future.

All in all, the government, through its expenditures, contributed greatly to the capital accumulation by the key industries at the stage of postwar rehabilitation. However, the role has become less important in recent years, and it is expeced that the government expenditures will be directed towards increased investment in social-overhead capital.

The second major role played by the government in the postwar economic growth is found in the field of taxation. This is outlined below.

1) REVALUATION OF ASSETS: With the development of inflation after the war, there was a fear that the enterpriser's upkeep of net worth might be adversely affected by a decline in depreciation costs, for book value of profits and excessive taxes on enterprises and dividends would be increased if the valuation of fixed assets remained unchanged. Thus, revaluation was enforced three times, in 1950, 1951 and 1953. However, the revaluation having been on a voluntary basis, major enterprisers revalued their assets up to the limits, while many of the small and medium enterprisers either failed to revalue their assets or left them under-revalued. As a result, the revaluation helped the big enterprises with their capital accumulation, while it may have adversely affected the small enterprises by causing taxes to eat up the capital. In this sense, the enforcement of the voluntary revaluation had the effect similar to taxes being levied retrogressively in relation to the scale of enterprise.

17

2) EXTRAORDINARY DEPRECIATION SYSTEMS: This system is aimed to step up investment and modernization of industrial equipment by encouraging enterprisers to carry out advanced depreciation of fixed assets. For example, a 50 percent increased depreciation is approved for three years in respect of machinery, equipment and ocean-going ships which will contribute to the sound development of the national economy. A 50 percent extraordinary depreciation is approved in the initial year for the modernization of equipment and mineprospecting machinery by the designated industries. However, the enterprises that benefited from the application of the depreciation system were largely big enterprises. The enterprises with a capital of ¥100 million and over accounted for 92.8 percent in terms of value for the year ending January, 1955, and here as well the system proved to be advantageous for the capital accumulation by big enterprises.

3) SYSTEM FOR VARIOUS RESERVES: This system is aimed at stabilizing the management bases of enterprises by counting up additions to the following reserves as losses:

Reserves for bad loans, retirement allowance reserves, price fluctuation reserves, and, in the designated industries, drought reserves (electric power industry), reserves for extraordinary casualties (non-life insurance), resereves for special repairs (shipping and iron and steel), reserves for losses from breach of contract (exchange) and reserves for export losses (trading).

In this case as well, only big enterprises have benefited from the systems. For instance, big enterprises with a capital of ¥100 million or more accounted for 85.2 percent in terms of cumulative additions to reserves for the year ending January, 1955. The total capital used of all corporations increased 3.17 times during 1952–59, of which tax-exempted reserves rose 10.2 times. This fact indicates how greatly the system has been contributing to the capital accumulation of big enterprises. According to the report of the Tax System Research Council of the

total profits of 136 (sample) large corporations, the amount deducted from the total profits and exempted from taxation in the form of reserves and extraordinary depreciation accounted for 20.5 percent in 1959. This is noteworthy since the same ratio for small and medium corporations (300 sample companies) was only 8.8 percent. As the industry-wise averages for the large enterprises benefiting from the above special measures, the percentages of tax relief by the reserve and extraordinary depreciation systems in total incomes in 1957–59 were: mining, 21.2 percent; spinning and weaving 20.1 percent; chemical fibers, 43.8 percent; paper manufacturing, 26.2 percent; fertilizer, 51.5 percent; iron and steel, 47.1 percent; electrical machinery, 20.9 percent; foreign trade, 36.9 percent; and electric power, 39.5 percent. Thus, the tax system has had favorable effects on the big enterprises as regards capital accumulation.

4) In addition, we cannot overlook the importance of measures which encouraged savings and equity investment, such as tax exemption for interest income, reduction of taxes for dividend income, tax exemption for dividends among corporations and that for gains from transfer of capital stocks.

7. Protection and Competition

There is no denying the fact that the brisk competition will always operate as a strong impetus to the high rate of growth. In the postwar Japanese economy it is claimed that the inter-firm competition was very keen, and the word "excessive competition" was often used to delineate this peculiar characteristics of the Japanese economy, although its meaning was not always clear in academic terms. I believe that there were three factors which accelerated the so-called "excessive competition": (1) The existence of a large number of small enterprises based on abundant cheap labor has become an incessant source of new entry into industry despite the prevalence of big enterprises which formed an oligopoly among themselves. In reality many small-medium enterprises belong to the big enterprises through subcontracting, and so we have a monopsonistic situation as concerns products supplied by the subcontract small-medium enterprises. An element of the "excessiveness" of competition in selling is found among small-medium enterprises. (2) The state intervention in the form of fixed investment regulation in some oligopolistic industries, e.g., iron and steel, and petroleum refining, has caused keen investment competition among firms in the acquiring hopes of higher share in their market. (3) The high growth potential of the economy due to the gap between the nation's potential technological capability based on the existing high-level education and the present technology employed, has caused a cutthroat competition in the introduction of foreign technology not only among big enterprises but also among small-medium enterprises.

Such an "excessive competition" may have been one of the mainsprings which brought about the high-pitched growth, although one could also argue that the excessive competition was a consequence of high growth rate.

However, it should also be noticed that the competition with foreign countries has been much more limited since the early postwar years. Under import restrictions, many industries which were "infant" about fifteen years ago have now grown up as powerful export industries. If the foreign trade liberalization had already been enforced in the early postwar period, I feel that such quick emergence of highly competitive industries, e.g., iron and steel and automobile, etc., would not have been made possible. If so, the combination of import restriction and the internal "excessive competition" could be considered one of the many factors responsible for the extraordinary growth. The growth of "infant industries" was not limited to a few sectors, but spread to the other sectors of the postwar economy. Consequently many of export industries developed and proved to be important contributors of high growth rate.

I do not maintain that an eternal import restriction will contribute to the high rate of growth. It is quite natural that after establishing an internationally strong competitive power in many industries, Japan has begun to take away her import barriers, and further moved into the phase of the liberalization of capital transaction. However, it must be noticed that, in the catching-up process, import restriction for some period of time may sometimes become an important factor prompting growth, provided that the nation has a strong willingness and potential to introduce new technology and expand the economy through internal competition.

8. *Capacity to Transform*

Using the phrase employed by Kindleberger, the "capacity to transform", we can say that the postwar Japan has probably displayed a distinguished willingness or capacity to transform her industrial structure. For the fifteen years between 1950–65, the farm labor force decreased by 33%. Her heavy industry ratio increased to about 60%, the highest in the capitalist world. The speed of emergence of new products, in various industries was marvellous. The introduction of excellent methods of production and high-level technology, and the flexible way of financing the more promising or growing sectors of the industry by financial institutions are also a representation of her high capacity to transform.

Of course, the high capacity to transform may partly be a reflection of the high rate of growth, but to some extent the causation may be the other way around. The prewar British economy of 1920's and 1930's was in the so-called secular stagnation, and one of the reasons may have lied in her extremely low willingness to transform her industrial structure in the face of the emergence of the strong rivals in the world mearket, e.g., Japan and Germany. In contrast, the postwar Japanese economy has exhibited a high flexibility in the transformation of her industrial structure.

B.   LONG-TERM FACTORS

9.   Financial Structure and Investment Behavior

As already stated, the rapid growth of the Japanese economy attained in the postwar period is attributable to the entrepreneurs' strong propensity to invest.   It is a well known fact that Japanese entrepreneurs are vigorous in investing.   They care less about excess equipment in the future than about the reduction of their market shares.   They continue to increase their investment outlays as long as they can borrow from the banks. They look ahead with bullish sentiment in contrast to foreign businessmen who are very bearish in undertaking business.

They are not only bullish in nature.   They will not confine their fixed investment within the limit of their gross profits or internal accumulation, unlike in the case of enterprises in other advanced countries.   Even if the fixed investment is over and above their gross profits, the enterprisers will undertake investment so long as bank financing is available.   In this sense, it may be considered that the foundation for pushing vigorous investment lies in the pattern of financing or in the Japanese financial strucutre.

In other words, Japanese commercial banks advance a large amount of funds for investment in plant and equipment, which would not seem to fall in line with the practices followed by their European counterparts.   However, the lending tends to be preferential in nature concentrating on affiliated big companies than on a wide range of enterprises.   As a result, major enterprises are able to introduce large sized and efficient equipment.   The more than four fold expansion of private fixed investment during 1955–61 period has been made possible with the help of this type of financial structure.   But for these banks the enterprises would hardly have been in a position to finance the greatly expanded fixed investment with their own profits or by raising funds in the capital market.   Thus this preferential and intensive provision of loans for fixed investment to big enterprises must have been an important factor in the high growth rate. This system of selective financing to major companies in the key industries even using state funds was carried further in the postwar period through such channels as the Reconstruction Finance Bank, Counterpart Fund Account and Japan Development Bank.

Such a pattern of financing was supported ultimately by means of loans from the Bank of Japan. This so-called postwar phenomenon has, in fact, continued to exist since the end of the nineteenth century. The pattern can be criticized on the grounds that this method of financing is based on the prematurity of the capital market, it results in excessive investment and runs counter to the interest rate mechanism. Despite these criticisms, however, such a pattern is an inevitable means by which we could catch up with the advanced countries. The typically Schumpeter type development, namely, credit creation and carrying out of "new combinations", applies in the case of Japan since the later part of 1800's more markedly than in the case of other advanced countries.

It is well known that similar to the Japanese economy the postwar growth rate of the other advanced countries was very high compared with that of prewar period. One of the important causes common to both the rest of the advanced countries and Japan is the change in the monetary system i.e.; a shift from the gold standard to managed currencies. However, another important factor unique to both pre-and postwar Japan, namely, the financial structure explained above, may be regarded as an important factor in Japan's economic growth.

10. Dual Structure and Export Growth Potential

When a country which is a later comer in development has both the zeal and strength to attain a growth it will tend to have a dual structure at home. The term "dual structure" implies the coexistence of the modern and pre-modern industries in a country. Japanese economy may be typical of dual structure,

23

since it has more small and medium enterprises than the other industrial countries, while at the same time has developed modern industries comparable to those in advanced countries. Such a dual structure may be absent in the other industrial countries since these countries have developed gradually over a long period. But the economy that is underdeveloped can introduce in a short period of time the technology which has required a long period of time for advanced countries to develop. This may suggest a combination of relatively low income level with a high level of technology, with the results of the benefits of low price, high rate of export growth and high rate of domestic growth. It may be partly due to this situation that West Germany and Italy, both having no dual structure but possessing relatively abundant labor force, have achieved a high rate of export growth. Of course, at least three other factors may be mentioned in Japan's case as responsible for the formation of the dual structure in addition to the historical circumstances under which it made a late start in economic development. They concern the nature of the labor market, product market and capital market.

It was from around 1920 that the wage differential between big and small businesses began to expand. From about that time, heavy industries began to develop. There was surplus unskilled labor in the areas of light industry and small-and-medium firms. During the period 1920–31, when prices fell significantly, wages also tended to fall. However, in heavy and chemical industries and big enterprises there was a relative shortage of skilled labor. The enterprises, for the purpose of retaining skilled workers in their jobs, introduced the systems of "life-time employment" and "payment-by-seniority". As a result, wages of skilled labor did not fall even during the depression for 1920–31. This caused large wage differential between big firms and small-and-medium firms, between heavy and light industries, and between skilled and unskilled laborers, which, we may say, have persisted until today.

24

In the product market, there was a wide disparity between oligopoly prices of big enterprises and competitive prices of small-and-medium enterprises during the same period, and this wide price dispersion led to the enlarging of the wage discrepancies between major and minor enterprises.

Many banks went bankrupt in the financial panics which occurred in the recessions during 1920–31. The total number of city banks in Japan fell to one-third, from 2,069 in 1919 to 663 in 1932. The result was that more bank loans came to be made to major enterprises and less to small-and-medium enterprises. This was a role that the selective financing in the capital market played in the formation of the dual structure.

Thus, so far as the three markets, labor, product and capital are concerned, it is apparent that the circumstances which helped to enlarge the dual structure existed in the 1920-31 period, and the institutional background of the three markets remained unchanged and was carried over to the postwar period.

Of the three aspects of the dual structure, capital concentration with the backing of the financial structure native to this country constituted a big push for the rapid economic growth on the one hand, and played an important role in enlarging the dual structure on the other.

The dual structure thus formed seems to have laid the basis for low wage level in the country giving rise to the higher savings ratio and lower prices. However, with the emergence of strong unions after the war, the basis for low wages in comparison to prewar period became weak. In the past several years, wage differentials were tending to be narrower. It will be interesting to watch how the probable decrease in the rate of increase of labor force will correct the dual structure and reduce the export growth potential during the coming ten to fifteen years.

11. The Role of Small-and-Medium Enterprises

It goes without saying, that due to the selective financing favorable for the growth of big enterprises, these enterprises

25

have always been leaders in the technological innovation in Japanese economy. This did not result in any decline in the role of the small-and-medium enterprises. We may cite several instances of wonderful rise of small enterprises to the rank of big enterprises in the postwar period, e.g., the Sony Corporation and Honda Motor Co., Ltd. It is also true that, while larger loans have been provided for big enterprises, the nature of financing has become markedly flexible in contrast to the prewar practice in which emphasis by banks was placed on financial affiliates.

Above all, it should be noticed that small-and-medium enterprises purchased machinery at low prices from big enterprises, which found them unnecessary after introduction of new efficient equipment, and have continued to maintain the growth rates comparable to those of the big enterprises. According to the *Census of Manufactures* for 1954, the percentage of purchases of used equipment in the total equipment investments stood at 4.6 percent for factories employing 1,000 workers and over, but it was higher as the scale of business became smaller, accounting for 48.8 percent for factories employing 4~9 workers. Since these are the assessment of the purchases in terms of value, the percentage of the purchases of used equipment will be far larger in terms of the units of machinery. Meanwhile, the percentage of the purchases of used equipment has been declining for every scale of enterprises, showing the spread of technological innovation to the small-and-medium enterprises. However, in Japanese economy, small-and-medium enterprises develop side by side with the expansion of big enterprises in the capacity of parts manufacturers or subcontractors and by becoming their affiliates. Big enterprises, for their part, have not rejected but rather taken advantage of this phenomenon for making use of the lower wages of the small-and-medium enterprises. In fact, with the exception of the smallest scale of enterprises, the big and minor enterprises have continued to make a parallel development over a long period, and hardly any marked difference is to be found in the pace of growth between the two.

Thus, the unused equipment in big enterprises has been utilized by the small-and-medium enterprises without scrapping. This may well be a truly economical pattern of development. The small-and-medium enterprises, in addition to the advantage of the low wage differentials, have thus been able to grow side by side with the major enterprises and, furthermore, to save machinery costs by purchasing unused equipment at substantially low prices.

However, with the permeation of the technological innovation into every industrial field, and the recent shortage of young labor it is now becoming gradually diffficult to follow the above mentioned pattern of development. The small-and-medium enterprises, too, have to introduce an advanced technology. This is especially the case with those affiliated with big enterprises. The accommodation of funds to the small-and-medium enterprises has been promoted since 1959, and consequently is causing a considerable change in the pattern of our economic growth based on the dual structure.

Recently, the percentage share of the cost in the automobile industry accounted for by the subcontracting part makers is said to amount to about 70%. Therefore, in order to reduce the total cost of automobile industry in the face of the liberalization of trade and capital transaction, the reduction of the above is also urgent. The subcontracting small-medium enterprises are now asked to shift from the dependence upon low wages to the promotion of their productivity by the introduction of new technology, increasing the scale of production and so on. In some cases, they may be forced to go out from the business of subcontract in future, in order to realize the mass production, for if they continue to stick to the sales of their parts to a specified big enterprise it will interrupt the realization of mass production, which can be easily brought about by selling these to unspecified several big enterprises. Therefore, the small-medium enterprises are now obliged to have their characteristic transformation, not only in the face of labor shortage but also of the international competition.

12. Savings Ratio

The proportion of personal consumption expenditure in the gross national product accounted for 54.8 percent in 1966, which was lower than 62.7 percent for the United States, 64.2 percent for the United Kingdom, 63.7 percent for France, 63.1 percent for Italy and 57.2 percent for West Germany. Moreover, Japanese share of personal saving in the personal disposable income being 18.5 percent, was higher than 6.0 percent for the United States, 7.1 percent for the United Kindgom and 9.3 percent for France. The personal savings ratio in the national income statistics does not mean the household saving ratio, for it includes those of non-profit organizations and private enterprises. Although this figure may involve some statistical errors, it is a very high savings ratio and would serve as a support for the high rate of growth.

This high rate of personal savings ratio is, to a fairly large extent, the reflection of a high rate of investment. That is, under the high rate of growth, a high rate of investment cannot but take place, and thus the savings by individual enterprises will increase in physical form (expanded factories and improved shops). While the savings in the form of deposits and securities will not be so large, the increase of the savings in physical form will be substantial. This is the case not only with the individual enterprises. A certain portion of the savings of general households also may increase somewhat as a reflection of increased investment.

Bonuses may be increased in the period of business prosperity. When such an extra income increases, the saving ratio will rise, as the hypothesis of Professor M. Friedman indicates. After the war the share of bonus in earned income has been on the increase. As if in response to this, the propensity to save on the part of urban workers rose from 2 percent in 1951 to 17.9 percent in 1967, and therefore we cannot say that the household savings ratio is independent of the investment ratio.

That the savings ratio of the Japanese workers' households reached about 17 percent in recent years in contrast to the average of 5 percent for the other advanced countries may reflect the fact that even if no influence is exercised by the increased investment, the workers' savings ratio is bound to be high for some reason or other.

Furthermore, the high rate of savings in the family budget is not a phenomenon peculiar to the postwar period alone. Although the family budget survey, prepared by the Cabinet Bureau of Statistics before and during the war, was based on the relatively lower income bracket (approximately ¥ 100 and below per month), the savings ratio stood somewhere between 10–15 percent. If the higher income bracket were included, the ratio would have been still higher.

Thus the savings ratio may be considered to have been autonomously high and was not a mere reflection of a high investment rate. The reasons are yet to be explored. But it may be said at least that the workers' savings ratio tends to be higher in Japan because the workers have to provide against old age and illness since the social security services rendered are not as adequate as in the other advanced countries. In the postwar period, the ratio has tended to rise because of the housing shortage, and because of the liquid assets and income levels falling below the prewar levels throughout the country. After all, something remains to be explained objectively. It may be the traditional character of the nation. By geographical distribution, high savings ratios are rather observed in prefectures with a lower income level, and this would mean that a high savings ratio remains in the districts into which the demonstration effect of the Western type of consumption has not yet penetrated. In any case, it is natural that the high rate of economic growth should come into existence when the high ratio of savings is combined with the high investment zeal of enterprisers.

Thus, there would be no doubt that, since the savings ratio has been high throughout the pre- and postwar period, the high savings ratio has constituted an important support for the high rate of the Japanese economic growth over the long period.

13. The Role of Education

The recent studies by Theodore Schultz, E. F. Denison, etc., point out the role of education in the long-term economic growth. However, we are not trying here to explore any detailed quantitative relationship between education and growth, but rather present two available statistics, Tables 5 and 6, clearly pointing out the long-term effort of education on Japan's economic development.

The number of college and university students per ten thousands of population in Japan stood as third in the world in 1958, following the United States and the Soviet Russia, and the radical decline in illiterate population as well as the increase in the number of graduates of middle and higher educational institutions is conspicuous.

According to a survey of the Ministry of Education, among new graduates of the middle schools the proportion of those who

Table 5. Composition of Working-Age Population by School Career

unit: ten thousands

	Working-age population	Without school career	Graduates of primary schools	Graduates of middle schools	Graduates of colleges and universities
1895	2279(100.0)	1916(84.1)	357(15.7)	4(0.2)	2(0.1)
1905	2437(100.0)	1396(57.3)	1015(41.6)	21(0.9)	5(0.2)
1925	3293(100.0)	659(20.0)	2447(74.3)	161(4.9)	26(0.8)
1935	3825(100.0)	255(6.7)	3154(82.5)	355(9.3)	61(1.6)
1950	4735(100.0)	117(2.5)	3718(78.5)	743(15.7)	157(3.3)
1960	5699(100.0)	31(0.5)	3639(63.9)	1713(30.0)	316(5.5)

Source: Ministry of Education, *Nihon no Seichō to Kyōiku* (Growth and Education in Japan), November 1962, p. 58.

Table 6. Number of College and University Students per Ten Thousands of Population—International Comparison in 1958

	Students per ten thousands of population		Students per ten thousands of population
Japan	69 persons	Spain	48 persons
U.S.A.	185	Yugoslavia	53
U.K. (1957)	42	India	21
W. Germany	33	Ceylon	9
France	50	Thailand	22
U.S.S.R. (1959)	108	Mexico	38
Sweden	38	Brazil	14
Denmark	31	Egypt	39
Italy	33	Nigeria	5

Source: Same as Table 4.

proceeded to higher schools was 67.4% in 1965, and those who went on to universities among graduates of high schools was 24.5% in the same year. A cutthroat competition of applicants for admission to universities represents the people's extremely high desire to have their boys and girls enter universities.

14. Other Factors, e.g., Entrepreneurship

In addition to the above, there may be various long-term factors contributing to the high rate of growth. For example, they sometimes take up the role of entrepreneurship, nation's character, etc. Once, Max Weber discussed the role of the protestantism for the development of industrial capitalism. We had almost no protestantism in the early phase of industrialization. But, the Confucianism which prevailed in the Tokugawa period impressed upon the people that the frugality and assiduity are respectable virtues. After Meiji Restoration, many *samurais* worked in banks, railroad, etc., and other public works. It must be pointed out that they were strong nationalists in their thinking and by their efforts tried to promote their industry, enrich the nation and eventually strengthen the defence power.

It should be noted that the intellectuals then mostly consisted of *samurai*. They wished to transform the nation into a modern state, and to that end they travelled all around the world exploring avenues of new knowledge. Typical and famous among them was *Eiichi Shibusawa*.[1]

There was another group, individual enterprisers with the adventurous and intrepid spirit which came into being during the days of storm and stress. For instance while *Mitsui* and *Iwasaki* (*Mitsubishi*) took advantage of the politico-business relationship with the Meiji government and, accumulated an extraordinary wealth, *Yasuda* earned a tremendous amount of profit in the inflationary period before and after the Restoration. Those who were successful, extended the field of their business. While *samurai* who worked in the corporations tried to steadily develop their own businesses, these individual enterprisers tried to expand to variety of other businesses. *Mitsui* encroached on to the fields of mining, foreign trade, and manufacturing, in addition to banking. *Iwasaki* began to enter into such fields as banking and mining besides their main business, namely shipbuilding and shipping. These marked the beginning of the formation of Zaibatsu in the economy.

Thus one saw an interesting combination of forces in that the *samurai* class with a strong and steady feeling of social responsibility only worked in industries with a public flavor like banks, insurance and railroad, while the individual enterprisers with active vitality and adventurous spirit tried to expand their influence into various other industries. The former laid the foundation which enabled the "take-off" of the Meiji economy, and the latter provided the dynamic stimulus which pushed forward the Japanese economy in that direction.

Of course, the nature and role of entrepreneurship may have changed afterwards. When the big Zaibatsus were constructed in the Taishô period, the "personal" nature of entrepreneurship

---

1) See, for instance, Johannes Hirschmeier, *The Origins of Entrepreneurship in Meiji Japan*, Harvard University Press, 1964.

was considerably blurred. And particularly in the postwar period which saw a phenomenal economic progress, some different viewpoint must be adhered in order to tackle this problem. However, studies pertaining to these fields are still in an infant stage.

3. Future of High Rate of Growth

The postwar rapid economic growth has thus been caused by the essentially long-term and structural factors such as financial structure, dual structure, high investment and savings ratios, export growth, high educational standard and entrepreneurship on the one hand, and on the other by such postwar factors as rehabilitation factors, expansion of domestic market, sharp decrease in military expenditures and the government measures for capital accumulation, the unique combination of import restriction for promoting "infant industries" and keen interfirm competition, in addition to the technological innovation, which is the most important of all. While the innovation may give rise to high surges in the long-term swing of the postwar economy, question is how long this rapid growth will last.

With the extremely dynamic expansion in the sixties, the gross national product of Japan in 1967 reached $ 115.5 billion, which constituted 14.6% of the United States ($ 789.7 billion), but surpassed France ($108.9 billion), the United Kingdom ($ 109.8 billion) and Italy ($ 67.0 billion) and approached the level of West Germany ($ 120.9 billion). It is expected that Japan's GNP will definitely exceed that of West Germany in 1968 and so from 1968 onward Japan will be placed the third in the world, in terms of level of GNP succeeding the United States and the Soviet Union.

However, despite such increase in aggregate GNP level it is often pointed out that the GNP or national income per capita of population in Japan is extremely low; i.e., her national income per capita in 1967 is $ 921, while that of the United States

33

Table 7. Alternative Courses of Japan's Future Per Capita Income

	Assumptions		
	14% growth	9% growth	7% growth
1967	$921	$921	$921
68	1050	1004	985
69	1197	1094	1054
70	1365	1193	1128
71	1556	1300	1207
72	1773	1417	1292
73	2022	1545	1382
74	2305	1684	1479
75	2627	1835	1582
76	3000	2000	1693
77	3414	2180	1812
78	3892	2377	1939
79	4437	2590	2074
80	5059	2824	2219
81	5767	3078	2375
82	6574	3355	2541
83	7494	3657	2719
84	8544	3986	2909
85	9740	4344	3113

is $ 3,279, that of Sweden, Switzerland, Canada, etc. are $ 2,400–2,000, and that of Denmark, New Zealand, Australia, West Germany, Norway, France, the United Kingdom, Belgium, Netherlands, etc. are $ 1,900–1,400. Nevertheless, we can easily anticipate that given the present high rate of growth, even in terms of per capita income, Japan will soon catch up with the present level of advanced Western countries. Table 7 is a numerical computation of alternative courses of per capita national income of Japan in current prices under the three assumption of annual per capita income growth rates (14%, 9% and 7%). If we assume 14% per capita growth rate, then Japan will catch up with the *present* U.S. level of per capita income in 1977 (after ten years from 1967). If 9% is assumed, then 1982 (fifteen years later) will be the year when she will catch up. If a more modest growth rate of 7% is assumed, then she can catch up only after nineteen years. In the past several years the 14% per capita growth (in money terms) has been found to be realistic, but if we take into account price rise and stick to real terms then 9% per capita growth should be selected. Even so, during coming fifteen years Japan is expected to catch up with the *present* U.S. level. The *present* European level can be more quickly surpassed.

However, these inferences are based on the assumption of a constant growth rate. Are there any factors which will negate this assumption, and slow down her growth rate? First, the increase in birth rate consequent to the baby boom immediately after the war has tended to decline, resulting in a slower rate of increase in labor force in the near future. Thus, Japan is expected to shift from the phase of semi-unlimited supply of labor to that of limited supply of labor, which may cause some slowing-down of growth rate through increase of wage cost in more labor-intensive industries and its indirect contribution to general cost-push inflation. This will weaken Japans price-competing capability in the world market and may dercease her export potential and consequently the domestic growth rate. However, such an analysis assumes away, the role of an accelerated technical progress in future. According to the U.S. experience (see Denison's study)[2], a considerable part of the economic growth for 1909–29 can be attributed to an increase in labor and capital, while for 1929–57 the contribution of labor and capital to the overall growth rate decreased to less than one-third thereby increasing the relative role of education and technology. If Japanese economy is to be subject to such similar influences as in the United States, then the above labor-shortage bottleneck will, to that extent, be mitigated. But, we must also take into consideration the contrary experience of West

---

2) E.F. Denison, *The Sources of Economic Growth in the United States and the Alternatives before Us*, New York, 1962.

Germany, where with a drop in the migration of refugees from East Germany, the resulting labor-shortage seems to have decidedly brought about a decline in growth rate.

Second, another point to be considered is that in the sixties the high capacity to transform in the case of big-business groups became one of the mainsprings of high rate of growth. However, in the future if the capacity to transform of small enterprises and peasants is not sufficiently high, it may turn out to be one of the important bottlenecks to future growth. If the transformation (shift to the production of more growing commodities, adoption of more cost-reducing method of production, etc.) is not readily resorted to, the price rise of food and small-industry products may be inevitable. In recent years since 1960, the rise of food price has been conspicuous and has constituted about 40% of the rise of overall consumer price index. If these are transferred to the general price increase, it will begin to have some effect upon the government policy and economic growth. Probably, the maintenance of high capacity to transform is more difficult in the case of small enterprises and peasants than of big enterprises.

However, we must also pay attention to a favorable aspect of the future growth. As a result of tremendous rise in fixed investment since 1956, the competitive power of Japanese industries was condiserably strengthened. Future increase of exports of heavy industrial product may probably follow in the wake of heavy industrialization which occurred during 1956–61. Before the war, an enhanced export of cotton textile goods followed a tremendous increase in their domestic production. An expansion of the scale of domestic production will reduce cost due to the economies of scale and thereby entail an increase of exports. This was particularly true in the case of light industries before the war, but probably a similar long wave may manifest itself after the war in the case of heavy industrial products. It should be noticed in particular that the growth rate of Japanese exports still continues to exceed that of the world exports (say, by twice

Table 8. Per Capita Stock of Crude Steel and the Growth Rate in Production (An International Comparison)

	Accumulated total of crude steel for 1910–1963	Population in 1963	Per capita stock of crude steel	Growth of crude steal production between 1935–39 and 1960–63
	million tons	million	ton	time
Japan	303.6	95.90	3.17	4.8
Italy	142.6	50.46	2.83	4.3
U.S.S.R	1040.6	224.76	4.61	3.5
France	400.5	47.85	8.37	2.5
U.S.A.	3121.5	189.38	16.50	2.2
U.K.	662.2	55.43	12.15	1.9
W. Germany	827.0	53.44	15.45	1.7

Sources: Computed by Nihon Sangyô Zairyô Kenkyûsho (Institute of Industrial Material Research in Japan), but minor adjustments were conducted by the author.

as much) since postwar years. If this tendency continues, despite some price rise (assuming it will not surpass the price rise in other advanced countries) Japan's growth rate will still maintain its higher pitch compared to other countries in the future.

Thus within fifteen years her per capita income will probably reach the *present* U.S. level. This will necessitate implementation of drastic programs concerning city planning, plant location, regional allocation of labor force and so on, as well as institutional changes. Japan has to face increasing difficulties in coping with a succession of new problems. Third, owing to a rapid expansion of key industries, the saturation of iron and steel, automobiles, and other consumer durables, is anticipated to come near. For instance, the production of crude steel in Japan in 1968 amounted to 66.89 million tons, but on the assumption of 12% growth rate, it will reach 117 million tons in 1972. Compared with the production of crude steel in the United States (99.11 million tons in 1968) and West Germany (34.30 million tons in the same year), one may understand how high the level of iron and steel production in Japan is. However, as Table 8 indicates, the accumulated total of crude steel production for 1910–1963 per unit of 1963 population is 3.17 tons in Japan, which is still far below the levels of the United States (16.50 tons), West Germany (15.45 tons), etc. Moreover, we can note from Table 8 that there exists an international inverse relationship between the growth of crude steel production and its per capita accumulated total. In other words, even though the Japans' level of steel production is conspicuously high, her per capita stock of crude steel is still low, and this accounts for the reason why in the flow (production) terms the Japan's level of iron and steel is excessively high. But, assume for instance 12% increase of crude steel production in Japan for 1968–77, then the per capita stock of crude steel production is computed to increase from 5.54 tons of 1968 to 15.05 tons in 1977 (almost the same figure as that of the United States and West Germany!), provided that we use a population projection by the Institute of Research of Population Problems, Ministry of Welfare, as a deflator.

The automobile industry is one of the most growing industries in Japan. They say that the kink point in the growth of passenger car production in Western countries seems to lie around 13–15 million cars in use per 100 million population. Compared with it, the passenger cars in use of Japan is 5.21 million in 1968, which is extremely lower than the above kink point. However, given an excessively high rate of growth of the passenger car in use (the average growth rate for past four years was more than 30% per annum), we can easily figure out that, in about 1970, the number in concern will reach about 14 million cars, and this seems necessarily entail the saturation and kink in the growth of automobiles industry.

These conclusions were emphasized by the Institute of Industrial Material Research in Japan, as well as by Ryôzô Yamada and Yoshiro Miwa, the member of the above Institute. In view of the fact that iron and steel, and automobiles are important industries, the influence of their retardation of growth upon the rest of the economy must not be underestimated. All the problem rests upon the extent of an emergence of new commodities which will be enough to offset the saturation of these goods. Certainly, in the past, the pace of an advent of new commodities surpassed the retardation of some commodities, but we cannot say that the same will also happen in the near future.

CHAPTER 2

THE ROLE OF SAVINGS

1. Problem

Among many other accelerating factors, the high savings ratio in the Japanese economy may have played a great role not only in the nation's extraordinarily high postwar economic growth, but also in the long process of its prewar development. The mere emphasis on one growth factor, the high savings ratio, will naturally mislead readers and blur their understanding of the intricate causal relationships of various other factors, such as technological progress, entrepreneurial propensity to innovate, an abundant labor force, an export growth potential, the financial framework which accelerated its growth, the government's role, etc. However, we will focus in this chapter upon the causes behind this high rate of savings as well as the role which savings play in Japanese economic development.

As the late Professor Nurkse pointed out, Japanese economic development has been successfully isolated from the impact of the Western mode of living, thus enabling a relatively high savings ratio to be maintained over a long period of time. In other words, the Japanese economy has shown a particularly strong "demonstration effect" with respect to the introduction of technology and high-level productive equipment from the advanced countries, while in the consumption sphere, the Japanese people have continued to follow the traditional "reserved" mode of living not only in their home life but in their current consumption of various commodities as well. In this way, the strong motivation toward investment as seen in the demonstration effect with respect to the introduction of foreign technology, on the one hand, and the high savings ratio resulting from the negation of the demonstration effect with respect to consumption, on the other, have contributed to Japan's high rate of growth. In contrast, economic growth of less-developed countries today is being disrupted with the permeation of the demonstration effect on consumption, and, in this sense, one important growth factor may be assumed to be absent in their development. The expansion of effective demand only, without a proper amount of savings, is apt to bring about inflation and a balance-of-payments deficit, since, for sustained growth, it is necessary to provide an investment fund which will be sufficiently large enough to increase productive capacity continually without inflation. Unfortunately, in the less-developed economies, capital is almost always in short supply.

Of course, savings are not independent of fluctuations in investment, If investment increases, national income will increase and savings will also increase until they become equal to investment. In this sense, savings are a reflection of investment. While this is true, at the same time, a high savings ratio, coupled with a high investment motivation, will no doubt accelerate a high rate of growth from the long-term point of view.

2. *Some International Comparisons*

In its rapid postwar economic growth, Japan's investment (or savings) ratio amounted to one of the highest among the capitalist countries. From United Nations or other statistics, we can compute the ratios of gross domestic fixed investment as well as inventory investment to the GNP of various countries as indicated in Table 1. In some Scandinavian countries, the concept of investment is somewhat broader than in other countries, and thus the fixed investment ratio appears always to be a bit higher. However, Table 1 does indicate the rank of these countries in terms of their gross domestic investment ratio. In

Table 1. International Comparison of Investment Ratios, for 1967

Country	Fixed inv. GNP	Inv. inv. GNP	Dom. inv. GNP
Japan	32.3%	5.2%	37.5%
Norway	31.0	−0.1	30.9
Union of South Africa	23.7	5.3	29.0
Australia	26.3	1.3	27.6
Netherlands	25.5	1.3	26.8
Thailand	25.4	0.1	25.5
Sweden	24.4	—	24.4
Taiwan	21.8	2.2	24.0
France	21.9	0.7	22.6
Denmark	21.6	0.7	22.3
W. Germany	22.8	−0.7	22.1
Philippines	20.5	1.6	22.1
Belgium	21.7	−0.3	21.4
Italy	19.1	1.5	20.6
Canada	19.9	0.4	20.3
U.K.	18.2	0.4	18.6
Burma (64)	15.7	2.2	17.9

Source: Bank of Japan, *Nihon Keizai o chushintosuru Kokusaihikaku Tōkei* (Japan and the World: A Comparison by Economic and Financial Statistics) 1969, except for Japan, for which the Economic Planning Agency's revised estimate has become available recently.

countries where the growth rate is relatively higher, the gross domestic investment ratio is higher as well. Japan's 37.5% surpasses those of other countries.

Turning to the personal savings ratio (personal savings divided by personal disposable income), we have Table 2, in which the highest ratio in Japan can be found again.

Probably the personal sector, including households and individual proprietors, can reserve enough funds for their internal investment needs from this high rates of savings and may even provide a surplus for the corporate and other sectors. This can be shown by the combination of the national income estimate and the Bank of Japan's "Money-Flow Table" in Table 3.

Table 2. Personal Savings Ratio in 1966 or 1967

Japan	20.2%	⎫
U.S.A.	7.6	⎪ 1967
U.K.	7.6	⎬
W. Germany	12.2	⎭
France	9.3	⎫
Canada	9.6	⎪
Belgium	12.6	⎪
Netherlands	14.4	⎪
Denmark	9.0	⎪
Sweden	9.1	⎬ 1966
Philippines	14.0	⎪
Taiwan	18.0	⎪
Korea	5.0	⎪
Austria	11.0	⎪
Chily	−2.9	⎪
New Zealand	9.4	⎭

Source: See the footnote for Table 1.

From this table, we can see that, for twelve years on average, 66.9% of personal net savings was transferred as a financial surplus to other sectors, not being invested in the personal sector. If we take personal gross savings, including capital consumption allowances, then the corresponding ratio will become 53.9%. This indicates the proportion which gross personal savings flow out as a financial surplus.

We can construct a similar table for the corporate sector by utilizing the money flow table, but it will be sufficient here to present Fig. 2 in order to highlight a peculiarity of Japanese corporations in their pattern of investment financing. Fig. 2 merely takes up fairly large corporations, but clearly indicates how Japanese corporations are highly dependent upon external financing (debts, bonds and others=64.3%) rather than upon internal financing which is quite low (profit accumulation plus depreciation=23.4%). The internal financing ratio is 54.4% in West Germany, 60% in the United Kingdom and

Table 3. Financial Surplus in the Personal Sector

unit: billion yen

Fisc. Year	Personal savings	Investment in personal sector		Capital consumption allowances	Financial surplus in personal sector	$\dfrac{c}{a}$	$\dfrac{c}{a+b_2}$
		Net	Gross				
	(a)	(b)	(b_1)	(b_2)	(c)	(d)	(e)
1956	1272.9	263.9	603.1	339.2	1009.0	79.3%	62.6%
1957	1133.3	365.6	697.4	331.8	767.7	67.7	52.4
1958	1176.7	461.1	827.9	366.8	715.6	60.8	46.4
1959	1604.3	494.9	892.7	397.8	1109.4	69.2	55.4
1960	1971.5	609.1	1064.5	455.4	1362.4	69.1	56.1
1961	2533.2	716.5	1219.5	503.0	1816.7	71.7	59.8
1962	2584.8	843.6	1442.9	599.3	1741.2	67.4	54.7
1963	3026.2	1120.2	1806.2	686.2	1906.0	63.0	51.3
1964	3950.4	1369.1	2160.0	790.9	2581.3	65.3	54.4
1965	4409.7	1820.3	2733.7	913.4	2589.4	58.7	47.6
1966	5514.0	2031.3	3133.8	1102.5	3482.7	63.2	52.6
1967	6748.8	2478.4	3857.5	1379.1	4270.4	63.3	52.5

Notes: 1) Personal savings (a) do not fit in with the counterpart in the new national income estimate, for (a) is defined as the total of (b) and (c). The difference indicates the statistical discrepancies between the national income estimate and the money flow table.

2) (c) comes from the Bank of Japan's money flow table; *Flow of Funds Accounts in Japan 1954–64*, 1966 and *Flow of Funds Accounts in Japan 1963–1966*, 1967, and also from *Economic Statistics Annual*, 1968.

66.8% in the United States. Japan's internal financing ratio is only 23.4%.

From these analyses, it will be evident that personal savings have played a greater role in Japan than in other countries. By sustaining a considerably high personal savings ratio, the personal sector can be a most important source of investment funds. Of course, we do not deny here that personal savings in "gross" terms may be somewhat smaller, but we do wish to emphasize that when financing from personal savings is internationally compared, its importance becomes clearly evident.

Fig. 2. Comparison of Patterns of Investment Financing among Certain Countries

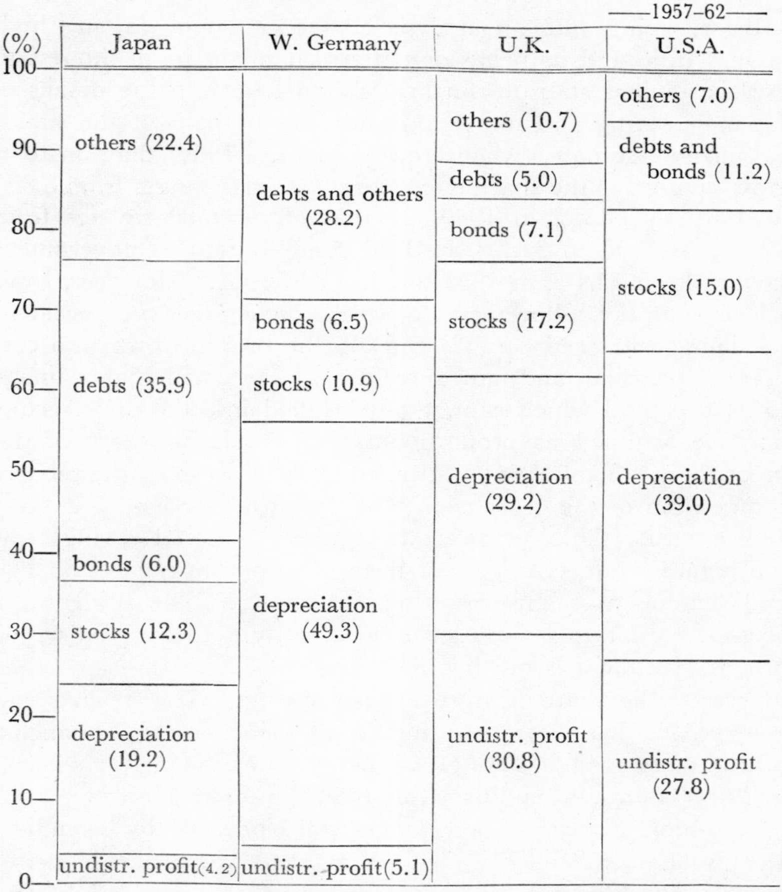

————1957–62————

(%)	Japan	W. Germany	U.K.	U.S.A.
100				
90	others (22.4)	debts and others (28.2)	others (10.7)	others (7.0)
80			debts (5.0)	debts and bonds (11.2)
			bonds (7.1)	
70	debts (35.9)	bonds (6.5)	stocks (17.2)	stocks (15.0)
60		stocks (10.9)		
50			depreciation (29.2)	depreciation (39.0)
40	bonds (6.0)	depreciation (49.3)		
30	stocks (12.3)			
20	depreciation (19.2)		undistr. profit (30.8)	undistr. profit (27.8)
10				
0	undistr. profit (4.2)	undistr. profit (5.1)		

Sources: Japan: Bank of Japan, *Shuyôkigyô Keiei Bunseki Chôsa* (Analysis of Financial Statements of Main Industrial Corporations); W. Germany: *Wirtschaft und Statistik*, Die Abschlusse der Aktiengesellschaften; U.K.: *Annual Abstract of Statistics;* U.S.A.: Dept. of Comm. and SEC, *Quarterly Financial Report for Manufacturing Corporations.*
Note: In "others", inter-firm credit is included.

3. Savings Composition and Savings Ratios

Before going into an analysis of the causes of Japan's high savings ratio and its behavior pattern, it might be of interest to explore savings statistics further and to look into the details of Japanese savings. Table 4 indicates, on the basis of the national income estimate, (wholly revised in May 1969) that, in total gross savings, 1) the share of corporate savings ranges from 8.8% in 1965 to 17.3% in 1960, 2) that of personal savings from 39.2% in 1955 to 31.2% in 1961, and 3) that of government savings from 15.4% in 1955 to 23.4% in 1962. However, capital consumption allowances (depreciation charges and accidental damage to fixed capital) can also be broken down into corporate, personal and government sectors (accidental damage to fixed capital which cannot be classified into the three sectors may be assumed as proportional to the relative share of depreciation). Table 5 is constructed in order to show the relative composition of the gross savings of the three sectors. For these twelve years, the average share of gross personal savings was the highest with 44.2%, that of gross corporate savings 33.6%, and that of gross goverment savings 23.0%. The rising share of gross corporate savings for 1956–60 may be attributed to the heavy investment boom in this period, which at the same time decreased the share of gross personal savings. It is striking that government has been continually and increasingly financing a little more than 20% of gross domestic investment. However, in "net" terms, excluding capital consumption allowances, the composition in terms of percentages will be drastically reshuffled. In this case, as Table 6 shows, the average proportion of personal savings becomes 50.3%, government savings 30.7%, and corporate savings 20.1%, for the same period. The share of corporate savings is thus considerably reduced. In order to derive net savings, capital consumption allowances are generally subtracted although this entails a somewhat upward bias, because, in such a rapid growth as Japan has experienced, replacement has always been lower than the depreciation charges. However, this does not deny that, even if the correct figures for replacement could be computed, personal savings may amount to a little less than 50%, with government savings almost one-third and corporate savings less than one-fourth.

Next let us consider a comparison of various savings data in Japan (Table 7). First, the total gross savings ratis is defined here as the ratio between gross capital formation (including surplus on foreign current account) and gross national product, assuming that the former is equal to total gross savings. It indicates that in the sixties about one-third of the GNP has been saved. On the other hand, the personal savings ratio as compared with personal disposable income was 17~20% for the same period. A problem remains: Why is the nationwide personal savings ratio higher than the personal savings ratio as computed on the basis of family budget surveys. For instance, in 1961, the personal savings ratio was 18.5% in the macro-data, but the urban workers' savings ratio was 16.5% and the farmer's savings ratio was 10.5% by the micro-data. This apparent contradiction between the macro- and micro-data can be reconciled by assuming that the savings ratio for individual proprietors and wealthy families may be much higher than for workers and farmers.

The *National Survey of Family Income and Expenditures* conducted by the Statistics Bureau of the Prime Minister's Office for September-November in 1959, covered a rather wide sampling of about 31,000 households. This involved not only big and medium cities but also smaller cities, towns and villages in all prefectures. Although it excluded farm households, it did include not only workers, but also company executives or directors, merchants, individual proprietors, craftsmen, professionals, etc. The savings ratios of these households are summarized in Table 8. From this, we see that the savings ratio for both manual and white collar workers is about 10.9%, while

Table 4. Gross Savings for 1955–67

Fiscal year	Gross capital formation			Total
	Total	Domestic	Surplus on foreign current a/c	
1955	2324.3	2229.3	95.0	2324.3
1956	2889.7	3011.0	−121.3	2889.7
1957	3494.5	3599.4	−104.9	3494.5
1958	3387.9	3293.5	94.3	3387.9
1959	4371.2	4285.9	85.4	4371.2
1960	5704.4	5709.3	−4.9	5704.4
1961	7659.2	8024.4	−365.4	7659.2
1962	7567.9	7573.7	−5.9	7567.9
1963	8994.7	9380.1	−385.4	8994.7
1964	10411.3	10401.3	10.0	10411.3
1965	11105.3	10728.1	377.2	11105.2
1966	13655.0	13297.2	357.8	13655.0
1967	16847.1	16959.8	−112.8	16847.1
				Proportions
1955	100.0	95.9	4.1	100.0
1956	100.0	104.2	−4.2	100.0
1957	100.0	103.0	−3.0	100.0
1958	100.0	97.2	2.8	100.0
1959	100.0	98.0	2.0	100.0
1960	100.0	100.1	−0.1	100.0
1961	100.0	104.8	−4.8	100.0
1962	100.0	100.1	−0.1	10010
1963	100.0	104.3	−4.3	100.0
1964	100.0	99.9	0.1	100.0
1965	100.0	96.6	3.4	100.0
1966	100.0	97.4	2.6	100.0
1967	100.0	100.7	−0.7	100.0

unit: billion yen

Gross	savings			
Capital consumption allowances	Corporate	Personal	Government	Statistical discrepancies
810.2	224.4	912.1	357.5	20.1
983.2	348.3	1029.9	580.8	−52.5
1059.2	597.1	1124.5	759.0	−45.3
1149.7	371.8	1242.7	626.6	−3.0
1361.4	617.5	1485.3	842.7	64.4
1676.9	989.4	1906.5	1248.6	−116.9
2165.9	1111.5	2392.0	1697.1	292.7
2465.9	907.3	2674.3	1769.4	−248.7
3000.8	1059.4	2968.0	1729.5	37.2
3667.1	1062.7	3307.0	1999.0	375.6
4090.0	972.7	3800.6	1957.0	285.1
4836.2	1718.3	4473.7	2139.9	486.8
5705.1	2416.0	5672.2	2784.3	269.5
(%)				
34.9	9.7	39.2	15.4	0.9
34.0	12.1	35.6	20.1	−1.8
30.3	17.1	32.2	21.7	−1.3
33.9	11.0	36.7	18.5	−0.1
31.1	14.1	34.0	19.3	1.5
29.4	17.3	33.4	21.9	−2.1
28.3	14.5	31.2	22.2	3.8
32.6	12.0	35.3	23.4	−3.3
33.4	11.8	33.0	21.5	0.4
35.2	10.2	31.8	19.2	3.6
36.8	8.8	34.2	17.6	2.6
35.4	12.6	32.8	15.7	3.6
33.9	14.3	33.7	16.5	1.6

Table 5. Composition of Gross Savings, for 1956–67

Fisc. year	Total gross savings	Gross corporate savings	Gross personal savings	Gross government savings	Statistical discrepancies
1956	100.0	31.2	47.4	23.2	−1.8
1957	100.0	35.0	41.7	24.6	−1.3
1958	100.0	30.9	47.5	21.7	−0.1
1959	100.0	33.5	43.1	21.9	1.5
1960	100.0	36.5	41.4	24.2	−2.1
1961	100.0	33.9	37.8	24.5	3.8
1962	100.0	34.3	43.3	25.7	−3.3
1963	100.0	35.2	40.6	23.8	0.4
1964	100.0	35.3	39.4	21.7	3.6
1965	100.0	34.1	42.4	20.9	2.6
1966	100.0	35.8	40.8	19.8	3.6
1967	100.0	37.1	41.9	19.4	1.6

Notes: 1) Total gross savings=total gross investment.
2) Accidental damage to fixed capital is alloted to the corporate personal and govermnent sectors in the same proportion as those of depreciation charges.

Table 6. Composition of Net Savings for 1955–67

	Net savings	Proportions (%)		
		Corporate	Personal	Government
1955	1514.1	14.8	60.2	23.6
1956	1906.5	18.3	54.0	30.5
1957	2435.3	24.5	46.2	31.2
1958	2238.2	16.6	55.5	28.0
1959	3009.8	20.5	49.3	28.0
1960	4027.5	24.6	47.3	31.0
1961	5493.3	20.2	43.5	30.9
1962	5102.3	17.8	52.4	34.7
1963	5993.8	17.7	49.5	32.2
1964	6744.2	15.8	49.0	29.6
1965	7015.3	13.9	54.2	27.9
1966	8818.8	19.5	50.7	24.3
1967	11142.0	21.7	50.9	25.0

Notes: The proportions in percentages of corporate, personal and governmental savings will not add up to 100% due to statistical discrepancies.

THE ROLE OF SAVINGS

Table 7. Savings Ratios in Macro- and Micro-data

	National income statistics (Fisc. year)		Family budget surveys**		Private deposit increase / National income* after tax (Fisc. year)
	Total gross savings / GNP	Personal savings / personal disp. income	Workers' savings ratio (Cal. year)	Farm households' savings ratio (Fisc. year)	
1952	25.6%	9.0%	4.4%	7.6%	—%
1953	25.4	7.0	5.8	6.1	13.5
1954	22.0	9.4	7.4	3.4	12.8
1955	26.2	13.9	9.2	11.5	15.1
1956	29.0	14.4	11.8	4.1	17.8
1957	31.0	14.4	12.5	5.7	12.6
1958	28.7	14.7	12.6	7.0	19.0
1959	32.1	15.7	13.9	8.2	18.9
1960	35.2	17.4	14.9	10.5	20.6
1961	38.6	18.5	16.5	10.5	16.2
1962	34.9	18.1	16.2	13.8	27.1
1963	35.2	17.2	15.7	13.5	23.9
1964	35.3	16.8	16.8	14.7	20.9
1965	34.0	17.1	16.8	15.8	23.4
1966	35.8	17.6	17.5	17.5	23.8
1967	37.7	19.2	17.9		21.5

Sources: National income data: Economic Planning Agency, National income data revised in May 1969; Workers' family budget data: Statistics Bureau of the Prime Minister's Office, *Kakeichôsa Nempô* (Annual Report on Family Income and Expenditure Survey); Farm household data: Ministry of Agriculture and Forestry, *Nôkakeizai Chôsa* (Farm Household Economic Survey); Private deposit increase: Bank of Japan's data.

    *   National income minus personal and corporate taxes.

  **   Savings ratios in these surveys are computed with disposable income as the denominator.

***   It deducts the increase of bills and checks which financial institutions hold.

Table 8. Savings Ratios in the *1959 National Survey of Family Income and Expenditures*

————September–November————

Occupation		Savings ratios
1. Regular laborers	12.6%	Manual workers
2. Temporary and daily laborers	5.5	12.2%
3. Non-governmental employees	11.0	Salaried employees
4. Government employees	8.8	10.2
5. Merchants and craftsmen	27.2	Individual proprietors
6. Managerial staffs of unincorporated enterprises	46.0	29.2
7. Managerial staffs of corporate enterprises	28.7	Managerial staffs of corporate enterpries 28.7
8. Professionals	22.0	Others 16.2
9. Others	9.6	
10. Retired and not gainfully occupied	2.9	

Worker households 10.9%

Other households 27.1

All households 18.0

Source: Computed by Toshiyuki Mizoguchi and Yuichi Kanda from the *1959 National Survey of Family Income and Expenditures* in their paper, "A Statistical Analysis of Savings Behavior by Occupation" (in Japanese), *Riron-Keizaigaku,* June, 1962.

the individual proprietors' savings ratio is 29.2%. There appears to be a contradiction between this worker's ratio of 10.9% and the figure of 13.9% for the identical year in Table 7. However, the apparent difference may be due to the exclusion of December and June in this large-scale 1959 survey, because it is customary in Japan for workers to receive large bonuses in December and June, and the savings ratio is destined to rise considerably in these two months. Thus, since the savings ratio for both individual proprietors, and wealthy households is so high, the latter being indicated by the ratio for the managerial staffs of corporate enterprises, a reconcilia-

Table 9. Savings Ratios by the *Savings Behavior Survey*

Occupation	1963	1964	1965	1966	1967	Simple av. of 1963–67
All households	18.5%	19.4%	23.3%	18.1%	23.6%	20.6%
Worker households	14.4	15.8	18.9	16.6	19.4	17.0
Regular manual	10.0	13.8	17.6	15.9	17.4	14.9
Temporary and daily	6.0	12.7	6.0	7.5	0.1	6.5
Non-governmental	16.9	17.1	20.4	18.1	22.2	18.9
Governmental employees	16.8	16.4	17.7	14.7	17.8	16.7
Other households	25.5	25.7	30.7	20.5	30.7	26.6
Merchants and craftman	21.6	22.5	27.4	17.4	28.4	23.5
Managerial staffs of unincorporated enterprises	49.0	28.3	60.9	24.0	54.9	43.4
Managerial staffs of corporate enterprises	28.2	48.9	40.3	40.6	36.9	39.0
Professionals	30.3	11.7	26.5	18.8	20.3	21.5
Others	26.9	17.4	5.9	−2.6	25.2	14.6
Retired and not gainfully Occupied	13.2	10.2	7.6	13.9	17.5	12.5

Source: Statistics Bureau of the Prime Minister's Office, *Chochiku Dôkô Chosa* ("Savings Behavior Survey").
Notes: The ratios are percentages as to income before taxes.

tion between the macro- and micro-personal savings ratios can easily be made.

Another survey, the *Savings Behavior Survey* (Table 9), gives the savings ratios of worker as well as non-worker households. In the *1959 National Survey of Family Income and Expenditures*, savings were derived from the difference between disposable income and consumption expenditures. However, in the *Savings Behavior Survey*, savings were derived from each component; e.g., "the increase of liquid assets" plus "the purchases of physical assets", minus the "increase of liabilities". Theoretically, both should be equal to each other, but in the latter survey, the coverage of the increases in assets and liabilities was not perfect. Moreover, the savings ratio was computed with reference not to disposable income but to income before tax. Thus, the savings ratio of entrepreneurial households in the *Savings Behavior Survey* may have upward as well as downward biases:

(Downward biases)
1. The denominator is the income before tax.
2. Excludes inventory investment.

(Upward biases)
3. Includes depreciation.
4. No account taken of sales of fixed assets.

5. No account taken of the difference in inter-firm credit.

We feel that (1) and (2) may be almost cancelled by (3) and (4), and that (5) is indefinite as to its plus or minus sign. Therefore, although the *Savings Behavior Survey* may involve some biases, we believe it is not too far from the actual situation. Thus we have persuasive statistical evidence in postwar data that the savings ratios of individual proprietors and others are relatively high.

What about prewar data? It is very interesting to note here the results of a special survey, known as the *Sozei Futan Chosa* (Survey of Tax Burdens), conducted in September, 1917, by the Ministry of Finance. Although the object of this survey was limited to the relatively higher income classes which were

Table 10. Savings Ratios by the Ministry of Finance from the *Survey of Tax Burdens*, 1917

Occupation	Average savings ratios
Farmers	41.0%
Individual proprietors	38.1
Governmental employees	16.7
Landlords	52.1

Table 11. Workers' or Urban Families' Savings Ratios in Three Countries

Country	Dates	Consumer units	Average savings ratio
	1888—90	Selected wage-earner families	10%
	1901	Selected wage-earner normal families	8
	1917—19	Selected wage-earner families	9
U.S.A.	1935—36	Non-relief non-farm families	11
	1941	Urban families	8
	1947	Urban families	8
	1950	Non-farm families	9
Great Britain	1951—52	Income units of one or more persons, urban plus rural	1
	1913	Industrial workers and low grade employees	1
Sweden	1923	″	0
	1933.	″	2
	1943	Middle-class families	4

Source: Milton Friedman, *A Theory of the Consumption Function*, 1957, p. 41.

subject to taxation and may have omitted expenditure on luxurious items, the number of samples amounted to 3,349 individual proprietor households. As a 1917 survey, it was an amazingly large-scale one in nature. Table 10 summarizes the savings ratios. It can be seen how high the savings ratios of individual proprietors were even before the war, even after taking account of its statistical exaggeration.

The high savings ratio of individual proprietors is evident. Let us now consider the savings ratio of urban workers. This has been increasing from 2.0% in 1956, through 9.2% in 1955, up to 17.9% in 1967. By 1967, the workers' savings ratio seems to have reached a ceiling and further increases have been limited. This workers' savings ratio is again surprising in an international comparison. If we quote statistics from Professor Milton Friedman's book, *A Theory of the Consumption Function*, 1957, we can see how low are the workers' savings ratios in advanced coun-

Table 12.   Worker's Savings Ratio for 1931—40

Year	Savings ratio	Year	Savings ratio
Sept., 1931—Aug.1932	11.7%	Sept., 1936—Aug. 1937	12.2%
// 1932— // 1933	12.7	// 1937— // 1938	14.5
// 1933— // 1934	12.7	// 1938— // 1939	16.8
// 1934— // 1935	11.3	// 1939— // 1940	15.7
// 1935— // 1936	11.6		

Source: Statistics Bureau of the Prime Minister's Office, *Sengo Jûnen no Kakei* (Household Budget in Ten Postwar Years), 1956.

Note: The basic data were published by the Statistics Bureau of the Cabinet (former name of the Prime Minister's Office), and included here are salaried and manual workers.

tries (see Table 11).   Although an explanation of original sources is omitted here, the savings ratios for workers or urban families are almost 8–11% in the United States, 1% in Great Britain, and 0–4% in Sweden.   Compared with these, the 16–17% savings ratio of worker households in postwar Japan is to be looked upon as phenomenal.

This is the postwar savings ratio for workers.   However, even in the prewar period, their savings ratio seems to have been very high as indicated in Table 12.   The savings ratio ranges from 11.3 to 16.8%, but what is made important is that the objective of this survey was the below-middle income classes (households with a monthly income of less than ¥40,000 in 1963 prices).   Even in such low income classes, these was 11–12% savings ratio on the average even in the depression years, increasing up to 16% in the war-time period.   If we assume that the same large-scale family budget surveys were conducted then as in the postwar period, it is natural to expect that the savings ratio, statistically speaking, would have been much higher, approaching, say, 16%.

4. *Causes of the High Savings Ratio*

From the analysis set forth so far, it appears almost without doubt that Japan has a high ratio of savings. The next problem is to explore the reasons why such a high savings ratio has prevailed in Japan. Concerning the savings of corporate enterprises, we can expect that it is a reflection of their investment. In a heavy investment boom, their profits will naturally increase as a function of the higher rate of growth, and therefore their corporate savings will increase as well. As regards the propensity of corporate enterprises to save, it is always very high in any country. In postwar Japan, the corporate savings ratio (corporate savings divided by corporate income after tax) was 74.7% for 1956–67 as a whole. It fluctuates, as indicated in Fig. 3, together with the annual rate of increase of the real GNP, reflecting the cyclical changes of corporate profits and the steady increase of dividend payments.

Therefore, what we should consider here, are the reasons why the personal savings ratio is so high in Japan. It is very diffi-

Fig. 3. Corporate Savings Ratio and GNP Growth Rate

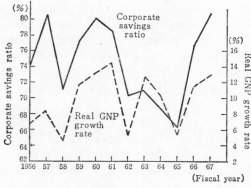

cult to explain in quantitative terms or in some econometric model all the causes of this high ratio of personal savings, since there may be many different factors operating. However it is possible to enumerate certain causes which may be important or significant.

1. The High Savings Ratio of Individual Proprietors

Since the personal savings ratio reflects the individual proprietors' high savings ratio as well as the worker's ratio, and in Japan the proportion of individual enterprises is very high, the personal savings ratio will naturally be high. In this case, the high savings ratio of individual proprietors will be strongly influenced by the high investment ratio in the national economy as a whole, and as long as there existed an excess demand situation, the small enterprises could increase their production in parallel with that of the larger enterprises, thus attaining a high rate of profit and a high savings ratio.

2. Insufficiency of Social Security Benefits

In a country where the social security system is imperfect, people need to provide for old age and illness, with the concomitant requirement of maintaining a higher savings ratio. Of course, we cannot get a good statistical correlation between the personal savings ratios and the ratios of social security expenditures to national income in an international comparison. This may be because many other factors are involved, but we admit that this factor will govern a part of the saving motives in a country like Japan, where social security is still inadequate, although improvements have been witnessed in recent times.

3. Bonus Effect

In explaining the size of a savings ratio, Milton Friedman has postulated a very useful theory, the "permanent income hypothesis." He emphasizes that the proportion of transitory or temporary income, as against permanent income, in total meas-

THE ROLE OF SAVINGS

ured income will be a vital factor in deciding the propensity to save. For example, if one receives a windfall income in addition to his regular income by writing a best-seller, his savings ratio may naturally increase, say from 10% to 40% in that particular year.

In the same way, the increased proportion of bonus payments in a worker's income may increase his savings ratio from the time-series point of view. This, however, may hold true even in an international comparison. Table 13 indicates how the proportion of temporary earnings (bonus, etc.) is higher in Japan, as compared with other countries. This ratio was 16.4% in Japan, 7–8% in Italy, Yugoslavia, Greece and Turkey, about 3% in Austria and West Germany and around 1% in the United States, the United Kingdom, France and Belgium. In general, the size of this proportion seems to correspond to the growth rate

Table 13. International Comparison of Wage Composition in Manufacturing (1955–57)

unit: %

Country	Basic wages	Special benefits for non-scheduled labor on holidays, etc.	Temporary earnings, bonus, etc.	Non-work allowances (e.g., for holidays)	Total
Japan	71.7	11.1	16.4	0.8	100.0
U.S.A.	90.5	—	1.4	8.1	100.0
U.K.	92.9	—	0.8	6.3	100.0
W. Germany	86.6	1.7	3.3	8.4	100.0
France	88.1	3.7	1.6	6.6	100.0
Italy	80.2	1.4	8.3	10.1	100.0
Austria	81.9	2.6	3.9	11.6	100.0
Belgium	91.8	—	0.7	7.5	100.0
Denmark	90.5	—	—	9.5	100.0
Greece	83.5	1.7	7.5	5.3	100.0
Turkey	63.0	15.4	7.5	14.0	100.0
Yugoslavia	77.7	4.5	8.9	8.8	100.0

Source: Ryôhei Magota, "International Comparison of Real Wages", in Miyohei Shinohara and Naomichi Funabashi, ed., *Studies in the Japanese-Pattern Wage Structure* (in Japanese), 1961, p. 377.

of each country, and Friedman's permanent income hypothesis may be extremely useful in explaining the high savings ratio of urban worker households.

4. Assets Effect

As a result of the hyper-inflation during 1945–51, the real value of the people's liquid assets holdings was drastically reduced. Table 14 shows that the ratio of cash and deposit holdings to national income was 1.71% in 1935, but had decreased to 0.79 in 1952. In the immediate postwar years of 1946–50, this ratio was undoubtedly much lower. This ratio, as a barometer of the holdings of liquid assets, has been increasing since 1951, and finally surpassed the 1935 ratio in 1965. As a matter of course, this ratio is not that of the urban-rural workers, but of the Japanese economy as a whole. Nevertheless, a similar situation probably prevailed in worker households as well.

In the situation where the liquid assets ratio had been drastically reduced, the desired level of liquid assets would have been much higher than the actual one, and this might have created a strong impetus for increasing the savings ratio.

Table 14. Cash and Deposits versus National Income

unit: billion yen

	National income (a)	Cash currency (b)	Deposits (c)	$\frac{b+c}{a}$
1935	14.4	1.4	23.2	1.708 (100.0)
1952	5012.5	545.9	3432.0	0.794 (46.5)
1955	7112.6	632.8	6277.0	0.971 (56.9)
1960	12816.5	1106.5	16396.3	1.366 (80.0)
1965	25461.6	2264.5	41381.4	1.714 (100.4)
1967	34543.3	3113.6	56321.0	1.721 (100.8)

Sources: As for financial figures, Bank of Japan, *Economic Statistics Annual*. National income is an estimate revised in May 1969.

Notes: (1) National income is for calendar year. Cash and deposits are for the end of calendar year.

(2) Deposits include the usual types, e.g., current deposits, time deposits, and ordinary deposits, of all financial institutions except for the Bank of Japan, and are adjusted by overlapping accounts.

Moreover, the discrepancy between desired and actual levels was not restricted to liquid assets. In physical assets, as well, there was in actuality an acute housing shortage, compounded by the wish of many to move from apartments into their own homes. This situation probably led many households to accumulate liquid assets in order to provide the necessary funds for residential building, thus raising their savings ratio in the postwar period. Without question, these factors operated after the war, although it is not so clear whether they were of importance in the prewar period.

5. *Age Composition*

The age composition of the Japanese population is younger than that of the United States and the United Kingdom. According to Professor Colin Clark, "Savings are generally accumulated by the young and decumulated by the old, so a rapidly growing population with a high proportion of young men should have a high rate of accumulation, an elderly population a lower rate."[1] His data suggest that, in the prewar period (about 1935–40), the proportion of persons over 60 as a percent of persons 20–39 years old was 41% in the Great Britain, 52% in France, 39% in Germany, and 32% in the United States, while it was only 26% in Japan. In the postwar period, too, the proportion of the persons over 60 years old in the total population is 29.5% in the United States (1955), 23.2% in the United Kingdom (1958), while it is only 8.3% in Japan (1960).

However, Hisao Kanamori has presented a very persuasive Comment against the above hypothesis. Based on the *1959 National Survey of Family Income and Expenditures*, he constructed Fig. 4, in which he compared savings as classified by income classes (·········) curve with those by age groups (·—·—·) curve. The latter indicates the savings-income relationships based upon the data classified by the ages of the heads of house-

---

1) Colin Clark, *The Conditions of Economic Progress*, 2nd ed., London, 1951, p. 505.

holds. From this he has concluded that, in the younger age group of less than 30 years old, the savings ratio is less than the average savings ratio of the same average income class classified without taking into account the ages of household heads. And, in the case of older heads of households, the savings ratio surpasses, on the contrary, that of the same average income class. In other words, the savings curve, taking age differences into consideration, rises more steeply than that when age is not considered. Thus, he insisted that, in postwar Japan, the savings ratio is higher in the older age households.

However, Mizoguchi has pointed out that the Japanese household with old head may sometimes include young couple, and

Fig. 4. Savings by Income Classes and by Age Classes of Urban Workers

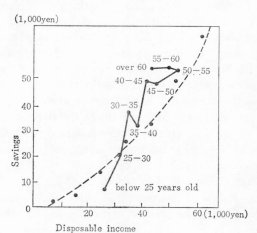

Source: Hisao Kanamori, "Why is the Japanese Savings Ratio so High?" (in Japanese), Economic Planning Agency, *Keizai Geppô* (Monthly Economic Bulletin), Oct. 30, 1961

2) Yasukazu Emi and Toshiyuki Mizoguchi, *Kojin Chochiku Kôdô no Kokusaihikaku* (International Comparison of Personal Savings Behavior), Iwanami-Shoten, 1968, pp. 102–104.

is also influenced by the lumpsum retire payment, thus increasing the total household income and savings ratio.

6. *Income Distribution*

If the relative share of wages and salaries in the value added is lower in such a rapidly growing economy as Japan, then the personal savings ratio may become higher, other things being equal, for the savings ratio is generally higher for dividend and rent recipients than for wage and salary earners. Actually, the relative share of wages and salaries in the gross value added in manufacturing is considerably lower in Japan than in other industrial countries, as indicated in Fig. 5. Compared to a 50—55% ratio in many other industrial countries, Japan's figure was only 36.9% in 1958, and 34.1% for a 1960—62 average, although in the less-developed countries we find countries in which the share is less than 30%. As a matter of course, the difference between the value added and wages and salaries in manufacturing consists not only of profit but also rent, advertisement costs, and other payments to the tertiary industry. These, in turn, will be again distributed into wages, profit and other costs in the teritary industry. However, the composite savings ratio, taking into account other industries, is expected to be higher, if the ratio of wages and salaries to the value added is lower in manufacturing.

The peculiarity of labor's relative share of income is thus clear in Japanese manufacturing. At the same time we see still another inequality in the wage payments of enterprises of different sizes. There is a tremendous wage differential between big and small enterprises. (In 1958, the average for wages and salaries in manufacturing establishments with employees of 4—9 persons was 37.8% of those with employees over 1,000 persons, and the same ratio was 44.9% in 1961). One of the most important causes of this wage differential by size of enterprise lies in the fact that we have in Japan a very strong wage payment system based on seniority in the sector of big enterprises. And the wage level

63

Fig. 5. Relative Share of Wages and Salaries in Manufacturing Industry

A. Labor's Relative Share in Japan for 1953–66

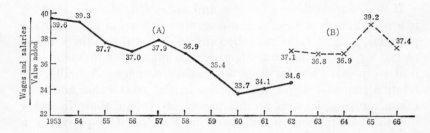

(A) → Ratios to *gross* value added for establishments *with 4 employees and more.*
(B) → Ratios to *net* value added for establishments *with 10 employees and more.*

B. International Comparison (1958)

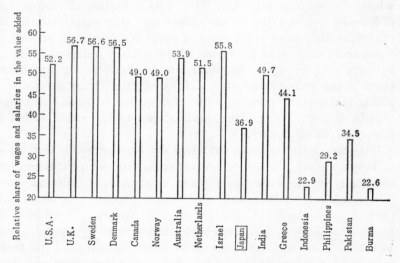

Sources: Japan: Ministry of Industry and Foreign Trade, *Census of Manufactures;* U.K.: *Census of Production;* Others: U.N., *The Growth of World Industry, 1938–1961,* 1963.

Notes: There are some differences in the scope or coverage of the Census or similar sampling surveys among countries.

Fig. 6. Wages in Big and Small Enterprises

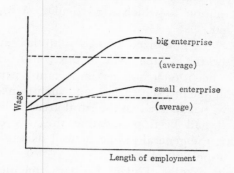

as a function of the length of employment can be shown as a much steeper curve in Japan than in other countries. Such being the case, the average wage in big enterprises will naturally be higher than that in the small enterprises, in which the wage curve is not so steep, as indicated in Fig. 6.

Professor Ryûtaro Komiya, with respect to the workers' high savings ratio, maintains that, since the wage curve as a function of the length of employment is considerably steeper in Japan from the standpoint of an international comparison, the savings ratio is particularly higher for the older generation.[3] Komiya seems to emphasize the peculiarity of the life-cycle pattern as a cause of the high savings ratio, but it can be viewed also from an income distribution aspect, for in this case both the steep wage curve as a life-cycle and the tremendous wage differential by the size of the enterprise may be identical phenomena.

7.   The Character of a Nation and the Demonstration Effect

We have enumerated so far a number of causes for the high personal savings ratio of the Japanese, but it appears quite clear that saving habits would still be different among countries, even

---

3)   Ryûtaro Komiya, "The Supply of Personal Savings" (Chapter 8) of Komiya ed., *Postwar Economic Growth in Japan*, University of California Press, 1966.

if these causes were assumed to operate equally to the same extent in all countries. This residual part should be ascribed to the character of a nation to which a particular savings hypothesis cannot be applied.

What should be emphasized here is that thriftiness is a very notable characteristic of Japan, for in this country frugality and thriftiness have been esteemed as important virtues from the Tokugawa feudal age or even earlier, and such thinking continues to exist even now, particularly in the rural areas. The Confucian influence, which had been permeating the way of life of the people, including the general public as well as the *samurai* class, was a decidely important element.

A Confucianist scholar, Ekiken Kaibara, mentioned, "Those who would like to govern with benevolence should esteem the spirit of frugality." Jinsai Itô, also a Confucianist, said, "Thriftiness is the soul of ruling the country." In the real economy, which the monetary system was still insufficiently developed, thriftiness was imperative for the Tokugawa Shogunate and other of the various clans in order to improve their financial conditions through the accumulation of cereals, particularly rice. This way of thinking has remained among people, even after the Meiji Restoration, and into the age of the money economy. The proverb, "Chiri mo Tsumoreba Yama to Naru" (Many drops make a shower), is still prevalent in the mind of the people, representing the traditional attitude toward saving.

It is not possible to analyze quantitatively this residual part, the thriftiness of a nation, as a legacy from past, but the following statistical analysis may be of some use in trying to clarify the regional distribution of this traditional attitude toward saving. Fig. 7 has been constructed, with the use of the large-scale survey of family budgets of worker's households conducted in September-November, 1959. The chart seems to indicate that there is no correlation, at first sight, between the savings ratios and the disposable incomes in the various prefectures covered. However, if we draw two freehand lines, we can see that, around the

Fig. 7. Inter-Prefectural Differences of the Urban Worker's Savings ratio

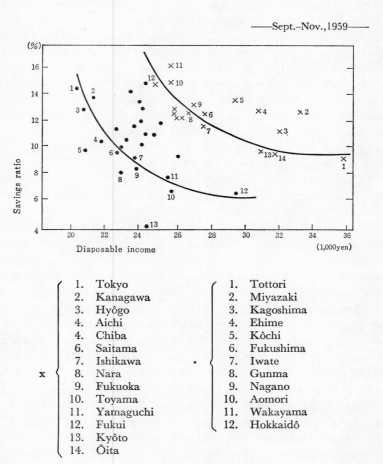

——Sept.–Nov.,1959——

1. Tokyo
2. Kanagawa
3. Hyôgo
4. Aichi
4. Chiba
6. Saitama
7. Ishikawa
8. Nara
9. Fukuoka
10. Toyama
11. Yamaguchi
12. Fukui
13. Kyôto
14. Ôita

1. Tottori
2. Miyazaki
3. Kagoshima
4. Ehime
5. Kôchi
6. Fukushima
7. Iwate
8. Gunma
9. Nagano
10. Aomori
11. Wakayama
12. Hokkaidô

Source: Statistics Bureau of the Prime Minister's Office: *The 1959 National Survey of Family Income and Expenditures.*

downward sloping curve to the right the relatively industrialized prefectures, e.g., Tokyo, Kanagawa, Hyôgo, Aichi, Toyama, Yamaguchi are scattered, while, around the curve to the left, the relatively non-industrialized prefectures, e.g., Tottori, Kagoshima, Miyazaki, Iwate, Aomori, Hokkaidô, are scattered. And, between these two groups, semi-industrialized prefectures are scattered as if they were a bridge connecting both groups.

Surprising is the phenomenon that, in taking each curve respectively, we have a reciprocal relation between the levels of disposable income and the savings ratios. In other words, as income rises, the savings ratio declines. This phenomenon contradicts in a conspicuous way Lord Keynes' contention that as income grows, the propensity to save rises. Therefore, it may be designated here as the "contra-Keynes law".

This empirical law is based upon the fact that as urbanization proceeds and income rises, the so-called demonstration effect will operate, and the propensity to consume will rise, while, in the lower income area in which the traditional notion of thriftiness still persistently exists, the propensity will be relatively lower. The inverse relation between the savings ratio and income thus holds true, among industrial as well as non-industrial prefectures.

A remaining problem is why these scattered points split into the two curves. It is difficult to explain, but the following may be termed at least as a partial explanation. In the case of employees in big enterprises, they receive benefits such as a good dormitory or a house the maintenance costs of which are charged to the company's account, and therefore they are required to pay only a very nominal rent. However, this is not the case for employees in small-medium enterprises. They are obliged to pay large sums of money as rent for their residences. In Fig. 7, disposable income refers to only money income, excluding incomes or benefits in kind. Therefore, if these housing facilities provided by the big enterprises are added to disposable income, the two curves will come much closer together, for in the non-industrialized prefecture those manufacturing enterprises which exist will mostly be small-medium ones, while a large portion of enterprises on the upper curve will be the relatively big enterprises. On the other hand, in the industrial prefectures, consumer prices will be a bit higher than in the non-industrial ones, and this also would play a role in reducing the gap between the two curves.

At any rate, Fig. 7 seems to indicate that in the lower income regions, the permeation of the modern mode of life is still limited

Table 15. Income Elasticity of Consumption and Marginal Propensity to Consume by *The 1959 National Survey of Family Income and Expenditures*

	Area Classification	Income elasticity of consumption	Marginal propensity to consume
	Whole country	0.7501	0.6136
	All cities	0.7695	0.6239
	Cities with more than 50 thousand population	0.7752	0.6281
Total households	Six largest cities	0.8505	0.6776
	Medium cities	0.7157	0.5834
	Small cities A (50–150 thousands)	0.7103	0.5867
	Small cities B (less than 50 thousands)	0.6853	0.5581
	All towns and villages	0.4599	0.3847
	Whole country	0.8857	0.7893
	All cities	0.8921	0.7931
	Cities with more than 50 thousand population	0.8917	0.7964
Worker's households	Six largest cities	0.9378	0.8544
	Medium cities	0.8199	0.7253
	Small cities A (50–150 thousands)	0.8090	0.7156
	Small cities B (less than 50 thousands)	0.8251	0.7260
	All towns and villages	0.7020	0.6306

Sources: *The 1959 National Survey of Family Income and Expenditures*, Abstract Report, p. 278–85.

Note: The elasticity of consumption and the propensity to consume were derived from among different income classes.

and the typically traditional way of thinking about thriftiness is still powerful, while, in the higher income regions, the degree to which modern life prevails is higher and the demonstration effect reduces the people's propensity to save. So, it may be expected from the analysis here that, as urbanization proceeds and the traditional attitude toward thriftiness gradually disappears, the people's savings ratio will decrease as an inevitable consequence in the future. Fig. 7 only takes up the income-saving data for the September-November, 1959 period and excludes the bonus payment months of June and December, thereby being able to explore the pure net effect by isolating the bonus effect.

This result can be reinforced by Table 15. When the marginal propensity to consume (the increment of consumption divided by that of income) and the income elasticity of consumption (the rate of increase of consumption divided by that of income) are computed from among income classes, we find in general that as we go from small cities to towns and villages, these coefficients become increasingly lower, while in the nation's six largest cities they are the highest. For example, with respect to total households, the marginal propensity to consume is 0.6776 for the six largest cities, 0.5834 for medium cities, 0.5867 for small cities (A), 0.5581 for small cities (B) and 0.3847 for towns and villages. Therefore, the marginal propensity to save is higher for the small cities and towns and villages than for the larger cities, and perfectly coincides with our speculation set forth in relation to Fig. 7.

5. Postwar Changes in the Savings Ratio

The total savings ratio is liable to change in accordance with the business cycle. Particularly, the movement of the corporate savings ratio closely corresponds with the rate of increase in the GNP (as indicated in Fig. 3) or with the investment ratio. In the same way, the savings ratios of individual proprietors will also follow a similar path with the corporate savings ratio, for it is also under the strong influence of the business cycle. Further, if the transitory portion of income (bonus, etc.) moves also according to the business cycle, even the workers' savings ratio will be influenced to some extent by business fluctuations. In this way, savings are not purely independent from investment.

However, the savings ratio of urban worker households had been rising very quickly from 2.0% in 1951 to 16.5% in 1961, and then remained almost constant for 1961—65 (In 1965, it was 16.8%).

Therefore, it can be assumed that this ratio is no longer rising as would be expected in a projection of the 1951—61 trend, although in 1966—67 it surpassed 17% level. As regards the behavior of the urban workers' savings ratio, a few explanations can be given.

1) As a result of the abnormal fall in real income for workers after the war, their savings ratio was abnormally low, but once their desired level of income, as compared with the prewar peak or with surveys modern mode of life introduced after the war, was arrived at their average savings ratio will stop rising. Of course, whether a 16—17% savings ratio was normal before the war or not is quite uncertain, in view of the fact that prewar family budget surveys were of limited scope. However, since the workers' savings ratio has become fairly stable for about six years, we can safely assume that it has now reached a normal ratio.

2) This apparent stabilization of the savings ratio may be due not only to the fact that their normal income[3] level has already been reached, but also to the fact that their normal liquid assets ratio (compared with their incomes) has been almost arrived at around this time (cf. Table 14).

---

3) By the phrase, "normal income", we do not mean here a constant income level but the situation in which abnormal declines of incomes have been removed and a normal trend of income re-established.

Fig. 8. Savings Ratio and Transitory Income Ratios for Urban Worker Households, 1951–67

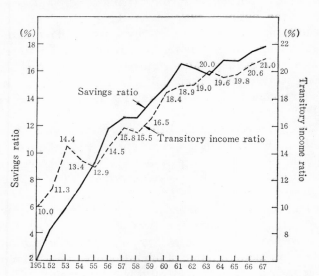

Source: Statistics Bureau of the Prime Minister's Office, *Kakeichôsa Nempô* (Annual Report on the Family Income and Expenditure Survey).

3) We may theorize that changes in the workers' savings ratio take place in correlation with changes in the ratio of temporary income (incl. bonus etc.) to total income before tax. Figure 8 indicates that at least for 1955—67 both had moved almost in parallel, if we ignore small fluctuations for the 1961—64 period.

The fact that the workers' savings ratio kept rising quickly from 1951 can be explained mostly in terms of their lower postwar income level rather than their prewar one, but the stabilization of their savings ratio from 1961 on can be ascribed to a number of causes, the priority for which is difficult to decide. The prewar peak, the new postwar consumption standard, the

Fig. 9. Savings Ratio and Increase of Real Income for Farm Households

———All prefectures excluding Hokkaidô———

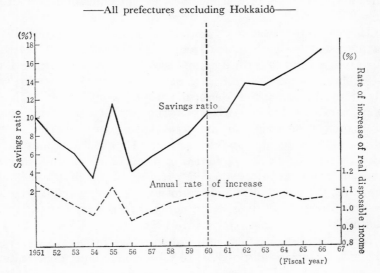

Source: Ministry of Agriculture and Forestry, *Nôka Keizai Chôsa* (Farm Household Economy Survey).

liquid assets ratio, the temporary income proportion (bonus effect, etc.) may all be important and interrelated.

With respect to farm households, Fig. 9 will be useful for understanding their savings behavior in postwar Japan. In this figure one notable fact is that for 1951—60 the savings ratio (net, excluding depreciation from both income and savings) and the annual rate of increase for real disposable income moved up and down almost parallel with each other. From such a relation, we see that the farmers' savings ratio did not have a rising trend like the urban workers', but rather fluctuated together with the rate of increase of their real income or, in other words, with their harvests. Further, we can interpret this to mean that these movements depended upon the fact that the farmers' real income

73

had already supassed its prewar peak around 1951, and this is why their savings ratio can be assumed to be only a function of the rate of increase of real income with no indication of a rising trend.

However, the situation has completely changed since 1961, as suggested by Toshiyuki Mizoguchi.[4] In Fig. 9, we see that the savings ratio of farm households kept increasing during 1960 —67, but nevertheless the rate of increase of real income was about the same for the identical period. Some other explanation seems warranted. Mizoguchi suggests that the rising share of "nonfarm income" in the total farm household income is primarily responsible, and he sets up a statistical equation in which gross savings are explained in terms of agricultural income as well as non-farm income. Moreover, although the assumption that the trend of savings ratio was not rising holds true for periods before 1960, it is to be noted that the savings ratio has continued to rise for six years since 1956.

Now, we are using here the gross savings ratio (gross savings divided by gross disposable income, including depreciation

Table 16. Nonfarm Income Ratio, Gross Savings Ratio, and Propensity to Deposit in Farm Households

Class	$\dfrac{Y^G_{nag}}{Y^G}$		$\dfrac{S^G}{Y^G_d}$		$\dfrac{S_D}{Y^G_d}$	
	1955	1961	1955	1961	1955	1961
I	62.6%	79.1%	14.3%	15.8%	6.6%	11.1%
II	30.7	46.9	19.3	19.7	6.8	13.8
III	17.4	27.6	23.1	25.3	7.7	12.3
IV	12.4	18.5	24.7	27.9	9.9	13.7
V	9.0	11.9	26.8	31.3	8.9	16.3

Notes: 1) I, II, III—V indicate the classes according to the size of cultivated land. I (less than 0.5 *chô*), II (0.5—1.0 *chô*), III (1.0—1.5 *chô*), IV (1.5—2.0 *chô*) and V (over 2.0 *chô*), where "*chô*" stands for 2.45 acres.
2) Y^G_{nag}=gross non-agricultural income; Y^G=total gross income; S^G=gross savings; Y^G_d=gross disposable income; S_D=increase of deposits outstanding.

4) Toshiyuki Mizoguchi, *Shôhi-Kansû no Tôkei-teki Bunseki* (A Statistical Analysis of the Consumption Function), Iwanami-shoten, 1964.

74

charges), and in view of the radical change in the survey method in 1958, we have standardized the basic data in order to maintain a continuity for the period of our analysis (This is too technical and will be explained in chapter 3). Table 16 indicates how the non-farm income ratio for each of the five classes of farm households increased during 1955—61 and how the savings ratio as well as the propensity to deposit also increased for the same period. We can see a kind of coincidence among the increases and this leads us to believe that there exists some kind of causal relationship. Furthermore we can also see that in the small size farm households, the proportion of non-farm income is extraordinarily high, reaching 79.1% in 1961 in Class I and 46.9% in Class II.

If we construct Figs. 10 and 11 for depicting the movements of the propensity to deposit and the savings ratio, we find the following fact:

1) In gross terms, including depreciation charges, the rising trend of the savings ratio is more conspicuous, and that of the propensity to deposit is much more clearly discernible.

2) In the case of the propensity to deposit, the differences in the coefficients by size of farm households are not so large, while in the case of the savings ratio, it is systematically higher as the size of the farm households increases. Since gross investment plus the increase in liquid assets, minus the increase of debt, is equal to savings, and the increase of debt is almost negligible in a farm household, we may roughly assume the following relation; gross savings＝gross investment+increment of liquid assets. Since deposits are a major part of liquid assets, we can now understand that the difference between the savings ratio and the propensity to deposit can be almost accounted for by the size of gross investment. The big difference in the savings ratio among the different classes of farms can now be explained by that of gross investment.

We can now see that the savings ratio has a close relationship to the fluctuations in the rate of increase of real income, since

Fig. 10. Propensity to Deposit for 1952–61, Classified by Size of Farm Household

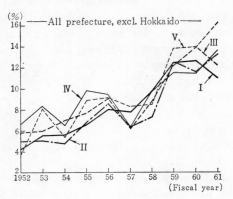

Fig. 11. Gross Savings Ratio for 1952–61, Classified by Size of Farm Household

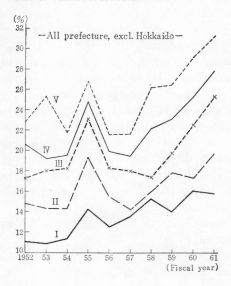

the latter may have an intimate bearing on the changes of gross investment (particularly, inventory investment). However, once the proportion of non-farm income develops a steadily rising trend, then the savings ratio may move under different influences. Although it may continue to fluctuate with the changes in farm income, it will probably be more directly influenced by the changes in the non-farm income level.

During 1952—61, agricultural income increased very little, while, for the same period, non-farm income increased very rapidly. Therefore, the rise in the savings ratio, if any, should be primarily ascribed to the increase of non-farm income. Since we can see a covariation as a trend between the non-farm income proportion and the savings ratio, it will be necessary for us to carefully direct our attention to the former proportion.

As for the reasons for the marginal propensity to save from non-farm income to be higher than that from agricultural income, we may speculate as follows:

1)   Since non-farm income has risen so fast while agricultural income has been extremely stagnant, it is very probable that the higher marginal propensity to save corresponds to the higher rate of income growth.

2)   Since in the urban worker sector, the proportion of transitory income to total income has increased very rapidly, it may be assumed that income earned by members of farm households working in nearby factories may also involve an increasing portion of transitory income. This again will raise the savings ratio from non-farm income.

3)   The increasing relative position of non-farm income as compared with agricultural income in farm households can also be recognized as contributing to the higher marginal propensity to save for the former.

6. Conclusion

We have so far explained the nature of the savings and the savings ratios of the Japanese people. The personal savings ratio has been influenced in intricate ways by quite a number of different causes and it would appear that we should not overemphasize the effect of traditional concepts of thriftiness in the postwar period in Japan. For instance, the bonus effect is quite a new phenomenon, completely different from traditional ones, and is still a powerful influence in raising savings ratio of workers.

Furthermore, we have the increase in the proportion of non-farm income, also a consequence of postwar industrialization. Many young sons of farmers now work in factories located near their parents' homes, and add into total family income an increasing amount of non-farm income. This again is playing a vital role in raising the savings ratios of farming households.

However, at the same time, we cannot deny that the traditional attitude toward thriftiness still survives in no less a degree than in the prewar period especially in the rural areas.

Thus, Japan's high rate of growth over a long period of time can be explained as a consequence of an ingeneous combination of the traditional-type thriftiness and an aggressive willingness to invest or a propensity to innovate in the sphere of entrepreneurship. In this sense, Japan's economic development can be characterized as dualistic even in its motivation.

CHAPTER 3

SAVINGS BEHAVIOR OF THE FARM
HOUSEHOLD

1. Problem

Farmer's savings behavior seems to have been greately influenced by the process of high postwar growth rate. Different
aspects of this influence such as the increasing proportion of
side-work incomes acquired by family members of farm households from non-agricultural enterprises will be dealt with, but
first we intend to examine certain extensive studies made on the
savings behavior of farm households.

To date quite a few studies relating to the farm household
savings function have been made. A study by the author in
1958[1] has pointed out the fact, first, that the Duesenberry- or
Mack-type savings function (which assumes the savings ratio in
a particular year to be either a function of the relative income
in the same year compared with the preceding highest real
income, or to be function of the annual percentage rate of increase
of current real income) is a useful analytical device for research
on postwar savings data.

Hiroshi Kawaguchi[2] (together with Kyôichi Hasebe, his col-
laborater) has made a tremendous contribution toward the
advancement of the study of the farm household savings behavior.

---

1) M. Shinohara, *Shôhi Kansû* (The Consumption Function), Tokyo, 1958. See
also my article "The Structure of Saving and the Consumption Function in Postwar
Japan", *Journal of Political Economy*, Dec. 1959.
2) Hiroshi Kawaguchi, *Chochiku Kôzô no Bunseki*, (Analysis of Savings Structure),
Tokyo, 1960.

He attempted a time-series analysis of farm households classified by the size of cultivated land and found that in the lowest-size farm household a time-series relationship—in which savings are a linear function of absolute disposable income—holds true, but in higher-sizes, the Duesenberry or Mack-type function fits very well. Yasuhiko Yuize[3] and Toshiyuki Mizoguchi[4] take a different approach in which they assume that savings (or consumption) of farmers is a function of both agricultural and non-agricultural incomes. Mizoguchi has further divided the latter income into wages and salaries acquired from industries and other income. Analyses of the various farm savings functions thus extended include those broken down by farm size, by type of farm household income and by farm region as' well.

In our analysis here, the deposit function as well as the savings function, is computed not only for time-series, but also for cross-section data (by cross-section data we mean the data based on the area of cultivated land and on the agricultural regions; data in each of these groups are mutually cross-related in our analysis). Since savings are defined as the difference of disposable income and consumption and at the same time an increase of net worth (assets minus liabilities), an increase in the deposit outstanding is a part of (and a form of) savings. The relationship between the two is given in the following formula:

Savings+Depreciation=Increase of deposit+Increase of other liquid assets+Gross investment in the real assets—Increase of liabilities

By taking up the deposit function together with the savings function, we believe we can explore the characteristics of farmer's savings behavior in a more penetrating and interesting way.

3) Yasuhiko Yuize, "Gyôtai-betsu Nôka no Shôhikansû" (Consumption Function of Farm Households by Different Farm Operation), Nôgyô Sôgô Kenkyû, Vol. 15, No. 2, 1961.

4) Toshiyuki Mizoguchi, Shôhikansû no Tôkeiteki Bunseki (Statistical Analysis of the Consumption Function), Tokyo, 1964.

2. *Adjustment of Statistical Data*

The *Farm Household Economy Survey* published annually by the Ministry of Agriculture and Forestry is one of the largest scale, most detailed surveys taken in Japan and provides us with substantial data for the study of the farmer's savings behavior. However, we must be careful in using this data as a time series because of the existence of the discontinuities owing to the intermittent revisions of the survey method; the particularly large revision in 1957. For instance before 1956 total samples were divided into five classes, but after 1957 they were broken down into six. Again, before 1956 the samples were comparatively biased toward the upper classes which tended to give a slightly overestimated figures for income, consumption, and saving per household. However, after 1957 an additional survey was introduced dealing with the smallest households whose area of cultivated land was less than three *tan;*[5] also, the sampling was conducted in such a way that it almost corresponds to the numbers of the household universe.

The criterion for the valuation method of fixed assets also underwent several changes which may have invalidated the continuity of *net* saving data excluding the depreciation charges. This inclines us to adopt the gross concept with regard to the savings, investment, disposable income, agricultural income and non-agricultural income.

The existence of discontinuity between 1956 and 1957 can be clearly discerned in the time-series data, and the filling of this gap was once attempted by Hiroshi Kawaguchi in his *Analysis of the Savings Structure.* Basically, we have followed his approach in order to construct a continuous series. The three basic surveys, (*Census of Agriculture in 1950, Temporary Basic Survey of Agriculture in 1955,* and the *World Census of Agriculture and Forestry in 1960*) were taken as benchmarks, and the numbers of farm

5)   1 tan = 0.245 acre.

81

households in the three years—classified by size as well as farm region—were assumed as the populations; the intermediate years were then estimated by linear interpolation. Having these figures of farm households classified by size and by region as weights, we have estimated the average disposable income and savings per household by size in each region and year. As a period of analysis, we selected the ten years 1952–61, and the 1961 weights were extrapolated by their trends for the 1955–60 period.

The detailed statistics will not be presented here; we will use the following notations for variables employed in our analysis (these are converted to real terms by the farm consumers' price index with 1955 = 100).

Y^G_{ag}	gross agricultural income	Y^n_{ag}	net agricultural income
Y^G_{nag}	gross non-agricultural income	Y^n_{nag}	net non-agricultural income
Y^G	gross income	Y^n	net income
Y^G_d	gross disposable income	Y^n_D	net disposable income
S^G	gross savings	S^n	net savings
I^G	gross investment	I^n	net investment
S_D	increase of deposits outstanding	L	increase of liabilities outstanding
C	consumption including D_h	C^n	consumption excluding D_h
D_{ag}	depreciation charges accruing to and due to farm operation		
D_{nag}	depreciation charges to be included in nonfarm expenditures (mostly due to nonfarm business)		
D_h	depreciation charges to be included as household expenses (in relation to residences, etc.)		

The "gross" concept normally includes depreciation charges, but in dealing with the data of the *Farm Household Economy Survey* special care must be taken since the mere addition of $(D_{ag}+D_{nag}+D_h)$ to the net value will not always lead exactly to the gross value. In terms of the above notations the numerical relationship among the different magnitudes can be set up as follows:

$$Y^G_{ag} = Y^n_{ag} + D_{ag}; \qquad\qquad Y^G_{nag} = Y^n_{nag} + D_{nag}$$
$$Y^G = Y^n + D_{ag} + D_{nag}; \qquad Y^G_d = Y^n_d + D_{ag} + D_{nag}$$
$$Y^g_d - C^n = S^G; \qquad\qquad Y^n_d - C^n = S^n + D_h$$
$$S^G = Y^n_d + D_{ag} + D_{nag} - C^n$$
$$= S^n + D_h + D_{ag} + D_{nag}$$

In other words, in order to convert Y^n_{ag}, or Y^n_{nag} to gross terms the mere addition of D_{ag} or D_{nag} will do, and the shift from Y^n_d to Y^G_d requires an addition of $(D_{ag} + D_{nag})$. However, in order to "grossify" S^n, we need further to add D_h in addition to $(D_{aG} + D_{nag})$. This also holds true in the "grossification" of investment. These relationships can be more clearly seen in Fig. 1.

Fig. 1. Gross and Net Concepts in the *Farm Household Economy Survey*

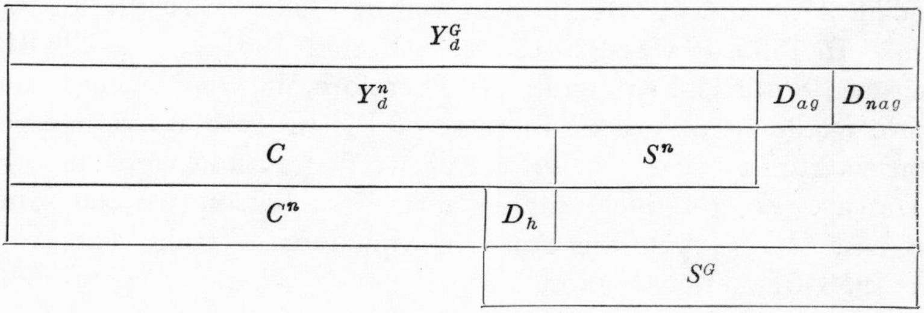

Y^G_d				
Y^n_d			D_{ag}	D_{nag}
C		S^n		
C^n	D_h			
		S^G		

We are going to make an analysis of the farmer's savings behavior in gross terms. This will not simply entail an analysis of the household net savings behavior. Since the valuation of fixed assets as the base of the computation of depreciation charges changes very often and the depreciation rate is not always the same, however, it becomes inevitable that we adopt the "gross" concept and minimize the irregularity factors in the time-series analysis of savings behavior.

3. *Deposit Function*

Before taking up the savings function, the deposit function will be computed to explore the liquid assets form of savings behavior, particularly in its deposit form. We will then compare it with the behavior of all savings as well as investment in assets and changes in liability.

After a few experimentations with functions, we have found the following formula to be preferable:

$$S_D = a + b Y^G_{nag} + c Y^G_{ag} + d \Delta Y^G_d$$

By fitting the above over the period 1953-61 for each class farm determined by cultivated land area (for all prefectures, excluding Hokkaidô), we have obtained those results indicated in Table 1.

Actually, the increase of Y^G_{ag} (real gross agricultural income) in this period was very minor. There are fluctuations in it, and in 1952 it was 201,211 yen, but in 1958, it was still 200,979 yen. In 1955, it was 228,168 yen, but in 1961 it was 228,818 yen (see Statistical Appendix). Therefore, it would seem that there would be almost no increase of Y^G_{ag} in its total average per household of all size-classes if the above fluctuations were smoothed away. In relatively higher farm-size classes, we see some increase of Y^G_{ag}, but it is not so conspicuous. Its increase rate for 1958–61 in the highest size (the fifth) class was only 23%. In the lowest size (the first) class, Y^g_{ag} actually decreased from 87,643 yen in 1953 to 77,826 yen in 1961. Turning to the non-agricultural income per household, we see the very surprising result that the lower the size, the higher the level of non-agricultural income and that its increase rate for 1953–61 was relatively higher in the relatively lower size-classes (78% increase in the first size-class, and 20% in the fifth size-class).

Any changes in the total income or the disposable income should be viewed as involving such changes of composition. In this sense, the procedure of Yuize and Mizoguchi which adopts

Table 1. Time-Series Deposit Function for All Prefectures by Area of Cultivated Land

$$S_D = a + b\,Y^G_{nag} + c\,Y^G_{ag} + d_\Delta Y^G_d$$

By Area	a	b	c	d	R^2
	−28,709.75	0.41258			0.86487
Average of	(9,485.74)	(0.06164)			
all	− 80,300.40	0.35151	0.29046		0.92489
prefectures	(24,766.18)	(0.05693)	(0.13264)		
	−102,140.61	0.37395	0.38826	−0.13545	0.93581
	(34,498.50)	(0.06258)	(0.17116)	(0.14683)	
	− 23,044.10	0.23595			0.90789
	(6,278.15)	(0.02840)			
I size-class	− 45,389.87	0.26301	0.19607		0.91713
	(28,051.95)	(0.04404)	(0.23958)		
	− 47,065.57	0.27808	0.19410	−0.08875	0.92055
	(30,304.75)	(0.05734)	(0.25701)	(0.19138)	
	− 27,917.03	0.43612			0.84686
	(9,507.26)	(0.07009)			
II size-class	− 96,779.08	0.42349	0.34639		0.91811
	(31,058.21)	(0.05564)	(0.15160)		
	−114,314.52	0.46279	0.41475	−0.12554	0.92288
	(45,676.42)	(0.09221)	(0.20275)	(0.22593)	
	− 18,019.79	0.61741			0.73093
	(13,385.96)	(0.14159)			
III size-class	− 50,639.75	0.51313	0.13251		0.76751
	(36,158.83)	(0.17812)	(0.13637)		
	− 98,069.83	0.46316	0.29994	−0.10855	0.79083
	(73,813.93)	(0.19884)	(0.26529)	(0.14513)	
	− 19,172.32	0.83789			0.61209
	(20,706.98)	(0.25211)			
IV size-class	−135,787.37	0.44369	0.34944		0.87820
	(34,559.39)	(0.18744)	(0.09651)		
	−137,366.29	0.44460	0.35326	−0.00833	0.87827
	(47,971.34)	(0.20597)	(0.12748)	(0.15536)	
	−112,354.62	2.42982			0.59129
	(56,889.28)	(0.76354)			
V size-class	−284,166.66	1.14793	0.44705		0.93011
	(40,748.40)	(0.41568)	(0.08289)		
	−291,091.48	1.13316	0.46147	−0.02945	0.93100
	(52,038.40)	(0.45615)	(0.10654)	(0.11550)	

Fig. 2. Patterns of Changes in Agricultural and Non-agricultural Incomes for All Prefectures

——in 1955 prices——

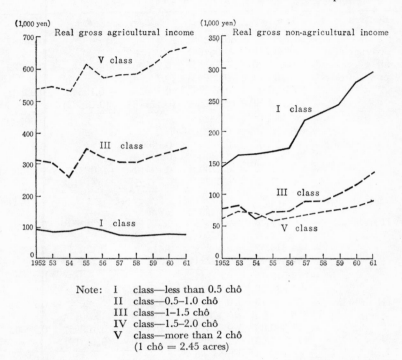

Note:　I　class—less than 0.5 chô
　　　　II　class—0.5–1.0 chô
　　　　III　class—1–1.5 chô
　　　　IV　class—1.5–2.0 chô
　　　　V　class—more than 2 chô
　　　　（1 chô ＝ 2.45 acres）

the agricultural as well as nonagricultural incomes as explanatory variables may be appropriate for this period in the sense that it stresses the compositional change of income. The pattern of changes of Y_{ag}^G and Y_{nag}^G by size of cultivated land is depicted in Fig. 2.

The computing result in Table 1 indicates, first, that even the one variable (Y_{nag}^G) function fits, unexpectedly, very well, and the coefficient of determination ranges from 0.591 to 0.908. Moreover, in the first size-class, (less than 0.5 *chô*) the non-

86

Fig. 3. Deposit Function Fitted to the Farm Size of Less than 0.5 *Chô* in All Prefectures for 1952–61

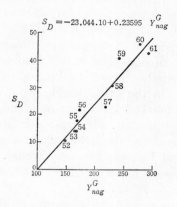

$$S_D = -23{,}044.10 + 0.23595 \, Y_{nag}^G$$

agricultural income level is the highest, and its rate of increase is also the highest; here we have $R^2 = 0.90789$. This is the finest fit among the five size-classes. In this size-class, the proportion of non-agricultural income in total income $\{Y_{nag}^G / (Y_{ag}^G + Y_{nag}^G)\}$ reached the very high figure of 79.1%, and the variation of Y_{nag}^g can almost explain about 90% of that of S_D (the increase of deposits outstanding).

Fig. 3 merely depicts this relationship. Consequently, in the case of the first size-class, the addition of other variables, Y_{ag}^G and ΔY_d^G, will bring about only a minor improvement in the coefficient of determination, but the standard error of the coefficients c and d is not statistically significant. However, in relation to the classes higher than the second size-class, the coefficient d is almost insignificant, but the coefficient c is significant except in the case of the two-variable function of the third size-class.

Upon examination of the two-variable (Y_{nag}^G and Y_{ag}^G) function, we are strongly impressed with the fact that in any class the coefficient of Y_{nag}^G ($= b$) is invariably higher than that of Y_{ag}^G ($= c$). If we take into account the greater rise of Y_{nag}^G than Y_{ag}^G for this period, it is now evident that the variation in the absolute magnitude of $(b\ Y^G_{nag})$ is far greater than that of $(c\ Y^G_{ag})$.

The coefficient b of Y^G_{nag} indicates, on the one hand, an almost consistent rise from the lowest to the higher size-class (from I to IV class, 0.263, 0.423, 0.513, 0.444, and 1.148). This probably suggests a higher proportion of agricultural income in the higher size-classes, a decline of non-agricultural income as a basic income, and also a strengthening of the "marginal income" character in the latter. On the other hand, the coefficient of Y^G_{ag} ($= c$) manifests no marked consistent tendency for variation, and so we may conclude that the possible inter-size differences of the marginal propensity to deposit in association with the changes of agricultural incomes are very trivial. This observation will be strengthened more by the smaller variation of the absolute changes in $(b\ Y^G_{ag})$.

Next, we intend to consider the computation of the cross-section deposit function fitted among the ten agricultural regions, the results of which are indicated in Table 2. In 1953 and 1956, the coefficients of determination are not high, but in other years the fit is fairly good. In the single-variable (Y^G_{nag}) function, the coefficient b ranges from 0.209 in 1955 to 0.361 in 1959; except 1953 and 1956, when R^2 is particularly low. We cannot see any conspicuous differences in the coefficient b in these years.

In the two-variable $(Y^G_{nag}$ and $Y^G_{ag})$ function, we find that the coefficients of b and c in every year are significant. In this case, the value of b, on the one hand, ranges from 0.228 (1953) to 0.381 (1959) — the average is 0.283 — except for 0.144 of 1956. On the other hand, the coefficient c of Y^G_{ag} is between 0.070 of 1958 and 0.197 of 1961, and in every year it is far lower than the coefficient b of Y^G_{nag}. Similar results were already obtained in our time-series deposit function shown in Table 1.

Our time-series, as well as our cross-section, analysis of the deposit function seems to have confirmed that non-agricultural income played a greater role in the determination of the deposit behavior. This point is made clearer in Fig. 4 where 1952–61

Table 2. Cross-Section Deposit Function among 10 Agricultural Regions Excluding Hokkaidô

$$S_D = a + b\, Y_{nag}^G + c\, Y_{ag}^G + d \varDelta Y_a^G$$

	a	b	c	d	R^2
1953	2,598.37 (14,308.458)	0.12589 (0.11240)			0.13554
	−30,443.30 (23,447.111)	0.22819 (0.11807)	0.10536 (0.06244)		0.38549
	−12,377.88 (27,857.936)	0.13619 (0.14080)	0.06028 (0.07271)	0.15504 (0.03556)	0.49548
1954	−11,234.56 (13,109.488)	0.23684 (0.10658)			0.38165
	−41,112.72 (16,365.911)	0.31115 (0.09047)	0.10856 (0.04458)		0.65698
	−26,896.76 (17,772.441)	0.24943 (0.09078)	0.07820 (0.04539)	0.13733 (0.08894)	0.79262
1955	370.66 (9,810.436)	0.20918 (0.07998)			0.46092
	−25,543.87 (15,476.341)	0.26107 (0.07311)	0.08809 (0.04423)		0.65590
	−26,712.99 (16,848.842)	0.31171 (0.16018)	0.09045 (0.04771)	−0.21813 (0.60239)	0.66326
1956	19,366.62 (9,138.484)	0.07166 (0.07130)			0.11211
	− 5,967.66 (15,826.719)	0.14429 (0.07367)	0.07879 (0.04247)		0.40475
	− 471.50 (17,962.199)	0.09745 (0.09895)	0.07215 (0.04481)	−0.18103 (0.24414)	0.45473
1957	−14,058.34 (12,993.785)	0.24634 (0.08456)			0.51478
	−37,970.05 (16,161.640)	0.25581 (0.07194)	0.11706 (0.05782)		0.69397
	−26,297.66 (37,567.298)	0.19759 (0.18330)	0.09404 (0.09027)	0.09638 (0.27544)	0.70009
1958	− 8,215.60 (6,189.930)	0.25193 (0.03855)			0.84221
	−23,210.83 (9,961.731)	0.25984 (0.03435)	0.07011 (0.03893)		0.89218
	−23,060.01 (10,807.172)	0.26087 (0.03789)	0.06930 (0.04244)	−0.01538 (0.11813)	0.89248

Table 2. (Continued)

	a	b	c	d	R^2
	−14,314.93	0.36136			0.70223
	(14,472.591)	(0.08320)			
1959	−45,132.98	0.38071	0.13457		0.77216
	(25,005.417)	(0.07891)	(0.09180)		
	−37,532.89	0.32616	0.10264	0.36144	0.80670
	(25,937.83)	(0.09455)	(0.09640)	(0.34907)	
	− 1,548.93	0.27342			0.64153
	(14,244.176)	(0.07226)			
1960	−44,379.48	0.29857	0.17855		0.83660
	(18,033.383)	(0.05288)	(0.06176)		
	−41,179.11	0.27861	0.16401	0.11902	0.84329
	(20,096.929)	(0.06845)	(0.07137)	(0.23523)	
	3,812.41	0.24403			0.57607
	(15,827.351)	(0.07401)			
1961	−45,227.10	0.27079	0.19720		0.82710
	(18,798.178)	(0.05122)	(0.06208)		
	−45,275.18	0.29502	0.22913	−0.41579	0.88989
	(16,203.632)	(0.04605)	(0.05604)	(0.22479)	

Fig. 4. Propensity to Deposit and Y^G_{nag}/Y^G Ratio in All Prefectures

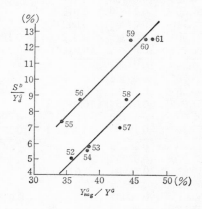

Fig. 5. Propensity to Deposit and Y_{nag}^G/Y^G Ratio by Area of Cultivated Land

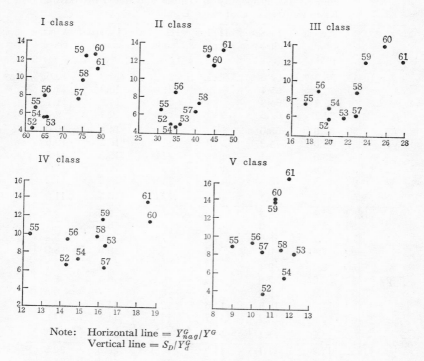

Note: Horizontal line $= Y_{nag}^G/Y^G$
Vertical line $= S_D/Y_d^G$

prefectural data (excluding Hokkaidô) are presented with reference to the relationship between the propensity to deposit and the ratio of non-agricultural income to all farm household income (in gross terms in Table 3). We see here some correlation of the propensity to deposit with the ratio of non-agricultural income, although this relationship is split into two lines. Fig. 5 indicates the same relation by area of cultivated land. Although in the fifth size-class the relation is not evident, we can find in other classes some positive correlation between the two variables. In other words, there is a rising tendency of the propensity to depos-

91

Table 3. National (excluding Hokkaidô) Non-Agricultural Income Ratio, Propensity to Deposit and the Gross Savings Ratio by Area of Cultivated Land

		Average of all pref.	I size-class	II size-class	III size-class	IV size-class	V size-class
	1952	35.8(%)	62.0(%)	33.5(%)	20.2(%)	14.3(%)	10.6(%)
	53	38.6	65.4	36.2	21.6	16.3	12.2
	54	38.3	65.3	34.8	20.0	14.9	11.7
	55	34.2	62.6	30.7	17.4	12.4	9.0
$\dfrac{Y^G_{nag}}{Y^G}$	56	37.0	65.0	34.5	18.8	14.4	10.0
	57	43.0	74.2	39.8	22.7	16.2	10.6
	58	43.8	75.1	40.9	22.8	15.9	11.5
	59	44.4	75.8	42.9	23.6	16.1	11.2
	60	46.5	78.1	44.6	25.6	18.6	11.2
	61	47.5	79.1	46.9	27.6	18.5	11.9
	1952	5.1	4.3	5.0	5.9	6.7	3.8
	53	5.8	5.6	5.1	6.0	8.4	8.1
	54	5.7	5.6	4.8	7.0	6.6	5.4
	55	7.4	6.6	6.8	7.7	9.9	8.9
$\dfrac{S_D}{Y^G_d}$	56	8.7	8.1	8.6	9.1	9.5	9.2
	57	7.0	7.8	6.5	6.2	6.4	8.3
	58	8.8	9.8	7.3	8.9	9.7	8.5
	59	12.5	12.5	12.6	12.2	11.6	13.8
	60	12.6	12.7	11.7	14.1	11.5	14.0
	61	12.6	11.1	13.3	12.3	13.7	16.3
	1952	15.2	11.1	14.8	17.3	20.6	22.8
	53	15.2	10.9	14.3	18.0	19.2	25.3
	54	15.1	11.4	14.3	18.2	19.5	21.6
	55	19.6	14.3	19.3	23.1	24.7	26.8
$\dfrac{S^G}{Y^G_d}$	56	16.0	12.6	15.5	18.3	19.9	21.5
	57	15.7	13.5	14.2	18.0	19.5	21.6
	58	17.3	15.3	16.0	17.4	22.2	26.2
	59	18.1	14.0	17.8	19.7	23.2	26.5
	60	19.6	16.1	17.3	22.5	25.3	29.2
	61	21.3	15.8	19.7	25.3	27.9	31.3

it in association with the rise of the Y^G_{nag}/Y^G ratio. At the same time, we recognize without exception that, in every class, both the 1955 value (where the agricultural income increased conspicuously) and the values for 1956, 59, 60 and 61 (where the economy as a whole was in a boom situation) deviate upwards. The propensity to deposit seems to have reflected business cycle situations very clearly.

We find the association of the rise of the propensity to deposit and the rise of Y^G_{nag}/Y^G ratio not only in the time-series, but also in the cross-section studies. What hypothesis can adequately explain this relationship?

Non-agricultural income consists of two types: (1) the income from non-agricultural enterprises of forestry, fishery, commerce, manufacturing and mining, and (2) the incomes from wages and salaries, and rent and interest. Among these items, the lower the size-class, the higher the proportion of wage and salary incomes and the proportion of farm household members who engage in side-works.

The problem is why the propensity to deposit from non-agricultural income is higher than that from agricultural income. Some considerations will follow:

(1) The non-agricultural revenue mostly consists of cash revenue, while a considerable part of the agricultural revenue, the source of the agricultural income, consists of income in kind, namely farm products which will be consumed by the farmers themselves. Taking a look at the 1961 prefectural (excluding Hokkaidô) data, all prefectural average of total farm gross revenue per household was 377,637 yen in 1961, but cash revenue was 228,117 yen. Therefore, cash revenue occupied 71% and revenue in kind 29%. The portion of self-consumption becomes income as well as the consumption when the change of inventories is assumed away. This cannot feasibly take the form of deposits, and accounts for one of the reasons why the propensity to deposit from the non-agricultural income is higher than that from the agricultural income.

(2) During the period in question the growth rate of non-agricultural incomes was much higher than that of agricultural incomes. In terms of the data for all prefectures (excluding Hokkaidô) and for all farm sizes, the real gross agricultural income increased by 13.7% for 1952–61, but the real gross non-agricultural income by 84.7% per household during the same period. There exists a considerable contrast between the stagnation of agricultural incomes and the growth of non-agricultural incomes. Since the propensity to deposit and save tends to rise and fall in association with the magnitude of the income growth rate, it is easily anticipated that the propensity to deposit from the non-agricultural income will become comparatively higher.

(3) The proportion of the transitory income (e.g., bonuses) in the total income for the urban-worker household has manifested a consistent increase for the period in concern. Similarly, the transitory proportion in the non-agricultural income for the farm household may have also tended to increase. According to the family budget survey for the urban-worker household, the propensity to deposit was 3.25% in 1953, 8.16% in 1958 and 10.49% in 1961. Therefore, the propensity to deposit of farm households from wages and salaries (in non-agricultural income) will also be destined to follow a similar process. Moreover, the proportion of the non-farm business revenue to be ascribed to commerce, manufacturing and mining was 53.1% in 1961, but the growth rate in these sectors was in general higher than that in agriculture. Here, we can also see a factor making for a higher propensity to deposit from non-agricultural incomes. The same speculation will naturally hold true for the savings ratio as well.

(4) In general, non-agricultural income has been, more or less, of a household-supplementing type. At present, however, its supplementation is not so trivial as it was in the case of pre-war female workers in the cotton spinning industry, but is gradually becoming a powerful supplement, thus transforming the structure of farm incomes tremendously. Be that as it may,

94

as a rule, agricultural income is the basic income, and the non-agricultural income is complementary and marginal to the farm household. Consequently, it is only natural that this marginal income has a higher marginal propensity to deposit or save, as compared with the basic income, the agricultural income.

(5) Another problem is to ascertain which is higher the agricultural income or the non-agricultural income, in terms of incomes per capita of earners. From the *Farm Household Economy Survey* of 1961, we can cite the following unadjusted figures. Net agricultural income was 229,196 yen, and the net non-agricultural income was 226,210 yen in the household average of all prefectures (excluding Hokkaidô). However, if we deduct the non-working persons from the regular residential family members of the 5,550 households surveyed we have 15,616 persons left. Those whose main occupation is agriculture amount to 10,863 persons; the residual is 4,753 persons who are supposed to be earning the non-agricultural income. In the average household with a labor force of 2.81 persons, roughly 1.96 persons earn the agricultural income, and 0.85 persons earn the non-agricultural income. If this is correct, the agricultural income will be 116,937 yen, while the non-agricultural income will be 266,130 yen, per capita of labor force. The per capita non-agricultural income is thus more than twice higher than the per capita agricultural income. Since the growth rate of the non-agricultural income was relatively higher for 1952–61, this gap in 1952 will have been much smaller than that in 1961. Therefore, the non-agricultural income injected into the farm household has not only enlarged its relative proportion, but it has also raised its relative income position per capita of the labor force. If the ordinary relative income hypothesis is applied mechanically, the demonstration effect from the non-agricultural income should reduce the savings ratio and the propensity to deposit of farm households. Actually, however, the relatively higher non-agricultural income does not exercise any "conspicuous consumption" effect, since both incomes accrue to the

95

same household. Since the non-agricultural income which is relatively higher and is increasing its relative share enters the traditional mode of life, the "contra-demonstration effect" from the agricultural income to the non-agricultural income prevails, and this operates to raise the savings ratio and the propensity to deposit.

The above are hypotheses explaining the rising trend of the farmer's propensity to deposit and save. Milton Friedman[6] once stressed that the variability and the transitory character of farmers' incomes due to good or bad harvests may explain their marginal propensity to save which is higher than that of non-agricultural workers. However, these workers' incomes in the postwar period included an increasing proportion of bonus payments, thus strengthening the transitory income character. This is also reflected in the non-agricultural income of farm households. On the contrary, agricultural income was virtually unchanging despite the continuation of good harvests, thus strengthening its permanent income character. The higher marginal propensity to deposit from the non-agricultural income should be understood by taking these factors into account.

The propensity to deposit, the gross savings ratio and the Y_{nag}^G/Y^G ratio have shown rising trends over 1952–61; Table 3 indicates their computed values by size-class (average of all prefectures excluding Hokkaidô). It is noticed that the Y_{nag}^G/Y^G ratio has shown a jump around 1957–58 in association with the further development of side work in farm households, but it is interesting that the propensity to deposit as well as the gross savings ratio also increased abruptly.

However, when we examine Table 3, even if the Y_{nag}^G/Y^G ratio is relatively higher in the lower size-classes, the propensity to deposit is somewhat higher in the fifth class than in the first class. In the case of the gross savings ratio, that of the fifth class is about double that of the first class. These facts can be well explained with a joint application of the ordinary relative income

6) Milton Friedman, *A Theory of the Consumption Function*, 1957, pp. 58–69.

hypothesis. The inter-class differences of the gross savings ratio and the propensity to deposit is not explainable solely by the differences of the Y_{nag}^G/Y^G ratio. We may need another hypothesis.

4. Savings Function

The *Farm Household Economy Survey*, makes use of the concept of "the farm household economy surplus" which corresponds to that of net savings. However, we use here the gross savings concept without excluding depreciation; agricultural income, non-agricultural income, and disposable income are all used in gross terms. Therefore, the savings functions, here computed, are all in terms of gross magnitudes (Table 4).

In the gross savings function, which is fitted for the time-series data of 1953–61 for all prefectures and all farm sizes, the coefficient b of Y_{nag}^G is lower than the coefficent c of Y_{ag}^G; the reverse is true in the case of the deposit function. Since the coefficient d of ΔY_d^G is not all significant, the two variable (Y_{nag}^G and Y_{ag}^G) function will be examined here. In the savings function, b and c are 0.30516 and 0.56293, respectively, but in the deposit function, they are 0.35151 and 0.29046 respectively. It is not adequate to use the investment function with the same variables here, but we did so for convenience of comparison, and b and c are 0.21260 and 0.28679, respectively. It is interesting that in this investment function, too, the coefficient c is higher than b as indicated in the savings function. From this, we may tentatively infer that the higher c is, than b in the savings function, the greater involvement of investment in savings. This is the case because

$$S^G = S_D + I^G - L$$

if the increment of the liquid assets other than deposit is assumed away. Since L is not a large item and the L function with the same variables results in an extremely bad and insignificant correlation, we may roughly assume that the summation of coeffi-

Table 4. Comparison of Savings, Deposits and Investment Functions (Time-Series) for All Prefectures and All Sizes of Cultivated Land

$$S^G = a + b\,Y^G_{nag} + c\,Y^G_{ag} + d\varDelta Y^G_d$$

	a	b	c	d	R^2
1	65.01 (12,969.55)	0.42352 (0.08427)			0.78294
2	−99,919.84 (14,912.98)	0.30516 (0.03428)	0.56293 (0.07987)		0.97660
3	−95,108.02 (22,245.70)	0.30021 (0.04036)	0.54138 (0.11037)	0.02984 (0.09468)	0.97706

$$S_D = a + b\,Y^G_{nag} + c\,Y^G_{ag} + d\varDelta Y^G_d$$

	a	b	c	d	R^2
1	−28,709.75 (9,485.74)	0.41258 (0.06164)			0.86487
2	−80,300.40 (24,766.18)	0.35151 (0.05693)	0.29046 (0.13263)		0.92489
3	−102,140.61 (34,498.50)	0.37395 (0.06258)	0.38827 (0.17116)	−0.13545 (0.14683)	0.93381

$$I^G = a + b\,Y^G_{nag} + c\,Y^G_{ag} + d\varDelta Y^G_d$$

	a	b	c	d	R^2
1	− 4,924.00 (12,640.93)	0.27290 (0.08214)			0.61191
2	−55,862.68 (38,496.21)	0.21260 (0.08850)	0.28679 (0.20617)		0.70655
3	−58,985.01 (57,966.85)	0.21581 (0.10516)	0.30077 (0.28760)	−0.01936 (0.24683)	0.70691

cients c in the deposit and the investment functions will naturally be equal to the coefficient c of the savings function. The coefficient c of the deposit function is equal to 0.29046, and that of the investment function is equal to 0.28679. The sum of the two is 0.57725 and roughly equal to 0.56293, the c of the savings function. Thus the relation $c > b$ in the savings function may

Table 5. Time-Series Savings Function for All Prefectures by Area of Cultivated Land

$$S^G = a + b Y^G_{nag} + c Y^G_{ag} + d \Delta Y^G_d$$

By Area	a	b	c	d	R^2
	65.01	0.42352			0.78294
	(12,969.55)	(0.08427)			
Average of	− 99,919.84	0.30516	0.56293		0.97660
all pref.	(14,912.98)	(0.03428)	(0.07987)		
	− 95,108.02	0.30021	0.54138	0.02984	0.97706
	(22,245.70)	(0.04036)	(0.11037)	(0.09468)	
	− 6,434.50	0.22612			0.92968
	(5,194.87)	(0.02350)			
I size-class	− 53,458.46	0.28306	0.41261		0.97534
	(14,489.42)	(0.02275)	(0.12375)		
	− 52,431.91	0.27382	0.41382	0.05437	0.97677
	(15,516.59)	(0.02936)	(0.13160)	(0.09799)	
	11,697.02	0.33907			0.65573
	(12,595.01)	(0.09286)			
II size-class	−116,358.90	0.31559	0.64415		0.97137
	(16,226.46)	(0.02907)	(0.25046)		
	− 96,767.29	0.27168	0.56779	0.14026	0.97898
	(21,067.83)	(0.04253)	(0.09352)	(0.10421)	
	12,157.55	0.76913			0.66710
	(19,414.71)	(0.20535)			
III size-class	− 87,174.27	0.45156	0.40352		0.86664
	(35,709.53)	(0.17590)	(0.13467)		
	− 70,316.63	0.46932	0.34402	0.03858	0.86838
	(76,349.67)	(0.20357)	(0.27440)	(0.15011)	
	4,203.97	1.32667			0.61459
	(32,613.56)	(0.39708)			
IV size-class	−210,079.93	0.60233	0.64211		0.97448
	(24,996.15)	(0.13557)	(0.06980)		
	−172,671.83	0.58083	0.55164	0.19734	0.99018
	(21,522.62)	(0.09241)	(0.05720)	(0.06970)	
	− 63,003.07	3.08373			0.61377
	(68,888.08)	(0.92458)			
V size-class	−270,664.68	1.53436	0.54033		0.93276
	(49,787.50)	(0.50789)	(0.10127)		
	−223,550.80	1.63479	0.44224	0.20039	0.95940
	(49,722.43)	(0.43585)	(0.10180)	(0.10036)	

99

be, by and large, due to the existence of farm investment, which includes the inventory investment as a major component, and oscillates in association with good and bad harvests.

Now moving to Table 5, we compute the time-series gross savings functions (average of all prefectures except Hokkaidô), but these are broken down into five size-classes. The observations resulting from them are as follows.

(1) In this case the coefficient d of ΔY^G becomes significant, excepting the first and the third classes. Except for those two classes, we may say that the marginal effect of income changes upon the gross savings is greater as the size-class becomes higher.

(2) The inter-size-class differences of the coefficient c of the agricultural income are trivial and are between 0.34 and 0.56. But, the coefficient b of the non-agricultural income tends to increase as the size-class increases (from 0.28 to 1.64). In the fifth size-class, it is 1.64 and seems to be too high. But, we may guess that in the higher classes the amount of non-agricultural incomes is not so large, and not only is all of it saved, but also considerable amount will be saved from agricultural incomes.

(3) In the first and second size-classes, the marginal propensity to save from Y^G_{ag} is higher than that from Y^G_{nag}. However, in the third-fifth classes, the marginal propensity to save from Y^G_{nag} is rather high. This may be due to the reversal of the basic and the marginal income relationship in the lower and higher size-classes.

By applying similar methods using the non-agricultural and agricultural incomes the cross-section gross savings functions among ten agricultural regions were computed in Table 6. In the cross-section analysis we find that the coefficients b of Y^G_{nag} is, by and large, higher than c of Y^G_{ag} which completely contradicts our former speculation. We cannot set up any positive theory to explain this phenomenon, but one of the factors may lie in the greater regional differences of Y^G_{nag} than those of Y^G_{ag}. For instance, in 1955, the absolute difference of Y^G_{nag} between the highest (Kinki) and the lowest (Minami Kantô) was 64,591 yen,

SAVINGS BEHAVIOR OF THE FARM HOUSEHOLD

and that of Y^G_{ag} between the highest (Tôhoku) and the lowest (Nankai) was 121,185 yen. These characteristics of regional distribution of Y^G_{nag} and Y^G_{ag} probably account for a part of the divergent consequences resulting from the time-series and the cross-section functions.

In light of the above, how do we evaluate the relative merit between our own analysis with Y^G_{nag} and Y^G_{ag} as variables and the Duesenberry- or Mack-type analysis which assumes the savings ratio to be a function of the year-to-year relative incomes (compared with the preceding peak income or the income in the preceding year)? We must take into account the fact that, in the computation of the latter type function, we used net income and net savings exclusive of depreciation, but in the present computation, we used the gross income and gross savings inclusive of depreciation. Moreover, we have here removed certain time-series discontinuities by the standardization of data in this analysis, while we used unadjusted data in the other approaches. Therefore, even if both show fine fits, they are not mutually comparable.

Therefore, we computed a savings function in which the gross savings ratio (S^G/Y^G_d) is assumed to be a linear function of the relative real gross income of the preceding year (Y^G_d/Y^G_{d-1}). The results are shown in Table 7. Compared with the result we obtained earlier in net terms, the correlation is much worse. For all sizes the coefficient of determination is 0.5482 which is lower than the $R^2 = 0.8767$ of the 1951–59 net analysis.[7] This may be due to the inclusion of depreciation in association; Hiroshi Kawaguchi[8] also obtained a high coefficient of determination in his computation when he based his computation upon the standardized, but "net", data.

However, from Table 7, we can recognize that the fit of this type of savings function is extremely bad, particularly in the first,

---

7) See, for instance, Chapters 9 and 10 of M. Shinohara, *Growth and Cycles in the Japanese Economy*, Tokyo, 1962.
8) Hiroshi Kawaguchi, *ibid.*

Table 6. Cross-Section Savings Function among 10 Agricultural Regions

$$S^G = a + b Y^G_{nag} + c Y^G_{ag} + d \Delta Y^G_d$$

	a	b	c	d	R^2
	32,992.22	0.12520			0.04214
	(26,865.679)	(0.21105)			
1953	−40,801.48	0.35369	0.23530		0.43399
	(40,138.702)	(0.20212)	(0.10689)		
	28,598.47	0.00025	0.06213	0.59561	0.94421
	(16,523.738)	(0.08351)	(0.04313)	(0.08040)	
	13,679.91	0.27802			0.25461
	(20,686.520)	(0.16819)			
1954	−45,474.20	0.42515	0.21493		0.77708
	(18,962.047)	(0.10482)	(0.05306)		
	−22,590.50	0.32581	0.16606	0.22106	0.90355
	(15,750.118)	(0.08247)	(0.04153)	(0.07882)	
	28,066.26	0.32111			0.42813
	(16,094.251)	(0.13121)			
1955	−33,528.11	0.44444	0.20938		0.86231
	(15,593.430)	(0.07361)	(0.04457)		
	−31,487.43	0.35606	0.20527	0.38075	0.87115
	(16,600.884)	(0.15782)	(0.04701)	(0.59352)	
	48,118.29	0.03277			0.00878
	(15,775.968)	(0.12309)			
1956	− 4,120.56	0.18251	0.16246		0.47487
	(24,287.844)	(0.11306)	(0.06518)		
	−14,007.34	0.26676	0.17439	0.32564	0.53543
	(27,088.899)	(0.14922)	(0.06758)	(0.36819)	
	2,127.18	0.34392			0.53728
	(17,340.399)	(0.11284)			
1957	−42,699.64	0.36167	0.21945		0.87449
	(14,144.118)	(0.06296)	0.05060)		
	−16,630.62	0.23165	0.16804	0.21526	0.89084
	(30,973.084)	(0.15112)	(0.07443)	(0.22709)	
	22,983.03	0.24584			0.60793
	(11,206.995)	0.06980)			
1958	− 7,433.83	0.26190	0.14222		0.76377
	(16,935.601)	(0.05840)	(0.06618)		
	−10,517.09	0.24082	0.15872	0.31443	0.86003
	(14,162.517)	(0.04965)	(0.05562)	(0.15480)	

Table 6.   (Continued)

	a	b	c	d	R^2
	24,155.53	0.26276			0.61301
	(12,844.658)	(0.07381)			
1959	179.31	0.27782	0.10469		0.75315
	(20,256.302)	(0.06392)	(0.07437)		
	5,076.90	0.24266	0.08412	0.23292	0.76303
	(22,350.054)	(0.08147)	(0.08307)	(0.30080)	
	34,658.73	0.23606			0.46635
	(17,598.402)	(0.08928)			
1960	−29,744.62	0.27387	0.26849		0.89651
	(14,532.163)	(0.04261)	(0.04977)		
	−25,860.75	0.24965	0.25084	0.14444	0.90612
	(15,750.919)	(0.05365)	(0.05594)	(0.18436)	
	47,891.78	0.21531			0.43776
	(18,448.644)	(0.08627)			
1961	−16,340.00	0.25037	0.25829		0.85791
	(17,251.494)	(0.04700)	(0.05677)		
	−16,297.75	0.23091	0.23262	0.33404	0.89747
	(15,828.715)	(0.04498)	(0.05475)	(0.21955)	

third and fifth classes in which the coefficients of determination remain in the range of 0.32–0.38.

However, if we use the function $S^G = a + b Y_d^G + c Y_{d-1}^G$ for $S^G / Y_d^G = a + b \ (Y_d^G / Y_{d-1}^G)$, we obtain the result summarized in Table 8.   Since the variable to be explained in the functions in Table 8 is the absolute magnitude, R^2 becomes much better here than that in the equations in Table 7.   If we compare the results in Table 8 with those in Table 5 in which Y_{nag}^G and Y_{ag}^G are employed as explanatory variables, we may be impressed by the fact that magnitudes of R^2 are not so different.   However, it is also evident that the standard errors of the coefficient c in the functions in Table 8 are fairly high, except for the fourth class, and this suggests an intrusion of the multicollinearity. Consequently, if we were to remove Y_{d-1}^G, we would have a very simple function with one variable ($S^G = a + b Y_d^G$), still with a relatively high R^2,   This may be due to the upward trend of

Table 7. $S^G/Y_d^G = a + b(Y_d^G/Y_{d-1}^G)$

——1953–61——

		a	b	R^2
Average		−0.15717	0.27818	0.54820
I	size-class	−0.15553	0.41165	0.32632
II	size-class	−0.26192	0.13781	0.64100
III	size-class	0.05803	0.53973	0.37931
IV	size-class	−0.33164	0.35496	0.55146
V	size-class	−0.11091	0.15777	0.37942

Table 8. $S^G = a + b\,Y_d^G + c\,Y_{d-1}^G$

——1952–61——

		a	b	c	R^2
Average		− 47,312.44	0.44558 (0.08902)	−0.14275 (0.11443)	0.94837
I	size-class	908,376.92	−0.73938 (0.32169)	−0.41745 (0.32099)	0.58264
II	size-class	− 52,167.80	0.32007	*	0.86340
III	size-class	− 75,382.58	0.41922 (0.07513)	−0.03297 (0.09669)	0.85974
IV	size-class	− 167,640.58	0.72674 (0.07295)	−0.16622 (0.09672)	0.97772
V	size-class	− 216,845.42	0.68834 (0.09796)	−0.09429 (0.11792)	0.94421

* The addition of Y_{d-1}^G led to an unsolved result.

the gross savings ratio for the period in question. But if this rising trend of the savings ratio has something to do with the increasing share of Y_{nag}^G, the function with Y_{nag}^G and Y_{ag}^G should be more useful than that with one variable, Y_d^G.

The peried covered by our analysis was from 1952 to 1961, and we did not deal with the post-1961 period during which the farmer's savings ratio has been still rising. However, we believe that the rising trend for that period would have also been associated with the increasing proportion of non-agricultural income.

Statistical Appendix

Major Variables in the Farm Household Economy in All Prefectures (excluding Hokkaidō) by Area of Cultivated Land

unit: yen, in 1955 prices

Y_d^G

	1952	1953	1954	1955	1956	1957	1958	1959	1960	1961
Average	309,245	322,295	305,932	340,244	331,416	347,114	358,305	380,821	412,865	443,115
I	241,623	256,338	255,476	269,124	270,442	295,637	310,601	324,105	362,465	384,849
II	299,596	308,327	300,587	323,604	315,176	324,675	334,007	358,411	380,789	413,643
III	380,281	391,707	321,078	415,805	391,069	395,464	393,964	425,639	456,108	490,278
IV	444,250	456,797	453,302	494,201	466,337	472,144	487,350	509,065	535,815	571,383
V	563,215	604,705	566,764	632,023	594,030	616,777	626,577	663,905	712,862	741,409

Y_{ag}^G

	1952	1953	1954	1955	1956	1957	1958	1959	1960	1961
Average	201,211	196,684	189,736	228,168	211,553	197,609	200,979	210,663	219,587	228,818
I	91,230	87,643	88,160	101,699	94,133	75,656	76,651	77,640	78,180	77,826
II	200,249	194,751	195,397	226,647	207,161	192,507	194,541	201,131	206,642	213,866
III	310,787	306,036	258,969	350,736	324,023	307,226	305,367	325,101	338,914	352,253
IV	398,730	384,322	397,092	452,965	416,241	404,968	419,513	433,310	444,485	472,666
V	539,015	545,344	531,077	615,902	573,634	581,008	583,978	609,981	655,886	671,438

Y_{nag}^G

	1952	1953	1954	1955	1956	1957	1958	1959	1960	1961
Average	112,168	123,792	117,784	118,767	124,051	149,364	156,847	168,067	190,750	207,165
I	148,719	165,364	165,667	170,005	174,786	218,099	231,399	242,874	279,520	295,234
II	100,688	110,675	104,228	100,347	109,277	127,056	134,890	130,858	166,681	188,609
III	78,691	84,205	64,866	73,849	75,180	90,084	90,182	100,322	116,691	134,585
IV	66,799	74,688	69,686	64,038	70,211	78,500	79,387	83,156	101,799	107,274
V	64,219	75,650	70,415	60,596	64,048	68,527	75,995	77,108	82,733	90,804

S^G

	1952	1953	1954	1955	1956	1957	1958	1959	1960	1961
Average	47,071	48,928	46,072	66,557	52,891	54,610	62,107	69,000	80,758	94,198
I	26,752	27,879	29,209	38,382	33,958	40,041	47,413	45,227	58,339	60,981

	1952	1953	1954	1955	1956	1957	1958	1959	1960	1961
II	44,354	44,005	43,107	62,478	48,838	46,148	53,533	63,971	65,967	81,607
III	65,652	70,642	58,563	96,064	71,652	71,251	68,986	83,862	102,507	124,240
IV	91,344	87,768	88,342	122,155	92,678	92,069	108,194	118,284	135,564	159,579
V	128,338	153,272	122,395	169,458	127,939	133,199	164,255	176,120	207,802	231,917

I^G

	1952	1953	1954	1955	1956	1957	1958	1959	1960	1961
Average*	28,655	31,195	30,051	35,993	25,610	33,572	29,858	32,904	42,544	64,164
I	12,304	12,265	14,649	18,295	18,447	14,144	15,510	19,934	24,434	25,812
II	29,854	31,778	30,381	35,263	21,032	33,847	30,543	27,821	36,382	61,628
III	42,913	49,072	41,174	52,139	33,440	51,874	37,724	39,596	60,129	98,146
IV	53,694	57,942	59,782	71,788	50,877	57,607	50,491	74,221	84,656	118,760
V	83,465	98,738	87,323	92,456	61,405	97,098	88,318	92,174	102,402	168,584

S_D

	1952	1953	1954	1955	1956	1957	1958	1959	1960	1961
Average	15,625	19,021	17,363	25,054	28,695	24,142	31,375	47,582	52,083	56,004
I	10,391	14,313	14,379	17,867	21,874	22,942	30,569	40,513	45,898	42,694
II	14,906	15,435	14,479	21,887	26,999	21,093	24,520	45,245	44,383	54,830
III	22,593	23,578	22,516	32,210	35,665	24,608	35,300	52,062	64,107	60,208
IV	29,959	38,340	30,122	49,019	44,282	30,030	47,489	58,956	61,760	78,053
V	21,180	48,837	30,457	56,264	54,706	51,064	53,043	91,821	99,992	120,584

L

	1952	1953	1954	1955	1956	1957	1958	1959	1960	1961
Average	5,548	9,235	6,210	2,075	4,274	7,879	2,512	6,075	5,704	7,157
I	4,880	6,572	3,481	2,030	2,575	5,266	1,673	3,455	3,327	407
II	6,388	10,179	7,053	1,996	4,232	8,035	3,605	5,464	7,253	8,700
III	6,760	10,710	8,134	1,696	5,417	9,082	3,346	8,347	6,950	10,375
IV	3,765	11,307	10,205	4,933	11,354	11,406	− 822	8,698	6,967	15,601
V	2,243	18,343	12,221	43	4,272	20,610	3,046	20,494	6,398	23,535

Notes: 1. I, II, III, IV, V are the classes classified by the area of cultivated land. See the footnote of Fig. 2.
2. All variables are deflated by the farmer's consumer price index (1955=100), which takes into account the food consumed by farmers themselves at farm prices.
3. Based upon the standardized data, the procedure of which is explained in the text. Basic data are taken from the *Farm Household Economy Survey.*

106

CHAPTER 4

THE 1955–61 INVESTMENT SUPER-BOOM
AND ITS AFTERMATH
——Evaluation of A Postwar Fixed Investment Cycle——

1. *Introduction*

For 1955–61, private fixed investment (excluding residential construction) in Japan had increased from 960 billion yen to 4.23 trillion yen, an increase of slightly more than 4.4 times in only six years. This is quite an unprecedented event. Thus, the Japanese economy would be said to have entered a phase of "high rate of growth," although by international standards the growth rate of the Japanese economy has, in both the prewar and the postwar periods, always been high.

When the recession occurred from 1961 to 1962, most people could not clearly recognize that this recession might be different from those ones we had experienced in 1954 and 1957-58. The writer was among a minority[1] who insisted that the ordinary short-run recession based on the inventory cycle would be inadequate for the adjustment process from 1962. The adjustment process would involve changes in the fixed investment cycle, the occurrence of which can be seen already twice in the postwar twenty years. In other words, the recession could have been due not only to the excess of inventories, but also to the excess capacity which has been entailed by the strong fixed investment boom of 1955–61.

---

1) E.P.A., *Keizai-hakusho* (Economic White Paper) of 1962 also expressed a similar opinion, and used the catch-phrase, "Tenkeiki" (transition period), to account for the adjustment process after 1962.

The actual course the Japanese economy has taken for several years following 1962, by and large, seems to substantiate this way of thinking. Therefore, in the following the writer would like to analyze to what extent his judgment and analysis were correct and highlight two phases: (1) the capacity shortage situation, 1955–61 and (2) the excess capacity situation from 1962 onward. By doing so, he wants to make clear the altered pattern of private fixed investment behavior as well as the so-called process of "prosperity without profit." By the latter is meant the situation of increasing bankruptcy and dishonored bills, on the one hand, and the high rate of growth, approaching 10% per annum for 1962–1965, on the other.

2. *Private Fixed Investment Cycle*

In postwar Japan every economic barometer has indicated a phenomenal increase, and private fixed investment is no exception in this respect. A cycle, the duration of which is about ten years, is discernible, however, if we take the ratio of the private fixed investment (excluding personal residential construction) to GNP. As indicated in Fig. 1, the first fixed investment cycle of nine years ranges from 1946 to 1955, and the second one of ten years from 1956 to 1965. The third upswing seems to have begun from 1966.

Noteworthy is the fact that the periodicity is about the same as the "Juglar cycle," and that the upswing phases are in each case six years and the downswing ones are three and four years, respectively. It will be certainly erroneous to believe in the mechanical regularity of the fixed investment cycle. However, as the six-year period from 1955 to 1961 was characterized by the extraordinarily rapid expansion of private fixed investment amounting to an annual growth rate of about 30% on the average in money terms, we may be easily led to hold a view that the next phase will show a decline in the ratio of private fixed

Fig. 1. Fixed Investment Cycle

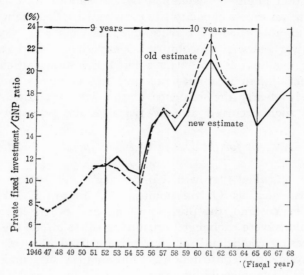

investment to GNP (hereafter fixed investment ratio) at least three or four years.

As we may recognize, the fixed investment ratio has a close bearing with the capacity growth rate. Since it reached 21.3% in 1961 and since a 21.3% ratio is considered to be much higher than the normal ratio which makes it possible to sustain a 10% growth rate, it is quite natural for us to expect that the fixed investment ratio should now begin to fall. Therefore, it seems to be beyond doubt that the fixed investment ratio which had risen to this point will not continue to rise or even maintain a constant level.

However, there were many peple who held the vague view that, since the Japanese ecomony is very young, has abundant labor, and is further endowed with rich investment opportunities, it was unthinkable that the fixed investment ratio would decline.

Such was the generally held view, and only a few insisted that the transition might be explained by the shift from a capacity shortage to an excess capacity situation and by the change from a rising to a levelled-off private fixed investment.

In postwar years, every country has experienced fairly marked inventory cycles, but not always fixed investment cycles. In this respect, Japan is among the very few countries indicating particularly clearly the existence of the fixed investment cycle which as such occurred already twice in the postwar period.

3. Reasons for the Declining Fixed Investment Ratio

In the so-called "growth controversy"[2] in which several economists, such as O. Shimomura, T. Tsuru, S. Ôkita, T. Uchida, T. Yoshino, the present writer, and others have taken part, opinions were exchanged on, among other topics, the "capacity-increasing coefficient" of *gross* private fixed investment (excluding residential construction). Shimomura first maintained that this coefficient would be unity whereas Tsuru and I contnded that it would be around 0.7 for the period 1951–56 or 1951–57. Because Shimomura has since changed his view and now maintains that the capacity-increasing coefficient of *net* private investment (excluding replacement) would be unity, we may roughly assume that in *gross* terms, the capacity-increasing coefficient of the gross private fixed investment (the reciprocal of the gross marginal fixed capital-output ratio) would be around 0.7, which Shimomura may now admit. However, as there was some tendency for the marginal fixed capital-ouput ratio to increase from 1957 on, we may safely imagine that the capacity-increasing coefficient would have moved toward 0.6 in more recent years.

Assume, for instance, that the real GNP growth rate for 1955–61 is, on the average, 10% per annum and the capacity-increas-

2) See M. Shinohara, *Growth and Cycles in Japanese Economy*, (Tokyo, Kinokuniya), 1962, Chapter 5, Section 4.

Fig. 2. Fixed Investment Ratio: Illustration

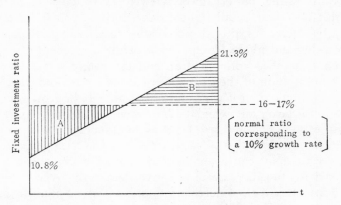

ing coefficient is 0.6. The required private fixed investment ratio would be derived by dividing 10% by 0.6, which is 16.7%. Now, if the 16–17% fixed investment ratio is assumed as normally required for the attainment of the average growth rate of 10% for the same period, then it is evident that the fixed investment ratio of 10.8% in 1955 was too low for the attainment of the 10% growth rate. Therefore, it is an inevitable consequence that the fixed investment ratio should rapidly be increasing up to around 16–17%. However, even if it reached this ratio, the fixed investment ratio would be still too low, because, as indicated in Fig. 2, the shaded area A must be offset by another one B. And this is why the fixed investment ratio did not stop at about 16–17% level but rushed up to 21.3% in 1961.

Provided that the growth potential was about 10% for 1955–61, the fixed investment ratio of 10.8% in 1955 was too low, and a disproportionate rise of fixed investment was inevitable. Therefore, an apparently unbalanced growth of fixed investment was perfectly consistent with and required by the situation prevailing in 1955–61 because there was a sudden jump of the average growth rate from about 8% (1951–55) to about 10%

111

(1955–61). Thus, from another point of view, the superficially disequilibrating path can be viewed as roughly equilibrating. This view will be all right for the period 1955–61 as a whole; only by means of this disproportionate growth process can the excess-demand phase (compared with the movement of capacity) be understood as coming to an end in around 1961. However, the continuation of the 21.3% fixed investment ratio thus arrived at is too high, even if we assume the same 10% growth potential for several years following 1962. Since the 16–17% fixed investment ratio was discussed here as being normally required for the attainment of the 10% growth rate, the 21.3% fixed investment ratio may cause an excessive capacity expansion as compared with the increase of effective demand. Were the 21.3% fixed investment ratio necessary to bring forth an equilibrium path between capacity and effective demand, we should assume then that the required rate of growth has to be raised to 12.8% (21.3% ×0.6). However, we came across the problems of a 5–8% rise in consumer prices as well as balance of payments difficulties, even under the 10% growth rate which has been maintained in the recent past. Therefore, the 12.8% growth rate would not have been a reasonable path from 1962 on. The unavoidable course would be a declining fixed investment ratio (say, from 21.3% in 1961 to around 15–16%, even under assumptions of the continued 10% growth rate and some decline in the capacity-increasing-coefficient of gross fixed investment).

As was the case during 1955–61, the decrease of the fixed investment ratio from 21.3% only to 16–17% will not be enough. It may have to decrease further down to, say, 13–14% to wipe out the excessive tendency of capacity. However, in the excess capacity situation, the firms may try to replace old-fashioned equipment more quickly than in the capacity shortage situation, where even old-fashioned facilities must be fully used to cope with excess demand. Therefore, the capacity increasing-coeffcient of gross fixed investment may be forced to decline somewhat in the capacity-surplus situation due to increasing replacement.

112

Taking this factor into account, the trough level of the fixed investment ratio would not be 13–14%, but 15–16% because a higher fixed investment will be required per unit increase of output under the assumption of the decreased capacity-increasing coefficient of gross fixed investment.

Such was the reasoning behind why I felt the post-1962 Japanese economy would necessarily move into a different phase from that of 1955–61 where excess demand or capacity shortage strongly prevailed.[3] There were many who could not under-

---

3) In order to understand the transition from the excess-demand to the excess-capacity phase, we should keep in mind the so-called the Capital Stock Adjustment Principle, in which the investment is assumed to be determined by the difference between the desired capital stock in the period K_t^e and the actual capital stock existing at the beginning of the period K_t.

Denoting expected income by Y_t^e, intended investment by I_t^e, and the coefficient of induced investment by v, we have the following relation.

$$I_t^e = K_t^e - K_t = vY_t^e - K_t,$$

where $K_t^e = vY_t^e$ is implied. On the other hand, if there is a technical relation between K_t and the productive capacity C_{at},

$$\beta C_{at} = K_t,$$

where β indicates the capital coefficient, then the above equation may be further rewritten as,

$$I_t^e = vY_t^e - \beta C_{at}.$$

If we assume $\beta = v$, and divide the both sides of the equation by Y_t^e, we derive

$$\frac{I_t^e}{Y_t^e} = v\left(\frac{Y_t^e - C_{at}}{Y_t^e}\right).$$

This clearly indicates that the investment ratio in "ex ante" terms (I_t^e/Y_t^e) will increase (or decrease) in consonance with a rise (or a fall) in the degree of excess demand or capacity $\left(\frac{Y_t^e - C_{at}}{Y_t^e}\right)$.

If, we have a relation where $v > \beta$ in the upswing, then

$$\frac{I_t^e}{Y_t^e} = (v - \beta) - \beta\left(\frac{Y_t^e - C_{at}}{Y_t^e}\right),$$

and the extent of a rise in the investment ratio may be accelerated. If we have a contrary relation $v < \beta$ in the downswing, $(v - \beta)$ will be negative, and the cyclical oscillation of the investment ratio will be more evident.

This formulation, however, explains only the behavior of *net* investment. Actually, in addition to net investment, we need an explanation of replacement investment. At any rate, this gives us a mechanism wherein I_t^e/Y_t^e decreases in the excess capacity phase, and increases in the excess demand (or capacity shortage) situation.

113

stand or accept such a line of thinking for they presumed that in such a rapidly growing economy the unbalanced growth of investment might be inevitable; moreover, a presumption of a decline of the fixed investment ratio or the levelling-off of its absolute amount even for three or four years seemed to have been too pessimistic. To those who had been accustomed to an extraordinarily high rate of growth in Japan, the mere thought of a cessation of a rise in fixed investment in absolute terms seemed to have been too unrealistic and too stagnationistic. To elucidate such an apprehension, the following illustration, although designed for the layman, may be of some use.

Let us assume a socialist planned economy in which the dictator intends to make a fixed investment amounting to 1.5 trillion yen for the coming three years which will increase the productive capacity by 0.9 trillion yen. In order to realize this plan, he may have various options among which we may enumerate the following three:

1) In the first year, a 0.3 trillion yen investment, in the second, 0.5 trillion yen and in the third 0.7 trillion yen.
2) In each of the three years, a 0.5 trillion yen investment.
3) In the first year, a 0.7 trillion yen investment, in the second, 0.5 trillion yen, and in the third, 0.3 trillion yen.

These three options all entail a fixed investment of 1.5 trillion yen and a capacity expansion of 0.9 trillion yen for the three years, assuming that the capacity-increasing coefficient is 0.6. The only difference lies in their growth paths.

In the perfectly same way, a capitalist economy is able to grow, say, with a 10% annual growth rate, whether or not its investment growth path is rising, levelling off, or falling, provided that no disadvantageous factors will creep in such as cumulative speculation and that the adjustment of other demand components in GNP is swiftly and flexibly made. Japan's growth paths for 1955–61 and the post-1962 years closely correspond to cases (1) and (2), respectively, still maintaining about the same 10% growth rate in GNP.

114

Someone once took my assertion as a kind of secular stagnation thesis, but in reality it is nothing of the kind. Still maintaining an optimistic view as to the 10% GNP growth potentiality, the writer has admitted the possibility that the fixed investment ratio might decline from 1962 on or the absolute amount of private fixed investment might level off over the coming few years. Such a view does not stand for a secular stagnation but for a medium-term stagnation of private fixed investment at a very high level amounting to 4–5 trillion yen. Since the fixed investment ratio was still extremely high, the Japanese economy may have expanded her capacity by about 10% per annum. This cannot be called pessimistic, but should be recognized as an indication of the mechanism and rhythm of fixed investment in a rapidly expanding, dynamic economy.

4. Prediction of Fixed Investment for 1961–65

Before going into analyses of the post-1962 situation it will be appropriate to explain what type of computation I employed in relation to private fixed investment requirements (excluding residential construction) for 1961–65. This did not depend upon any sophisticated econometric model, but on a very simple algebraic equation. Although in the first computation I used the old national income statistics, I would present here another one based on the newly revised estimates of GNP and its components which were published in may 1969.

According to this series, the real GNP growth rate for 1955–61 is, on the average, 10.0% per annum. This means an increase of 77% in real GNP for these six years. Although, potentially, the excess demand situation had prevailed in this period, the actual effective demand can be supposed to have increased hand in hand with increases in realized capacity. Consequently, we assume that the total demand as well as the capacity had increased by 77% in the six years. Denoting the six-year growth

115

rate of the total demand by d and the same growth rate of the capacity by s, we have the following relation:

$$d = s = \frac{x \sum_{55}^{60} I_f}{C_{a55}} \quad \cdots \cdots \cdots \cdots (1)$$

In this equation, I_f stands for gross private fixed investment (excluding residential construction), so $\sum_{55}^{60} I_f$ is equal to the cumulative total of I_f for 1955–60. All items are expressed in terms of 1965 calendar year constant prices. The denominator C_{a55} denotes the total capacity in 1955 and x the capacity-increasing coefficient of I_f. In this equation it is assumed that the private gross fixed investment would give rise to an increase of capacity in the next year with one year time lag. This is why we take a cumulative total of fixed investments for 1955—60 and not for 1955–61. The fixed investment in 1960 is, thus, supposed to bring about the capacity increase in 1961.

We assume that the capacity in 1955 is 11.146 trillion yen under the assumption that GNP = capacity and we compute $\sum_{55}^{60} I_f = 11.651$ trillion yen in real terms. Suppose $d = s$ at the rate of 77%, but C_{a55} and $\sum_{55}^{60} I_f$ are already known. Therefore, the only unknown in equation (1) is x, which can be solved as 73.7%.[4] This coefficient may be imagined as almost appropriate in view of the discussions in the "growth controversy" previouoly mentioned.

We now extend this equation over the five years 1961–66 which gives us the following:

$$d = s = \frac{x \sum_{61}^{65} I_f}{C_{a61}} \quad \cdots \cdots \cdots \cdots (2)$$

In this equation, we can assume that the known variables are x, C_{a61}, d and s. $C_{a61} = C_{a55} + x \sum I_f$. Since $C_{a55} = 11.146$

---

4) The capacity-increasing coefficient thus computed to be 0.737 is a bit higher than the one we have discussed already, 0.6 − 0.7. This is because we have here compared the capacity expansion with the preceding year's gross fixed investment which will mostly be less than the present year's investment. Thus, the superficial difference between 0.737 and 0.6 − 0.7 is merely due to the introduction of a year's lag.

trillion yen and $x \sum_{55}^{60} I_f = 8.587$ trillion yen, C_{a61} becomes 19.733 trillion yen. Let us presume for the time being that x is also 73.7% for 1961–66. However, it was very difficult to estimate the real GNP growth rate for 1961–66. I have tentatively assumed that it would be 10.0% annually (61% for five years) in view of the still prevailing, extremely high fixed investment ratio, but the actual result for 1961–66 has almost coincided with this assumpiton.

Consequently, the only unknown in equation (2) will be $\sum_{61}^{65} I_f$, and it will be solved as 16.332 trillion yen. However, this is a total for five years, so the average annual figure may be derived roughly as 3.26 trillion yen by dividing 16.332 trillion yen by five. Since it is still valued in 1965 constant prices, it should be converted to a 1961–65 average price which amounts to 3.302 trillion yen. This is a solution derived under the assumptions that effective demand and total capacity grow parallel with an annual rate of 10% and that a constant capacity-increasing coefficient $x = 73.7\%$ prevails.

However, the figure of 3.302 trillion yen for private fixed investment was not correct in view of the actual figures, and the writer himself did not accept it at its face value. In a paper written in Japanese in the autumn of 1962, I stated a view that the average private fixed investment for 1961–65 (inclusive of 1961) would be around 4 trillion yen instead 3.302 trillion yen. The reasoning is as follows.

(1) As already mentioned, the capacity-increasing coefficient x will not be constant after 1961. Owing to the pressure of our excess capacity situation, the proportion of replacement in the gross fixed investment may have increased, and the gross fixed investment may have a smaller counterpart in the increase of capacity after 1961. The entrepreneur would like to have utilized any old equipment to satisfy an increasing demand in the excess demand situation of 1955–61, but once some reserve emerges in their capacity, they would tend to scrap old equipment to a greater degree than in a situation of excess demand.

117

This naturally reduces the coefficient x, and the required amount of fixed investment would be raised to the extent that x is reduced. However, if $x = 60\%$ instead of 73.7% then the fixed investment derived will be 4.0086 trillion yen.

(2) Our equation presupposes that the effective demand and the capacity will grow proportionally, but the actual process might be different in the post-1962 excess capacity phase. Probably, the capacity may have increased faster than the effective demand, and the condition $d = s$ should be replaced by $d < s$. The entrepreneurs may have been forced to invest even if they have some excess capacity, particularly in the face of rapid technological progress and cutthroat competition among domestic firms as well as with foreign firms. If so, the condition $d = s$ should be loosened again in order to take this into account although (1) and (2) may overlap with each other to some extent. Thus, the private fixed investment projection which was revised upward by the reduction of x to 60% should be raised even higher by replacing the $d = s$ condition by that of $d < s$. My prediction that private fixed investment may be around 4 trillion yen for 1961-65 depends not only upon the mechanical calculation of simple algebra, but also upon the consideration of the tendency for x to decrease somewhat and the disequilibrium growth process $(d < s)$.

Such is a very global, macroscopic judgment based on GNP data. However, at the same time, I have attempted to estimate fixed investment requirements in manufacturing industry (corporate sector only) for 1961-65, based on the *Corporate Enterprise Quarterly Survey* (Hôjinkigyô Tôkeikihô) according to the same procedure. The method and assumptions of our computation are as follows: 1) The capacity-increasing coefficients x in gross terms are computed on the bases of both the corporate enterprise sales and fixed investment data; both series are reduced to real terms (1955 constant prices). 2) In estimating $\sum_{61}^{65} I_f$, the growth rate of corporate enterprise sales in real terms for 1955-61 is assumed to persist for 1961-66. 3) Although

Table 1. Estimates of x and $\sum_{51}^{65} I_f$ by Industry Based on the *Corporate Enterprise Quarterly Survey*

	Capacity-Increasing Coefficients (1955–61)	Estimates of $\sum_{61}^{65} I_f$ (1955 prices)	$\sum_{61}^{65} I_f /5$ (1961 prices)	Acutal Amount of I_f in 1961	Assumed Growth Rate of Real Sales (the same as those for 1951–61)
Manufacturing	2.88	8,165.6 bil. yen	2,021.6 bil. yen	1,919.0 bil. yen	20.2%
Food	4.56	422.1	104.5	113.5	13.5
Textiles	2.67	473.6	117.2	85.4	11.5
Chemicals	1.97	1,026.1	254.0	290.3	19.8
Iron and Steel	2.00	1,879.1	465.2	420.3	25.5
Machinery	4.88	390.6	96.7	103.8	26.2
Electric Machinery	3.88	1,040.6	257.6	197.4	28.4
Transp. Equipments	4.78	1,164.5	288.3	216.4	32.5

Note: The corporate enterprises covered do not include those having paid-up capital which is less than two million yen. The proportion of the latter in fixed investment was about 8% in early 1965.

a preliminary attempt was made to adjust sales by the capacity utilization ratio of the Ministry of International Trade and Industry to make them approach the capacity figures, quite unnatural results came about in some industries; for this reason we have decided to start from a tentative assumption that sales = capacity for 1955–61.

Table 1 indicates that in manufacturing as a whole the average fixed investment per annum for 1961–65 is almost the same as that of 1961, the peak year of fixed investment in the 1955–61 boom. As a matter of course this calculation is based on very simple assumptions that the same sales growth rates will continue to prevail for 1961–65 and that the capacity-increasing coefficients remain the same.

However, our computation of the fixed investment requirements in manufacturing indicates quite evidently that the fixed investment for 1961–65 will not show so spectacular an increase as its counterpart for 1955–61. Rather, its rate of increase falls tremendously, approaching zero %. For 1961–65, on the average, its absolute level may be the same as the preceding peak level in 1961, and our computations tell us that fixed investment will transform its behavior pattern radically. It is of interest to see that almost the same results come about, not only in the national economy as a whole, but also in the manufacturing sector although the extent of this behavior pattern varies from industry to industry.

Such were the computational results. We now intend to check this considerable body of data to see how good our predictions were, and as to what extent we did not take into account new developments.

5.   Post-Mortem

According to the new national income statistics, private fixed investment (excluding residential construction) was 960.1 billion yen in 1955 (fiscal year, the same below) and 4,227.4 billion yen in 1961. However, it was 4,229.2 billion yen in 1962, 4,670.2 billion yen in 1963, and 5,467.0 billion yen in 1965. The average of the five years, 1961–65, 47,213 billion which exceeds our prediction, 4,000 billion yen, by 18.0%. Although ours was not a precise prediction, it seems to be clear that we have not guessed so badly. On the basis of our computational procedure, the transformation of the fixed investment behavior pattern was by and large elucidated. For the four years 1957–61, private fixed investment increased by about 2.3 times, but for the four year period 1961–65 it increased only by 18.6%. This is really tremendous transition in investment behavior. Nevertheless, we must admit that our estimate was a bit low.

Another source of fixed investment in the corporate enterprise sector is the Ministry of Finance's *Corporate Enterprise Quarterly Survey* concerning the corporate enterprises whose paid-up capital is greater than two million yen. Table 2 takes up some industries and indicates on a quarterly basis how their fixed investments have changed so far. A casual look at this table will lead one to the following observations: 1) For 1958 IV– 1961 IV (Roman numeral indicates quarter) (period of heavy investment boom), the fixed investment in manufacturing increased by 3.36 times, and in all industries (excluding financial institutions and insurance companies) by 2.68 times; for 1961– 1965, it increased by 0.95 and 1.10 times, respectively. 2) In manufacturing and electricity and gas, the post-1961 rate of increase of fixed investment is very low, but it is surprising to see that in retail and wholesale trades, real estates, transportation and communication as well as other service industries, the fixed investment demonstrated an increase of close to twice as much, thus presenting a sharp contrast of investment behavior in the excess capacity phase between manufacturing and, electricity and gas, on the one hand, and the tertiary industry in general, on the other.

Although the fixed investment of all industries in 1964 slightly exceeds that in 1961, it is to be noticed that the fixed investment

Table 2.   Fixed Investment in Corporate Enterprises

Cal. year by quarter	All industries	Manufacturing	Retail and whole trades
1958.III	337.1	161.1	15.3
IV	311.9	145.3	15.7
1959.I	317.3	156.5	14.5
II	331.2	172.7	20.2
III	399.4	199.3	26.1
IV	446.6	238.0	22.6
1960.I	489.3	286.6	22.1
II	465.5	302.9	20.6
III	594.9	354.6	30.7
IV	645.7	401.2	33.0
1961.I	695.6	410.3	30.6
II	708.1	429.4	36.1
III	869.5	539.5	41.4
IV	902.4	541.1	42.1
1962.I	802.8	466.3	43.3
II	766.0	464.3	49.4
III	772.1	414.7	48.5
IV	732.3	403.4	51.2
1963.I	673.1	378.8	38.1
II	689.4	394.2	54.8
III	780.8	424.6	69.4
IV	849.9	490.6	84.1
1964.I	847.2	491.8	65.1
II	846.0	480.2	73.7
III	1039.7	555.0	83.4
IV	994.6	559.9	93.7
1965.I	892.3	468.0	61.8
II	817.1	465.0	67.0
III	919.1	443.0	70.8
IV	858.1	441.4	73.9
1961.IV/1958.IV	2.68	3.36	2.75
1965/1961	1.10	0.95	1.82

Source: The Ministry of Finance, *Hôjin Kigyô Tôkei Kihô* (Corporate Enterprise Quarterly Survey).

unit: billion yen

Real estates	Transp. and communication	Electricity and gas	Other service industries
5.8	43.2	75.7	6.2
4.7	43.2	70.7	8.1
6.2	49.7	64.4	4.6
3.9	43.3	60.5	6.9
4.9	54.1	72.3	9.1
8.6	64.9	67.0	8.5
9.5	53.8	66.8	16.5
6.7	39.9	63.2	5.3
9.4	72.0	76.5	7.1
14.6	58.2	81.6	6.9
9.0	78.8	102.4	6.3
19.0	65.0	72.7	14.6
17.9	79.1	92.1	12.2
18.3	82.5	110.9	24.3
22.5	88.4	95.0	14.1
17.1	64.2	83.7	17.8
20.1	90.8	106.5	13.5
17.6	74.5	110.7	13.4
15.4	82.6	96.5	8.0
11.9	85.2	71.4	16.2
18.0	86.6	105.1	21.7
15.3	89.6	87.4	24.2
18.4	103.6	86.7	22.7
32.0	90.1	70.3	23.0
35.9	129.0	90.4	34.0
47.8	106.8	83.1	50.7
38.3	126.3	94.8	32.4
21.3	102.1	74.6	28.1
36.3	140.5	125.7	32.9
25.8	132.6	116.5	31.3
3.16	1.91	1.47	3.92
1.90	1.64	1.09	2.17

Note: Financial institutions and insurance companies are excluded from all industries.

began to decline from 1964 IV on. In all industries, fixed investment declined by 17.5% from 1964 III to 1965 IV, and, in manufacturing it decreased by 21.2% from 1964 IV to 1965 IV. This seems to be a downward adjustment of fixed investment due to its excessive expansion from 1963 to 1964; for 1963 I–1964 IV it recovered by 47.7% in all industries and by 47.8% in manufacturing. This fixed investment recovery, which seems to have far surpassed the amount required by the growth rate, may be destined to have a relapse. At any rate, the average amount of fixed investment in manufacturing for 1961–65 was 1,769 billion yen less than the 1961 fixed investment of 1,920.3 billion yen by 7.9%. This underlines our view that fixed investment in manufacturing will also have stopped rising for several years after 1962.

The actual figures were thus even lower than our prediction and the 1961 peak, reflecting the fact that the per annum rate of increase in industrial production is lower for 1961–65 than for 1955–61 whereas our prediction presupposes the continuation of the same growth rate.

Our prediction was not intended to yield perfect results, but rather to suggest the fundamental transition which occurred from 1962 in private fixed investment behavior. However, if we take the above into account, even as a quantitative measure, our prediction was reasonably successful.

As another post-mortem, the following comparison (Fig. 3) may be of value. Here we have compared the 1957 II–1960 III period, starting from the peak of the so-called "Jimmu boom" (Emperor Jimmu was the legendary founder of Japan) when the tight money policy began to be enforced, and the 1961 IV–1965 I period, the main objective of our observation.

From Fig. 3, we see very clearly that, although in the corporate sector the rates of increase of sales (in money terms) are not so different between the two periods, there is a decisive difference in the behaviors of fixed investment. In the former period, the fixed investment moves up hand in hand with sales, and, although

Fig. 3. Transition in Fixed Investment Behavior

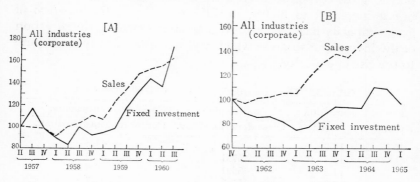

Source: The Ministry of Finance, *Corporate Enterprise Quarterly Survey.*

1961 was omitted in the graph [A], the rate of increase of fixed investment surpassed that of sales in 1961,. However, in the latter period, fixed investment almost levels off although there are some ups and downs in its behavior. In the former period fixed investment in 1960 III exceeds the 1957 II level by 76.8%, but in the latter it is 12% lower in 1965 I than the level of 1962 I. Such is the remarkable change in the pattern of fixed investment between the two periods.

However, we could not take into consideration beforehand the rising share of tertiary industry as well as the increasing proportion of construction in total private fixed investment. Naturally, the banks and other financial institutions may have lent their funds much more to industries in which there exists no over-capacity. Even in manufacturing the investment structure may have changed in such a way that the building and structures will increase their share vis-à-vis machinery and equipments.

The new national income statistics published in May 1969, indicates how the construction's share increased particularly from about 1960 or 1961 as shown in Table 3. The proportion of total construction in GNP was 16.2% in 1957–61, but it increased to 18.2% in 1962–65. The ratio of corporate construction to gross corporate fixed investment was 35.1% in 1957–61, but it increased to 38.0% in 1962–65. Thus, the pressure of excess capacity has been absorbed to some extent in the direction of the investment to areas which will not immediately contribute to the rise of capacity.

Table 3. The Construction Share in Fixed Investment

Fisc. year	Construction / GNP	Construction / Gross dom. fixed inv.	Corporate construction / Corporate gross fixed inv.
1956	14.9%	60.6%	41.2
57	15.4	57.6	33.0
58	14.5	56.9	33.6
59	15.8	57.1	34.7
60	16.9	54.2	35.7
61	18.5	54.9	38.4
62	18.6	55.3	37.1
63	18.3	56.5	41.8
64	18.3	56.4	36.2
65	17.5	57.7	37.0

Source: Economic Planning Agency's new national income estimates, revised in May 1969.

6. Excess Capacity Phase and the Ensuing Consequences

Even if we have come across a radical decrease in the increase of fixed investment from 1962 onward, we may, nevertheless, theoretically be able to assume an equilibrium growth path between effective demand and capacity. However, in the actual process a growth pattern with increasing excess capacity may inevitably happen because the private fixed investment is apt to have a strong downward rigidity. If it were unbalanced, it may exert a powerful influence on the creation of excess capacity.

We do not restrict our data only to the capacity utilization ratio announced by the Ministry of International Trade and Industry. If we only use that data, we may come to the conclusion that the excess capacity view is nothing but an illusion because the capacity utilization ratio in manufacturing has never followed a declining trend so far. This may be partly due to the fact that construction of a capacity index is very difficult and not yet so satisfactorily done for Japan as for other countries. For example, even if no overcapacity exists in strip-mills, considerable overcapacity may exist in blast-furnaces. This makes it difficult to construct an unambiguous measure of capacity. Moreover, the definition of capacity depends upon the kind of shift systems the workers are placed in, and this may differ from factory to factory. However, let us accept for the time being the official capacity data at its face value, and then ask if we have any evidences of increasing excess capacity.

According to my opinion, the implicit excess capacity tendency, emerging from a fixed investment ratio which exceeds the equilibrium ratio (given by the growth rate), may be absorbed as follows: 1) a decline of the capacity utilization ratio; 2) an unintended piling-up of stocks of finished as well as intermediate commodities; 3) an extraordinary upward deviation of interfirm credit from the normal rising trend; 4) exhorbitant increases of dishonored bills and bankruptcy even in the period of increasing production; 5) a decreasing trend in the profit rate; and 6) a depressed state of the stock market.

The index of the capacity utililization ratio (1965 = 100) in manufacturing was 107.5 in 1961, and from 1962 on it was 100.8, 100.0, 106.1 and 100.0 respectively, according to the Ministry of International Trade and Industry data. However, as referred to already, we are somewhat reluctant to accept this data at its face value. With regard to the producer's stocks of finished commodities in mining and manufacturing (1965 = 100), it was 46.5, 56.6, 75.0, 77.4, 88.1 and 100.0 for 1960-65. In terms of the inventory ratio (a ratio to sales), it was 82.7, 78.9, 81.3, 99.6, 92.7, 91.7 and 100.0 for 1959-65, surpassing the past trend for 1962-65.

Table 4. Dishonored Bills and Bankruptcies

	Dishonored bills	Bankruptcies Number	Amount
1956	115.2 bil. yen	1,123	46.4 bil. yen
1957	168.7	1,736	76.7
1958	155.5	1,480	58.0
1959	154.6	1,166	48.4
1960	185.3	1,172	65.2
1961	208.5	1,102	80.4
1962	280.5	1,779	184.0
1963	349.2	1,738	169.5
1964	526.5	4,212	463.1
1965	557.5	6,141	562.4

Source: See the footnote of Figure 4.

Thus, although the capacity utilization ratio indicates no decreasing trend, the inventories of finished commodities (and their ratio to sales) are increasing particularly from 1962. The statistical biases of the capacity figures aside, it may be expected that the heavy investment boom has entailed an increasing trend in depreciation and interest changes to any firm. Therefore, the relative stability of the utilization ratio could be ascribed to the entrepreneurial consideration that any reduction of output level or output increase will increase the per unit overhead cost and that the incremental overhead cost of curtailed production is higher than the disadvantages of holding unsold stocks.

However, the holding of an excessive stocks still may not be a good policy, so the firms are obliged to push their sales even at the sacrifice of an abnormal increase of interfirm credit. Therefore, the implicit pressure of excess capacity, resulting from an unbalanced high fixed investment ratio, will show up not only in increasing stocks, but in the abnormal rise of interfirm credit as well. The latter tendency is presented quite evidently in the sudden shift of the account receivable-sales ratio of firms in 1962 as indicated in Fig. 4. However, if the transactions are sustained by such an abnormal rise in interfirm credit, there may

Fig. 4. Interfirm Credit, Bankruptcies, and Dishonored Bills

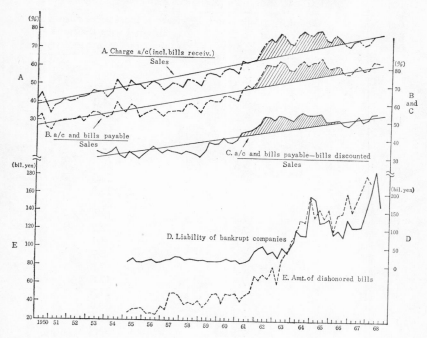

Sources: A, B, C. The Ministry of Finance, *Corporate Enterprise Quarterly.*
D. Tokyo Shôkô Kôshinsho (Tokyo Commercial and Industrial Inquiry Agency), Nationwide Survey on the Bankruptcy of Companies.
E. Tokyo Tegata Kôkansho (Tokyo Clearing House), Annual and Monthly Reports of Tokyo Bank Clearing.

also arise the danger that any small friction or strain in the transaction may bring forth an increase of the dishonored bills and bankruptcies. For 1961–65, we have a very high growth rate of real GNP of near 10% per annum; and still it is to be noted that dishonored bills and bankruptcies have kept rising very steeply from around 1962. Even in the 1963 recovery,

Table 5. Operating Profit Rate and the Rate of Increase of
Sales: All industries (corporate sector)

Cal. year by quarter	Operative profit rate to total capital	Rate of increase of sales (compared with the same quarter of the previous year)
1959.I	7.5%	17.4%
II	8.1	23.6
III	8.3	30.7
IV	9.4	34.0
1960.I	9.2	43.3
II	9.4	27.0
III	9.0	20.4
IV	9.0	17.9
1961.I	9.0	14.8
II	9.0	23.5
III	8.4	29.5
IV	7.7	23.1
1962.I	7.5	18.8
II	7.4	12.2
III	6.8	4.1
IV	6.4	5.7
1963.I	7.2	7.8
II	7.3	17.6
III	7.1	27.3
IV	7.3	30.0
1964.I	7.5	28.9
II	7.5	23.6
III	6.8	19.2
IV	6.4	14.0
1965.I	6.8	15.2
II	6.4	11.0
III	5.8	10.4
IV	5.9	13.6

Source: The Ministry of Finance, *Corporate Enterprise Quarterly Survey.*

when the private fixed investment and industrial production began to increase so rapidly, the above indicators were still rising.

From these observations, it will be understood that the excess capacity pressure has been embodied in rising stocks and interfirm credit and also in the increasing bankruptcies and dishonored bills. Another factor in the aftermath of the 1955–61 investment boom is the tendency for the profit rate to decrease. In Table 5, we see this tendency, and it is of interest to note that from 1963 III to 1964 II the average profit rate was 7.4% and the average rate of increase of sales was 27.5%, while for 1959 II– 1960 IV the average profit rate was 8.9% and the average rate of increase of sales was 28.1%. In other words, at corresponding growth rates the profit rate tended to decline during this period.

This decline was probably due to several causes. Some point out that the operating profit rate to total capital has tended to decline, but the operating profit to sales has shown no tendency to decrease although we see its ups and downs in accordance with minor cycles. Therefore, the decline in profit rate to total capital can be regarded as resulting mainly from the decline of the sales/total capital ratio, but the ratio of profit rate to sales has shown no declining tendency. However, such a decrease in the turn-over rate of total capital is further attributable to the preceding spectacular investment boom of 1955–61 as well as the post-1962 abnormal rise in interfirm credit; it should be noted here the "account and bills payable" is also an item of total capital on the corporation's balance sheet. It is to be emphasized that these two are not short-term but medium-term factors, so the decreasing trend in profit rate also reflects some-what the intractable impact of the fixed investment cycle.

Among other factors, excessive competition among firms, caused by pressures resulting from the piling up of stocks, may have exerted a strong influence upon the decreasing profit rate. The Bank of Japan and the Economic Planning Agency have demonst-rated that the decreasing trend in the nominal profit rate computed from the corporation's balance sheet is de-emphasized because in booms they would like to conceal their profits and in depressions their losses.[5]

---

5) E.P.A., *Keizai-hakusho* (Economic White Paper) of 1965, and the Bank of Japan, "The Tendency of Corporate Profit" (in Japanese), *Chôsa Geppô* (Monthly Research Bulletin), 1965.

Fig. 5. Stock Prices and Fixed Investment

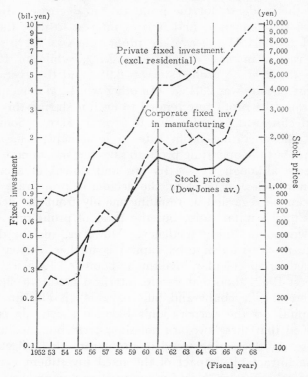

(Fiscal year)

Sources: (1) Stock prices: Tokyo Stock Exchange; *Tôshô Tôkeinempô*, and *Geppô* (Annual and Monthly Reports of Tokyo Stock Exchange).
(2) Private fixed investment: Economic Planning Agency's revised estimate of national income statistics in 1969, and Ministry of Finance, *Corporate Enterprise Quarterly Survey*.

Such being the case, it is quite natural that the stock market stagnated. It is the first time in the postwar period, that a more than five years stagnancy has persisted in the stock market. It is very interesting to see the positive correlation prevailing between the Dow-Jones average stock prices on the Tokyo stock exchange and the private fixed investment (Fig. 5). This correlation probably means that under conditions of excess demand in which the fixed investment and its ratio to sales are pushed up, stock prices will also increase, but under excess capacity in which the fixed investment ratio will be forced to fall (and its absolute level tends to level off) the stock prices will naturally decrease. From Fig. 5, we can assume that the stagnancy of stock prices also reflects the medium-term fixed investment cycle, and so it will be erroneous to imagine that the slump in stock market has been a result merely of bad monetary policy.

There is another interesting phenomenon the cause of which may also be attributable to the post-1962 excess capacity. As indicated in Table 6, the Marshallian k (total money supply divided by GNP) suddenly increased from 23.9% in 1962 to 26.1% in 1963 and 27.4% in 1965. Although there is an upward tendency in the Marshallian k (21.3% in 1955, 23.9% in 1962

Table 6. The Marshallian k

Cal. year.	Money supply / GNP	Cash currency / GNP	Deposit currency / GNP
1955	21.3%	5.9%	15.4%
56	21.6	5.8	15.8
57	21.5	5.6	15.9
58	21.7	5.5	16.2
59	22.5	5.6	16.9
60	22.5	5.4	17.1
61	22.8	5.4	17.4
62	23.9	5.6	18.3
63	26.1	5.6	20.5
64	25.9	5.5	20.4
65	27.4	5.7	21.7
66	27.7	5.7	22.0
67	26.7	5.7	21.0
68	27.1	5.9	21.2

Source: Bank of Japan: *Keizai Kansoku Kiso Tōkei* (Basic Statistics on Economic Forecasting), and national income statistics revised in May 1969.

Note: Money supply data are the annual average of the figures at the end of twelve months.

and 27.1% in 1968), its ratio of 26.1% for 1963 marks a sharp, and abrupt, upward shift. The cash currency/GNP ratio is comparatively stable, and so the increase of the Marshallian k is caused mainly by the increase of the deposit currency/GNP ratio. There is a particular explanation as to why the Marshallian k suddenly increased in 1963. In the autumn of 1962, the Bank of Japan adopted a new monetary policy of open market operation, and in May 1963 it lifted the long-standing regulation on city bank's loans. Because the city banks no longer found it necessary to conceal the actual amount of their loans, loans which had thus far remained hidden suddenly appeared on the financial statistics. This apparently also raised the amount of deposits, because loans and deposits almost always move in consonance with each other under the double-entry bookkeeping.

However, this does not explain all of the increase in either loans and deposits or the Marshallian k. Generally, the hidden loans at that time were estimated as amounting to 400–450 billion yen, concentrated in big banks in large cities. Therefore, it does not explain all of the increase in the Marshallian k. Even if the hidden loans were removed (for June-December period), the Marshallian k of 26.1% for 1963 would decrease only to 25.3–25.2% which still leaves an abrupt jump compared with the 23.9% of 1962. Moreover, in January of 1964, the Bank of Japan's regulation has come to life again together with the revival of the tight money policy, yet the Marshallian k still remained at 25.9% in 1964.

Such an abnormal increase in the Marshallian k was largely a result of the unusual increase of loans and deposits, which again may have come from the exhorbitant increase of interfirm credit. The interfirm credit consists of the charge account and bills receivable. The latter, however, must be transformed soon into cash or current account by discounting at a bank. In this sense, the interfirm credit cannot but be changed into bank credit in a short period, and the former is therefore one of the most important causes of the abnormal rise of deposit currency and also of the Marshallian k. If this speculation is correct, we come to the conclusion that the growth of the excess capacity pattern, even if the growth rate is high, has necessarily brought about the interfirm credit increase deviating from normal trend and that, at the same time, the latter must be followed by an exhorbitant increase in the Marshallian k.

The above is an explanation of the aftermath of the 1955–61 investment boom and may highlight to some extent as to why the high growth rate for 1962–65 cannot but be accompanied by the rather peculiar occurrences of the so-called "prosperity without profit," the stagnancy of the stock market, increases in inventories, interfirm credit and the Marshallian k.

We have insisted so far that the pattern of growth may have changed, with 1961 as the turning point, from the period of high-tempo increase in fixed investment to the period of stagnation in fixed investment and also from excess demand to excess capacity. However, many people have recently tended to understand it rather differently. These people think that since the impact of excess capacity and depression has been felt particularly strongly for 1964–65, the transition is thought to have occurred during 1964–65, not 1961. In our opinion, the transition had already occurred in 1961–62, and the rapid increase in production and fixed investment for 1963–64 is of a rather temporary nature; much confusion might have been created if the Japanese economy were under the prewar-type capitalism and the gold standard. Actually, by being able to spread interfirm credit and to support it with increasing bank loans, the Japanese economy could be emancipated from the deep depressions we experienced in the prewar period. In this sense, in terms of potential, the Japanese economy has entered a new phase in 1962, but this has been concealed by a loose monetary policy as well as an aggressive fiscal policy. In 1962 and 1963, the rate of increase of government expenditures for goods and services, including public investment, was 23.0% and 23.2%, the highest for 1952–1967 period. The implicit tendency for the economy to move to a new phase is evident in view of the decreasing trend of profit rates and the remarkable increase of stocks, interfirm credit and bankruptcies, even if the apparent movement of the capacity utilization ratio seems to be relatively stable in manufacturing as a whole.

7. Respurt of Fixed Investment in 1966

The fixed investment stagnation thus prevailed for 1962–65, but after 1966 we had a renewed investment boom. In fiscal 1966, the private fixed investment (excl. residential construction) indicated a 25.4% rise, and in fiscal 1967, it exhibited a higher increase, 27.1%. Now, it became a problem when the upswing of a new fixed investment cycle would start, but Toshio Shishido has pointed out that the four year period of investment stagnation would reach to an end in around 1965.[6]

To make this point clear, it will be more useful to have a chart based on the *Corporate Enterprise Quarterly Survey* (Fig. 6) rather than that based on the national income statistics. Fig. 6 is the fixed investment-sales ratio in all industries (excluding financial institutions) and manufacturing as concerns corporations with paid-in capital of 2 million yen and more. From this, the medium-term cycle of fixed investment is by and large evident, and it is extremely interesting to see that the trough in early 1966 of the fixed investment ratio came down very close to the 1955 trough. Thus, the roughly ten year cycle presents itself in the behavior of private fixed investment.

If we look at the cycle of the fixed investment-GNP ratio, based on the national income statistics, we may be misled by a still higher ratio prevailing in 1965 than in 1955, and we may doubt whether or not 1965 was the end of investment stagnation, for the 1965 fixed investment ratio was still higher than that of 1955. However, Fig. 6 tells us that the investment ratios in both troughs are comparatively equal. The apparent difference may

---

6) Toshio Shishido, "Tenkei-ki wa Owatta" (End of the Transition Period), *Ekonomisuto*, January 17, 1967.

Fig. 6. Fixed Investment-Sales Ratio in Corporate Enterprises

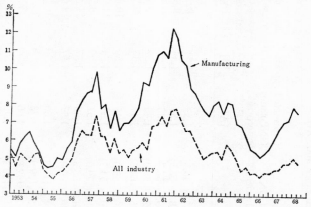

Source: The Ministry of Finance, *Corporate Enterprise Quarterly Survey*.
Note: (1) "All industry" excludes financial institutions.
  (2) Corporate enterprises cover those with paid-in capital of 2 million yen and more.

be due to the fact that, according to the national income statistics, the agriculture total is included, while in the *Corporate Enterprise Quarterly Survey* almost all figures for agriculture are excluded (except for corporate farm enterprises), even in "all industries". Since the share of agriculture had decreased considerably for past several years and the role of fixed investment in agriculture is not so important, it is expected that the optimum fixed investment ratio, as compared with *GNP*, may probably increase. Nevertheless, it is also true that the trend of the fixed investment ratio will not be upward in manufacturing or non-agriculture proper. In this way, Fig. 6 presents the conjecture that the fixed investment ratio may begin to rise from around 1966 in so far as it had already reached the 1955 low early in 1966. At that time I was not aware of this and still hesitated to insist that the medium-term investment stagnation had ended,

Table 7. Gross Private Fixed Capital Stock and GNP

unit: billion yen

Fisc. year	Private fixed investment (1960 prices)	Gross fixed capital stock in private enterprises		Real GNP (1960 prices)	Gross fixed capital-GNP ratios in private enterprises		Rate of increase of fixed capital stock
		[A]	[B]		[A]	[B]	[A]
1950	—	9515.8(37.7)	10554.9(41.8)	—	—	—	—
1951	817.4	10333.2(40.9)	11290.6(44.7)	7455.8(46.5)	1.39	1.51	8.6%
1952	930.5	11263.7(44.6)	12128.1(48.1)	8418.8(52.5)	1.34	1.44	8.8
1953	1124.4	12388.1(49.1)	13140.1(52.1)	9089.9(56.7)	1.36	1.45	10.0
1954	1049.6	13437.7(53.2)	14084.7(55.8)	9292.9(58.0)	1.45	1.52	8.5
1955	1140.3	14578.0(57.8)	15111.0(59.9)	10355.8(64.6)	1.41	1.46	8.5
1956	1582.2	16160.2(64.0)	16614.1(65.8)	11056.6(69.0)	1.46	1.50	10.9
1957	1871.0	18031.2(71.4)	18391.6(72.9)	11979.7(74.7)	1.51	1.54	11.6
1958	1786.5	19817.7(78.5)	20088.8(79.6)	12658.4(79.0)	1.57	1.59	9.9
1959	2269.8	22087.5(87.5)	22245.1(88.1)	14161.2(88.3)	1.56	1.57	11.4
1960	3151.7	25239.2(100.0)	25239.2(100.0)	16030.7(100.0)	1.57	1.57	14.4
1961	4076.6	29315.8(116.2)	29112.0(115.3)	18314.4(114.2)	1.60	1.59	16.2
1962	4126.0	33441.8(132.5)	32701.6(129.6)	19373.4(120.9)	1.73	1.69	14.1
1963	4538.6	37980.4(150.5)	36650.2(145.2)	22897.0(142.8)	1.66	1.60	13.6
1964	5261.8	43242.2(171.3)	41228.0(163.3)	24106.5(150.4)	1.79	1.71	13.9
1965	4782.9	48025.1(190.3)	45389.1(179.8)	25417.2(158.6)	1.89	1.79	11.1
1966	5782.5	53807.6(213.2)	50593.4(200.5)	28301.6(176.5)	1.90	1.79	12.0
1967	7260.9	61068.5(242.0)	57128.2(226.3)	31956.8(199.3)	1.91	1.79	13.5

Sources: Revised national income estimate (May, 1969) by the Economic Planning Agency; *Shihon Suttoku to Keizai Seichō* (Capital Stock and Economic Growth), 1962 and the journal *Keizai Bunseki* (Economic Analysis), February 1966.

Notes: (1) From "An Estimate of Gross Capital Stock" in the above *Keizai Bunseki*, we obtain 23955.1 billion yen, the sum of the gross tangible fixed assets of corporate enterprises (all industries, excl. temporary construction account) and those of unincorporated enterprises at the end of the calendar year 1960, and then add to it the temporary construction account of corporate enterprises, 445.7 billion yen, adjusting it upward by making a further addition of the 95 per cent of real private fixed investment for January-March of 1961, 838.4 billion yen. We apply 95 per cent in order to subtract the probable replacement. The figure finally arrived at is the gross capital stock at the end (March) of fiscal year 1960.

(2) The capital stock [A] is derived by a continuous addition or deduction of real private fixed investment for each year, as based on the capital stock at the end of fiscal 1960. The capital stock [B] is derived by further assuming that the replacement-private fixed investment ratio is 10% for 1951–55, 5% for 1956–61, 13% for 1962–65, and 10% for 1966–67. [A] is estimated on a "gross" investment basis, while [B] is estimated on that of "net" investment.

Fig. 7. Gross Private Fixed Capital Stock and GNP

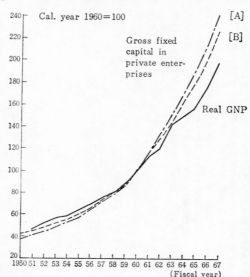

but Toshio Shishido correctly pointed out the upward transition of private fixed investment will soon occur.

In relation to the future alternative trends of private fixed investment, we can now compute values under differnet assumed growth rates of GNP and varying gross fixed capital-GNP ratios. For 1950–67, we estimate, as enumerated in Table 6, the series of the gross fixed capital stock (in 1960 calendar year prices) of private enterprises which is some cumulative value of private fixed investment (excluding housing) in 1960 prices. The base year of this cumulation is 1960, and the method of its calculation is shown in the footnote of Table 7. We have here two series of fixed capital stock, one of which [B] takes account of the deduction of rejected plant and equipment (replacement) and another of which [A] does not account for any such replacement. The latter merely continually adds or deducts each year's gross fixed

Fig. 8. Gross Private Fixed Capital-GNP Ratio [A]

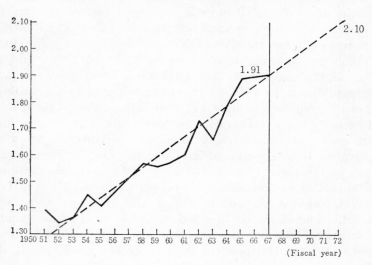

Note: The straight line is fitted in free hand.

investment to or from the 1960 value of gross fixed capital.   In comparison with the real GNP, we get the gross private fixed capital-GNP ratios [A] and [B], both of which indicate increasing tendencies.   The gross capital stock [A] and [B] and GNP at 1960 constant prices are depicted in Fig. 7, and trend of the gross private fixed capital-GNP ratio [A] for 1951–67 is indicated in Fig. 8.

On the basis of the above statistics for 1951–67, we are trying to figure out the 1968–72 trend of private fixed investment in Table 8.   For this period we assume alternative growth rates of 12%, 10% and 8%, as well as the probable capital coefficients ((1) a constant coefficient of 1.91 and (2) an increase in it from 1.91 to 2.10), thus deriving gross private fixed capital [A] and its annual increment, gross private fixed investment, for 1968–72.

Before going into an examination of private fixed investment for 1967–72, we have to discuss what assumptions are most adequate as to the GNP growth rate and gross private capital-GNP ratio. On the one hand, for the five year period 1963–67, the average growth rate of real GNP was 10.6%, but if we exclude the 1965 growth rate, it increases to 11.9% (12.8%, 10.4%, 5.4%, 11.4% and 12.9% for 1963–67). From this, we may anticipate that if the 1966–67 growth rate continues, the assumption of 12% will be adequate, but if we include that of 1965, 10% will be more likely. Therefore, we select 10% and 12% as probable real GNP growth rates, although a calculation based on 8% growth is also presented in Table 8. On the other hand, as far as the three years of 1965–67 are concerned, the gross capital coefficient tended to level off (in terms of [A], from 1.89 to 1.91), whereas, as seen in Fig. 8, the long-term trend was upward. Therefore, we decided to select a constant capital coefficient of 1.91 and also one that increases from 1.91 (1967) to 2.10 (1972). However, in the case of 8% growth, only the latter assumption (1.91 to 2.10) is adopted because a rise is always indicated in the low annual growth rate.

Now, according to the Economic Planning Agency's projection of January 27, 1969, the real GNP growth rate was 12.6% in 1968 and 9.8% in 1969. Private fixed investment (excluding housing) was 9,200 billion yen in 1968 and 10,700 billion yen in 1969. If this is the actual trend, the Japanese economy in 1968 and 1969 can best be explained in terms of a 12% GNP growth rate, but, as concerns an assumption of capital coefficient, an intermediate case of the two (a constant capital coefficient and one that increases from 1.91 to 2.10) may be appropriate, as manifested in Table 8. If this were correct, the upswing of the fixed investment cycle will be certain to continue *at least* until 1969 (as it has for the four years from 1966). In view of the fact that in the 1955–61 investment boom the upswing period was six years, although interrupted by the 1958 recession, the continuation of rising fixed investment ratio for four years seems to convince us

Table 8. Alternative Private Fixed Investment Projected for 1967–72

I. 12% GNP growth

Fisc. year	Assumed gross capital coefficient A	Private gross capital stock (1960 prices)	Private fixed investment (1960 prices)	Private fixed investment (current prices)	(3) / Real GNP
	(1)	(2)	(3)	(4)	(5)
1967	1.91	61037.5	7260.9(actual)	7987.0	22.7%
1968	1.91	68362.0	7324.5	8489.1	20.5
1969	1.91	76565.4	8203.4	9639.0	20.5
1970	1.91	85753.3	9187.9	10942.8	20.5
1971	1.91	96043.6	10290.3	12420.4	20.5
1972	1.91	107568.9	11525.3	14095.4	20.5
1967	1.910	61037.5	7260.9(actual)	7987.0	22.7%
1968	1.948	69722.0	8684.5	10065.3	24.3
1969	1.986	79612.0	9890.0	11620.8	24.7
1970	2.024	90871.5	11259.0	13409.5	25.1
1971	2.062	103686.9	12815.4	15468.2	25.5
1972	2.100	118269.5	14582.6	17834.5	25.9

II. 10% GNP growth

Fisc. year	Assumed gross capital coefficient A	Private gross capital stock (1960 prices)	Private fixed investment (1960 prices)	Private fixed investment (current prices)	(3) / Real GNP
1967	1.91	61037.5	7260.9(actual)	7987.0	22.7%
1968	1.91	67141.3	6103.8	7074.3	17.4
1969	1.91	73855.3	6714.0	7889.0	17.4
1970	1.91	81240.9	7385.6	8796.2	17.4
1971	1.91	89365.1	8124.2	9805.9	17.4
1972	1.91	98301.4	8936.3	10929.1	17.4
1967	1.910	61037.5	7260.9(actual)	7987.0	22.7%
1968	1.948	68477.1	7439.6	8622.5	21.2
1969	1.986	76794.0	8316.9	9772.4	21.5
1970	2.024	86089.8	9295.8	11071.3	21.9
1971	2.062	96476.9	10387.1	12537.2	22.2
1972	2.100	108080.1	11603.2	14190.7	22.5

III. 8% GNP growth

Fisc. year	Assumed gross capital coefficient A	Private gross capital stock (1960 prices)	Private fixed investment (1960 prices)	Private fixed investment (current prices)	(3) / Real GNP
1967	1.910	61037.5	7260.9(actual)	7987.0	22.7%
1968	1.948	67231.9	6194.4	7179.3	17.9
1969	1.986	74027.0	6795.1	7984.2	18.2
1970	2.024	81479.0	7452.0	8875.3	18.5
1971	2.062	89649.4	8170.4	9861.7	18.8
1972	2.100	98605.5	8956.1	10953.7	19.1

Notes: (1) GNP at 1960 prices × (1) = (2); Δ(2) = (3); (3) × Private fixed investment deflator = (4).

(2) GNP at 1960 constant prices in 1967 is 31956.8 billion yen, and its series for 1967–72 is derived by each real GNP growth rate.

(3) The private fixed investment deflator (1960 = 100) employed is 115.9, 117.5, 119.1, 120.7 and 122.3 for 1968–72, according to the Economic Planning Agency's economic plan's data.

143

that the Japanese economy came into the upswing phase of fixed investment cycle in 1966.

When compared with other calculations based on more moderate assumptions, the actual path of private fixed investment is more exactly consistent with a case of 12% growth and an intermediate case of the two capital coefficient assumptions, as far as the period of 1967–69 is concerned. Of course, it is not clear whether or not this will continue and whether or not this will be shifted to a 10% growth rate from around 1969 or 1970. However, it is evident that for 1966–69 the growth path of the Japanese economy was extremely high, very close to the highest growth path computed in Table 8.

Table 9. Gross Fixed Capital-Sales Ratio and the Rate of Change of Gross Fixed Capital Stock in Corporate Enterprises of Manufacturing

Fiscal year	Gross fixed capital-sales ratio		Rate of change of gross fixed capital stock
	[A]	[B]	
1953	0.53	0.59	16.9%
1954	0.54	0.59	12.9
1955	0.55	0.59	12.3
1956	0.53	0.56	19.5
1957	0.55	0.56	20.1
1958	0.55	0.57	14.7
1959	0.52	0.52	19.0
1960	0.51	0.51	25.5
1961	0.53	0.52	26.3
1962	0.57	0.56	17.6
1963	0.55	0.53	16.0
1964	0.54	0.52	15.7
1965	0.56	0.53	11.3
1966	0.51	0.48	11.4
1967	0.49	0.45	16.3

Source: Ministry of Finance, *Corporate Enterprise Quarterly Survey.*
Notes: (1) [A] and [B] of the gross fixed capital-sales ratio correspond to [A] and [B] in the preceding Table, in accordance with whether or not the replacement is neglected in the computation of the gross capital stock.
(2) Corporate enterprises with paid-in capital of 2 million yen and more.

It is of some interest to see that the rate of increase of fixed capital stock [A] followed a medium-term cycle movement as indicated in Table 9. In the same way, that in corporate manufacturing enterprises also indicated a similar cycle (12.3% in 1955, 26.3% in 1961, 11.3% in 1965 and 16.3% in 1957). Table 9 shows this as well as the trend of the gross fixed capital-sales ratio. It is very important to see that in the corporate enterprise sector of manufacturing the gross capital coefficient was relatively stable for 1953–65 and even tended to decline for 1966–67. This seemingly contradicts its rising trend in the national economy as a whole. Probably, the latter is due to the declining share of agriculture in which fixed investment is not so significant, as well as a relative increase of fixed capital stock in the tertiary industry in which the relation between fixed capital stock and capacity is comparatively flexible.

The relative stability of the gross fixed capital coefficient in manufacturing thus coexisted with its rising trend in the national economy as a whole.

8. Conclusion

1. Following the unprecedented investment boom of 1955–61 we have a stagnant fixed investment even while GNP is growing at a rate of 10%. Both periods can be characterized as the excess demand and the excess capacity phases of medium-term fixed investment cycle; this has occurred twice, at intervals of 9–10 years in the postwar fixed investment ratio.

2. Therefore, the situation for 1962–65 was completely different from an ordinary phase of inventory recession. Owing to the downward rigidity of private fixed investment and to the persistence of an investment ratio too-highly rigid vis à vis the growth rate, we have a continuing excess capacity pheno-menon which has been reflected in the following: the increasing stocks of finished commodities; an upward deviation from the trend of interfirm credit; a rapidly increasing number of bank-

ruptcies and dishonored bills (even during the 1963 minor recovery); a decreasing trend in the profit rate; and a continuing depression of the stock market. The extraordinary increase of interfirm credit, in turn, extraordinarily augmented bank loans which entailed a sudden increase of the Marshallian k. Therefore, for 1962–63, the excess capacity situation was merely implicit, but from 1964 on a severe depression was experienced as soon as the tight money policy was enforced.

3. The postwar second "Juglar cycle" of fixed investment ended in 1965, and from 1966 we had a renewed investment spurt. This suggests that the Japanese economy has been on the postwar third upswing of the fixed investment cycle.

9. Technical Appendix

This appendix aims to analyze the formal relationship between the marginal gross fixed capital-output ratio and the growth rate of gross fixed investment and thus fill the gap we could not discuss in detail as to the variability of the capacity increasing coefficient of gross fixed investment (the reciprocal of the above ratio) in accordance with the change of the growth rate.

We will use the following notation: I^n and I^G, net and gross fixed investment, respectively; R, replacement investment (or the equipment rejected); τ, the effective years of durability of the equipment; and g, the average annual rate of growth of gross fixed investment for the period in which the equipment is durable. It should be noted that gross fixed investment before τ years, $I^G_{-\tau}$, is equal by definition to R. Thus,

$$\frac{R}{I^G} = \frac{I^G_{-\tau}}{I^G_{-\tau}(1+g)^\tau} = \frac{1}{(1+g)} \qquad \cdots\cdots\cdots\cdots (1)$$

$$\frac{I^n}{I^G} = 1 - \frac{R}{I^G} = \frac{(1+g)^\tau - 1}{(1+g)^\tau} \qquad \cdots\cdots\cdots\cdots (2)$$

When marginal gross fixed capital-output ratio is defined as

$$I^G/\Delta C_a = \frac{I^n + R}{\Delta C_a} = \frac{I^n + \dfrac{I^G}{(1+g)^\tau}}{\Delta C_a} = \frac{I^n}{\Delta C_a}\left[1 + \frac{I^G}{I^n(1+g)^\tau}\right]$$

$$= \frac{I^n}{\Delta C_a}\left[1 + \frac{(1+g)^\tau}{[(1+g)^\tau - 1](1+g)^\tau}\right]$$

β_G and β_n, refer to the marginal gross and net fixed capital-output ratios respectively. The former relation can be simplified as follows:

$$\beta_G = \beta_n\left[1 + \frac{1}{(1+g)^\tau - 1}\right]\quad\cdots\cdots\cdots(3)$$

This can be called the fundamental equation of the relationship between the marginal gross and net fixed capital-output ratios.

Assuming the effective years of durability as 20 years, we present in Table 7 the difference which will be brought about between β_G and β_n by the change in the average growth rate of gross fixed investment.

Table 7. The Growth Rate of I^G and Its Relationship with R/I^G and $\beta_G \cdot \beta_n$
——in case of 20 year durability——

g	β_G/β_n	R/I^G
20%	1.0746	0.0694
10%	1.1746	0.1486
4%	1.8396	0.4564
2.5%	2.5659	0.6103
0%	∞	1.0000

The result shows very clearly that when the growth rate of I^G is extraordinarily high, the difference between $\beta_G - \beta_n$ will be reduced extremely. When g is 20%, β_G/β_n is only 1.0746; this is because of the very low R/I^G (= 0.0694). However, if g is 2.5%, R/I^G will become very high (0.6103), and therefore β_G/β_n becomes 2.5659. It seems to me that $g = 20\%$ looks like the case of Japan, $g = 4\%$ that of EEC, and $g = 2.5\%$ that of the United Kingdom. If we further assume that the inter-

147

national differences in β_n are not considerable and that there is a positive correlation between the growth rate of the gross fixed investment and that of GNP, we may find a negative correlation between the GNP growth rate and β_G. The meaningful relations shown here might be a formal explanation for the historical as well as the international differences of the marginal gross capital output ratios, which were once empirically analyzed in my book, *Growth and Cycles in the Japanese Economy*, (Kinokuniya 1962), pp. 126–33.

CHAPTER 5

JAPAN'S INDUSTRIAL LEVEL IN INTERNATIONAL PERSPECTIVE

1. Measurement

In an article published in the *Weltwirtschaftliches Archiv* the writer has previously attempted to compute an inter-country index of industrial production in 1956 for the following seven countries: the United States, the United Kingdom, West Germany, Italy, France, Sweden, and Japan.[1] It was not an ordinary time-series, but a *cross-section* index of production indicating the relative levels of industrial production for these countries in the year 1956. Here we have felt it desirable to make a number of important revisions in the above-mentioned work. The number of countries considered earlier was limited to seven, but it was felt that any our comparison here should have a much wider scope including not only other industrial countries (capitalist as well as socialist countries), but also under-developed countries. Second, in choosing the year 1958 for the new computation, the comprehensive *Census of Manufactures* is available for the United States as well as corresponding statistics for the United Kingdom, thus making it possible to set up the detailed weight systems in terms of value added in the various industries of the United States, the United Kindgom,

---

1) Miyohei Shinohara, "Relative Production Levels of Industrial Countries and their Growth Potentials," *Weltwirtschaftliches Archiv*, Band 86, Heft 1, 1961 (incorporated with amendments in the book, *Growth and Cycles in the Japanese Economy*, Tokyo, Kinokuniya Bookstore, 1962).

and Japan. Third, this present effort affords an opportunity to remedy the inadequacies of the index number of the earlier work.

Most of the physical volumes of the various commodity items come from the *Statistical Yearbook* of the United Nations, and the individual cross-section indices of the physical volume of production of the various commodity items are combined into the total index with each individual index being weighted by its respective value added figure. In this way, three types of indices arise: (1) the index with the United States = 100 using the U. S. value added weights, (2) the index with the United Kingdom = 100 using the U. K. value added weights and (3) the index with Japan = 100 using Japan's value added weights. These three indices are then compared with each other with the United States = 100 or with Japan = 100. In most cases the geometric averages of the three indices are computed and then used for analytical purposes.

The countries covered in this survey number more than eighty, and the commodity items amount to more than seventy. However, as far as the manufacturing index is concerned, we used fifty-three items which were further classified into the following twelve industries; (1) food, (2) tobacco, (3) textiles, (4) lumber, (5) pulp and paper, (6) chemicals, (7) rubber products, (8) petroleum products, (9) coal products (cokes), (10) cement, (11) metals and (12) machinery and construction. It may be strange that the machinery industry and the construction activity are combined in the last category. But, in computing the physical volume of machinery, we come across the difficulty that each type of machinery, even if it has the same name say, the machine tools, consists of products which vary in quality, size, etc., and are heterogeneous. Therefore, we gave up measuring these products from the output side, and instead used an input approach. Since steel is one of the most important raw materials, we may grasp the relative level of machinery production approximately by the steel consumption in the machinery industry. Of course, the unit requirements of steel consumption in machinery production may differ from country to country in accordance with the differences in the intra-composition of the machinery industry as well as with the technological differences. Even if we put aside this problem, it is very difficult to estimate the machinery industry's proportional share in steel consumption after excluding that used for the purposes of construction in every country. Consequently, the scope of the category has been enlarged here to include the construction industry as well as the machinery industry. However, in this case the weighted average of the indices of the volume of the following major inputs was used: the apparent domestic consumption of crude steel, cement, and lumber after allowance had been made for exports and imports in the broader category of industry as defined above. The resulting index thus covered the machinery industry as well as the construction industry as steel, cement and lumber are the major inputs in the construction and machinery industries.

Besides the index of manufacturing production, we have computed an index of mining production (based only on the Japanese value added weight system) consisting of twenty commodity items and also an index of public utilities consisting of electricity and gas (based on the three weight systems of the United States, the United Kingdom and Japan).

The detailed results of computed indices of manufacturing, mining, and public utilities are indicated in the attached tables in the Appendix. Concerning the manufacturing index, we have calculated a "total" index and an index which excludes the food industry using the weights of the U. S., the U. K. and Japan, respectively. The reasons why extremely big differences emerge between the three "total" indices using different weight systems when they are converted to the United States = 100 calls for special consideration.

In relation to the total index (including the food industry), we denote Japan's weight index by Q_j, U. K.'s, by Q_u, the U.

S.'s, by Q_a. When they are converted to the United States $=$ 100, by $Q_j(a)$, $Q_u(a)$, and Q_a, respectively. The indices excluding the food industry, converted to the U. S. $= 100$, are expressed here as $\hat{Q}_j(a)$, $\hat{Q}_u(a)$, $\hat{Q}_a$. We indicate in Table 1 how the differences between $\hat{Q}_j(a)$, $\hat{Q}_u(a)$, and $\hat{Q}_a$ are so small in spite of the fact that in some countries we see tremendous gaps existing between $Q_j(a)$, $Q_u(a)$, and Q_a.

Table 1. Variations Entailed by Inclusion or Exclusion of Food Industry

	$Q_j(a)$	$Q_u(a)$	Q_a	$\hat{Q}_j(a)$	$\hat{Q}_u(a)$	$\hat{Q}_a$
Argentina	9.33	3.61	4.72	1.64	1.71	2.04
Austria	6.76	4.62	5.12	3.76	3.90	3.91
Cuba	2.48	0.47	1.23	0.22	0.20	0.26
Denmark	2.74	1.45	1.53	0.87	1.04	0.93
France	26.70	17.25	20.63	16.07	15.65	17.66
Greece	1.40	0.70	0.86	0.42	0.46	0.55
Italy	20.24	9.68	12.74	8.48	8.06	9.71
New Zealand	2.54	1.45	1.22	0.72	1.27	0.67
Portugal	2.17	0.98	1.32	0.61	0.69	0.71
Spain	6.96	3.77	4.90	2.88	2.99	3.46
Uruguay	0.64	0.26	0.34	0.12	0.12	0.16

Since $\hat{Q}_j(a)$, $\hat{Q}_u(a)$, and $\hat{Q}_a$ are, for the most part, not so different in value, we can see from Table 1 that the differences in the indices due to the different weight systems are, by and large, due to the inclusion or exclusion of the food industry. At first sight, it is strange that the food industry, the value added weight of which is only 10–13%, introduces such a large bias in the total indices.

However, there are eleven commodity items included in the food industry index: meat, butter, cheese, canned fish, salted fish, animal feeding stuffs of aquatic animal origin, wheat flour, sugar, margarine, wine, and beer. Compared with other industries, the number of items adopted is not particularly small, but what is relevant here is the degree of representativeness of

152

these samples. For example, *saké* is not included, although wine and beer are included. In the same way, polished rice is not included, although wheat flour is included. Therefore, the eleven commodity items will not be enough for an international comparison. The food industry consists of too many items, but none of these can be regarded as being a major commodity by which its level of production can be approximated.

In addition, the food industry shows no parallel relation with the production level of manufacturing as a whole as it is the case for the iron and steel and machinery industries. For instance, the production of meat in Argentina amounts to 2,893,000 tons, coming up almost to the levels of France and West Germany, and about 10 times as high as Japan's level of 291,000 tons. The production of wine is 47,734,000 *hls* in France, 67,994,000 *hls* in Italy, and 19,834,000 *hls* in Spain, but only 257,000 *hls* in Japan. The unusually low production level of some foods, coupled with their higher relative prices, brings forth a situation whereby Japan's food weight index becomes extremely raised when compared with other weight indices in those countries where the production of these foods is relatively abundant. These could have been overcome to some extent by computing the alcohol content and the calorie indices, but this was not done. Moreover, the inclusion of *saké* and rice would entail further difficulty since their production may be zero in the United Kingdom; these items would be dropped out of the U.K. weight index The above are the special difficulties pertaining to the food industry and are also the reasons for computing the two indices excluding and including food industry.

2. Relative Industrial Levels of the Industrial Countries

Since we have computed the three indices according to the three weight systems (those of the U.S. weight, the U.K. weight and Japan's weight) it may be convenient for our analysis to use

Table 2. Manufacturing Production Index per Head in Relatively Industrialized Countries

—1958—

	Geometric mean of three indices		Population	Manufacturing production per head of population	
	I.F.	E.F.		I.F.	E.F.
U.S.A.	100.00	100.00	100.00	100.00	100.00
U.S.S.R.	59.40	60.10	118.28	50.22	50.81
W. Germany	23.00	21.44	29.77	77.26	72.02
U.K.	19.54	18.91	29.64	65.92	63.80
France	21.18	16.44	25.49	83.09	64.50
Italy	13.57	8.72	27.87	48.69	31.29
Japan	15.64	17.68	52.34	29.98	33.78
Austria	2.64	2.22	4.01	65.94	55.36
Belgium	4.14	3.83	5.18	79.92	73.94
Denmark	1.83	0.94	2.58	70.93	36.43
Finland	1.71	1.63	2.49	68.67	65.46
Netherlands	3.72	3.09	6.40	58.13	48.28
Ireland	0.57	0.23	1.63	34.97	14.11
Sweden	4.14	4.10	4.24	97.64	96.70
Switzerland	1.46	1.23	2.97	49.16	41.41
Norway	1.69	1.55	2.01	84.08	77.11
Greece	0.95	0.47	4.67	20.34	10.06
Spain	5.05	3.10	16.96	29.78	18.28
Portugal	1.41	0.67	5.14	27.43	13.04
Czechoslovakia	5.60	5.67	7.70	72.73	73.64
E. Germany	3.19	1.95	9.29	34.34	20.99
Hungary	2.19	1.61	5.65	38.76	28.50
Poland	7.73	6.84	16.45	46.99	41.59
Canada	10.28	10.20	9.79	105.01	104.19
Mexico	2.19	1.69	18.81	11.64	8.98
Argentina	5.41	1.79	11.47	47.17	15.61
Brazil	5.22	3.10	18.87	27.66	16.43
Australia	5.43	3.86	5.63	96.45	68.56
New Zealand	1.65	0.85	1.30	126.92	65.39
South Africa	2.82	2.19	8.60	32.91	25.47
Israel	0.29	0.27	1.14	25.44	23.68

the geometric mean of the three indices after converting them to the United States=100. This is presented in Table 2 where the manufacturing production per head of population in 1958 is also shown. Table 2 also indicates the two indices which include and exclude the food industry (hereafter I.F. and E.F., respectively).

Naturally, it must be admitted that Table 2 may involve a wide margin of error due to the lack of data for some commodities and underreporting in the relatively less developed countries (e.g., Greece, Mexico, etc.), but it does provide a rough picture of the relative industrial levels of industrial countries. It makes clear the following facts: 1) As the geometric mean of the three indices shows that the level of Soviet Russia was 59.4% (I.F.) or 60.1% (E.F.) of the United States' level of manufacturing production which confirms the generally held opinion. 2) West Germany, France, and the United Kingdom followed these two big countries, and Japan was the sixth largest industrial country in the world in 1958, surpassing both Italy and Canada. 3) The Western European countries combined gave 106.6% (I.F.), and 88.57 (E.F.), and the EEC countries together, a figure 65.61% (I.F.) or 53.52% (E.F.) that of the United States. The latter percentages are higher than the relative industrial level of the U.S.S.R., in terms of the I.F., but slightly lower in terms of the E.F. basis. 4) In terms of the I.F. basis, the United Kingdom (19.54%) is lower than both West Germany (23.00%) and France (21.18%), but in terms of the E.F. basis, the United Kingdom (18.91%) is lower than West Germany (21.44%), but higher than France (16.44%). But it is decidedly true that the British economy was surpassed in 1958 by West Germany in any terms of manufacturing production index and that she is being overtaken even by France, owing to the very low economic growth rate of the United Kingdom. 5) It is interesting that in such countries, as France, Italy, Denmark, Greece, Spain, Portugal, Australia, New Zealand, etc., the I.F. index surpasses the E.F. index. If we take the Q_a index of food production, relative to the United States, the figures are 40.28% (France), 32.80% (Italy), 5.51% (Denmark), 2.91% (Greece), 14.46% (Spain), 5.37% (Portugal), 13.11% (Australia), and 4.88% (New Zealand), and they are always higher than the indices of manufacturing production E.F. which coincides with our analysis developed so far. 6) The manufacturing production indices per capita are not so widely diversified as the total manufacturing levels themselves. In Table 2, putting aside the particularly low per capita production areas such as Greece (I.F., 20.34% or E.F., 10.06%), Spain (I.F., 29.78% or E.F., 18.28%), or Portugal (I.F., 27.43% or E.F., 13.04%), the European countries range from Sweden (97.64% or 96.70%) which ranks among the highest down to Italy (48.69% or 31.29 %). Other countries like the United Kingdom, Austria, Denmark, and Finland are all around 60%. 7) In the levels of per capita manufacturing production, Soviet Russia, Italy, and Switzerland are approximately the same, 50.22%, 48.69%, and 49.16% on an I.F. basis. 8) It is to be noticed that in Australia, Canada, and New Zealand the manufacturing production per population is tremendously high, approaching the U.S. level or even surpassing it. Among them, Australia and New Zealand will fall to 68.56% and 65.39%, respectively, if the food industry is omitted in the computation of the index. Only Canada exceeds the United States by 4–5%. 9) In relation to the East European countries, East Germany (34.34% or 20.99%), Hungary (38.76% or 28.50%), and Poland (46.99 % or 41.58%) fell behind the industrial countries of West Europe except for Czechoslovakia (72.7%).

These are the observations on the computations relating to 1958. However, several years have passed, and it is interesting first to contrast these with similar figures for 1963 and 1967, for during this nine year period the manufacturing production of Japan has more than trebled. This may be roughly approximated by combining the cross-section indices of production with the time-series indices of production constructed for each country

	1963/1958 ratio of manufacturing production (1)	Manuf. production index for year 1958 (2)	Manuf. production index for year 1963 (3)	1967/1958 ratio of manufacturing production (4)	Manuf. production index for year 1967 (5)	Population index 1963 (6)	Population index 1967 (7)	Per capita manuf. production index 1963 (8)	Per capita manuf. production index 1967 (9)
U.S.A.	1.333	100.00	100.0	1.707	100.00	100.00	100.00	100.00	100.00
U.S.S.R.	1.613	59.40	71.87	2.242	78.01	118.67	118.29	60.56	65.95
W. Germany	1.389	23.00	23.97	1.597	21.52	29.26	28.98	81.92	74.26
U.K.	1.205	19.54	17.67	1.534	17.56	28.34	27.66	62.35	63.49
France	1.299	21.18	20.64	1.571	19.49	25.26	25.06	81.71	77.77
Italy	1.695	13.57	17.25	2.169	17.24	26.74	26.28	64.57	65.60
Japan	2.174	15.64	25.51	3.565	32.67	50.63	50.18	50.39	65.11
Austria	1.316	2.64	2.60	1.487	2.30	3.79	3.68	68.60	62.50
Belgium	1.429	4.14	4.44	1.629	3.95	4.90	4.81	90.61	82.12
Finland	1.515	1.71	1.94	1.864	1.87	2.40	2.34	80.83	79.91
Netherlands	1.429	3.72	3.99	1.658	3.61	6.32	6.33	63.13	57.03
Ireland	1.429	0.57	0.61	1.786	0.60	1.50	1.46	40.67	41.10
Sweden	1.408	4.14	4.37	1.775	4.30	4.01	3.95	108.98	108.86
Norway	1.316	1.69	1.66	1.658	1.64	1.94	1.90	85.57	86.32
Greece	1.299	0.95	0.93	1.844	1.03	4.48	4.38	20.76	23.52
Portugal	1.471	1.41	1.56	—	—	4.77	4.74	32.70	—
E. Germany	1.449	3.19	3.47	1.792	3.35	8.50	8.04	40.82	41.62
Czechoslovakia	1.429	5.60	6.00	2.000	6.56	7.37	7.18	81.41	91.36
Hungary	1.639	2.19	2.69	2.197	2.82	5.33	5.13	50.47	54.97
Poland	1.538	7.73	8.92	2.138	9.68	16.20	16.04	55.06	59.75
Canada	1.015	10.28	10.15	1.697	10.22	9.99	10.27	101.60	99.51
Mexico	1.429	2.19	2.35	2.100	2.69	21.05	22.94	11.16	11.73
Argentina	0.943	5.41	3.83	—	—	11.45	11.57	33.43	—
South Africa	1.408	2.83	2.99	1.944	3.22	9.00	9.41	33.22	34.22

Notes: International cross-section manufacturing production indices for 1963 (or 1967) were derived by first multiplying 1958 international indices by repsective production increase ratio (1963/1958 or 1967/ 1958), and then by converting them again to USA = 100.

157

and collected by the United Nations. By multiplying the former by the latter and by converting them to U.S.A. = 100, the relative levels of manufacturing production for the years 1963 and 1967 may be derived, and per capita figures may also be obtained (Table 3).

Major changes occurred during the period 1958–1963 in relation to Japan, which had ranked sixth in manufacturing; she had moved up to third place, following the United States and the Soviet Union. This dramatic change arose as a result of her phenomenal twofold increase in industrial production for 1958–1963. Thus, the Japanese relative level of production increased from 15.64% in 1958 to 25.51% in 1963. In 1967, Japan considerably surpassed West Germany (21.52%) which ranked fourth.

Secondly, the Soviet Union which was about 60% relative to the United States in 1958, now moved up to about 78% in 1967. On the other hand, the United Kingdom, which was about 19% relative to the United States in 1958, fell further to about 17% in 1967, and is in about the same position as held by Italy (17.56% vs. 17.24%), but lags behind France by about 2 points (17.56% vs. 19.49%).

When the relative manufacturing production index in 1963 is deflated by the population index in the same year, we get the 1963 and 1967 per capita production index. Japan ranks only seventeenth in 1963, but advanced to twelfth in 1967. However, Japan's per capita position of 65.11% is quite similar with that of the Soviet Union, the United Kingdom, and Italy which are in about the 60–65% level, running ahead of Austria, the Netherlands, Poland, Ireland, East Germany, Hungary, Portugal, Argentina, and the Union of South Africa. Thus, Japan's level may be still low, as far as it is being compared with Sweden (108.86%), Canada (99.51%), Norway (86.32%), Belgium (82.12%), France (77.77%), Czechoslovakia (91.36%), and West Germany (74.26%). But, the gaps existing between Japan and

West Germany and France, for instance, are greatly reduced, as compared with 1958.

Although the per capita level of Japan's manufacturing production is still below that of West Germany, France, and Sweden, doubtless, Japan will soon reach the levels of the advanced industrial countries in West Europe even in terms of the per capita manufacturing production.[2]

3. Divergences between Physical Volume and Dollar Value of Output

The preceeding conveys the impression that after 1963 Japan became the third ranking industrial power. However, this sharply contradicts a generally held conception among Japanese that, although her growth rate is high, her international level is still tremendously low. We must ask whether our analytical results or the commonly held view is right. One of the reasons that Japan's status is deemed very low comes from the dollar per capita income levels of the *Yearbook of National Accounts Statistics* of the United Nations. In 1967, the national income of Japan was $92.7 billion, surpassing West Germany ($90.4 billion). However, the national income ($) per head of population for the same year in Japan was only 28.1% when compared with the United States, despite the fact that West Germany was 47.8%, the United Kingdom, 41.3%, France, 50.1%, and Italy, 31.1% of the United States level. However, this data conveys a different picture from the computations of the preceeding section. This difference may be, to a great extent, due to the undervaluation of Japan's exchange rate from the viewpoint of its purchasing power parity when compared

---

2) The writer should naturally use the labor force or employees in manufacturing when the level of manufacturing production is converted to per capita basis. Since the statistical data is restricted, he was forced to use the population figure as its deflator. Therefore, the per capita index in each country reflects not only the level of industrial productivity, but also the proportion of labor force absorbed in non-manufacturing sector.

with the United States. The divergence between output, in terms of physical volume, and income, in dollar terms, must have been one of the secrets why the Japanese export growth rate has been higher than that of any other advanced country.

This may be demonstrated as follows: From the *Yearbook of National Accounts Statistics*, 1962 of the United Nations, the income originating in the manufacturing and construction sectors are taken up in 1958 and adjusted to the same concept (i.e. gross domestic product at factor cost), if in some countries different concepts (e.g., gross domestic product at market price or net domestic product at factor cost) are used. When they are converted to dollar values and reduced to the relative numbers, U.S.A. = 100, it is surprising to note that the Japanese dollar income index in the manufacturing and construction sectors was only 6.02% of U.S.A., while the index of physical volume of manufacturing production (inclusive of the construction industry) was 15.64% in 1958, as indicated in Table 4. This is a really big difference between the two. Naturally, this gap may be partly due to the undervaluation of the Japanese national income statistics, but it alone will not fill this gap. One of the major factors for this gap is the undervaluation of Japanese *yen* in international exchange rates.

When the dollar income indices in the manufacturing and construction sectors are divided by the physical volume indices we computed, we get in Table 4 the "dollar income-physical output ratios" for various countries. These ratios in column (G) tell us, first, that, as compared with the United States, the United Kingdom is 87%, the percentages for Canada, France, West Germany, and Belgium are in the 70's, those for Netherlands, and Denmark, in the 60's, those for Italy and Norway, in the 50's, and Japan is 38%. Even when Japan's weight index (13.62% relative to the United States) is used as a deflator, this ratio for Japan will merely be raised to 44.2%. Second, most interesting is the fact that we get a negative correlation between

Table 4. Dollar Income-Physical Output Ratios and Export Growth Rates (1958)

	Income in manufacturing and construction sectors (A)	Exchange rate per US dollar (B)	A/B (C)	Income concepts (D)	Adjusted income (GF concept) (E)	Index of manufacturing production (USA=100) (F)	E/F (G)	Export index (1963/1958) (H)
			mil. $		mil. $			
Japan	2,799(bil. Yen)	360	7,776	NF	8,732 (6.02)	15.64	38.49	198
U.S.A.	129,122(mil. Dollar)	—	129,122	NF	145,004 (100.00)	100.00	100.00	126
Canada	10,878(mil. Dollar)	0.971	11,203	GF	11,203 (7.73)	10.28	75.19	133
U.K.	8,869(mil. Pound)	0.357	24,843	GF	24,843 (17.13)	19.54	87.67	120
France	109.8(bil. N. Franc)	4.20	26,143	GM	22,039 (15.20)	21.18	71.77	162
W. Germany	115,920(mil. D. M.)	4.20	27,600	GM	23,819 (16.43)	23.00	71.43	156
Norway	8,912(mil. Krone)	7.14	1,249	GF	1,249 (0.86)	1.69	50.89	155
Netherlands	12,753(mil. Guilder)	3.80	3,356	GF	3,356 (2.31)	3.72	62.10	149
Belgium	226.0(bil. Franc)	50.0	4,520	GF	4,520 (3.12)	4.14	75.36	173
Italy	5,858(bil. Lira)	625	9,373	GF	9,373 (6.46)	13.57	47.61	206
Denmark	11,892(mil. Krone)	6.91	1,721	GF	1,721 (1.19)	1.83	65.03	141

Sources: U.N., *Yearbook of National Accounts Statistics*, 1962 [for (A) and (B)] and *Monthly Bulletin of Statistics*, Oct. 1964 [for (H)]

Notes: 1) NF (net domestic product at factor cost); GF (gross domestic product at factor cost); GM (gross domestic product at market price)

2) NF's and GM's are adjusted into GF's in column (E) through the following simple calculations, although more precision may be achieved with much difficulties.

U.S.A. (NF × 1.105 = GF); Japan (NF × 1.123 = GF); W. Germany (GM × 0.863 = GF); France (GM × 0.843 = GF)

In estimating the NF-GF ratios and GF-GM ratios in manufacturing sectors, we borrowed those ratios for entire national economy.

3) Austria, Finland, Switzerland, Ireland, and Sweden have not been included here either because it was impossible to single out the income originating in manufacturing and construction sectors or because estimated incomes by industry were not available.

4) "F" has been calculated by first converting manufacturing production indices under USA-weight, UK-weight and Japan-weight into USA base and then taking the geometric averages.

Fig. 1. The Dollar Income-Physical Output Ratios in Manufacturing and Export Growth Rates

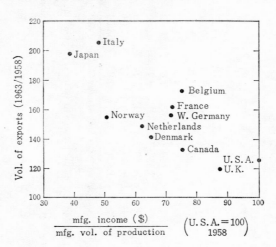

the dollar income-physical volume ratios and export growth for 1958–63, as indicated in Fig. 1.

Putting aside the first problem, we will focus our attention upon the second. Suppose for a moment that there are neither statistical nor computational errors in the measurement of the dollar income-physical output ratio. Under this assumption, the relative low ratios of Italy and Japan may be due to the undervaluation of their exchange rates. In the two country comparison (A and B), if A's exchange rate with B were undervalued when compared with A's relative price level of general commodities to B, then there will be a tendency for A's exports to become cheaper when compared with B's, and the undervalued exchange rate of A will have some stimulating effect on A's exports. Of course, country A may have to pay relatively high prices for her imports, but the increase of the relative prices of her imported raw materials can be offset to some extent by the increase of productivity or the suppression of wage increases. If so, Fig. 1 demonstrates very cogently that the more one country's exchange rate is undervalued, the higher the growth rate of exports in that country. Incidentally, the exports (1963/ 1958) in the vertical axis of Fig. 1 merely compares the two years, 1958 and 1963, and so may be accompanied by some cyclical biases. However, even admitting this point, we are tempted to interpret the upward deviations of Italy, Belgium, France, and West Germany in Fig. 1 as an additive accelerating effect of the EEC integration upon their exports.[3]

Some may hold a different view on the question that Japan's exchange rate might be undervalued. The other view asks that a different criterion should be used in judging the under-or overvaluation of the *yen*, i.e. whether an exchange rate will bring about a continuing export or import surplus in a situation where there prevails no significant export and import restrictions. This thinking is based on the "balance-of-payments" doctrine as opposed to the "purchasing power parity" doctrine. Of course, as a theory of the determination of exchange rate the simple purchasing power parity may not be so effective. At least it does not hold true so far as the purchasing power parity is measured in the consumer price indices (including service prices),[4] but it can still survive in so far as it is based on the "commodity" relative price level. However, we do not insist here that the exchange rate which will satisfy the purchasing power parity is the "equilibrium" one nor that the actual rate will tend towards it. We only maintain that the exchange rate undervalued relative to the purchasing power parity will be more exports-stimulating, as compared with a rate not so undervalued. Now, let us assume that exports expand, owing to the

---

3) We get a similar negative correlation among seven countries in 1956, in *Growth and Cycles in the Japanese Economy*, p. 33. In that case, on the vertical axis were measured the export growth rates per annum which were derived after fitting logarithmic curves to the export volume indices of seven countries respectively.

4) Bela A. Balassa, "Purchasing-Power Parity Doctrine: a Reappraisal", *Journal of Political Economy*, Vol. 72, (Dec., 1964) pp. 584–94.

undervaluation of the exchange rate, that the balance of payments ceiling rises upward, that domestic growth is consequently accelerated, and that imports rise parallel with the increase in exports. In that case, we have no objection to the view that a certain exchange rate is an equilibrium rate because on that rate the exports and imports have just balanced. Our opinion, however, is that, whether or not the equilibrium holds true between exports and imports, we may have a higher export growth rate than otherwise when the exchange rate is undervalued compared with the purchasing power parity.

To prevent misunderstanding, I must add my use of the purchasing power parity concept which differs from the conventional use based on a "particular year". Ordinarily, the under-or overvaluation of exchange rate is discussed by comparing two country price indices as "time series" and with relation to the prevailing exchange rate. Mostly, they choose the year when the exports and imports balanced as the base year. However, what we are trying to discuss here is not such a time-series purchasing power parity compared with a particular "would-have-been" equilibrium year, but a cross-section purchasing power parity compared with a "particular country". Some call the former the "relative" purchasing power doctrine and the latter the "absolute" purchasing power doctrine.

It seems to me that this is a very misleading expression, for even when comparing with a particular country, the purchasing power parity is never an "absolute" but only a "relative" concept. There is nothing absolute in my logic. Nevertheless, R. Komiya and R. Tachi[5] have paid too much attention to the term absolute, criticized that the writer is swayed excessively by an "absolute" way of thinking and seems to assume that the *yen* has an intrinsic value in itself.

To repeat my points. 1) We use the phrase, "the purchasing power parity" with a particular country as its base. This

5) Ryûichirô Tachi and Ryûtarô Komiya, *Keizai-seisaku no Riron* (Theories of Economic Policy), Tokyo, 1964, pp. 317–321.

is to make a cross-section comparison of price levels of various countries (in our case, indirectly), and then to compare them with their prevailing exchange rates. 2) All the same, the writer is not of the opinion that the "equilibrium" exchange rate will be determined by the purchasing power parity irrespective of the balance of payments. We are not concerned here with the discussion on the "equilibrium" exchange rate nor with the need to appreciate the exchange rate since it is undervalued. What we would like to do is merely to bring to the fore, through an international comparison, the fact that the exchange rate undervalued from the viewpoint of cross-section purchasing power parity, will have a stimulative effect on export growth. The present exchange rate ($1 = ¥360) fixed under the IMF system at its undervalued level, we beleive, has a considerably favorable influence upon Japan's export growth rate. However, we have, of course, not urged appreciation but rather to continue it in order to maintain the high export growth rate. The confusion of my opponents is probably be due to the fact that they assume we are insisting that the purchasing power parity doctrine be viewed as a theory of the determination of the exchange rate.

4. Our Manufacturing Index vis-a-vis Other Indices

As far as the interpretation of the results of Fig. 1 are concerned, we could stop here. However, there is still the problem of whether the statistical figures in Fig. 1 are correct or not. Consequently, we need to examine in more detail our result that in 1963 Japan ranked as the third biggest industrial power in the world following the United States and Soviet Russia.

Table 5 indicates the rank of each country in 1967 and its relative position vis à vis to the first-rank country with regard to twenty-four major manufacturing commodities. These items do not represent enough of those in the machinery and food industries. However, pig iron and crude steel represent

Table 5. Ranking by Production of Major Manufacturing Commodities (1967).

Pig iron (1000 ton)			Crude steel (1000 ton)		
1. U.S.A.	79,512	(100.0)	1. U.S.A.	115,404	(100.0)
2. U.S.S.R.	74,808	(94.1)	2. U.S.S.R.	102,240	(96.2)
3. Japan	41,040	(51.6)	3. Japan	62,148	(53.9)
4. West Germany	27,492	(34.6)	4. West Germany	36,744	(31.8)

Commercial vehicle (1000 car)			Shipbuilding* (1000 reg. ton)		
1. Japan	1,798	(100.0)	1. Japan	6,685	(100.0)
2. U.S.A.	1,536	(85.3)	2. West Germany	1,184	(17.7)
3. U.S.S.R.	827	(45.9)	3. Sweden	1,161	(17.4)
4. U.K.	385	(21.4)	4. U.K.	1,084	(16.2)

Television set* (1000 set)			Sulphuric acid (1,000 ton)		
1. U.S.A.	11,174	(100.0)	1. U.S.A.	25,596	(100.0)
2. Japan	5,652	(50.6)	2. U.S.S.A.	9,744	(38.1)
3. U.S.S.R.	4,415	(39.5)	3. Japan	6,276	(24.5)
4. West Germany	2,276	(20.4)	4. West Germany	3,768	(14.7)

Pulp* (100 ton)			Newsprint (1000 ton)		
1. U.S.A.	32,324	(100.0)	1. Canada	7,308	(100.0)
2. Canada	14,519	(44.9)	2. U.S.A.	2,112	(28.9)
3. Sweden	6,553	(20.3)	3. Japan	1,320	(18.1)
4. Finland	5,706	(17.7)	4. Finland	1,217	(16.7)
[Japan=5th]					

Cement (1000 ton)			Cotton yarn* (1000 ton)		
1. U.S.S.R.	84,828	(100.0)	1. U.S.A.	1,9986	(100.0)
2. U.S.A.	62,364	(73.5)	2. China	?	(?)
3. Japan	43,260	(51.0)	3. U.S.S.R.	1,323.0	(66.2)
4. West Germany	31,740	(37.4)	4. Japan	493.6	(24.7)

Rayon and acetate filaments fibres (1000 ton)			Woven cotton fabrics (1000 ton)		
1. U.S.A.	630.0	(100.0)	1. U.S.A.	1,125	(100.0)
2. Japan	523	(83.0)	2. India*	1,090	(96.9)
3. West Germany	244	(38.7)	3. U.S.S.R.	911	(81.0)
4. U.K.	240	(38.1)	4. China*	877	(78.0)
			[Japan=5th]		

Passenger car (1000 car)			Tire (1000)		
1. U.S.A.	7,440	(100.0)	1. U.S.A.	163,188	(100.0)
2. West Germany	2,292	(30.8)	2. Japan	39,900	(24.5)
3. France	1,752	(23.5)	3. France	28,728	(17.6)
4. U.K.	1,522	(19.4)	4. West Germany	24,024	(14.7)
[Japan=6th]					

Radio set* (1000 set)			Beer* (1000 hl)		
1. Japan	27,925	(100.0)	1. U.S.A.	128,759	(100.0)
2. U.S.A.	24,537	(87.9)	2. West Germany	70,206	(54.5)
3. U.S.S.R.	5,842	(20.9)	3. U.K.	49,424	(38.4)
4. West Germany	4,356	(15.6)	4. U.S.S.R.	34,370	(26.7)
			[Japan=5th]		

Nitrogenous fertilizer* (1000 ton)			Caustic soda (1000 ton)		
1. U.S.A.	5,535.0	(100.0)	1. U.S.A.	7,164	(100.0)
2. U.S.S.R.	2,920.0	(52.8)	2. Japan	1,644	(22.9)
3. Japan	1,801.2	(32.5)	3. U.S.S.R.	1,524	(21.3)
4. West Germany	1,501.3	(27.1)	4. France	875	(12.2)

Other paper* (1000 ton)			Plastics and resins (1000 ton)		
1. U.S.A.	38,231	(100.0)	1. U.S.A.	5,736	(100.0)
2. Japan	7,018	(18.4)	2. Japan	4,092	(71.3)
3. U.S.S.R.	4,324	(11.3)	3. Italy	1,148	(20.0)
4. West Germany	4,106	(10.7)	4. U.S.S.R.	1,112	(19.4)

Woolen yarn (1000 ton)			Woven rayon and acetate fabrics (10^6m)		
1. U.S.A.	305	(100.0)	1. Japan	1,742	(100.0)
2. U.K.	228	(74.8)	2. U.S.A.	1,464	(84.0)
3. Italy*	179	(58.7)	3. U.S.S.R.	927	(53.2)
4. Japan	164	(53.8)	4. India	875	(50.2)

Woven woolen fabrics (1000 ton)			Electricity (10^6 kwh)		
1. U.S.S.R.	237	(100.0)	1. U.S.A.	1,314	(100.0)
2. Japan	115	(48.5)	2. U.S.S.R.	589	(44.8)
3. U.S.A.	94	(39.7)	3. Japan	238	(18.1)
4. U.K.	75	(31.6)	4. U.K.	208	(15.8)

in fair approximation the level of the iron and steel industry, while sulphuric acid, superphosphate, caustic soda, and plastic resin do likewise for the chemical industry. Pulp, newsprint and paper other than newsprint may represent the paper and pulp industry and cotton yarn, woolen yarn, staple fiber, woven woolen fabrics, and woven cotton fabrics, the textile industry. Cement production in a sense reflects that of the ceramics industry.

In Table 5, there are twenty items accredited to Japan which rank in the first four (exclusive of the passenger cars, beer, pulp, and cotton fabrics). Among these twenty items, there are four items, which rank first, seven that rank second, seven that rank third and two that rank fourth. In other words, it is interesting to note that among twenty commodities eighteen items are in categories above the third rank. Of course, if we include commodities in the food industry, then the items lower than the third rank will increase. However, in view of radio and television sets, in which category Japan ranks first and second in the world, we may guess that the electrical machinery industry of Japan will rank at least third in the world. It is not clear to what extent the sixth ranking of passenger cars neutralizes the high ranking Japan holds in the world for shipbuilding, and trucks and buses (top in each). Since the apparent consumption of crude steel increased to third place in 1963, outrunning West Germany, we may not be too far off in speculating that the level of the total machinery industry of Japan (inclusive of general, electrical, transportation, and other machineries) is also third in the world. On the other hand, it seems to be a consensus among those in the chemical industry that Japan's international level is that, or better than Soviet Russia which ranked second until now. Such being the case, it is still possible to maintain that Japan ranks third internationally on the basis of these commodity observations. Concerning light industry, the food industry is very low, but it is beyond doubt that the Japanese textile industry also ranks third in the world.

Fig. 2. Production Ratios vis-à-vis to the U.S.A. of Manufacturing Commodities

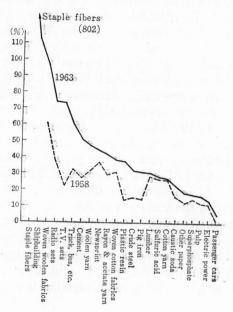

Note: In 1958, staple fibers production was 134, that of shipbuilding, 282

Fig. 2 depicts the percentages of the output of the twenty-three commodities relative to the United States arranged in order of the magnitude in 1958 and 1963. From this chart we see that among the twenty-three items there are fifteen which exceed 30%. In our manufacturing production index for 1963 the index of Japan when compared with the United States was 26.11% (I.F.) and 29.51% (E.F.). The results of Fig. 2 suggests that our computational results are not spurious.

We have made a comparison of our manufacturing output index and the dollar income index in Fig. 1 and Table 4. How-

169

ever, the latter is dependent upon the national income statistics. Therefore, if we use the gross value added based on the *Census of Manufactures* or similar statistics, this will be another check for our analysis. Table 6 indicates the gross value added by manufactures for 1958 converted to the U.S. dollars, and its index (U.S.A. = 100) is comparable with the dollar manufacturing income index. It also computes the value added per employee. It is to be noted that the value added relates to manufacturing while the dollar manufacturing and construction income index refers to manufacturing and construction industries. In Table 6, there are no significant differences between the two indices of the following countries: West Germany, the United Kingdom, France, Italy, Japan, Norway, and Canada. But in so far as Belgium, Denmark, and the Netherlands are concerned, we see fairly big differences. To some extent, this may be due to the variation of the ratios of the construction industry to manufacturing. For instance, in 1958, the income originating in the construction industry in Belgium was 21.4% of the manufacturing income in the same country, and the same ratio was 25.5% in the Netherlands and 25.3% in Denmark while it was 17.0% in the United Kingdom and 14.6% in West Germany.

It is striking that the value added index of Japan when compared with the United States is also 6.26% (manufacturing and construction income index = 6.02%) in terms of U.S. dollars, whereas the values for the United Kingdom and France are about 15% which means they are about 2.5 times higher than Japan. West Germany is about 17%, which is about three times higher. On the other hand, according to our cross-section manufacturing production index of 1958, Japan is 15.64% of the United States; thus, the level of the United Kingdom (19.54%) and France (21.18%) surpasses Japan only by 25–35% in 1958. In other words, Japanese manufacturing production in terms of our index is much higher than the dollar income or value added index, not only in comparison with the United States, but also with the United Kingdom or France.

In Table 6, the coverage of the *Census of Manufactures* varies from country to country. This difference, however, may not entail any errors higher than 10% in industrial countries, but it can be expected that, in such a country like Greece where industrial development is still delayed, the errors will be considerable in view of the fact that in Greece only establishments with more than ten employees are surveyed. However, putting aside this problem we have also computed the value added per employee in Table 6. The value added per employee thus computed indicates that Japan is 16.52% of the United States and tremendously lower than Western countries (the United Kingdom and West Germany are 31–34%) in 1958. Probably, this gap would have been narrowed in 1967 due to the tremendous increase of Japanese productivity during 1958–67. But that the value added per employee of Japan, Italy, and Greece in 1958 were similar (in the range of 15–16%) deserves special notice.[6]

If we take into consideration the above points, we cannot but observe the existence of a gap between the dollar income or value added index, on the one hand, and our physical volume index, on the other. This gap may be reduced to some extent if we can take up more commodity items in the construction of the index. All the same, the difference is too large, and does not seem to be wiped out easily by some statistical manipulation. At least, one has to admit the rank or order of the dollar income-physical output ratios among countries, even if he may be still skeptical of the absolute differences of the two indices.

---

6) With regard to Japan, the population and the manufacturing employee indices are 52.34 and 37.71%, respectively, with the United States = 100. Therefore, the output index (be it the volume or value added indices) per capita of employee is higher than that per capita of population.

In the United Kingdom, however, the employee index is 48%, but the population index is about 30% of the United States. Therefore, when the output index is deflated by the number of employees, the per capita index will be reduced by about 40% more than it is deflated by the population figures.

Table 6. Value Added per Empolyee in Manufacturing (in U.S. Dollars) of Major Industrial Countries in 1958

	Gross value added by manufactures		Coverage	Converted to $ of (A)
	(A)		(B)	(C)
				mil.$
U.S.A.	141.5	(bil. dollar)	all	141500 (100.00)
W. Germany	92.7	(bil. D.M.)	108 & more emp.	22071 (15.60)
U.K.	7849	(mil. £)	all	21986 (15.54)
France	89.2	(bil. new france)	*	21238 (15.01)
Italy	4602	(bil. lira)	all	7363 (5.20)
Japan	3175	(bil. yen)	47 & more emp.	8819 (6.23)
Belgium	148.2	(bil. franc)	all	2964 (2.09)
Denmark	6867	(mil. krone)	6 & more emp.	994 (0.70)
Finland	2862	(mil. mark)	5 &more emp.	894 (0.63)
Netherlands	11274	(mil. gld.)	all	2967 (2.09)
Ireland	103.3	(mil. £)	3 & more emp.	289 (0.20)
Sweden	16789	(mil. krone)	5 & more emp.	3246 (2.29)
Norway	7564	(mil. krone)	all	1059 (0.70)
Greece	8637	(mil. drachma)	10 & more emp.	288 (0.20)
Canada	9791	(mil. $)	all	10083 (7.13)
Brazil	320	(bil. Cr. $)	5 & more emp.	5008 (3.54)
Australia	3536	(mil. A. $)	4 & more emp. or installed power equip.	3960 (2.80)
New Zealand	481.6	(mil. NZ $)	2 & more emp.	670 (0.47)
South Africa	1047	(mil. Rand)	3 & more emp. or installed equip.	1466 (1.04)

Source: United Nations, *Statistical Yearbook*, 1967.

Notes: (*) France includes fishing, quarrying of construction materials and distribution of petroleum products, and does not include manufacture of wine (only private sector). The number of employees in the Netherlands is in terms of man-years and should not be compared correctly with other figures.

Number of employees (D)		Value added per employee (in $) USA=100 (E)	Index of incomes orig. in manuf. and constr. ind. (F)	Population index (G)
Thousand				
16209	(100.00)	100.00	100.00	100.00
6616	(40.82)	38.22	16.43	29.77
7781	(48.00)	32.38	17.13	29.64
5280	(32.57)	46.09	15.20	25.49
5588	(34.47)	15.09	6.46	27.89
6112	(37.71)	16.52	6.02	52.34
1166	(7.19)	29.07	3.12	5.18
328.8	(2.03)	34.48	1.19	2.58
333.3	(2.06)	30.58	—	2.49
1176	(7.26)	28.79	2.31	6.40
144.4	(0.89)	22.47	—	1.63
827.6	(5.10)	44.90	—	4.24
315.7	(1.95)	35.90	0.86	2.01
211.7	(1.31)	15.27	—	4.67
1289	(7.95)	89.69	7.73	9.79
1547	(9.54)	37.11	—	18.87
1071	(6.61)	42.36	—	5.63
168.7	(1.04)	45.19	—	1.30
652.4	(4.01)	25.87	—	8.60

(2) Japan's gross value added covers those in *Census of Manufactures* and excludes that of tobacco (¥26,562 mil.). But, this does not improve too much Japan's index figure of about 6% level compared with the United States.

5. *Relative Industrial Levels of the Less Advanced Countries*

In less developed countries, the reliability of production statistics may decrease with the result that the computations may be subject to a wide margin of statistical error. Particularly, the difference in weight systems may produce extremely large differences in the computed indices for many countries. Moreover, the application of the value added weights in advanced economies to underdeveloped economies may entail great biases. Therefore, these computations are rather experimental, and there was no strong insistence on their statistical validity. In order to produce convincing results, a much more detailed examination of the statistical data of each country would be necessary.

In Table 7, we see the manufacturing indices of the various countries in 1958 in Asia, the Middle and Near East, Africa, and Middle and South America as well as some socialist countries whose per capita incomes are comparatively low. Per capita indices are also computed. Keeping in mind the limitations already stated, the following observations can be made in relation to Table 7.

1. In Asia, the manufacturing production of Communist China is about half and the Indian level is about one-fourth of Japan. In the other countries, the levels of manufacturing production are extremely low. However, if the manufacturing output of these two countries is deflated by their populations, the per capita output indices will only be about 7% in Communist China and about 6% in India as compared with Japan.

2. Malaya, Taiwan, and Hong Kong are very low, 3.5%, 4.7–3.2%, and 1.2%, respectively, of Japan, but since their population levels are also low, their per capita manufacturing production levels are relatively high, i.e., Malaya about

one half, Taiwan 44–30%, and Hong Kong 37–38% that of
Japan.
3. As those countries whose per capita manufacturing production levels are between 3 and 8% of Japan, we have
Communist China, India, Thailand, Korea, Pakistan,
Ceylon and Indonesia. The Philippines are 15.9% (I.F.)
or 7.5% (E.F.). Burma is extremely low (1.45–1.27%).
4. Moving to the Middle and Near East, Israel, which does
not appear in Table 7 but in Table 2, has a relatively high
per capita production level (84.86–70.10%). In Table 7
those with relatively high per capita manufacturing output
are Lebanon (59.7–52.6%), Syria (21.8–20.5%) and Turkey (18.0–12.0%). Iran, Iraq, and Afghanistan are less
than 5%.
5. In Africa, the Union of South Africa (in Table 2) is the
highest in per capita manufacturing production (109.77–
75.40% of Japan). In Table 7, the same are 105.5% in
South West Africa and 73.7–18.9% in Algeria. The I.F.
level is particularly high compared with the E.F. level in
Algeria, mostly because she is the fifth in the production
of wine, following Italy, France, Spain, and Argentina.
With per capita production of 20–30% of Japan are
Tunisia, Kenya, Congo, South Rhodesia, Morocco, and the
United Arab Republic, but Uganda, Angola, Madagascar,
Nigeria, Tanganyika and Ethiopia are at extremely low
levels, mostly around 3%.
6. In Middle and South America, per capita manufacturing
production is very high in Argentina (157.34–46.21%) and
Brazil (92.26–48.64% of Japan) according to Table 2. The
big difference between the I.F. and E.F. bases accounts
for extraordinarily high level of the food industry compared
with other industries in the two countries. Such is also
common in relation to Cuba (101.26–18.23%) from Table
7. At any rate, as those countries with per capita manufacturing production levels of 60–100% in the I.F. terms in

Table 7. Per Capita Industrial Production Indices in Lower Income Nations (1958)

		Manufacturing production index (U.S.A.=100)		Manufacturing production index (Japan=100)		Population (Japan=100)	Per capita manufacturing production index (Japan=100)	
		(I.F.)	(E.F.)	(I.F.)	(E.F.)		(I.F.)	(E.F.)
Asia	Japan	15.64	17.68	100.00	100.00	100.00	100.00	100.00
	China	7.89	9.29	50.42	52.54	706.27	7.14	7.44
	India	4.30	4.55	27.48	25.73	451.53	6.09	5.70
	South Korea	0.32	0.26	2.04	1.47	25.46	8.01	5.77
	Burma	0.05	0.05	0.32	0.28	22.13	1.45	1.27
	Thailand	0.28	0.32	1.79	1.81	27.20	6.53	6.65
	Pakistan	0.73	0.55	4.66	3.11	96.96	4.81	3.21
	Philippines	0.71	0.38	4.54	2.15	28.51	15.92	7.54
	Ceylon	0.05	0.06	0.32	0.34	10.26	3.12	3.31
	Fed. of Malaya	0.55	0.63	3.51	3.56	7.10	49.44	50.14
	Taiwan	0.74	0.56	4.73	3.17	10.76	43.96	29.46
	Hong Kong	0.18	0.21	1.15	1.19	3.12	36.86	38.14
	Indonesia	0.64	0.36	4.09	2.04	97.71	4.19	2.09
Middle & Near East	Turkey	0.72	0.61	4.60	3.45	28.67	18.04	12.03
	Syria	0.16	0.17	1.02	0.96	4.68	21.79	20.51
	Iran	0.54	0.51	3.45	2.88	97.71	3.53	2.95
	Iraq	0.16	0.16	1.02	1.07	21.50	4.74	4.98
	Lebanon	0.16	0.16	1.02	0.90	1.70	59.65	52.63
	Afghanistan	0.03	0.03	0.19	0.17	14.20	1.39	1.20
	Algeria	1.31	0.38	8.37	2.15	11.35	73.74	18.94
	Congo	0.67	0.74	4.28	4.19	16.60	25.78	25.24
	Angola	0.03	0.00*	0.19	0.00*	4.96	3.83	0.00*
	Kenya	0.32	0.26	2.04	1.47	7.45	27.38	19.73
	Madagascar	0.03	0.01	0.19	0.06	5.61	3.39	1.07
	Morocco	0.44	0.20	2.81	1.13	12.00	23.42	9.42

Region	Country							
Africa	Nigeria	0.04	0.05	0.26	0.28	36.93	0.70	0.76
	S. Rhodesia	0.12	0.09	0.77	0.51	3.19	24.19	15.99
	S W. Africa	0.09	0.00*	0.58	0.00*	0.55	105.45	0.00*
	T. nganyika	0.04	0.02	0.26	0.11	9.74	2.67	1.13
	Uganda	0.09	0.04	0.58	0.23	6.94	8.36	3.31
	U. A. R.	0.87	0.56	5.56	3.17	26.95	20.63	11.76
	Tunisia	0.24	0.13	1.53	0.74	4.42	34.62	16.74
	Ethiopia	0.01	0.00*	0.06	0.00*	23.60	0.25	0.00*
Central & South America	Cuba	1.13	0.23	7.22	1.30	7.13	101.26	18.23
	Nicaragua	0.02	0.02	0.13	0.11	1.51	8.61	7.28
	Chile	1.08	1.00	6.90	5.66	7.97	86.57	71.02
	Colombia	0.47	0.29	3.00	1.64	14.77	20.31	11.10
	Dominican Rep.	0.20	0.05	1.28	0.28	3.06	41.83	9.15
	El Salvador	0.02	0.02	0.13	0.11	2.66	4.89	4.14
	Bolivia	0.03	0.01	0.19	0.06	3.67	5.18	1.63
	Guatemala	0.07	0.02	0.45	0.11	3.87	11.63	2.84
	Jamaica	0.10	0.03	0.64	0.17	1.78	35.96	9.55
	Panama	0.04	0.01	0.26	0.06	1.12	23.21	5.36
	Honduras	0.10	0.08	0.64	0.45	1.89	33.86	23.81
	Peru	0.40	0.21	2.56	1.19	11.16	22.94	10.66
	Paraguay	0.04	0.00*	0.26	0.00*	1.84	14.13	0.00*
	Puerto Rico	0.27	0.11	1.73	0.62	2.51	68.92	24.70
	Uruguay	0.38	0.13	2.43	0.74	3.01	80.73	24.58
	Venezuela	0.91	0.84	5.81	4.75	7.51	77.36	63.25
	Ecuador	0.08	0.04	0.51	0.23	4.42	11.54	5.20
Eastern Europe	Yugoslavia	2.40	1.75	15.34	9.90	19.70	77.87	50.25
	Rumania	2.16	2.19	13.80	12.39	19.70	70.05	62.89
	Albania	0.02	0.02	0.13	0.11	1.65	7.83	6.67
	Bulgaria	1.13	0.89	7.22	5.03	8.44	85.55	59.60

Notes: 1) Production indices here are those computed by the geometric average of three indices (Japan, U.K. and U.S.A.) in the table below (appendix).
2) 0.00* is not to be taken as strictly zero; this results whenever at least one of the three indices is zero.

177

Table 7 we can enumerate Cuba, Chile, Uruguay, Venezuela and Puerto Rico. In the 20–30% range we have Jamaica, Honduras, Peru, Panama and Colombia. The percentages for Paraguay, Guatemala, Ecuador, Nicaragua, Bolivia, and El Salvador are on the order of 4–14%.

7. Among socialist countries included in Table 7 the per capita production level is 85.6–59.6% in Bulgaria, 70–62.9% in Rumania, and 77.9–50.3% in Yugoslavia, but Albania is very low, 7.9–6.7%.

Next, let us compute the value added index (Japan = 100) in dollar terms based on the *Census of Manufactures* or similar surveys in Asian countries (Table 8). Among the nine countries taken up here, the data for India and Pakistan relate to establishments with twenty employees or more, and Indonesia to those with ten employees or more, so there may be a considerable omission of small establishments in the two countries. India's value added index is 19.8; that of Japan which is considerably lower than our volume of manufacturing production index, 27.48% in Table 7. Pakistan is 3.19%, but it is also lower than our index 4.66%. In Korea, Burma, and the Philippines, the relation between both indices are reversed; Korea (2.76% vs. 2.04%), Burma (1.49% vs. 0.32%) and the Philippines (7.96% vs. 4.54%). Probably, in these three countries prices have continued to increase; thus, the value added indices in dollar terms may have had an upward bias compared with the volume indices. Particularly in the Philippines the exchange rate had been fixed at $1 = 2 pesos from before the war, but domestic prices (the wholesale as well as the consumer price indices) increased by four times from 1938 to 1958. This fact will demonstrate very clearly how the difference between the value added and the volume indices had become enlarged so tremendously. However, in Taiwan, the Federation of Malaya and Indonesia the opposite relation prevailed.

We have also prepared Table 9 in which we have computed the manufacturing income index in dollar terms, utilizing the

Table 8. Manufacturing Value Added and Its Productivity in Asian Countries in U.S. Dollars

	Manufacturing gross value added (A)	Coverage of Survey (B)	Gross value-added in dollar (C)	Number of employees (D)	Value added per emp. index in $ (E)
	mil. unit		mil. $	thousand	
Japan(1958)	3,174,836.3(yen)	4 & more emp.	8,819(100.00)	6,111.7(100.00)	100.00
India(1957)	8,310 (R.)	20 & more emp. & 10–19 emp. w/ installed power equipment	1,746(19.80)	3,490 (57.10)	34.68
Korea(1958)	15,754.9(won)	5 & more emp.	243.5(2.76)	260.6(4.26)	64.79
Burma(1958)	623.7(kyat)	All in urban districts	131.0(1.49)	233.8(3.82)	44.50
Pakistan(1958)	1,338.9(R.)	20 & more, w/ installed power equipment	281.3(3.19)	397.9(6.51)	49.00
Philippines (1958)	1,404.3(peso)	5 & more emp.	702.2(7.96)	228.4(3.74)	212.83
Fed. of Malaya(1959)	234.0(M.$)	*	76.47(0.87)	67.0(1.10)	79.09
Taiwan(1959)	6,280.6(N.T.$)	10 & more, or w/ installed power equipment	201.2(2.28)	173 (2.83)	80.57
Indonesia(1958)	8,480.1(R.)		290.4(3.29)	447.2(7.32)	44.95

Source: U.N., *The Growth of World Industry, 1938–1961*, 1963.

Notes: 1) *All establishments, excluding clothing, footwear and other fabricated textile products (ISIC 24), furnitures (ISIC 26) and printing and publishing (ISIC 28).

2) Japan's excludes the tobacco industry.

3) Employee figures in India, Pakistan, and Indonesia do not include proprietors and family workers.

179

Table 9. Manufacturing Incomes in Asian Nations (in dollars) (1958)

	Manufacturing incomes	Income Concept	Adjusting ratio	Incomes in G. F.	Exchange rates ($=)	Manufacturing incomes in U.S. dollar (G. F.) (mil. $)
Japan	2,155.0 (bil. yen)	NF	1.123	2,420.0	360	6,722 (100.00)
Korea (South)	14.72 (bil. won)	GF	1.000	14.72	4.76	227.5 (3.39)
Burma	713 (mil. kyat)	GM	902	642	64.7	135.1 (2.01)
Thailand	5,207 (mil. baht)	GM	.926	4,822	4.76	230.7 (3.43)
Philippines	1,677 (mil. peso)	NF	1.133	1,900	20.9	950.0 (14.14)
Ceylon	243.6 (mil. rupee)	GF	1.000	243.6	4.76	51.2 (0.76)
Taiwan	6,510 (mil. N.T.$)	GF	1.000	6,510	31.22	208.5 (3.10)

Source: U.N, *Yearbook of National Accounts Statistics*, 1962.

Notes: 1) NF (net factor cost), GF (gross factor cost), GM (gross market price). Manufacturing incomes in NF's and GM's are converted to GF's by the second-best method of multiplying each manufacturing incomes by GF/NF ratio or GF/GM ratio of each national economy as a whole.

national income statistics. It is surprising to see that the Philippines' manufacturing income index is raised to 14.14% probably due to the wider coverage in the national income statistics (far higher than the value added index, 7.96% in Table 8), and this again confirms the above mentioned speculation. From Table 9 we see that the manufacturing income indices are higher than our volume indices not only in the Philippines, but also in Korea, Burma, Thailand and Ceylon. This may be due to the fact that (1) their exchange rates are overvalued, (2) we have more omission of the manufacturing commodities in the volume index and (3) the relative prices of manufacturing commodities are far higher than those in advanced countries.

Another striking fact to be observed from Table 8 is the value added per employee index in dollar terms. The Philippines' value added per employee index is 212.8% of Japan, which reflects a tremendous overvaluation of the peso. However, the Federation of Malaya is about 80%, Korea is 65%, and Pakistan, Indonesia, Burma and India are in the 30–40% range. These again give us an impression of productivities that are much too high. But this may be partly due to the swift overseas propagation of modern technology. Also this shows us that even if the per capita manufacturing output is low in less developed countries, the productivity may be higher in manufacturing, particularly in the big enterprise sector. However, this is not the whole story, and we are tempted to speculate that the overvaluation of their exchange rates due to inflation under the fixed or inflexible exchange rates is very important in understanding the problem.

This tendency can be found not only in Asia, but also in other regions of the world. Table 10 will indicate this. It is again extremely surprising to see that of the thirteen countries in Middle and South America only three countries are lower than Japan in manufacturing value added per employee. Even these three countries indicate considerably high value added per employee indices; Chile (90.7%), Honduras (78.8%), and

181

Table 10. Manufacturing Value Added and Productivity in U.S. Dollar in Other Areas (1958)

	Gross value added by manufactures (A)	Coverage of surveys (B)	Gross value added conv. to U.S. $ (C) mil. $	Index of gross value added (Japan=100) (D)	Employees (E) thousand	Index of emp. (Japan =100) (F)	Value added per employee index in US $ (Japan=100) (G)
Chile (1957)	303.4 (bil. peso)	(5 & more emp.)	283.0	3.21	216.5	3.54	90.68
Columbia	3,234.0 (mil. peso)	(5 & more emp. or w/output of 24,000 peso & more)	682.3	7.74	236.8	3.87	200.00
Ecuador	853.6 (mil. sucre)	(output of 300,000 sucre & more)	563.4	6.39	30.4	0.50	1278.00
El Salvador	41.1 (mil. colon)	(6 & more w/ installed power equipment)	16.4	0.19	3.8	0.06	316.67
Guatemala	43.4 (mil. quetzal)	(3 & more emp.)	43.4	0.49	27.6	0.45	108.89
Honduras	46.0 (mil. lempira)	(5 & more equipment)	22.8	0.26	20.1	0.33	78.79
Panama	19.0 (mil. balboa)	(with paid-in capital of 500 balboas & more)	19.0	0.21	8.6	0.14	150.00
Paraguay	1,998.0 (mil. guarani)	(specified mfg. estab.)	18.0	0.20	19.4	0.32	62.50
Peru	4,602.0 (mil. sol)	(5 & more emp. or w/ output of 100,000 sol & more)	187.4	2.13	116.3	1.90	112.11
Puerto Rico	292.1 (mil. dollar)	All	292.1	3.31	72.3	1.18	280.51
Trinidad-Tobago (1957)	57.8 (mil. B.W.I.$)	(5 & more emp.)	33.7	0.38	18.3	0.30	126.67
Barbados	8.1 (mil. B.W.I.$)	(5 & more emp.)	4.7	0.05	3.2	0.05	100.00
Costa Rica (1956–57)	301.4 (mil. colon)	All	48.9	0.55	31.3	0.51	107.84

Central & South America

Region	Country	Value	Coverage					
Africa	Algeria (1957)	107.3 (bil. o. franc)	All	255.5	2.90	146.7	2.40	120.83
	Rhodesia-Nyasaland	56.4 (mil. R. £)	(6 & more emp.)	158.0	1.79	109.6	1.79	100.00
	Ghana (1959)	11.9 (mil. G. £)	(6 & more emp.)	33.3	0.38	21.7	0.36	105.56
	Kenya (1957)	20,739 (1,000 £)	(5 & more emp.)	58.1	0.66	52.4	0.86	76.74
	Libya	5,988 (1,000 L. £)	(urban districts)	16.8	0.19	13.03	0.21	90.48
	Morocco	97,388 (1,000 M. franc)	All	231.9	2.63	—	—	—
	Mozambique	1,509.7 (mil. escude)	All	52.5	0.60	87.4	1.43	41.96
	Nigeria (1957)	10.94 (mil. £)	(10 & more emp.)	30.6	0.35	—	—	—
	Suden (1959–60)	5,184 (1,000 S. £)	(Excl. handicraft)	14.9	0.17	18.46	0.30	56.67
	Tanganyika	4,898 (1,000 £)	(5 & more emp.)	13.7	0.16	25.0	0.41	39.02
	U.A.R.	81,626 (1,000 E. £)	(10 & more emp.)	187.6	2.13	264.5	4.33	49.19
Middle & Near East	Iraq	15,853 (1,000 I. dinar)	(20 & more emp.)	44.4	0.50	25.63	0.42	119.05
	Israel	603.6 (mil. I. £)	All	678.2	7.69	116.1	1.90	404.74
	Jordan (1959)	6,453.3 (1,000 dinar)	All	18.0	0.20	23.07	0.38	52.63
	Turkey	3,768.2 (mil. T. £)	(10 & more emp. w/installed power equipment)	558.3	6.33	295.3	4.84	130.79
	Portugal	8,510.3 (mil. escude)	All	295.5	3.35	254.9	4.17	80.34

Source: U.N., *The Growth of World Industry, 1938–1961*, 1963.
Note: The number of employees in El Salvador, Trinidad-Tobago, Barbados, Sudan and Iraq do not include those of proprietors and family workers.

Paraguay (62.5%). Ecuador's 1,278%, Puerto Rico's 280%, El Salvador's 317% and Columbia's 200% are all fantastically high figures. As a matter of course these do not account for relatively higher physical productivities, but merely reflect the galloping inflationary development and the lagging adjustment of exchange rates.

Moving to Africa, we come across again an apparently inconceivable phenomenon. Algeria (120.8%), the Federation of Rhodesia-Nyasaland (100%), Ghana (105.6%) and Libya (90.5%) are also amazing. It is quite unbelievable that the value added per employee in Ghana's manufacturing is almost the same as Japan's whose level of technology is so high. Although the value added per employee indices in other African countries are lower than Japan's, our general feeling is that they are still very high.

Further, turning our eyes to the Middle and Near East, we find the value added per employee is 119% in Iraq, 405% in Israel, and 131% in Turkey as compared with Japan's. Thus, we are impressed with the general prevalence of overvalued exchange rates (compared with Japan) in relatively less developed countries, but the overvaluation of exchange rates in so many countries can rather be understood reversely as the undervaluation of Japan's exchange rate. We have already arrived at a conclusion that Japan's exchange rate is undervalued compared with other industrial countries, but here again we have the same impression in re'ation to the underdeveloped countries too, although this does not mean that this is the case with respect to all the underdeveloped countries.

However, we must add that in the underdeveloped countries the proportion of manufacturing in total output may be very low, and, therefore, the share of manufacturing products in the total exports may also be low. Consequently, a comparison of the exchange rate and the relative prices of manufacturing commodities with other countries may not make sense, unlike a comparison among industrial countries whose proportions of manufacturing output and exports are considerably high. Moreover, many manufacturing industries in the underdeveloped countries used to be under government protection by protective tariffs, subsidies and the like. Therefore, a part of an apparent overvaluation of exchange rates so far discussed may be defined more exactly as higher relative prices of manufacturing commodities as compared with primary products. In this case, it will be misleading to use the word "overvalued" only from a comparison of exchange rates with relative prices of manufacturing products. High relative prices of manufacturing products may, to a large extent, be cancelled by low relative prices of primary products. Nevertheless, our "trial and error" type analysis seems to have made clear that the exchange rate is one of the most important factors which makes it difficult to obtain an exact international comparison of industrial levels.

6. Long-term Changes of Relative Industrial Levels of Major Industrial Countries

It is of some interest to estimate not only the present-day relative production levels of major industrial countries, but also of that of twenty or sixty years ago from a regressing of the cross-section manufacturing production indices we have computed.

As basic data we used the cross-section I.F. manufacturing production index (the geometric mean of the three value added weights indices) for 1958. By multiplying this by time series manufacturing production index of each country and converting it to the United States = 100, we estimate roughly the relative manufacturing production level of the following years: 1901, 1910, 1920, 1929, 1933, 1948, 1955, 1958, 1960, 1963 and 1967. As a time series production index, we used OEEC, *Industrial Statistics, 1900–1955*, and OECD, *Industrial Statistics, 1900–1962*, with the United Nations' *Statistical Yearbook* and *Monthly Bulletin of Statistics* as complementary materials. With regards to Japan,

Table 11. Time-Series (A) and International Cross-section (B) Production Indices in Manufacturing Industry

		1901	1910	1920	1929	1933
U.S.A.	(A)	12.4	19.3	27.8	41.9	25.9
	(B)	100.00	100.00	100.00	100.00	100.00
Canada	(A)			19.8	33.7	21.4
	(B)			7.34	8.26	8.49
U.K.	(A)	26.9	30.2	37.9	42.9	40.7
	(B)	42.42	30.57	26.65	20.00	30.69
Austria	(A)			22.0	43.3	26.7
	(B)			2.09	2.72	2.70
Belgium	(A)		31.0	37.2	77.1	54.1
	(B)		6.63	5.44	7.61	8.65
Denmark	(A)			22.8	38.8	40.9
	(B)			1.51	1.69	2.90
Sweden	(A)			19.2	28.6	27.2
	(B)			2.84	2.82	4.36
France	(A)	26.0	37.5	30.8	59.2	49.1
	(B)	44.35	41.14	23.45	29.93	40.15
Germany	(A)	19.0	26.8	18.0	37.0	24.9
	(B)	35.24	31.92	14.89	20.31	22.12
Japan	(A)	6.6	9.0	17.3	27.3	33.7
	(B)	8.32	7.29	9.73	10.19	20.4
Italy	(A)	14.5	23.8	24.2	40.1	31.9
	(B)	15.89	16.74	11.80	12.98	16.72
Netherlands	(A)				47.9	36.2
	(B)				4.25	5.21
Norway	(A)	14.8	20.8	27.5	32.0	29.1
	(B)	2.02	1.81	1.65	1.29	1.89
U.S.S.R	(A)					
	(B)					

Notes: (A)'s are the time series manufacturing production indices (1958 = 100). That of U.S.S.R. before 1958 is an index of total industry including electricity, gas and mining. (B)'s are computed by extrapolating the cross-section I.F. manufacturing production index (the geometric mean of the

1938	1948	1955	1958	1960	1963	1967
32.8	74.3	104.0	100.0	116.0	133.3	170.7
100.00	100.00	100.00	100.00	100.00	100.00	100.00
32.4	69.4	96.4	100.0	109.2	131.6	169.7
10.15	9.60	9.53	10.28	9.68	10.15	10.22
54.9	69.8	99.1	100.0	114.5	120.5	153.4
32.71	18.36	18.62	19.54	19.28	17.67	17.56
38.7	34.8	89.0	100.0	117.0	131.6	148.7
3.11	1.24	2.26	2.64	2.66	2.60	2.30
56.3	72.1	98.4	100.0	117.1	142.9	162.9
7.10	4.01	3.91	4.14	4.18	4.44	3.95
53.1	68.0	89.0	100.0	122.5	140.8	—
2.96	1.67	1.57	1.83	1.93	1.94	—
44.7	66.1	91.7	100.0	116.9	140.8	177.5
5.64	3.69	3.69	4.14	4.17	4.37	4.30
48.2	52.0	79.0	100.0	110.4	129.9	157.1
31.13	14.82	16.09	21.18	20.16	20.64	19.49
48.7	23.4	84.4	100.0	120.8	138.9	159.7
34.15	7.24	18.66	23.00	23.95	23.97	21.52
55.5	18.7	69.6	100.0	152.2	217.4	356.5
26.46	3.94	10.47	15.64	20.52	25.51	32.67
44.0	42.7	83.2	100.0	128.8	169.5	216.9
18.20	7.79	10.86	13.57	15.07	17.25	17.24
48.9	54.3	94.5	100.0	124.3	142.9	165.8
5.55	2.73	3.38	3.72	3.98	3.99	3.61
39.9	55.5	91.4	100.0	113.2	131.6	165.8
2.04	1.27	1.48	1.69	1.64	1.66	1.64
18.0	27.0	74.0	100.0	124.2	161.3	224.2
32.59	21.59	42.27	59.40	63.59	71.87	78.01

three value added weights indices) for 1901–63. Except for the Japan's time-series before 1938 which depends upon on my own estimate, we used OECD's *Industrial Statistics* for the period before 1958 and U.N., *Statistical Yearbook* after 1958.

Fig. 3. Comparative Manufacturing Production Levels and their Long-Term Changes

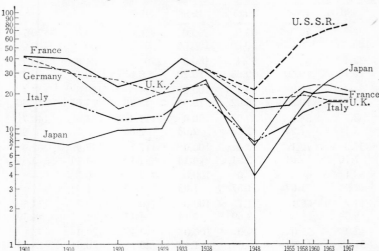

however, the Ministry of International Trade and Industry's manufacturing production index (1960 = 100, going back to 1930) and long-term production index of my own estimate were utilized as the time series for our regression.

The results are indicated in Table 11 and in Fig. 3 from which the folloing observations are derived:

1. After World War II the relative manufacturing production levels (to the United States) of various industrial countries fell and then, by and large, began to relapse to the prewar positions (Soviet Union, France, West Germany, Japan, Italy, and Austria). However, the recovery of relative levels to the United States in the postwar period cannot be seen in the United Kingdom, Canada, Belgium, Sweden and Denmark. This may have something to do with the extent of their fall in the area of relative production during

188

the immediate postwar years. The latter countries did not show any sharp decrease in their production in the immediate postwar years.

2. During the World Depression of the 1930's, the relative positions of various countries to the United States indicated a uniform increase due to the tremendous decline of manufacturing production in the United States.

3. Canada, Sweden, Denmark, and Italy give us no impression of a rising or declining trend in their relative positions to the United States. The movements and the relative levels of the United Kingdom and France are comparatively similar, indicating long-term downward trend. Although the postwar increase of West Germany in her relative industrial level is phenomenal, we see a slight downward tendency over the long run. Moreover, it is to be noted that her postwar relative level has been tapering off from around 1958.

4. Japan and the Soviet Union show a conspicuous increase in their relative levels. Japan was only 8.32% in 1901 but reached 26.46% in 1938, approaching the levels of the United Kingdom, Germany and France. She dropped sharply after the war, but arose markedly, arriving at 32.67% of the United States in 1967, and jumped up to the status of the third industrial power in the world.

5. In 1901, the population of the United States was 77,585 thousand, that of the United Kingdom, 38,237 thousand, and that of Japan, 44,358 thousand. Therefore, the relatives of population with the United States = 100 is 49.2% in the United Kingdom, and 57.17% in Japan. Consequently, the manufacturing production indices (the United States = 100) per capita were in 1901 the United Kingdom = 86.09, and Japan = 14.55. Probably, in the twenty or thirty years before 1901, there was no significant difference in the manufacturing production levels per head of population between the United States and the United Kingdom. Now, in

1967, the United Kingdom's level dropped to about 63% of the United States. On the other hand, Japan could jump up from 14.55% in 1901 to about 65% in 1967.

7. Relative Production Levels by Industry

We have already examined the rank and relative levels of production of major commodities in 1963 and 1967, but here we shall further check those by industry. Table 12 summarizes the 1958 geometric mean production indices (of the three weight

Table 12. Relative Production Levels by Industry (1958)

Rank	Food		Tobacco		Textiles	
1	U.S.A.	100.0	U.S.A.	100.0	U.S.A.	100.0
2	U.S.S.R.	52.7	U.S.S.R.	38.5	U.S.S.R.	55.7
3	France	42.1	U.K.	23.3	Japan	37.4
4	Italy	35.4	Japan	18.0	China	34.5
5	W. Germany	30.2	W. Germany	17.2	U.K.	32.3
6	Argentina	25.0	Bulgaria	12.6	India	28.0
7	U.K.	22.9	France	11.0	W. Germany	26.3
8	Brazil	15.9	Italy	10.7	France	25.4
9	Spain	14.5	Belgium	9.3	Italy	14.2
10	Australia	13.2	Poland	7.7	Poland	10.6
	Japan	6.1				

Rank	Rubber products		Petroleum products		Cokes	
1	U.S.A.	100.0	U.S.A.	100.0	U.S.S.R.	104.7
2	U.K.	17.4	Canada	6.7	U.S.A.	100.0
3	France	13.6	U.K.	6.4	W. Germany	89.6
4	W. Germany	13.0	France	5.7	U.K.	38.6
5	Japan	10.3	Venezuela	5.2	China	37.0
6	Canada	6.1	Italy	3.7	France	25.6
7	Italy	5.1	W. Germany	3.1	Czechoslovakia	15.2
8	Australia	3.7	Japan	3.0	Belgium	14.2
9	Brazil	3.1	Mexico	2.8	Poland	13.0
10	India	2.6	Netherlands	2.5	Japan	11.5
			Rumania	2.5		

Note: These production indices are the geometric averages of three indices computed with value added weights of Japan, U.K. and U.S.A., res-

indices already explained) broken down into twelve industries in manufacturing which are arrayed in the order of rank.

We see from Table 12 first, that Japan is outside the top ten and 6.1% of the United States in the food industry in 1958, holding the same rank as Algeria, seventeenth. Between the tenth and seventeenth there are Poland (11.9%), Canada (10.7%), East Germany (10.0%), Czechoslovakia (7.2%), the Netherlands (6.8%) and Denmark (6.2%). As far as the food industry is concerned, Japan is located in such a low position. However,

Lumber		Pulp & paper		Chemicals	
U.S.S.R.	118.8	U.S.A.	100.0	U.S.A.	100.0
U.S.A.	100.0	Canada	33.6	U.S.S.R.	20.8
Japan	28.2	U.S.S.R.	15.7	Japan	18.9
Canada	21.6	Japan	15.0	W. Germany	18.2
Sweden	10.1	W. Germany	13.7	U.K.	17.9
France	9.7	U.K.	13.2	France	15.1
Poland	8.6	Sweden	12.2	Italy	14.9
W. Germany	8.3	France	10.4	E. Germany	7.5
Brazil	8.3	Finland	8.9	Spain	7.1
Finland	8.3	Italy	5.5	Poland	7.0

Cement		Metals		Machinery & construction	
U.S.A.	100.0	U.S.A.	100.0	U.S.A.	100.0
U.S.S.R.	60.8	U.S.S.R.	48.0	U.S.S.R.	75.0
W. Germany	35.4	W. Germany	22.2	W. Germany	24.5
Japan	27.3	U.K.	22.0	U.K.	19.9
France	24.9	France	17.0	France	17.6
Italy	23.0	China	13.7	Japan	17.1
U.K.	21.6	Japan	13.2	China	9.3
China	17.0	Canada	12.1	Italy	9.1
India	11.3	Belgium	9.1	Canada	8.1
Canada	10.5	Poland	6.1	Poland	7.4

pectively, and are rearranged according to their ranks.

this may be a considerable underestimate, for if we take account of the indigenous production of *saké*, *shôyu*, *miso* and polished rice which were not included in our computation of the food industry index, Japan's level of food industry will be much improved, even if she will still be outside the top ten.

However, the table shows that Japan ranks fourth in tobacco, third in textiles, third in lumber, fourth in pulp and paper, third in chemicals, fifth in rubber products, fourth in cement, seventh in metals, sixth in machinery and construction, eighth in petroleum products, and tenth in cokes. In 1958, although the metal industry ranks in seventh, and the machinery and construction industries sixth, both the textile and the chemical industries are ranked third. Naturally, we can expect a tremendous transfiguration in the ranks of these industries during the several years after 1958 due to the conspicuous advance Japan has made in the area of manufacturing production.

This is estimated in Table 13 where the 1963 and 1966 cross-section indices are extrapolated from the 1958 cross-section indices by making use of the time series production indices for 1958–63 and 1958–66 by industry. In Table 12 we have only selected four industries; chemicals, metals, machinery and construction, and food. From the table we can observe a rise in Japan's chemical industry to the second rank in 1963. The Soviet Union is 25.4% while Japan is 27.3% of the United States in 1963. Taking into our further consideration a remarkable development of petrochemical industry (which was not considered in our index) in Japan, the level of Japan's chemical industry may have been much higher than our index shows. In the metal industry, the Soviet Union is still the second, but Japan which ranked seventh in 1958 advanced in 1963 to the third in the world (from 13.2% to 24.8%). The machinery and construction industries may involve some upward bias, in view of the fact that we used the time series machinery production index in order to extrapolate the cross-section machinery and construction index. Nevertheless, it is to be noticed that the

Table 13. Relative Production Levels by Industry in 1963 and 1966

	1958 International cross-section prod. index (A)	Time series prod. index 1963/1958 (B)	" " 1966/1958 (C)	Estimated cross-section index 1963 (D)	1966 (E)
Chemical Industry					
U.S.A.	100.0	147.1	186.8	100.0	100.0
U.S.S.R.	20.8	188.7	283.0	26.7	31.5
Japan	18.9	212.8	327.7	27.3	33.2
W. Germany	18.2	181.8	252.7	22.5	24.6
U.K.	17.9	142.9	172.9	14.8	16.6
France	15.1	163.9	223.0	16.8	18.0
Italy	14.9	208.3	300.0	21.1	23.9
Canada	6.3	129.9	167.5	4.9	5.6
Metal Industry					
U.S.A.	100.0	129.9	163.6	100.0	100.0
U.S.S.R.	48.0	153.8	195.4	56.8	57.3
W. Germany	22.2	120.5	134.9	20.6	18.3
U.K.	22.0	112.4	124.7	19.0	16.8
France	17.8	117.6	127.1	16.5	13.8
Japan	13.2	243.9	351.2	24.8	28.3
Canada	12.1	142.9	177.1	13.3	13.1
Belgium	9.1	131.6	151.3	9.2	8.4
Machinery & Construction Industries					
U.S.A.	100.0	142.9	194.3	100.0	100.0
U.S.S.R.	75.0	196.1	262.7	102.9	101.4
W. Germany	24.5	142.9	164.3	24.5	20.7
U.K.	19.9	117.6	134.1	16.4	13.7
France	17.6	131.6	153.9	16.2	13.9
Japan	17.1	285.7	408.6	34.2	36.0
Italy	9.1	185.2	185.2	11.8	8.7
Canada	8.1	137.0	191.8	7.8	8.0
Food Industry					
U.S.A.	100.0	117.6	129.4	100.0	100.0
U.S.S.R.	52.7	140.8	169.0	63.1	68.8
Italy	35.4	122.0	136.6	36.7	37.1
W. Germany	30.2	123.5	137.0	31.7	32.0
U.K.	22.9	114.9	124.1	22.4	22.0
Japan	6.1	135.1	154.1	7.0	7.3

Notes: (B) and (C) comes from U.N., *Statistical Yearbook*.

machinery and construction index of the Soviet Union, thus computed, is 91.7% of the United States in 1963. Japan's steep rise, from 17.1% in 1958 to 33.5% in 1963, made her outrun West Germany in 1963 who had ranked third in 1958.

8. A Comparison of Some Value Added Ratios

We have come across the strange result that in relation to Japan our cross-section volume index is considerably higher than the cross-section value added index (in dollar terms). Our tentative interpretation was focused on the undervaluation of Japan's exchange rate, together with other factors. However, one may still feel that it may not entirely explain the gulf between the two indices.

We have used the value added index in dollar terms in comparison with our volume index. Why do we not use the gross output index instead of the value added index? There may be a variation of the ratio of value added to gross output from country to country, and while country A is 50% of country B in terms of gross output, it can be 40% in terms of value added, if the value added ratio of A is sufficiently smaller than that of B. However, we did not take up the gross output or the gross shipments in our analysis for the definition of them may differ from country to country. Taking an example of the Japanese *Census of Manufactures*, the "value of shipments" in the postwar period covered only the final products in each establishment, but the "value of products" in the prewar period had covered not only the final products but also the intermediate products. According to the latter definition, the value of products or shipments is naturally larger than that of the former. Using the prewar definition, the value of intermediate products was included not only in the value of products, but also in the cost of raw materials, etc. This is the case in Japan, and the writer was afraid that the definition may also differ from country to country. The value added ratio will, therefore, be subject to

194

such a bias. This is why we preferred the value added index for the gross output index in terms of dollars. However, let us for the time being assume that the methods of survey on the gross output are the same in every country. Other things being equal, the value added ratio can naturally be lower in country *A* than *B*, when *A*'s exchange rate is sufficiently undervalued in comparison with her purchasing power parity. This presupposes that *A* imports mostly raw materials and exports finished commodities. The undervaluation of *A*'s exchange rate will, on the one hand, reduce her export prices in terms of foreign currency, but, on the other, may raise the import prices of raw materials in terms of domestic currency. Therefore, the proportion of the raw material cost in the value of products may become higher and the value added ratio may be lower than in the case when the exchange rate is not undervalued. Of course, this may not apply to a country whose dependency on imported raw materials is very low, but it will be important in such countries where the prices of raw materials are strongly influenced by foreign trade.

The *Census of Manufactures* of the United States in 1958 did not include the totals of the values of shipments and raw materials used, except for the four digit classification because their totals of manufacturing as a whole, or of the two digit classification, consist of a considerable amount of duplications and their overtime changes might not reflect their true production movement. In the United Kingdom, however, the *Census of Production* includes the totals of shipments although the definitions and survey methods are not well explained in the Census. However, we are going to make an international comparison of the value added ratios with the tentative provision that the definition of the shipments is the same as in Japan, and to check what results are obtained.

Table 14 makes a comparison of the ratios of the gross value added to the value of shipments or products in various industries, in relation to the United Kingdom, Japan, Denmark, West

STRUCTURAL CHANGES IN JAPAN'S ECONOMIC DEVELOPMENT

Table 14. International Comparison of Gross Value Added Ratios

	U.K. (1958)			Japan (1958)		
	Ship-ment	Gross value added	b/a	Ship-ment	Gross value added	b/a
	(a)	(b)	(c)	(a)	(b)	(c)
	mil. £	mil. £	%	bil. yen	bil. yen	%
Manufacturing Industry	21,947	7,849	35.8	9,880.9	3,174.8	32.1
Food	4,263.6	916.5	21.5	1,463.2	315.9	21.6
Textiles	1,882.6	615.3	32.7	1,294.6	324.2	25.0
Apparels	749.8	308.3	41.1	114.7	34.4	30.0
Leather	138.0	43.3	31.4	48.7	13.6	27.9
Chemicals	2,309.7	735.7	31.9	974.5	361.3	37.1
Coal & petroleum Prod.	(Included in Chemicals)			243.3	40.2	16.5
Rubber products	(Included in Others)			140.8	54.4	38.6
Pupl & paper	1,255.7	577	46.0	398.5	124.2	31.2
Printing & publishing				303.1	164.3	54.2
Ceramics & quarrying	591.7	296.6	50.1	337.4	154.0	45.6
Lumber & wood-works	510.9	211.9	41.5	456.1	139.9	30.7
Primary metals	2,318.6	689.3	29.7	1,259.7	318.3	25.3
Machinery exc. elec.	3,470.3	1,742.7	50.2	630.0	273.0	43.3
Electric machinery				652.6	274.9	42.1
Ship-building	496.0	227.0	45.8	886.2	322.9	36.4
Other transp. equip.	2,233.0	818.4	36.7			
Instruments & related products	(Included in Machinery)			114.9	49.4	43.0
Other fabricated metal products	1,183.6	439.3	37.1	345.9	133.0	38.5
Others	543.1	227.4	41.9	215.5	76.8	35.6

Sources: U.K.: *Census of Production 1958*, 1962; Japan: *Kôgyô Tôkeihyô* (Census of Manufactures), 1958; Denmark: Det Statistiske Department, *Industriel producktionsstatistik 1958, 1961*; W. Germany: U.N., *The Growth*

Denmark (1959)			W. Germany (1954)			Norway (1958)		
Production (a)	Gross value added (b)	b/a (c)	Shipment (a)	Gross value added (b)	b/a (c)	Production (a)	Gross value added (b)	b/a (c)
10,000Kr	10,000Kr	%	mil. DM	mil. DM	%	1,000Kr	1,000Kr	%
16,880.7	7,841.5	46.5	143,966	64,377	44.7	17,411.8	7,061.5	40.6
4,012.2	1,317.0	32.8	25,074	9,628	38.4	3,992.9	1,101.2	27.6
1,030.6	446.9	43.4	12,661	5,112	40.4	677.6	302.6	44.7
1,020.0	462.2	45.5	5,804	2,379	41.0	761.4	352.8	46.3
154.3	57.2	37.1	1,536	585	38.1	80.5	33.6	41.7
1,676.3	585.2	34.9	} 16,920	7 512	44.4	1,824.1	724.6	39.7
188.1	82.5	43.9				61.7	21.4	34.7
161.5	90.0	55.7	1,906	929	48.7	128.9	68.1	52.8
} 1,438.2	784.7	54.6	4,397	1,963	44.6	2,088.5	692.7	33.2
			2,502	1,517	60.6	392.4	252.0	64.2
775.4	525.1	67.7	6,286	3,857	61.4	480.5	283.2	58.9
762.2	393.4	51.6	5,735	2,497	43.5	1,057.6	427.5	40.4
515.6	147.1	28.5	17,125	6,661	38.9	1,950.9	718.5	36.8
1,714.7	987.2	57.6				529.5	293.9	55.5
1,224.4	619.8	50.6				603.9	334.8	55.4
} 1,414.3	649.5	45.9	} 40,758	19,909	48.8	} 1,692.6	871.0	51.5
(Included in Machinery)						(Included in Machinery)		
842.7	455.4	54.0				899.4	478.3	53.2
413.9	238.0	57.5	3,262	1,828	56.0	189.3	105.5	55.7

of World Industry 1958–1961, 1963; Norway: Statistisk Sentralbyra, Norges Industri, Produksjonsstatistikk 1958, 1961.

Germany and Norway; the United States is not included because no data is given on the total value of shipments.

This tells us that Japan's value added ratio in manufacturing is 32.1%, which is a slightly lower than the 35.8% of the United Kingdom, but considerably lower than the 46.5% of Denmark, 44.7% of West Germany, and 40.6% of Norway. (In the United States, the corresponding ratio was 40.6% in 1929 and 43.4% in 1939). If one entertains a judgment that the cross-section manufacturing production indices which we have computed express and correspond to the relative levels of *the gross output* including the cost of raw materials used rather than the net output or the value added, he should compare the index of the volume of production with the index of the gross value of output. If his judgment were correct, the value added index of Japan should be multiplied by 1.3926 (= 44.7 ÷ 32.1) when it is to be compared with that of West Germany.

By industry, Japan's value added ratio is particularly low, by about 30%, in textile industry (Japan 25%, the U.K. 32.7%, Denmark 43.4%, West Germany 40.4%, and Norway 44.7%). This is also true for apparels. In the machinery industry, it is 43.3% in Japan, 57.6% in Denmark, 55.5% in Norway and 50.2% in the United Kingdom (including the electrical machinery industry only in the United Kingdom). This shows that Japan's value added ratio is lower than others' by about 20%.

However, some may be skeptical against the presumption that the index of the volume of production represents the level of gross output rather than net because in the construction of the aggregate index the value added of each industry are used as weights. Since the weights used are in terms of net-concepts, one may speculate that the resulting index will also represent the level of physical net output or the value added in real terms. According to this opinion, we should rather compare the index of the volume of production with the value added index, and the comparison of the former with the gross value of output index is perfectly illusory; however, is this procedure correct?

The use of value added or net output weights in the computation of a cross-section aggregate production index, however, cannot take into consideration the difference of the value added ratios among countries. Of course, it makes possible to "nettify" the character of the index by using the value added weight at least in the "inter-commodity" and "inter-industry" relations of the index. However, it does not take account of the "inter-country" differences of the value added ratios.

Denoting by v the value added, by p and q the price and quantity of each commodity, by r the value added ratio and by the suffixes j and a, Japan and the United States, our formula for the quantity index with the U.S. value added weight will be as follows:

$$\frac{\sum v_a \left(\dfrac{q_j}{q_a} \right)}{\sum v_a} \equiv \frac{\sum r_a p_a q_a \left(\dfrac{q_j}{q_a} \right)}{\sum r_a p_a q_a} \equiv \frac{\sum r_a p_a q_j}{\sum r_a p_a q_a} \quad \ldots \ldots (1)$$

It is an indispensable condition for the construction of the quantity index to apply a common p_a to any country's quantity of production. However, not only p_a, but also r_a, the U.S. value added ratio, is commonly applied, so it is clear that equation (1) does not take into condiseration the actually existing inter-country differences of the value added ratios. If, instead of equation (1), the formula (2),

$$\frac{\sum r_j p_a q_j}{\sum r_a p_a q_a} \equiv \frac{\sum v_a \dfrac{r_j}{r_a} \left(\dfrac{q_j}{q_a} \right)}{\sum v_a} \quad \ldots \ldots (2)$$

is used in the comparison with the value added index in terms of dollars, then both indices become comparable. However, the ordinary quantity index, even if it employs the value added as weight, assumes the constancy of the value added ratio among countries. This is why we must take into account of the differences of the value added ratios in various countries.

Since the number of countries is very limited in the computation of the value added ratio and the definition of the value added ratio is some ambiguity, our conclusion is rather preliminary and conditional. However, we have had an impression that the value added ratio of Japan is comparatively lower due to the undervalued exchange rate. If this is correct, the apparent gap existing between the physical volume index and the dollar value index, as indicated already in Fig. 1, is attributable not only to the undervalued exchange rate, but also to the relatively low value added ratio which is again influenced by the undervaluation of exchange rate in so far as industrial countries whose dependency on the imports of raw materials is relatively high.

9. A Test of the Index for the Machinery and Construction Industries

The remaining problem is the reliability of our cross-section production index, particularly of our very peculiar index for the machinery and construction industries. In the advanced industrial countries the proportion of the machinery industry in the value added by all manufactures is considerably large. Therefore, our discussion on the undervalued exchange rate is, to a great extent, dependent upon the reliability of the index for the machinery and construction industries. Since it is simply a weighted average of the apparent consumption of crude steel, cement, and lumber, special reconsideration is needed.

Before computing the 1958 index, we have tentatively estimated the 1956 index for machinery and construction which can be conveniently checked by other three indicators in 1955 or 1956: (1) gross fixed investment in 1956 dollar terms, (2) the domestic product plus imports or domestic production plus imports minus exports of machineries in various countries in 1956 and (3) Milton Gilbert's estimate of fixed investment based on the purchasing power equivalent in 1955. These provide fairly satisfactory checks for the reliability of our index for the machinery and construction industries, and are indicated in Table 15.

Table 15. Indices for Machinery and Construction Industries and the Check Using Other Data, *circa* 1956

	(1956) Machinery & construction index (U.S.A. weight)	(1956) Total fixed investment (dollar)	(1955) Gilbert Estimated fixed investment (U.S.A. weight)	(1956) Machinery Production plus imports (mil. dollar)	(1956) Machinery Production plus imports less exports (mil. dollar)
U. S. A.	100.00	100.00	100.00		
Japan	13.72	8.38	—	805	717
Norway	1.29	1.41	1.89		
Sweden	3.00	2.59	—	2,293	1,810
Denmark	0.93	1.02	1.45	680	487
U. K.	16.99	11.88	15.26	11,750	8,087
Ireland	0.24	0.34	—		
Netherlands	2.64	2.87	3.49	2,237	1,793
Belgium	2.55	2.34	3.49	1,668	1,291
France	11.57	12.82	12.21	7,555	6,702
W. Germany	19.69	14.53	20.06	9,012	5,616
Switzerland	1.47	2.22	—	1,486	750
Portugal	0.47	0.38	—		
Italy	6.14	6.61	9.30	2,789	2,308
Finland	0.83	1.69	—		
Austria	1.50	1.27	—	610	479
Greece	0.38	0.54	—		
Canada	9.33	11.08	—		
Taiwan	0.38	0.20	—		
Philippines	0.53	0.50	—		
Australia	3.19	4.23	—		
New Zealand	0.67	0.84	—		

Notes: 1) Indices for machinery and construction are those the writer once computed for another purpose ("International comparison of Industrial levels and structures" in Japanese in *Keizai Kenkyu*, April, 1962).
2) Gilbert estimations are from Milton Gilbert and Associates, *Comparative National Products and Price Levels*, 1958.
3) Data on Production, Imports and Exports of Machinery are from the OEEC, *The Engineering Industries in Europe*, 1960.

Of course, there is no reason why the indices for the machinery and construction industries should correspond proportionally to the fixed investment among countries. This is because, first, the fixed investment is equal to the domestic production of plant and equipment plus imports minus exports while the index for machinery and construction industries is not adjusted by these imports and exports. Second, the production of consumer durables is included in the index for machinery and construction industries while the same is deducted in the estimate of fixed investment. However, it might be expected that the above-mentioned difference could be, to a great extent, blurred by the existence of construction investment which might amount to about half of the total fixed investment. The index for machinery and construction index would probably be roughly proportional to the index of fixed investment except for any deviation which might rise due to the under or overvaluation of exchange rates. Table 15 shows that the 1956 indices for machinery and construction industries with U.S. weights are in considerable agreement with the dollar term indices of fixed investment. Norway, Denmark, the Netherlands, Belgium, France, Italy, Austria, the Philippines and Canada are examples of countries in which the two indices are, by and large, close to each other.

However, Japan's index for the machinery and construction industries is 13.72% of the United States in 1956, but that of fixed investment is 8.38%. This gap exists despite the fact the proportions of the machinery exports and the consumer durables production are higher in the United States, the index-base country. Naturally, the index for machinery and construction industries estimated from the "input" aspect might exaggerate, to some extent, its true value, for it does not reflect quality differences or input coefficients of various types of machinery. Nevertheless, we see an enormous gap the major cause of which, we believe, cannot easily be anything other than the undervalued exchange rate.

It is very interesting to notice that the Gilbert indices of real fixed investment in the United Kingdom and West Germany are far closer to the corresponding indices of machinery and construction industries than to the fixed investment indices based on the conversion using present exchange rates. Of course, these comparisons are still not adequate, but it gives us an impression that our index for the machinery and construction industries can play a useful and credible role in the analysis of international comparison of industrial production.

Table 16. Machinery and Construction Index and Total Fixed Investment Index, 1958

	Machinery and construction index	Total gross fixed investment (mil. $)		Machinery and construction index	Total gross fixed investment (mil. $)
U.S.A.	100.0	72,367(100.00)	New Zealand	0.9	697(0.96)
W. Germany	24.5	11,976(16.55)	South Africa	2.9	1,497(2.07)
France	17.6	10,500(14.51)	Austria	1.9	1,108(1.53)
U.K.	19.9	9,625(13.30)	Spain	2.9	1,900(2.63)
Japan	17.1	7,404(10.23)	Argentina	2.3	2,033(2.81)
Italy	9.1	5,590(7.72)	Mexico	1.68	1,338(1.85)
Sweden	4.0	2,157(2.98)	Israel	0.36	342(0.47)
Norway	1.3	1,194(1.68)	Yugoslavia	1.73	1,302(1.80)
Finland	1.0	944(1.30)	Portugal	0.56	338(0.47)
Denmark	1.2	857(1.18)	Puerto Rico	0.13	295(0.41)
Netherlands	3.0	2,121(2.98)	Ceylon	0.10	143(0.20)
Belgium	3.0	1,792(2.48)	Fed. of Malaya	0.56	149(0.21)
Ireland	0.2	220(0.30)	Taiwan	0.65	204(0.28)
Greece	0.5	539(0.74)	Korea	0.20	339(0.47)
Canada	8.1	8,540(11.80)	Philippines	0.46	436(0.60)
Brazil	3.2	2,680(3.70)	Thailand	0.46	330(0.46)
Australia	3.6	3,601(4.98)	Turkey	0.40	727(1.00)

Source: Total gross fixed investment is based on U.N., *Yearbook of National Accounts Statistics, 1962*, and they are converted to U.S. dollar.
Note: The machinery and construction index is the geometric mean of the three indices based on the U.S.A., U.K. and Japan's weights.

Fig. 4. Machinery and Construction Indices and Total Fixed Investment Indices (1958)

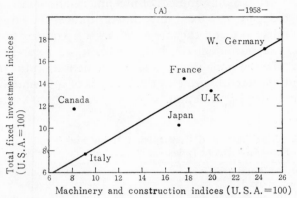

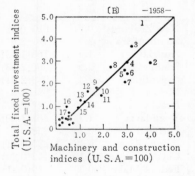

1. Australia
2. Sweden
3. Brazil
4. Netherlands
5. Spain
6. Belgium
7. South Africa
8. Argentina
9. Yugoslavia
10. Mexico
11. Austria
12. Norway
13. Finland
14. Denmark
15. New Zealand
16. Turkey
17. Greece

However, the above test concerns only the 1956 index and does not take up the 1958 index. Therefore, in Table 16 we shall make a comparison of the 1958 indices for the machinery and construction industries and fixed investment indices based on the conversion using present exchange rates. From **Fig. 4**, which is based on Table 16, we see that the fixed investment indices for West Germany, the United Kingdom, France, Italy

204

and Japan are consistently lower than our index for machinery and construction industries. In particular, Japan's fixed investment is extremely low. In Fig. 4, *B*, we have plotted seventeen countries which are very closely scattered around the 45° line except for some deviations as seen for Australia, Sweden and the Union of South Africa.

Thus, in spite of some differences in definitions of the two indices and some deviations due to the under or overvaluation of exchange rates, we are not going too far in saying that the index for machinery and construction industries we have computed is, by and large, dependable and a very good substitute for the index for machinery production, even if seemingly simple and unconventional.

10. *Specific Reconsiderations on the Machinery and Textile Industries*

So far, the machinery industry has been dealt with in combination with the construction industry. Since we have a detailed *Census of Manufactures* for 1958 for the United States and the United Kingdom, it will be a good check and complement to our analysis to make a comparison of the value of shipments of the machinery industry and its intra-industry structure between the following three countries: the United States, the United Kingdom and Japan.

However, in the *Census of Manufactures* of the United States for 1958, the value of shipments is stated only in the four digit industries in the new standardized industry classification of 1957 (in some industries, even these are not shown). Consequently, it becomes necessary to estimate the value of shipments in machinery industry and its subgroups under certain assumptions with reference to the United States and then to make a three-country comparison. In Table 17, the value of shipments in the total machinery industry (including general machinery, electrical machinery, transportation equipment and instruments and

Table 17.   Three-Country Comparison of Shipments in the
Subgroups of Machinery Industry (1958)

	U.S.A. (All)		U.K. (All)
	million $	%	million £
Machinery, ex_cl. electrical	22,491.8	(100.00)	1,951.8
Engines & turbines	2,017.5	(100.00)	113.4
Farm machinery & equipment	2,421.9	(100.00)	54.7
Construction & mining equipment	4,067.2	(100.00)	75.2
Metalworking machinery	3,171.5	(100.00)	212.4
Textile industry machinery	376.3	(100.00)	77.3
Other industry machinery	(8,752.2)	(100.00)	1,368.1
Machineries for office, service industry & households	1,685.2	(100.00)	50.7
Electrical machinery	19,290.5	(100.00)	1,265.8
Electric distribution products & electric industrial apparatus	4,715.7	(100.00)	542.3
Household appliances & electric equipment	3,295.3	(100.00)	102.3
Communication equipment, electronic apparatus & others	(11,279.5)	(100,00)	621.2
Transportation equipment	32,723.8	(100.00)	2,729.1
Motor vehicles & equipment	(15,672.3)	(100.00)	1,343.7
Railroad equipment	969.7	(100.00)	235.4
Motorcycle, bicycle, & parts	121.5	(100.00)	74.9
Ships & boats	1,954.6	(100.00)	496.0
Aircraft & parts	13,451.8	(100.00)	568.1
Transportation equipment, n.e.c.	553.9	(100.00)	11.0
Instruments & related products	4,666.4	(100.00)	186.9
Total Machinery industry	79,172.5	(100.00)	6,133.6

Sources: U.S.A., *Census of Manufactures*, 1958; U.K., *Census of Production*, 1958; Japan, *Kôgyô Tôkeihyô* (Census of Manufactures), 1958.

Japan (4 or more emp.)	U.K. (converted to $)		Japan (converted to $)	
million yen	million $	%	million $	%
629,951	5,467.0	(24.31)	1,749.9	(7.78)
70,606	317.6	(15.74)	196.1	(9.72)
34,680	153.2	(6.33)	96.3	(3.98)
38,483	210.6	(5.18)	106.9	(2.63)
79,963	594.9	(18.76)	222.1	(7.00)
52,481	216.5	(57.53)	145.8	(38.75)
290,417	3,832.0	(43.78)	806.7	(9.22)
63,316	142.0	(8.43)	175.9	(10.44)
652,614	3,545.5	(18.38)	1,812.8	(9.40)
269,791	1,519.0	(32.21)	749.4	(15.89)
88,131	286.5	(8.69)	244.8	(7.43)
294,690	1,740.0	(15.43)	818.6	(7.26)
886,233	7,644.2	(23.36)	2,461.8	(7.52)
387,787	3,763.7	(24.01)	1,077.2	(6.87)
55,622	659.4	(68.00)	154.5	(15.83)
29,499	209.8	(172.67)	81.9	(67.41)
388,457	1,389.3	(71.08)	1,079.1	(55.48)
18,806	1,591.2	(11.83)	52.2	(0.39)
6,060	30.8	(5.56)	16.8	(3.03)
114,932	523.5	(12.18)	319.3	(6.84)
2,283,730	17,180.2	(21.70)	6,343.7	(8.01)

Notes: The United States' bracketed figures for some industries are estimated by dividing the value added in those industries by the value added
ratios in the similar industries.

207

related products) is 8% in Japan and 21.7% in the United Kingdom as compared with the United States. This is much higher than Japan's 5.61% and the United Kingdom's 17.49% in terms of the value added index in dollars although the metal goods industry is included in the latter case. In other words, the level of the machinery industry becomes higher on a shipment basis than on a value added basis by 42.6% in Japan and by 24% in the United Kingdom. It is interesting to see that this 21.7% of the United Kingdom on the shipment basis is very close to the 19.9% of her index for machinery and construction industries. However, the 8% of Japan on the shipments basis is still far less than the 17.1% of her index for the machinery and construction industry. In the case of Japan, the figures cover establishments with four employees or more, but even if the value of shipments included those establishments with less than three employees, the level of shipments would increase only by 0.58% which is really negligible. Thus, the hypothesis of the undervaluation of exchange rate seems to remain valid.

When the subgroups of the machinery industry are examined, Japan is 7.78% of the United States in general machinery, 9.4% in electrical machinery, 7.52% in transportation equipment and 6.84% in optical, scientific and other machineries. Also noteworthy are the 38.75% of textile machinery, 67.41% of bicycles, 2-wheel cars, etc. and 55.48% of shipbuilding. However, that the value of shipments in Japan's shipbuilding of 55.48% of the United States and 77.7% of the United Kingdom seems thoroughly inconsistent with the following statistics of Lloyd's register of shipping (London) according to which tonnage launched in Japan is 2,067 thousand tons, but 1,429 thousand tons in West Germany, 1,402 thousand tons in the United Kingdom and 732 thousand tons in the United States, in 1958 (all in terms of gross registered tons). According to the *Census of Manufactures*, the level of shipbuilding in the United States is much higher than that in the United Kingdom and Japan while according to the statistics of Lloyd's register of shipping, Japan is ranked as the top in the world. This inconsistency problem is very difficult to deal with here in detail, but if the Census figure were correct, our computational result will naturally be subject to further consideration.

It is true that the Census figure might include war vessels, which accounted for 28.7% of the production in the United States and 1.3% in Japan in 1958. This percentage is in terms of current prices, but we must also take into account that prices of war vessels may be exceedingly higher (say ten times) than that of merchant vessels in terms of gross registered tons. It is very difficult to evaluate unit prices of vessels, but, according to the experts' information, the unit prices of vessel per gross ton is extraordinarily higher in the United States than in Japan. Particularly, they say, the United States' tanker's price doubles that of Japan's. In the United States, the 1958 value added ratio in shipbuilding was 56.2% while in Japan it was only 29.6%. If it is assumed that there are no significant differences in technology and raw material prices, then the difference in the value added ratios between the two countries might be understood as reflecting that in Japan the unit wage cost is exceedingly low and also that the unit price is much lower in Japan than in the United States.

They say that in the United States the proportion of repairs in the value of shipments in the Census is much higher and the sidebusiness ratio (other than shipbuilding) is also higher. Although the value of shipments and the value added in shipbuilding are much lower in Japan, it is to be further noticed that the number of employees in Japan is more than that in the United States (148,676 vs. 119,147). Although not complete, these are our explanations of the large gap between the Census data and Lloyd's statistics. However, we must admit that the puzzle has not been completely solved as yet, and one may cast some doubts on the generally established notion that Japan is the top shipbuilding country in the world.

209

Another problem which needs a special check is the level of Japan's textile industry. As we already pointed out, the value added ratio in the textile industry is tremendously low in Japan. Therefore, we shall try to make a comparison in Table 18 of the value of shipments of the textile industry in the following three countries: the United States, the United Kingdom and Japan.

When the value of shipments of the textile industry according to a narrower definition (excluding apparels) is compared, the United Kingdom is 42.35%, and Japan is 28.88% of the United States. If this is checked with our index of production, 32.3% in the United Kingdom and 37.4% in Japan, the United Kingdom is relatively higher and Japan lower. Now, when the value of shipments of the textile industry according to a wider definition (including apparels) is compared, the United Kingdom becomes 28.32%, and Japan 15.04%, of the United States. In this case the United Kingdom becomes lower by 12.3% and Japan by about 60% than the international production index.

This involves an important problem which needs a further check. When the value of shipments is compared between the textile industry, according to a narrower definition, and apparels, we have the following composition.

	(textiles)		(apparels)
U.S.A.	100.0	vs.	109.1
U.K.	100.0	vs.	39.8
Japan	100.0	vs.	8.9

The relative size of apparels compared with the narrowly defined textile industry is extremely high in the United States (109.1%), but tremendously low in Japan (8.9%). The United Kingdom is located in between them (39.8%). Since the proportion of apparels varies so widely among countries, it seems very important whether or not we should include it in the comparison of the value of shipments index with our volume of production index. The two alternatives may lead to very different results and conclusions. The following should be explored:

210

1. In the *Census of Manufactures* of Japan commercial enterprises are not included among its survey-objectives. Moreover, with respect to the subcontracter's processing of yarns brought in from commercial corporations, only the processing fee is mentioned in the Census. The value of shipments or production of woven fibers, etc., by the subcontracters of commercial enterprises, is entirely left out from the Census. However, in Japan, in which the proportion of the above is expected to amount to a large percentage, the exact value of shipments cannot be estimated without the inclusion of this portion.

In the estimate of 1955 clothing expenditures by the commodity flow method, the writer made an addition of the value of shipments of textile products made by the subcontracters of commercial enterprises (138,056 million yen) to the final domestic consumption of textile products according to the narrower definition (469,546 million yen), the estimate of which, however, depends solely upon the *Census of Manufactures*. The former amounts to 29.4% of the latter. With respect to apparels, the value of shipments by the subcontracters of commercial enterprises is 62,834 million yen while that mentioned in the *Census of Manufactures* is 64,537 million yen. Therefore, in our estimate, an addition amounting to 97.4% was necessary. If the same ratios were to prevail in 1958, the dollar value of shipments of Japan's textile industry should be enlarged as follows.

		million $	
Japan (1958)	textiles	4,653.5	(100.0)
	apparels	628.9	(13.5)
	total	5,282.4	

The ratio of apparels to the textile industry according to the narrower definition with respect to the value of shipments will thus increase from 8.9% to 13.5%, but we must bear in mind that it is still far less than the 39.8% of the United Kingdom. The above total of 5,282.4 million dollars stands for the 20.3% of the United States, an improvement of about 5 points compared with the 15.04% (the relative of Japan to the United States) in Table 18. However, it is still lower than the 37.4% of our international production index. It is lower than the latter by 45.7% and by 17.1 points. Also interesting is the fact that, if we take only the textile industry according to the narrower definition, the Japan-U.S. ratio becomes 37.4%, a chance coincidence with the 37.4% of our international index of production.

2. Another analytical suggestion is indicated in Table 18 where we are given the hint that, as the economy develops, the ratio of the apparels industry to the textile industry (according to the narrower definition) will increase. In the early stage of economic development we can expect that much of the processing of garments was done in the homes and by tailors and dress makers (like *kimono* in Japan), but in later stages, when mass production and standardization of commodities became inevitable, the tendency for garments to be produced increased. This is perceived not only in the cross-section relation of Table 18, but also in the time-series relation too (in Japan, the ratio in question was 8.9% in 1958, 11.4% in 1961 and 12.9% in 1962). In 1958, the value of shipments of the men, youths and boys' suits, coats, overcoats and furnishing was 49.7 times higher in the United States than Japan. The corresponding ratio for women's and misses' outwear and undergarments was 240.1 times higher in the U.S. and the figure for children's outwear was 209.4 times. There are astonishingly high figures which tell us that economic growth entails a tremendously great transfiguration even in the intrastructure of the textile industry.

Table 18. Shipments of Textile Industry in Japan, U.K. and U.S.A. (1958)

	Textiles (A)	Apparels (B)	Textile industry (A + B) (in broader sense)
U.S.A. (All)	12,451.1 mil. dollar	13,580.5 mil. dollar	26,031.6 mil. dollar
U.K. (All)	1,882.6 mil. pound	749.8 mil. pound	2,632.4 mil. pound
(in dollars)	5,273.2 mil. dollar	2,100.2 mil. dollar	7,373.4 mil. dollar
Japan (4 or more employees)	1,294,607 mil. yen	114,690 mil. yen	1,409,297 mil. yen
(in dollars)	3,596.2 mil. dollar	318.6 mil. dollar	3,914.8 mil. dollar
U.S.A.	100.00	100.00	100.00
U.K.	42.35	15.46	28.32
Japan	28.88	2.35	15.04

Sources: U.S.A., *Census of Manufactures*, 1958; U.K., *Census of Production*, 1958; Japan, *Kôgyô Tôkeihyô* (Census of Manufactures), 1958.

3.   Probably most of the value of shipments of textile products according to the narrower definition may flow into domestic consumption in the United States while a considerable portion of it may flow out of Japan as exports. This also may be a resaon why the difference in Table 18 arises.

4.   A final explanation is the relative cheapness of the commodities in the later stage of production in the less advanced countries. Assuming that the same price prevails in the raw material stage, but at the same time that the relatively low wage cost per unit of output prevails in the more fabricated commodities in the less advanced countries, it may be quite natural for us to reach the conclusion indicated in Table 18. In Japan the level of technology is relatively high, but wages are relatively low; therefore, the more fabricated or more labor-intensive a commodity is, the less its price will be.

These considerations suggest a need for a cautious handling of data in comparative studies on an international basis. Without going into detailed analyses with respect to peculiarities of survey methods, data, and empirical tendencies by industry or commodities in various countries, we may not reach satisfactory results.

In this sense, our attempt at the computation of an international index of the physical volume of industrial production may only be a first, preliminary attempt subject to much criticism and requiring further amendment and reformulation.

11. Notes on a New Hypothesis

The above analyses help us explain the discrepancies which exist between our index of production and that found in the *Census of Manufactures* pertaining to textile and machinery industries. Recently, however, I have developed a new hypothsisis on the relative expansion of the "fabricating" industries when compared with the "basic" industries. By introducing this hypothes is, we expect to fill the statistical gap mentioned above. The terms "fabricating" and "basic" are relative in nature. Textiles (threads and woven fabrics) are defined here as more "basic" than apparels, and the latter more "fabricating" than the former. In the same way, machinery, electrical machinery, transportation equipment, etc., are taken to be more "fabricating" than iron and steel or nonferrous metals.

Before going into an explanation of our hypothesis let me present two further statistics which indicate the increasing importance of the "fabricating" industries. The following statistics shows us that, in comparison with the shipments of primary metal products, proportion of the shipments of fabricated metals, machinery, electrical machinery, transportation equipment, and instruments and related products was the highest in the United States, medium in the United Kingdom, and the lowest in Japan in 1958.

214

	(Primary metals)	(Machinery and other fabricated metal products)
U.S.A.	100	370
U.K.	100	318
Japan	100	210

Thus the relatively higher importance of "fabricating" industries in more advanced economies beomes evident.

On the other hand, we find from Table 19 that during 1955–65 the increase in shipments of apparels was 5.13 times compared to an increase of 2.38 times in textiles. That was 6.18 times increase in furniture and fixture in comparison with 3.86 times in lumber and wooden products, and 7~9 times in various kinds of machinery industries, while primary metals increased by 4 times. It is interesting to note that the miscellaneous industry, which is often not attached much importance shows 7.34 times increase for these ten years. In other words, for the ten years, the growth of "fabricating" industries was more conspicuous than that of "basic" industries. A similar tendency can be discerned for the United States and the United Kingdom in the postwar period, but we shall not deal with it here.

It goes without saying that "fabricated" commodities are highly labor-intensive and even when the prices of "basic" commodities tend to decline those of "fabricated" commodities may increase particularly in a situation where the economy experiences acute labor shortage. Consequentry, this is reflected in the relatively higher rate of growth in the shipments of "fabricated" goods. But, Table 19 also indicates that employment increases in conformity with the growth of shipments, i.e., the employment increase in the "fabricating" industry is higher than that in the "basic" industry, although it should be noted that we did not measure the increases of shipments in constant prices.

Table 19. Relative Growth of the Basic and Fabricated Industries

	Shipments (bil. yen)			Employees (thousands)		
	1955	1965	1965/1955	1955	1965	1965/1955
Textiles	1096	2602	2.38	1061	1327	1.25
Apprarels	86	441	5.13	144	311	2.60
Lumber & Wood prod.	274	1057	3.86	383	528	1.38
Furniture and fixture	65	402	6.18	145	250	1.72
Iron and steel	651	2691	4.13	276	480	1.74
Nonferrous metal	283	1165	4.12	99	176	1.78
Machinery	312	2292	7.35	383	902	2.36
Electrical machinery	251	2301	9.17	233	851	3.65
Transp. equipment	371	2854	7.69	322	664	2.06
Instrument & related prod.	56	383	6.84	79	193	2.44
Other misc. industries	133	976	7.34	221	481	2.18

Source: Ministry of International Trade and Industry, *Census of Manufactures* (by Industry), 1955 and 1966.

What factors explain the widening share of "fabricating" industries as the economy grows? We may look for an explanation from factors relating to demand and supply sides.

As an economy grows and the per capita income or consumption of people rises, the diversification of demand will necessarily occur, and the degree of fabrication will accordingly increase. However, such changes in the demand structure will also necessitate some changes in the supply conditions. In order for the output of "fabricating" industries to increase relatively more than that of "basic" industries, there must be a reduction of raw material consumed per unit of output, on the one hand, and the enlargement of the portion of value added, on the other. Therefore, some technological progress must occur which brings about a revolution in raw material consumption, in order to expand the relative proportion of "fabricating" industries. In other words, the substitution of plastics or synthetic fibers for lumber or cotton, for example, is one of the processes which reduces the raw material consumption ratio and increases the share of "fabricating" industries.

This process will be particularly accelerated if new products with higher technology appear in succession. For instance, with the same or lesser amount of raw material input, the use of IC or LST has resulted in the production of more efficient and less noisy computing machine (electronics desk computer). Moreover, the size of the machines have become progressively smaller, but for the time being their prices will not show a clear decline owing to the existence of patents. Therefore, the continuous introduction of new "fabricated" products, may result in a situation in which the proportion of "fabricated" output rises in total output even if in some specific commodities the raw material consumption ratios do not show any decline (for example, the ratio of consumption of raw cotton in the cotton spinning industry.)

Therefore, we may be justified in arguing that some technological progress is a precondition for the relative increase in "fabricating" industries. In general, "fabricating" industries are more labor-intensive and include a large number of small enterprises than the "basic" industries. If there were no technological progress, the rising share of "fabricating" industries will merely cause an increase in unit wage costs and prices. Such a rise in wage costs and prices would weaken their competitive power in the world market. In order to sustain or strengthen their competitiveness in the world trade, it is of utmost importance to accelerate the technological progress in "fabricating" industries. If this is true, the technological progress is an indispensable link in the widening process of "fabricating" industries.

Our finding has something to do with the Leontief Paradox.[7] Leontief found that the United States exports relatively labor-

---

7) W. Leonticf, "Domestic Production and Foreign Trade, American Capital Position Reexamined" *Proceeding of the American Philosophical Society*, September 1953.

intensive commodities, while importing relatively capital-intensive commodities. This finding, which seems to contradict common sense in international economics, is, however, reasonable if we take into account the increasing degree of fabrication coupled with growth as well as the concomittent technological progress in "fabricating" industries. The United States exports a considerable amount of machinery, automobiles, etc., which are essentially labor-intensive, compared with other industries. What is important is that these apparently labor-intensive commodities have at the same time technology-intensive or research-and-development-intensive nature.

One point to be noticed is that there seem to be typically two kinds of "fabricated" commodities: (1) the "sophisticated" goods, on the one hand, and (2) the fashion goods, on the other. The former is represented by machineries, for example, and are essentially technology-intensive. However, the latter is indicated for instance, by high-class apparels, which embody high-level design, elegant colour, etc., but not always high rate of growth in technology. Therefore, the prices of the former tend to decline, but those of the latter tend to increase as a usual.

If these observation are valid, one of the important factors accounting for the discrepancies, particulary conspicuous in case of Japan, between the dollar-index of manufacturing income, and the inter-country index of physical manufacturing production, on the other, may be traced back to the differences of the degree of "fabrication" in the industrial structures of countries. We have already pointed out the role of the undervaluation of exchange rate in causing the discrepancies between the two indices. But probably, this may not be a sufficient or satisfactory explanation. Another more important factor can be found in the difference in the proportion of "fabricating" industries which tends to be greater in more advance countries.

It is very difficult to distinguish clearly the contribution of the undervaluation of exchange rate and the diffierence in the degree of "fabrication" towards causing the discrepancy. Laborious studies of the "real term" proportion of "fabricating" industries and also detailed studies of the price structure of "basic" and "fabricated" commodities, will have to be made before we can successfully explain differences in the industrial levels of different nations.

12. Conclusions

There will be other problems to be explained and analyzed in more detail in relation to these computations, particularly with reference to each category of the individual indices of production in manufacturing as well as the mining index and the public utilities index. Concerning individual indices, we have dealt with them up to some extent in my book written in Japanese, *Kôgyô-suijun no Kokusaihikaku* (International Comparison of Industrial Levels), (Tokyo, The Institute of Asian Economic Affairs), 1965. However, in this English version, it has been omitted.

Although our results may be subject to a wide margin of error, they provide a very rough indication of the industrial levels of various countries.

1. In terms of the dollar value of income per head of population, a great divergence of levels, even in industrial countries, may still be seen, but the index of the physical volume of manufacturing production per head of population does not indicate such wide differences. This suggests that the exchange rate is not a good conversion rate for the purpose of computing real income or output.

2. The most phenomenal advance may be seen particularly with respect to Japan where, in the brief five-year period from 1958 to 1963, she has moved up from sixth to third in rank, following only the United States and the Soviet Union in terms of the aggregate volume of manufacturing production.

3. Export growth rates in industrial countries seem to be positively correlated with their dollar income-physical output ratios in manufacturing. This may probably be one of the most important reasons why the Japanese export growth rate is so high.

4. It is highly probable that, even from the commodity comparison of twenty-three major products, Japan achieved third place by 1963. By industry, Japan was the number two in chemicals, number three in metals and also number three in the machinery and construction industries in 1963.

5. It is astonishing that the value added (in dollar terms) per employee in manufacturing is almost twice as high in the Philippines as it is in Japan, and the values for ten out of the thirteen countries of Middle and South Africa exceeds that of Japan. Such apparently unbelievable results come from a general overvaluation of exchange rate in quite a few underdeveloped countries. However, this comparison with underdeveloped countries reinforces our contention that Japan's exchange rate is also undervalued.

6. The gap between the dollar income and the physical volume indices of production may also be dependent upon the fact that in Japan the value added ratio is conspicuously lower when compared with other advanced countries. Although there exist some differences in the survey method of the value of shipments among countries, it is our hypothesis that the undervaluation of the exchange rate will necessarily reduce the value added ratio by increasing the relative prices of raw materials imported.

7. The case of the shipbuilding industry and the textile industry seems particularly puzzling. Even if Japan is called the top shipbuilding country in the world, a comparison of three-country Censuses reveals inconsistent and contradictory conclusions. The ratio of the output of apparels to the textile output in a narrower sense seems to have a marked tendency to increase with industrialization.

This may cause some problems in comparing of industrial levels on an international basis.

8. Just when this book is compiled, one hypothesis has come up. This emphasizes the increasing share of the "fabricating" industries, as compared with the "basic" industries, as the level of an economy grows. This throws a light not only upon the discrepancies between our production index and the dollar value of output, but also upon the interpretation of the so-called "Leontief Paradox".

Appendix 1 Total Manufacturing Production Index, 1958.

Japan = 100.00   U.K. = 100.00

	I.F.	E.F.	I.F.	E.F.
Afghanistan	0.12	0.12	0.16	0.18
Albania	0.12	0.09	0.09	0.09
Algeria	19.78	1.90	4.06	2.01
Argentina	68.48	9.56	20.86	10.12
Ausirtala	49.61	21.91	26.68	23.05
Austria	20.21	11.30	14.75	14.31
Belgium	32.35	22.55	19.27	18.76
Brazil	50.00	16.80	26.29	20.97
Bulgaria	8.79	5.33	6.74	5.72
Nicaragua	0.27	0.09	0.13	0.12
Canada	75.77	59.94	63.02	64.63
Ceylon	0.29	0.31	0.27	0.30
Chile	9.69	7.44	4.78	4.34
Colombia	4.10	1.55	1.82	1.50
Cuba	18.21	1.30	2.74	1.17
Trinidad-Tobago	1.01	0.49	0.27	0.23
Czechoslovakia	39.70	28.87	31.46	31.99
Denmark	20.14	5.06	8.39	6.13
Dominican Republic	2.95	0.26	0.56	0.28
Federation of Malaya	3.23	3.31	3.30	3.45
Finland	11.66	8.23	13.45	13.74
France	195.99	93.79	99.73	92.38
East Germany	32.35	12.13	12.93	9.31
West Germany	177.13	123.61	119.86	119.27
Saar	2.96	2.67	1.62	1.69
Congo	3.64	3.56	7.21	7.95
El Salvador	0.27	0.09	0.10	0.09
Angola	0.48	0.05	0.10	0.04
Taiwan	4.89	2.30	6.47	6.81
Hong Kong	1.15	1.21	1.01	1.13
Bolivia	1.10	0.07	0.07	0.04

U.S.A.=100.00		Japan weight, converted to USA=100		U.K. weight, converted to USA=100		Geometric average of 3 indices	
I.F.	E.F.	I.F.	E.F.	I.F.	E.F.	I.F.	E.F.
0.04	0.04	0.02	0.02	0.03	0.03	0.03	0.03
0.02	0.02	0.02	0.02	0.02	0.02	0.02	0.02
1.19	0.47	2.69	0.33	0.70	0.34	1.31	0.38
4.72	2.04	9.33	1.64	3.61	1.71	5.41	1.79
5.12	3.91	6.76	3.76	4.62	3.90	5.43	3.86
2.62	2.32	2.75	1.94	2.55	2.42	2.64	2.22
4.84	4.57	4.41	3.86	3.33	3.18	4.14	3.83
4.60	2.91	6.81	2.88	4.55	3.55	5.22	3.10
1.04	0.81	1.20	0.91	1.17	0.97	1.13	0.89
0.01	0.01	0.04	0.02	0.02	0.02	0.02	0.02
9.67	9.43	10.32	10.27	10.90	10.95	10.28	10.20
0.06	0.07	0.04	0.05	0.05	0.05	0.05	0.06
1.14	1.07	1.32	1.28	0.83	0.74	1.08	1.00
0.61	1.36	0.56	0.27	0.31	0.25	0.47	0.29
1.23	0.26	2.48	0.22	0.47	0.20	1.13	0.23
0.07	0.04	0.14	0.08	0.05	0.04	0.08	0.05
5.95	5.68	5.41	4.95	5.44	5.42	5.60	5.67
1.53	0.93	2.74	0.87	1.45	1.04	1.83	0.94
0.20	0.05	0.40	0.04	0.10	0.05	0.20	0.05
0.67	0.76	0.44	0.57	0.57	0.58	0.55	0.63
1.34	1.33	1.59	1.41	2.33	2.33	1.71	1.63
20.63	17.66	26.70	16.07	17.25	15.65	21.18	16.44
3.29	2.25	4.41	2.08	2.24	1.58	3.19	1.95
24.33	23.03	24.14	21.18	20.73	20.20	23.00	21.44
0.66	0.69	0.40	0.46	0.28	0.29	0.42	0.45
0.48	0.49	0.50	0.61	1.25	1.35	0.67	0.74
0.02	0.01	0.04	0.02	0.02	0.02	0.02	0.02
0.02	0.00	0.07	0.01	0.02	0.01	0.03	0.00
0.53	0.40	0.67	0.39	1.12	1.15	0.74	0.56
0.21	0.23	0.16	0.21	0.17	0.19	0.18	0.21
0.02	0.01	0.15	0.01	0.01	0.10	0.03	0.01

Appendix 1 Total Manufacturing Production Index, 1958 (Cont'd)

Japan = 100.00   U.K. = 100

	I.F.	E.F.	I.F.	E.F.
Greece	10.26	2.43	4.06	2.72
Guatemala	0.70	0.09	0.30	0.19
Hawaii	2.14	0.00	0.23	0.00
Hungary	19.87	8.87	9.99	8.78
Iceland	0.81	0.12	0.33	0.13
Indonesia	6.21	1.84	3.23	2.69
Ireland	6.34	1.23	2.28	1.43
Italy	148.57	49.46	55.94	47.60
Jamaica	1.36	0.20	0.27	0.14
Japan	**100.00**	**100.00**	104.96	113.17
Kenya	1.31	0.81	0.84	0.57
Korea (South)	2.76	1.75	1.72	1.49
Lebanon	1.00	0.87	0.85	0.88
Luxembourg	2.89	2.53	1.60	1.67
Madagascar	0.27	0.06	0.12	0.11
Mexico	19.66	10.56	9.43	8.26
Morocco	5.05	1.09	1.81	1.17
Netherlands	31.18	17.34	18.28	16.80
New Zealand	18.68	4.21	8.39	7.51
Norway	12.29	8.83	9.74	9.58
Pakistan	6.63	3.33	3.49	2.92
Panama	0.40	0.06	0.16	0.10
Philippines	6.86	1.75	3.26	2.74
Honduras	0.53	0.16	0.43	0.41
Israel	2.06	1.42	1.57	1.51
Nigeria	0.33	0.32	0.11	0.11
Peru	5.19	1.80	1.30	0.81
Paraguay	0.57	0.42	0.05	0.02

JAPAN'S INDUSTRIAL LEVEL IN INTERNATIONAL PERSPECTIVE

U.S.A.=100.00		Japan weight, converted to U.S.A.=100		U.K. weight, converted to U.S.A.=100		Geometric average of 3 indices	
I.F.	E.F.	I.F.	E.F.	I.F.	E.F.	I.F.	E.F.
0.86	0.55	1.40	0.42	0.70	0.46	0.95	0.47
0.06	0.02	0.10	0.02	0.05	0.03	0.07	0.02
0.12	0.00	0.29	0.00	0.04	0.00	0.11	0.00
2.24	1.83	2.71	1.52	1.73	1.49	2.19	1.61
0.15	0.02	0.11	0.02	0.06	0.02	0.10	0.02
0.54	0.33	0.85	0.32	0.56	0.64	0.64	0.36
0.54	0.24	0.86	0.21	0.39	0.24	0.57	0.23
12.74	9.71	20.24	8.48	9.68	8.06	13.57	8.72
0.10	0.04	0.19	0.03	0.05	0.02	0.10	0.03
15.46	16.81	13.62	17.14	18.16	19.17	15.64	17.68
0.10	0.07	0.18	0.14	0.15	0.10	0.14	0.10
0.29	0.23	0.38	0.30	0.30	0.25	0.32	0.26
0.18	0.19	0.14	0.15	0.15	0.15	0.16	0.16
0.63	0.68	0.39	0.43	0.28	0.28	0.41	0.43
0.03	0.02	0.04	0.01	0.02	0.02	0.02	0.01
2.41	1.90	2.68	1.81	1.63	1.40	2.19	1.69
0.40	0.20	0.69	0.19	0.31	0.20	0.44	0.20
3.84	3.48	4.25	2.97	3.16	2.85	3.72	3.09
1.22	0.67	2.54	0.72	1.45	1.27	1.65	0.85
1.72	1.51	1.67	1.51	1.68	1.62	1.69	1.55
0.72	0.61	0.90	0.57	0.60	0.49	0.73	0.55
0.04	0.02	0.05	0.01	0.03	0.02	0.04	0.01
0.69	0.39	0.93	0.30	0.56	0.46	0.71	0.38
0.19	0.21	0.07	0.03	0.07	0.07	0.10	0.08
0.33	0.33	0.28	0.24	0.27	0.26	0.29	0.27
0.09	0.10	0.04	0.05	0.02	0.02	0.04	0.05
0.41	0.22	0.71	0.31	0.22	0.14	0.40	0.21
0.10	0.10	0.08	0.07	0.01	0.00	0.04	0.00

Appendix 1   Total Manufacturing Production Index, 1958 (Cont'd)

Japan = 100.00   U.K. = 100.00

	I.F.	E.F.	I.F.	E.F.
Poland	60.82	38.70	43.43	42.16
Portugal	15.93	3.54	5.64	4.05
Puerto Rico	3.43	0.67	0.80	0.54
South Rhodesia	1.01	0.47	0.51	0.41
South Africa	24.75	11.86	13.36	12.03
S. W. Africa	0.96	0.00	0.37	0.00
Spain	51.07	16.81	21.79	17.67
Sweden	28.82	21.85	27.39	28.51
Switzerland	11.95	6.69	7.74	7.38
Syria	1.06	0.89	1.06	1.11
Tanganyika	0.37	0.12	0.18	0.13
Turkey	6.03	3.62	4.06	3.96
Uganda	0.94	0.25	0.50	0.35
U.S.S.R.	412.17	329.93	384.34	402.25
U.A.R. (Egypt)	9.50	3.36	3.90	3.03
U.K.	145.50	109.82	**100.00**	**100.00**
U.S.A.	734.15	583.48	578.06	590.31
Uruguay	4.73	0.72	1.49	0.69
Venezuela	7.22	5.31	4.53	4.39
Yugoslavia	21.99	9.92	12.23	10.79
Rumania	14.66	12.13	14.15	14.46
Tunisia	2.69	0.65	1.01	0.79
Communist China	50.54	53.50	43.40	48.06
Ecuador	0.72	0.26	0.35	0.30
Ethiopia	0.15	0.03	0.04	0.02
India	31.29	27.07	22.01	23.40
Iran	3.34	2.35	4.41	4.40
Iraq	0.90	0.99	0.92	1.02
Thailand	1.81	1.79	2.41	2.66
Burma	0.29	0.18	0.18	0.19

U.S.A.=100.00		Japan weight, converted to U.S.A.=100		U.K. weight, converted to U.S.A.=100		Geometric average of 3 indices	
I.F.	E.F.	I.F.	E.F.	I.F.	E.F.	I.F.	E.F.
7.42	6.77	8.28	6.63	7.51	7.14	7.73	6.84
1.32	0.71	2.17	0.61	0.98	0.69	1.41	0.67
0.30	0.14	0.47	0.11	0.14	0.09	0.27	0.11
0.13	0.11	0.14	0.08	0.09	0.07	0.12	0.09
2.90	2.53	3.37	2.03	2.31	2.04	2.83	2.19
0.09	0.00	0.13	0.00	0.06	0.00	0.09	0.00
4.90	3.46	6.96	2.88	3.77	2.99	5.05	3.10
3.82	3.82	3.93	3.74	4.74	4.83	4.14	4.10
1.43	1.28	1.63	1.15	1.34	1.25	1.46	1.23
0.17	0.18	0.14	0.15	0.18	0.19	0.16	0.17
0.03	0.02	0.05	0.02	0.03	0.02	0.04	0.02
0.64	0.55	0.82	0.62	0.70	0.67	0.72	0.61
0.07	0.03	0.13	0.04	0.09	0.06	0.09	0.04
56.15	56.35	56.14	56.55	66.48	68.14	59.40	60.10
0.76	0.59	1.29	0.58	0.67	0.51	0.87	0.56
21.76	21.20	19.82	18.82	17.30	16.94	19.54	18.91
100.00	100.00	100.00	100.00	100.00	100.00	100.00	100.00
0.34	0.16	0.64	0.12	0.26	0.12	0.38	0.13
0.98	0.89	0.98	0.91	0.78	0.74	0.91	0.84
2.17	1.71	3.00	1.70	2.12	1.83	2.40	1.75
2.05	2.05	2.00	2.08	2.45	2.45	2.16	2.19
0.22	0.14	0.37	0.11	0.17	0.13	0.24	0.13
9.49	10.75	6.88	9.17	7.51	8.14	7.89	9.29
0.08	0.04	0.10	0.04	0.06	0.05	0.08	0.04
0.02	0.01	0.02	0.01	0.01	0.00	0.00	0.00
4.88	5.12	4.26	4.64	3.81	3.96	4.30	4.55
0.47	0.43	0.45	0.40	0.76	0.75	0.54	0.51
0.20	0.23	0.12	0.17	0.16	0.17	0.16	0.19
0.22	0.24	0.25	0.31	0.42	0.45	0.28	0.32
0.13	0.14	0.04	0.03	0.03	0.03	0.05	0.05

Appendix 2   Mining Production Index   (Japan weight, Japan = 100) 1958.

	Value added weight 20-comm. total index	Coal convert. 4-comm. total index
Afghanistan	0.1	0.1
Albania	1.2	1.5
Algeria	4.3	1.7
Argentina	18.3	18.6
Australia	72.0	50.9
Austria	16.6	16.7
Belgium	43.1	52.9
Brazil	22.8	12.9
Bulgaria	14.1	12.3
Nicaragua	1.1	
Canada	171.8	109.2
Ceylon	0.0	
Chile	41.7	6.0
Colombia	24.6	26.7
Cuba	1.7	0.1
Trinidad-Tobago	15.3	18.8
Czechoslovakia	82.9	99.6
Denmark	1.8	2.2
Dominican Rep.	0.2	
Fed. of Malaya	2.1	0.1

	Value added weight 20-comm. total index	Coal convert. 4-comm. total index
Greece	2.3	1.1
Guatemala	0.3	
Hawaii		
Hungary	23.1	27.6
Iceland		
Indonesia	50.3	56.9
Ireland	0.4	0.4
Italy	26.2	17.5
Jamaica	0.0	
Japan	100.0	100.0
Kenya	0.1	
South Korea	6.6	5.2
Lebanon	0.0	
Luxembourg	2.3	
Madagascar	0.0	
Mexico	73.5	61.2
Morocco	7.4	1.2
Netherlands	25.3	29.0

	Value added weight 20-comm. total index	Coal convert. 4-comm. total index
Poland	164.8	192.9
Portugal	2.7	1.2
Puerto Rico	0.0	
South Rhodesia	14.5	6.9
South Africa	167.0	72.3
S.W. Africa		
Spain	37.8	30.7
Sweden	18.8	0.9
Switzerland	0.3	
Syria		
Tanganyika	0.6	0.0
Turkey	17.0	10.8
Uganda	0.7	
U.S.S.R.	1,111.8	1,232.0
U.A.R. (Egypt)	9.6	10.2
U.K.	364.0	427.3
U.S.A.	2,182.1	2,445.6
Uruguay		
Venezuela	380.4	452.8

Finland	9.0		New Zealand	2.9	3.3	Yugoslavia	24.7	64.0
France	130.6	120.0	Norway	3.3	0.6	Rumania	55.1	0.0
East Germany	162.5	195.3	Pakistan	3.6	3.2	Tunisia	1.7	
West Germany	309.7	359.1	Panama			China	466.0	533.2
Saar	26.4	32.4	Philippines	9.7	0.2	Ecuador	1.2	1.3
Congo	24.7	0.6	Honduras	0.1		Ethiopia	0.4	
El Salvador	0.0		Israel	0.3		India	96.6	91.0
Angola	0.6	0.2	Nigeria	3.0	0.3	Iran	108.1	132.4
Taiwan	6.3	6.3	Peru	22.0	2.6	Iraq	92.9	114.1
Hong Kong	0.1		Paraguay		8.4	Thailand	2.3	0.1
Bolivia	7.0	1.4				Burma	2.7	1.5

Note: The coal-converted 4-commodities total indices are derived as the "total" of coal, lignite, natural gas and crude petroleum.

Appendix 3 Public Utilities Production Index, 1958

	Japan weight index Q_j	U.K. weight index Q_u	U.S.A. weight index Q_a		Japan weight index Q_j	U.K. weight index Q_u	U.S.A. weight index Q_a
Afghanistan	0.1	0.1	0.0	Mexico	30.2	5.7	1.2
Albania	0.2	0.1	0.0	Morocco	3.1	0.6	0.1
Algeria	1.5	7.2	0.2	Netherlands	50.9	13.5	3.1
Argentina	10.9	6.3	1.3	New Zealand	34.8	3.7	0.8
Australia	27.6	15.4	3.3				
Austria	16.0	9.2	1.9	Norway	15.8	17.3	3.5
Belgium	23.2	12.5	2.8	Pakistan	5.5	0.8	0.2
Brazil	21.8	12.7	2.6	Panama	0.5	0.1	0.0
Bulgaria	3.2	1.9	0.4	Philippines	18.6	1.2	0.3
Nicaragua	0.2	0.1	0.0	Honduras	1.5	0.1	0.0
Canada	107.3	62.7	12.9	Israel	3.1	1.1	0.2
Ceylon	0.3	0.1	0.0	Nigeria	0.5	0.2	0.1
Chile	4.8	2.8	0.6	Peru	13.2	1.3	0.3
Colombia	3.2	1.9	0.4	Paraguay	1.0	0.1	0.0
Cuba	2.9	1.7	0.4	Poland	100.0	21.0	4.7
Trinidad-Tobago	0.4	0.2	0.1	Portugal	10.5	1.7	0.3
Czechoslovakia	31.0	16.9	3.7	Puerto Rico	12.0	10.0	0.2
Denmark	5.2	2.9	0.6	South Rhodesia	1.7	10.0	0.2
Dominican Rep.	0.3	0.2	0.0				
Fed. of Malaya	0.9	0.6	0.1	South Africa	40.1	13.4	2.8
Finland	8.6	5.0	1.0	S. W. Africa	0.3	0.1	0.0
France	88.5	49.0	10.6	Spain	41.7	10.2	2.1

East Germany	45.6	25.7	5.5
West Germany	166.9	89.3	20.0
Saar	8.2	4.1	1.0
Congo	2.7	1.6	0.3
El Salvador	0.2	0.1	0.0
Angola	0.1	0.1	0.0
Taiwan	3.2	1.9	0.4
Hong Kong	0.9	0.5	0.1
Bolivia	0.3	0.1	0.0
Greece	12.1	1.2	0.3
Guatemala	1.0	0.1	0.0
Hawaii	9.1	0.9	0.2
Hungary	23.2	4.6	1.0
Iceland	1.1	0.3	0.1
Indonesia	14.9	1.3	0.2
Ireland	9.7	1.4	0.3
Italy	179.5	31.1	6.5
Jamaica	4.7	0.2	0.1
Japan	100.0	57.7	12.0
Kenya	1.1	0.1	0.0
Korea (South)	2.0	0.9	0.2
Lebanon	0.7	0.2	0.0
Luxembourg	3.7	3.7	0.2
Madagascar	1.0	0.1	0.0

Sweden	42.4	19.4	4.0
Switzerland	16.0	11.0	2.3
Syria	0.8	0.2	0.0
Tanganyika	0.1	0.1	0.0
Turkey	9.6	1.8	0.4
Uganda	0.3	0.1	0.0
U.S.S.R.	476.4	179.1	38.5
U.A.R. (Egypt)	21.9	1.4	0.3
U.K.	156.5	100.0	22.2
U.S.A.	906.0	481.9	100.0
Uruguay	2.1	0.8	0.2
Venezuela	30.3	1.4	0.3
Yugoslavia	17.4	4.6	0.9
Rumania	20.2	4.3	0.9
Tunisia	1.8	0.1	0.0
Communist China	82.9	17.2	3.5
Ecuador	1.5	0.2	0.0
Ethiopia	0.5	0.1	0.0
India	56.1	9.6	2.0
Iran	10.1	0.4	0.1
Iraq	6.4	0.4	0.1
Thailand	2.4	0.3	0.1
Burma	0.9	0.2	0.1

CHAPTER 6

LONG-TERM CHANGES IN LEVEL AND STRUCTURE OF CONSUMPTION EXPENDITURES, 1874–1940

In this paper we have attempted to explore the long-term changes of the level and structure of personal consumption expenditures in prewar Japan, based upon our new estimates of them using the commodity flow and retail valuation methods. Our estimates have not only been checked by the official national income estimates, but also by family budget surveys on farms and workers' households. We believe that these checks will fortify the reliability of our estimates, and that they will provide us with a critical evaluation of the existing official estimates of consumption, thereby making clear the weakness of these official estimates.

1. Estimated Results of Consumption Expenditures

It is extremely difficult for economists in any country to estimate personal consumption expenditures over a long period. We might, indeed, be able to compute them indirectly, for instance, by subtracting from the gross national product government expenditures and capital formation, the long-term estimates of which are available in Japan today, and then adjusting balance of international payments. To our regret, however, although direct estimates of government expenditures and capital formation are available, direct estimates of long-term personal consumption expenditures have not been attempted. However, recently I estimated long-term personal consumption expenditures after several years of research. I have made up a long series of personal consumption expenditures from 1874 to 1940, computed year by year by means of the commodity flow method, the retail valuation method, and other procedures. The results were made public in a volume: Miyohei Shinohara, *Kojin Shôhi Shishutsu* (Personal Consumption Expenditures), *Chôki Keizai Tôkei* (Estimates of Long-Term Economic Statistics of Japan since 1868), No. 6, Tokyo, Oriental Economist, 1966.

Full data can be found in the volume above. The headings of every basic statistics table and the summary of estimating procedures are also given in English, but the analyses of the findings led from the estimated results are stated only in Japanese. Here I shall, therefore, confine myself to explaining the findings and their analyses in English. I hope readers interested in the more detailed estimating procedures will take the trouble to refer to the book itself.

Table 1 gives a series of personal consumption expenditures from 1874 to 1940 in current prices with the components shown in overlapping decades. Table 2 gives their percentage compositions. The constant price series, based on 1934–36 prices, are to be found in Table 3, and their percentages composition are shown in Table 4. It can be seen from Table 2, that food, including beverages and tobacco, dropped from 65.7% in the decade 1874–1883 to 49.5% in the decade 1931–1940, while clothing rose from 7.8% to 12.9%, during the same period, i.e., an increase of approximately 65% in percentage composition. The rapid growth of transportation together with communications, from 0.3% to 4.2%, may be due to industrialization and urbanization. Housing has increased from 7.2% to 12.4% and medical and personal care expenses have increased from 3.8% to 5.7%, while fuel and lighting fell from 5.5% to 4.4% with a little irregular oscillation during the period. Education, recreation and other expenses, which cover expenses for school fees, stationery, theatre, movies, radio fees, etc., rose from 3.9%

233

Table 1. Personal Consumption Expenditures in Current Prices

Year	Food	Clothing	Housing	Fuel & lighting
1874~1883	416,001	49,573	45,383	34,730
1877~1886	466,540	54,447	52,927	35,216
1882~1891	522,112	64,377	72,016	34,312
1887~1896	673,020	99,641	95,051	35,704
1892~1901	1,038,860	157,363	131,214	50,279
1897~1906	1,443,573	186,402	180,402	68,192
1902~1911	1,825,521	237,091	254,599	94,924
1907~1916	2,286,195	341,148	344,016	134,106
1912~1921	4,191,161	920,639	520,588	273,999
1917~1926	6,614,943	1,431,933	960,119	452,850
1922~1931	6,866,671	1,336,002	1,395,106	514,562
1927~1936	6,248,798	1,385,791	1,527,637	523,456
1931~1940	7,043,455	1,840,447	1,765,581	624,299

Table 2. Percentage Composition of Consumption Expenditures in Current Prices

Year	Food	Clothing	Housing	Fuel & lighting
1874~1883	65.7	7.8	7.2	5.5
1877~1886	65.4	7.7	7.4	4.9
1882~1891	63.8	7.9	8.8	4.2
1887~1896	63.1	9.3	8.9	3.3
1892~1901	63.0	9.5	8.0	3.0
1897~1906	63.7	8.2	7.9	3.0
1902~1911	63.2	8.2	8.8	3.3
1907~1916	61.9	9.2	9.3	3.6
1912~1921	60.4	13.3	7.5	3.9
1917~1926	58.9	12.8	8.6	4.0
1922~1931	56.0	10.9	11.4	4.2
1927~1936	52.1	11.6	12.7	4.4
1931~1940	49.5	12.9	12.4	4.4

Note: Computed from Table 1.

unit: thousand yen

Medical & personal care	Transpor- tion	Communi- cation	Social expenses	Education, recreation, & others	Total
24,253	1,514	478	36,915	24,695	633,542
30,242	1,753	720	43,329	28,295	713,469
38,806	3,157	1,035	49,240	33,147	818,202
47,580	7,064	1,818	63,564	42,852	1,066,294
69,084	16,181	3,725	116,394	66,258	1,649,358
87,126	28,851	6,644	174,324	93,287	2,268,472
87,574	46,114	10,148	208,050	123,079	2,887,100
108,918	70,159	14,923	224,621	167,882	3,691,968
228,159	150,868	27,478	270,246	356,534	6,939,672
419,888	292,447	45,887	384,053	624,440	11,226,560
508,599	383,467	62,351	417,560	766,730	12,251,048
611,225	398,948	76,267	352,955	867,787	11,992,861
815,055	493,476	95,646	405,661	1,135,128	14,218,748

(%)

Medical & personal care	Transpor- tation	Communi- cation	Social expenses	Education, recreation, & others	Total
3.8	0.2	0.1	5.8	3.9	100.0
4.2	0.2	0.1	6.1	4.0	100.0
4.7	0.4	0.1	6.0	4.1	100.0
4.5	0.7	0.2	6.0	4.0	100.0
4.2	1.0	0.2	7.1	4.0	100.0
3.8	1.3	0.3	7.7	4.1	100.0
3.0	1.6	0.4	7.2	4.3	100.0
3.0	1.9	0.4	6.1	4.6	100.0
3.3	2.2	0.4	3.9	5.1	100.0
3.7	2.6	0.4	3.4	5.6	100.0
4.2	3.1	0.5	3.4	6.3	100.0
5.1	3.3	0.6	2.9	7.3	100.0
5.7	3.5	0.7	2.9	8.0	100.0

Table 3. Personal Consumption Expenditures in 1934–36 Prices

Year	Food	Clothing	Housing	Fuel & lighting
1874~1883	2,065,956	94,270	400,494	83,590
1877~1886	2,197,342	104,774	412,477	87,818
1882~1891	2,460,638	138,141	435,296	96,413
1887~1896	2,797,112	227,331	474,178	106,644
1892~1901	3,110,852	319,654	520,895	117,191
1897~1906	3,267,191	327,547	608,433	130,919
1902~1911	3,475,123	361,929	716,409	153,614
1907~1916	3,972,546	473,747	703,688	201,738
1912~1921	4.703,622	703,251	737,673	284,651
1917~1926	5,536,744	893,231	1,038,815	374,139
1922~1931	6,078,622	1,017,462	1,304,782	456,639
1927~1936	6,356,584	1,349,934	1,440,466	519,570
1931~1940	6,542,951	1,565,213	1,627,959	572,159

Table 4. Percentage Composition of Consumption Expenditures in 1934–36 Prices

Year	Food	Clothing	Housing	Fuel & lighting
1874~1883	64.9	3.0	12.6	2.6
1877~1886	65.4	3.1	12.3	2.6
1882~1891	64.7	3.6	11.5	2.5
1887~1896	62.7	5.1	10.6	2.4
1892~1901	60.9	6.3	10.2	2.3
1897~1906	59.9	6.0	11.1	2.4
1902~1911	59.7	6.2	12.3	2.6
1907~1916	60.7	7.2	10.8	3.1
1912~1921	60.5	9.0	9.5	3.7
1917~1926	58.1	9.4	10.9	3.9
1922~1931	55.9	9.3	12.0	4.2
1927~1936	53.1	11.3	12.0	4.3
1931~1940	50.3	12.0	12.5	4.4

Note: Computed from Table 3.

unit: thousand yen

Medical & personal care	Transportation	Communication	Social expenses	Education, recreation, & others	Total
81,422	5,727	1,299	356,701	93,226	3,182,685
98,538	6,864	2,117	348,439	100,147	3,358,516
128,254	11,315	3,399	360,272	166,018	3,799,746
151,037	23,268	5,639	423,250	256,111	4,464,570
170,236	48,799	8,958	502,501	308,528	5,107,614
173,247	76,068	12,973	540,884	321,982	5,459,244
156,587	77,686	17,392	543,011	325,960	5,827,710
181,018	84,750	23,635	510,212	372,893	6,534,227
241,360	144,286	28,496	441,001	493,647	7,777,987
329,214	240,849	34,673	391,652	683,401	9,522,718
420,620	318,087	51,370	402,234	818,049	10,877,865
590,759	379,144	73,233	365,537	905,804	11,981,031
739,410	491,311	87,641	384,834	993,334	13,004,811

(%)

Medical & personal care	Transportation	Communication	Social expenses	Education, recreation, & others	Total
2.6	0.2	0.0	11.2	2.9	100.0
2.9	0.2	0.1	10.4	3.0	100.0
3.4	0.3	0.1	9.5	4.4	100.0
3.4	0.5	0.1	9.5	5.7	100.0
3.3	1.0	0.2	9.8	6.0	100.0
3.2	1.4	0.2	9.9	5.9	100.0
2.7	1.3	0.3	9.3	5.6	100.0
2.8	1.3	0.4	8.0	5.7	100.0
3.1	1.8	0.4	5.7	6.3	100.0
3.5	2.5	0.4	4.1	7.2	100.0
3.9	3.0	0.5	3.7	7.5	100.0
4.9	3.2	0.6	4.0	7.6	100.0
5.7	3.8	0.7	3.0	7.6	100.0

to 8.0%. Attention must be paid to the item of social expenses, which showed an increase during the take-off stage in the Meiji period (5.8% in 1874–1883 to 7.7% in 1897–1906), but which from then on showed a declining tendency throughout the period under review, with the sharpest drop in 1912–1921, and finally reaching a low of 2.9% in 1927–1940. Estimates of social expenses are based primarily on the income of service trades in the "*Shuzeikyoku Tôkei Nempô-sho* (Annual Statistical Report of the Tax Bureau). If this trend is correct, we are led to expect that social expenses may have shown relative cuts during the long recession in the 1920's and during the period of a wartime economy from the Manchurian Incident through World War II (1931–1945).

The series shown in Table 3 are the totals of commodity flows and flows of services to consumers in 1934–36 prices, classified by expenditures. A trend in the relative proportions of component expenditures in real terms derived from Table 3 is shown in Table 4. This result when contrasted with changes in the proportions in the current price series (Table 2) shows some interesting conclusions. First, no great differences are found as regards the percentages of food expenditures between the two tables. In the case of clothing expenditures, however, a marked difference is seen, in that the current price share rose from 7.8% to 12.9%, or a rise of approximately 65%. Similarly constant price share rose from 3.0% to 12.0%, or a sharp increase of fourfold for the period. This indicates that the relative price of clothing declined precipitously during the period. In any case such a sharp increase in the percentage for clothing in constant prices during the 67 years can be seen as one of the most important influences of prewar industrialization centering around light industries, and its effect on the consumption structure.

Meanwhile, the percentage for housing changed little (12.6% to 12.5%) in real terms despite an increase (7.2% to 12.4%) in current prices. Judging from the weights occupied by the house-and-land rents in our estimates of housing, these changes tell us that the relative prices of rents went upward. Fuel and lighting were reduced from 5.5% to 4.4% in current prices while they rose from 2.6% to 4.4% in real terms, owing to the long-term fall in the relative prices of gas and electric lighting. The less than proportionate increase of medical and personal care in current prices than that in real terms suggests that the cost of medical treatment and charges for the public bath and hair-cuts declined relatively. As is shown in the table, transportation and communications saw a drop in relative prices in the first half of the period.

Social expenses fell from 5.9% to 2.9%, by nearly 50% in current prices while in real terms they fell from 11.2% to 3.0% or a drop to about one-fourth. This naturally means a rise of relative prices for social expenses.

All the above mentioned findings become clearer when we divide the current price percentages by the constant prices per-centages. Table 5 shows the trend of relative price for each item. From this table we see that in the first half of the period the rate of fall in relative prices was remarkably high in case of such items as fuel and lighting, transportation, communications as well as medical and personal care.

This may reflect the influences of outstanding drops in the relative prices of electricity, railroads, communications, and medical treatment during the same period. We are especially interested in this finding, considering the fact that the trend increase in electricity, communication services, and railroad transportation were slowed down around the year 1900.

Next, it is necessary to analyse why there was little difference between the current and constant price series in food expendi-ture proportions. For, when Kuznets analysed the long-term changes in food expenditures in advanced countries, he found that, despite the growth in real income the percentage of food expenditures in current prices was comparatively stable, but

Table 5. Relative Prices of Flows of Goods and Services to Consumers

Year	Food	Clothing	Housing	Fuel & lighting
1874~1883	101.5	264.3	56.8	208.5
1877~1886	100.0	245.3	60.4	189.2
1882~1891	98.6	216.7	76.7	165.6
1887~1896	100.8	183.3	83.7	140.2
1892~1901	103.1	152.3	78.0	132.8
1897~1906	106.2	136.8	71.2	125.2
1902~1911	106.1	132.2	71.7	124.8
1907~1916	101.8	127.4	86.5	117.5
1912~1921	99.9	146.7	79.1	108.0
1917~1926	101.4	136.0	78.4	102.6
1922~1931	100.4	116.6	94.9	100.1
1927~1936	98.2	102.6	106.0	100.6
1931~1940	98.4	107.6	99.3	99.8

Table 6. Annual Growth Rates of Real Consumption Expenditures

Year	Food	Clothing	Housing	Fuel & lighting
1877~1886/1874~1883*	2.07	3.65	0.99	1.67
1882~1891/1877~1886	2.29	5.69	1.08	1.89
1887~1896/1882~1891	2.60	10.48	1.73	2.04
1892~1901/1887~1896	2.12	7.05	1.90	1.90
1897~1906/1892~1901	0.98	0.50	3.16	2.24
1902~1911/1897~1906	1.24	2.02	3.32	5.66
1907~1916/1902~1911	2.73	5.53	−0.36	5.60
1912~1921/1907~1916	3.29	8.22	0.95	7.13
1917~1926/1912~1921	3.31	3.84	7.09	5.61
1922~1931/1917~1926	1.89	2.64	4.66	4.07
1927~1936/1922~1931	0.90	5.82	1.99	2.62
1931~1940/1927~1936**	0.72	3.77	3.11	2.44

Notes: (1) *3 years, **4 years. (2) Computed from Table 4.

Medical & personal care	Transportation	Communication	Social expenses	Education, recreation, & others	Total
149.7	132.7	184.9	51.8	133.2	100.0
144.8	120.3	160.4	58.5	133.5	100.0
140.9	129.8	141.9	63.7	93.0	100.0
131.8	127.2	135.1	62.8	69.9	100.0
125.7	102.8	128.8	71.8	66.6	100.0
120.9	91.1	123.1	77.4	69.7	100.0
112.9	120.0	117.8	77.4	76.4	100.0
106.4	146.5	111.7	76.5	79.6	100.0
105.9	117.3	108.1	68.7	80.9	100.0
108.1	103.0	112.2	82.3	77.5	100.0
107.4	103.8	107.8	92.2	83.2	100.0
103.4	105.1	104.0	96.5	95.7	100.0
100.8	91.9	99.8	96.4	104.6	100.0

(%)

Medical & personal care	Transportation	Communication	Social expenses	Education, recreation, & others	Total
6.56	6.21	17.69	−0.78	2.41	1.81
5.42	10.51	9.94	0.66	10.64	2.50
3.33	15.51	10.65	3.28	9.06	3.28
2.42	15.96	9.70	3.49	3.79	2.73
0.36	9.29	7.68	1.48	0.86	1.34
−2.00	0.42	6.04	0.08	0.25	1.32
2.94	1.76	6.33	−0.85	2.73	2.31
5.92	11.22	3.82	−3.25	5.77	3.55
6.41	10.79	4.01	−2.35	6.72	4.13
5.03	6.37	8.18	0.53	3.66	2.70
7.02	3.02	7.35	−1.90	2.06	1.95
5.78	6.70	4.60	1.30	2.27	2.07

that the food expenditure proportion in real terms dropped.[1] Needless to say, the amount of food put on the market increases in proportion with economic growth. That alone accounts for rises in the relative price of food; even if market prices as well as farm prices are fixed, an increase in the percentage of food put on the market has in itself the effect of raising the weighted average price of both. Kuznets explained that this was why there was little change in the proportion of food expenditures in current prices despite a drop in the proportion in real terms. In Japan, however, both of them declined in the long run and, thereby, brought about only a slight difference in absolute levels of the ratios. The reason for this is that a rise in the relative price of services cancelled out the effect of the rise of the relative price of food which was promoted by an increase in the percentage of food marketed.

In comparison with Kuznets' findings, the following two points are noteworthy in the case of Japan. (1) The proportion of food expenditures has tended to decline (the rate of fall particularly food expenditures has tended to decline (the rate of fall particularly marked after the 1920's). (2) Only a small difference is to be found between the food expenditure percentages in current prices and those in real terms.

One more problem remains to be analysed with regard to the real term series, that is, the question of growth rates of real consumption expenditures. Table 6 shows changes in the annual growth rates. These rates were calculated from the increase ratios of the average values of two overlapping decades. The average decadal values have the effect of evening out cycles occurring during each decade. Therefore, the waves here will be longer than Juglar Cycles, which are about 10 years long. In examining the long waves drawn by some of the items and those by the total real consumption expenditures, we notice that

---

1) Simon Kuznets, "Quantitative Aspects of the Economic Growth of Nations: The Share and Structure of Consumption," *Economic Development and Cultural Change*, January 10, 1962.

the latter, in particular, show fairly regular long swings. 1.81% for 1877–86/1874–83 indicates the growth rate at the bottom of the Matsukata Deflation, making a period of 22 years from this to the next trough (let us suppose it to be 1899–1908, mid-term between 1897–1906 and 1902–1911). Next, the period from the peak of 1887–1896 (3.28%) to that of 1917–1926 (4.13%) is 30 years. In the same way there are 28 years between the two troughs of 1899–1908 and 1927–1936. These data must not be taken as proving positively that duration of a consumption swing was over 20 years, for the use of decade averages is naturally a crude statistical technique. Nevertheless, we may say that long waves of more than two decades in length probably existed in the course of the growth of real consumption expenditures.

In comparison with the growth rates of total consumption expenditures, the trend for clothing is interesting to follow. It should be noted that its peak growth rate during the time of World War I preceded that of total expenditures by a decade and further that each trough in the clothing growth rate was always a decade ahead of that of total expenditures.

In contrast, the growth rates for housing appear to have been moving inversely with the growth rates for total expenditures up to 1920. However, it is difficult to find out whether this was caused by possible defects in statistical data or whether it reflects actual trends.

The growth rates for food swayed slightly less than those for total expenditures and scarcely went up even during World War II, thus distinguishing itself from the rates for total expenditures and for clothing.

The growth rates for fuel and lighting interest us considerably. On the basis of common sense we may anticipate that there will be no distinct cycle in the consumption of fire-wood and charcoal which have been used long since in the past. However, since such new forms of energy as gas and electricity came into use, the fuel and lighting expenses began to grow at a rapid rate. In fact, as the table shows, the growth rate rose remarkably after the decade of 1897–1906. It reached a peak in 1912–1921 though they did not show any conspicuous long swings previously.

Long swings can also be found in education, recreation, etc., as well as in transportation and communications. Transportation and communications showed the widest swings. They showed surprising growth rates in the first half of the period when transportation and communication networks were expanded. Here I may have to mention a word of caution: we obtained these results in spite of the fact that we included the household expenses not only for modern transportation and communications but also for such conventional traffic services as carts, wagons, *rikishas*, etc., which occupied a larger proportion at the earlier stage of the period under review.

In Table 7 are given the average annual growth rates for as long periods as possible. Annual growth rates per capita are presented in the right column of the table. The rate for each item, such as food, clothing, etc., divided by that of the total expenditures, gives the expenditure elasticity. In computing it we should, if possible, subtract the effects caused by an increase in population. The figures on the right side of each growth rate in Table 7 shows in this sense a net expenditure elasticity; it is calculated from the per capita growth rate. According to the results the elasticity of food comes to a low figure of 0.713. Medical and personal care shows high figures of 1.843 (up to 1900) and 3.066 (from 1900 on). Clothing, transportation, and communications stand also high with indices of 2.772, 4.214, 5.088 respectively.

In Table 8 the calculation of expenditure elasticities of five items has been attempted for 12 overlapping decades. They are, of gross elasticities disregarding price elasticities, and not on per capita basis. It is to be noted from the table that a certain kind of long swing exists in the elasticity of food, and that as time goes on the elasticity declines from the 1.182 of 1907–

Table 7. Secular Growth Rates and Expenditure Elasticities of Real Consumption Expenditures

	Real consumption expenditures		R.C.E. per capita of population	
	Annual growth rate (%)	Expenditure elasticity	Annual growth rate (%)	Expenditure elasticity
Food				
(whole period)	2.12	0.841	0.97	0.713
Clothing				
(whole period)	4.96	1.968	3.77	2.772
Housing				
(whole period)	2.52	1.000	1.36	1.000
Fuel & lighting				
(up to 1910)	2.11	0.921	1.12	0.868
(from 1911 on)	4.05	1.436	1.42	1.044
Medical & personal care				
(1875–1900)	4.21	1.565	3.28	1.843
(from 1900 on)	5.99	2.147	4.66	3.066
Transportation				
(whole period)	8.14	3.230	6.92	5.088
Communication				
(from 1889 on)	6.76	2.661	5.52	4.214
Education recreation, & others				
(from 1890 on)	3.28	1.286	2.03	1.538
Total				
(whole period)	2.52		1.36	

Note: Annual growth rate is computed by the formula $\log X_i = \log a + bt$ (X_i = real consumption expenditures of each item). Annual growth rates of the above divided periods used in computation of expenditure elasticities are as follows:

	Real consumption	Per capita real consumption		Real consumption	Per capita real consumption
1874–1910	2.29	1.29	1900–1940	2.79	1.52
1911–1940	2.82	1.52	1889–1940	2.54	1.31
1875–1900	1.78	1.78	1890–1640	2.55	1.32

Table 8. Expenditure Elasticities Among Overlapping Decades

Year	Food	Clothing	Fuel & lighting	Housing	Education, recreation, & others
1877~86/1874~83	1.144	2.017	0.923	0.547	1.331
1882~91/1877~86	0.916	2.276	0.756	0.432	4.256
1887~96/1882~91	0.793	3.195	0.622	0.527	2.762
1892~1901/1887~96	0.777	2.582	0.696	0.696	1.388
1897~1906/1892~1901	0.731	0.373	1.672	2.358	0.642
1902~11/1897~1906	0.939	1.530	4.288	2.515	0.189
1907~16/1902~11	1.182	2.394	2.424	−0.156	1.182
1912~21/1907~16	0.927	2.315	2.008	0.268	1.625
1917~26/1911~21	0.801	0.930	1.358	1.717	1.627
1922~31/1917~26	0.700	0.978	1.507	1.726	1.356
1927~36/1922~31	0.462	2.985	1.344	1.021	1.056
1931~40/1927~36	0.348	1.821	1.179	1.502	1.097

Note: Computed from Table 6. Medical & personal care, transportation, communication, and social expenses are omitted. The figures show gross elasticities because they are computed not from the growth rates per capita expenditures.

1916 to a very low level of 0.348 in 1931–1940. Such a trend reflects a rapid fall of the Engel's Coefficient during this period. Broadly speaking, the elasticity of clothing follows a course corresponding to its growth rate. So does that of fuel and lighting, which also shows high figures for 1897–1921 when its growth rate increases. Housing keeps a consistently low elasticity before 1892–1901 as compared with the figures thereafter. At any rate, we can conclude that each item of expenditure does not always show a stable trend in the expenditure elasticity.

Following the analysis of real consumption expenditures, the next problem we must deal with is how these per capita expenditures changed during the entire period 1874–1940. Table 9 (p.249) shows this. The average annual rate of growth throughout the entire period amounts to 1.36%, the rate of food being 0.97%. The real per capita food expenditures stopped rising from about 1920 and after the peak (¥ 102) of 1923–1925 began

Table 9. Consumption Expenditures Per Capita of Population, 1874–1940

unit: yen

Year	Current prices		1934–36 prices		Year	Current prices		1934–36 prices	
	Total	Food	Total	Food		Total	Food	Total	Food
1874	12	8	82	52	1908	68	44	127	77
1875	14	9	84	54	1909	67	42	128	75
1876	13	8	85	55	1910	68	42	132	79
1877	13	9	87	56	1911	74	47	128	78
1878	15	9	86	55	1912	81	52	130	80
1879	19	13	90	58	1913	85	56	132	82
1880	23	16	96	63	1914	72	44	127	77
1881	25	16	91	59	1915	71	43	132	83
1882	22	15	92	60	1916	81	46	138	84
1883	18	11	90	58	1917	104	61	143	86
1884	18	12	94	63	1918	148	89	150	88
1885	20	13	89	59	1919	214	127	163	96
1886	19	12	94	62	1920	211	131	158	95
1887	20	13	101	66	1921	208	123	168	101
1888	20	12	101	65	1922	213	124	176	101
1889	22	14	107	67	1923	214	124	177	102
1890	25	17	103	65	1924	217	126	178	102
1891	26	17	112	71	1925	224	133	179	102
1892	25	16	109	68	1926	214	123	179	101
1893	27	18	117	74	1927	207	116	181	101
1894	28	18	113	70	1928	205	112	184	101
1895	32	20	109	67	1929	195	107	180	99
1896	36	22	122	74	1930	177	95	178	96
1897	42	27	121	73	1931	157	79	180	97
1898	48	31	127	75	1932	154	78	174	93
1899	47	29	128	77	1933	168	86	183	99
1900	50	31	124	74	1934	185	92	192	98
1901	49	31	124	77	1935	191	96	189	95
1902	50	32	122	74	1936	197	99	192	94
1903	52	34	121	71	1937	222	107	200	94
1904	54	36	123	74	1938	247	115	201	94
1905	54	34	115	68	1939	253	129	192	98
1906	56	35	113	66	1940	285	139	190	90
1907	60	37	115	67					

to decrease towards the ¥ 90 of 1940. In spite of the stagnation
of per capita food expenditures, however, rises in other items
encouraged the per capita total values to increase from the ¥178
of 1923–1925 to the ¥200 of 1937, although they could not arrest
a fall which began thereafter and resulted in the ¥190 of 1940.

2. Food Expenditures

In analysing the changes in the level and composition of personal consumption expenditures in Section I, the following two
adjustments were introduced with regard to food expenditures.
First, foods sold for market, except for farmers' own consumption, were adjusted to correct the overestimate which may have
arisen from the fact that the construction of estimates were based

Table 10. Food Expenditures in Current Prices

Year	Rice	*Mugi*	Miscel-laneous cereals	Wheat flour & starch	Fresh vegeta-bles, & fruit (fresh & dried)	Meat, eggs, milk & related products
1874~1883	166,609	20,183	7,876	600	47,491	4,409
1877~1886	176,435	23,641	8,576	764	57,918	5,906
1882~1891	181,077	30,145	10,024	1,063	66,102	8,845
1887~1896	235,778	42,029	13,421	1,504	81,753	14,399
1892~1901	342,159	59,902	17,827	2,307	111,898	26,957
1897~1906	496,907	78,478	24,133	3,299	158,535	43,947
1902~1911	637,978	91,004	28,927	4,059	243,684	63,511
1907~1916	771,168	106,739	34,336	4,942	322,935	80,118
1912~1921	1,388,039	174,819	63,594	8,836	551,610	153,315
1917~1926	2,037,213	203,449	93,383	13,530	761,629	325,549
1922~1931	1,980,870	145,143	89,184	12,937	696,340	444,685
1927~1936	1,764,906	108,507	75,041	15,011	574,834	452,468
1931~1940	2,069,313	156,420	77,725	23,390	685,571	526,292

Notes: 1) Valued higher than the expenditures shown in Table 1, since
the values above are without adjustments of overestimation by applying
Tokyo retail prices to all goods and include the food expenditures by the
army and navy.

248

on the Tokyo retail prices. The Tokyo retail prices were presumably higher than the average prices in the country as a whole. Therefore, the marketed portion of foods was adjusted *en bloc* by multiplying it by 95%; it was not possible to make adjustments for each item individually. The second adjustment is the exclusion of the *military* food consumption.

In examining the composition of foods in Section II, we will take up changes in the composition of "gross" food consumption without adjusting the figures as we did in Section I.

In Table 11, which is based on Table 10, the following changes in composition of food consumption are noted: (1) The ratio of rice expenditures to total food expenditures was reduced from the 37.9% of 1874–1883 to 27.2% in 1931–1940; the total of rice, *mugi*, miscellaneous cereals, wheat flour, and starch also

Unit: thousand yen

Marine products	Canned & bottled goods	Season- ings	Bread & confec- tionery	Liquor, beverages & tea	Other miscel- laneous	Tobacco	Total (unad- justed)
54,653		41,872	16,796	62,528	12,153	4,196	439,366
62,187		43,884	20,332	73,195	13,227	5,245	491,310
77,979		42,398	27,631	83,579	15,302	6,950	551,095
102,237		48,991	38,204	108,262	18,040	10,170	714,788
157,745		75,177	72,465	194,353	22,781	20,246	1,103,817
207,427		105,440	114,411	263,254	28,576	38,843	1,563,250
219,110	1,330	136,444	162,108	318,937	36,717	64,013	2,007,822
223,683	3,920	174,688	217,145	393,215	51,589	86,305	2,470,783
394,137	16,203	330,079	410,847	723,930	106,303	144,888	4,466,600
658,318	37,443	552,329	630,819	1,292,571	183,612	240,889	7,030,734
673,371	49,585	603,316	686,199	1,374,623	216,087	307,130	7,279,470
617,237	50,183	559,429	727,681	1,443,688	211,835	327,522	6,628,342
725,902	70,674	595,569	834,130	1,179,983	270,044	387,460	7,602,473

2) Canned and bottled goods are supposed to have been consumed unprocessed before 1908.

249

Table 11. Percentage Composition of Food Expenditures in Current Prices

Year	Rice	Mugi	Miscellaneous cereals	Wheat flour & starch	Fresh vegetables, & fruit (fresh & dried)	Meat, eggs, milk & related products
1874~1883	37.9	4.6	1.8	0.1	10.8	1.0
1877~1886	35.9	4.8	1.7	0.2	11.8	1.2
1882~1891	32.8	5.5	1.8	0.2	12.0	1.6
1887~1896	33.0	5.9	1.9	0.2	11.4	2.0
1892~1901	31.0	5.4	1.6	0.2	10.2	2.4
1897~1906	31.8	5.0	1.5	0.2	10.1	2.8
1902~1911	31.8	4.5	1.4	0.2	12.1	3.2
1907~1916	31.2	4.3	1.4	0.2	13.1	3.2
1912~1921	31.1	3.9	1.4	0.2	12.4	3.4
1917~1926	29.0	2.9	1.3	0.2	10.8	4.6
1922~1931	27.2	2.0	1.2	0.2	9.5	6.1
1927~1936	26.6	1.6	1.1	0.2	8.7	6.8
1931~1940	27.2	2.1	1.0	0.3	9.0	6.9

fell from 44.3% to 30.6%; (2) Meanwhile, dairy and meat products (meat, meat products, eggs, milk, dairy products) achieved a rise from 1.0% to 6.9%; if marine products, and bottled and canned goods are included this totals from 13.5% to 17.4%; (3) bread and confectionery increased from 3.8% to 11.0%, tobacco from 1.0% to 5.1%; (4) Seasonings in the broad sense (*miso*, soy sauce, monosodium glutamate, salt, margarine, vinegar, fats and oils, sugar) started at 9.5%, fluctuated slightly, and ended at 7.8% in 1940; (5) Alcoholic drinks, tea and other beverages varied in percentage generally corresponding to the long swings.

We cannot help but be surprised to find that during 57 years values of real food expenditures more than tripled. Meanwhile, however, population grew, too, from 36,080 thousand to 75,030 thousand, i.e., an increase of 2.08 times. Accordingly, a considerable portion of the great increase in food expenditures must

(%)

Marine products	Canned & bottled goods	Seasonings	Bread & confectionery	Liquor, beverages & tea	Other miscellaneous	Tobacco	Total
12.5		9.5	3.8	14.2	2.8	1.0	100.0
12.7		8.9	4.1	14.9	2.7	1.1	100.0
14.1		7.7	5.0	15.2	2.8	1.3	100.0
14.3		6.9	5.3	15.2	2.5	1.4	100.0
14.3		6.8	6.6	17.6	2.1	1.8	100.0
13.3		6.8	7.3	16.9	1.8	2.5	100.0
10.9	0.1	6.8	8.1	15.9	1.8	3.2	100.0
9.1	0.2	7.0	8.8	15.9	2.1	3.5	100.0
8.8	0.4	7.4	9.2	16.2	2.4	3.2	100.0
9.4	0.5	7.9	9.0	18.4	2.6	3.4	100.0
9.3	0.7	8.3	9.4	18.9	3.0	4.2	100.0
9.3	0.8	8.4	11.0	17.3	3.2	5.0	100.0
9.6	0.9	7.8	11.0	15.5	3.6	5.1	100.0

have been absorbed by the increase in population. In order to examine such relationships we shall attempt to estimate per capita real food expenditures. From Table 12 we find that: (1) Both rice and total food expenditures per capita had been stagnant, the former since 1912–1921 and the latter since 1917–1926. It is important to note that per capita food expenditures were almost stable in real terms for 20 years during the 1920's and 1930's. (2) On the other hand, meat and dairy products, as well as marine products increased during the same 20 years. Dairy and meat products increased by 86.3% from 1912–1921 to 1931–1940 and marine products by 48.5%, while alcoholic drinks, tea and other beverages fell by 21.9% during the same period. These increases and declines cancelled each other out so that total food expenditures remained on almost the same level from the 1920's on. (3) Examples of products following the total food trend from the 1920's were wheat flour and starch,

251

Table 12. Real Food Expenditures Per Capita of Population in 1934–36 Prices

Year	Rice	Mugi	Miscellaneous cereals	Wheat flour & starch	Fresh vegetables, fruit (fresh & & dried)	Meat, eggs, milk & related products
1874~1883	18.28	2.43	0.90	0.06	4.34	0.69
1877~1886	19.07	2.57	0.97	0.08	4.72	0.91
1882~1891	21.15	2.81	1.08	0.10	5.44	1.30
1887~1896	22.43	2.96	1.17	0.11	5.98	1.66
1892~1901	21.71	3.09	1.17	0.13	6.37	2.05
1897~1906	23.34	2.94	1.19	0.15	6.73	2.45
1902~1911	25.32	2.89	1.25	0.16	7.65	2.78
1907~1916	26.41	3.03	1.27	0.16	8.66	3.14
1912~1921	28.19	2.86	1.33	0.19	8.91	3.80
1917~1926	28.94	2.48	1.43	0.22	8.52	4.97
1922~1931	29.04	2.13	1.39	0.21	8.14	5.85
1927~1936	28.55	1.84	1.21	0.24	8.03	6.46
1931~1940	28.99	1.74	1.13	0.29	7.83	7.08

Note: Simple arithmetic means of annual real per capita food expenditures for every 10 years. Therefore, they may not be equal to the decade average

seasonings, tobacco, and other foods. Barley and wheat, miscellaneous cereals, and vegetables declined during the same period. (4) However, before this period, namely, from 1874–1883 to 1912–1921, consistent increases can be seen in many items, of which the most outstanding growth rates were found in dairy and meat products (450.7%), bread and confectionery (262.6%) tobacco (228.3%), wheat flour and starch (21.67%), and vegetables (105.3%). Other foods and beverages increased by 78.5%, rice by 54.2%, miscellaneous cereals by 47.5%, and seasonings by 37.4%. Barley and wheat (17.7%), alcoholic drinks, and

(unit: yen)

Marine products	Canned & bottled goods	Season-ings	Bread & confec-tionery	Liquor, beverages & tea	Other miscel-laneous	Tobacco	Total
5.82		5.14	1.82	18.41	1.44	1.13	60.46
6.53		5.21	2.20	17.54	1.53	1.24	62.57
6.78		5.09	2.97	17.44	1.61	1.49	67.26
6.80		5.56	3.72	19.62	1.68	1.79	73.48
6.44		6.10	5.10	21.77	1.81	2.08	77.82
5.50		6.17	5.63	20.06	1.92	2.17	78.25
4.85	0.05	6.24	5.38	18.91	1.99	2.33	79.80
5.52	0.14	6.55	5.48	19.34	2.17	2.65	84.52
6.66	0.30	7.06	6.60	20.86	2.57	3.71	93.04
7.75	0.54	7.79	8.87	23.72	3.08	5.12	103.43
8.68	0.73	8.06	10.70	22.28	3.41	5.42	106.05
9.89	0.78	8.03	11.51	18.22	3.33	5.01	103.10
9.89	0.91	8.19	11.42	16.30	3.45	5.16	102.38

of real consumption expenditures divided by the decade average of population.

tea and other beverages (13.3%) stand out clearly among others
in their lower growth rates. Alcoholic drinks are found to
have been stable in per capita real expenditures in the long run
despite various changes resulting from wars and business conditions.

Incidentally, Saburô Yamada and Yûjirô Hayami tried to
calculate changes in calorie-intake mostly on the basis of our
estimated results on food expenditures. With their permission
I shall show their data for the readers' reference in Table 13.

Table 13. Calorie-Intake per Capita of Population

unit: calories

Period	Nakayama's estimate			Yamada-Hayami's Estimate				
	Staple[1]	Livestock products	Total	Staple[2]	Livestock products	Others[3]	Total	Per unit[4] consumption
1874~1877	—	—	—	1,567	2	94	1,663	2,132
1878~1882	1,349	2	1,351	1,664	3	135	1,802	2,328
1883~1887	1,520	3	1,523	1,727	5	147	1,879	2,434
1888~1892	1,830	3	1,833	1,856	7	165	2,028	2,617
1893~1897	1,876	7	1,883	1,834	9	178	2,021	2,608
1898~1902	1,941	7	1,948	1,863	11	188	2,062	2,671
1903~1907	2,006	8	2,014	1,959	12	185	2,156	2,815
1908~1912	2,119	9	2,128	1,969	14	190	2,173	2,829
1913~1917	2,084	10	2,094	1,986	16	216	2,218	2,896
1918~1922	2,189	12	2,201	2,059	20	269	2,348	3,057
1923~1927	2,031	15	2,046	1,975	25	308	2,308	3,005
1928~1932	1,866	19	1,885	1,807	29	325	2,161	2,825
1933~1937	1,815	24	1,839	1,827	34	337	2,198	2,818
1938~1942	1,960	23	1,883	1,836	30	345	2,211	2,860

Notes: 1) Seiki Nakayama, "Shokuryō Shōhi Suijun no Chōkihenka ni tsuite" (On the Long-Term Changes in the Level of Food Consumption), *Nōgyō Sōgō Kenkyū*, Vol. 12, No. 4.
2) Cereals, potatoes, and beans. Beans refer to red beans and soy beans in Nakayama's estimate, but Yamada-Hayami's includes them and other beans.
3) Sugar, fruit, vegetables, and aquatic products.
4) Total calories divided by population represented by the equivalent unit of 20–29 aged males.

3. Comparisons with Official Data

We shall compare our estimates with the official data given in the *Kokuminshotoku hakusho* (Report on National Income) for 1963 by the Economic Planning Agency. Table 14 shows where numerical differences lie between our estimates and the personal consumption expenditures as reported in that report. On the whole, values in our estimates are much higher than those of the official data; there are conspicuous differences of 7.1% for 1930, 20.8% for 1935, and 6.3% for 1940. Our figures are very much higher for food expenditures, by 47.5% for 1930, 59.0% for 1935, and 21.6% for 1940. This may lead the readers to think that results are unreasonable.

I shall explain whether our results are exaggerated or not through the comparative examination of the results and underlying data of the two estimates. Figure 1 plots the correlations

Table 14. Comparison with Official Data in Current Prices

unit: million yen

Year	Personal consumption expenditures			Food expenditures		
	Official series (A)	Shinohara's series (B)	(B)/(A)	Official series (A)	Shino-hara's series (B) (A)	(B)/(A)
1930	10,572 (%)	11,325 (%)	1.0712	4,106	6,057	1.4752
1931	9,103(−13.9)	10,198(−10.0)	1.1203	3,463	5,120	1.4785
1932	9,504(+ 4.4)	10,154(− 0.4)	1.0684	3,729	5,171	1.3867
1933	10,186(+ 7.2)	11,228(+10.6)	1.1023	3,972	5,732	1.4431
1934	10,610(+ 4.2)	12,515(+11.5)	1,1795	4,313	6,222	1.4426
1935	10,833(+ 2.1)	13,081(+ 4.5)	1.2075	4,136	6,575	1.5897
1936	11,443(+ 5.6)	13,722(+ 4.9)	1.1992	4,701	6,892	1.4665
1937	12,809(+11.9)	15,583(+13.6)	1.2166	5,360	7,522	1.4034
1938	13,886(+ 8.4)	17,436(+11.9)	1.2557	5,824	8,114	1.3932
1939	16,475(+18.6)	17,913(+ 2.7)	1.0873	7,063	9,129	1.2925
1940	19,155(+16.3)	20,357(+13.6)	1.0628	8,185	9,955	1.2162

Note: Figures in the column of "Official series" are taken from the Economic Planning Agency, *Report on National Income*, Tokyo, 1963.

Fig. 1. Weakness in Official Estimate

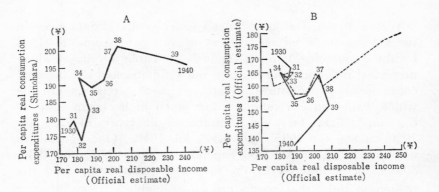

of per capita real disposable income and per capita real consumption expenditures. In Figure 1 the per capita real consumption and the per capita disposable income are compared with each other, but in Figure 1–A the per capita consumption expenditures of our estimates and the per capita disposable income in the official estimates in current prices are both deflated by the aggregate consumer price index (implicit deflator) we computed. In Figure 1–B, however, the two real per capita magnitudes are all based on the *Report on National Income*, 1963. In Figure B consumption and disposable income in current prices are from the official estimates. However, two aggregate consumer price indices have been used in deriving real term series for consumption and disposable income. The solid line was derived from the index made from the official estimates and the dotted line was derived from the Shinohara's implicit deflator.

At all events, the figures obtained out of our estimates seem to follow the ordinary course in the consumption-disposable income relation up until 1938. For 1930–1931 and 1934, with the business depression, the points become scattered above the usual line. Real expenditures began to fall in 1939–1940 when the war-time economy entered the last and the most serious stage. On the other hand, official unadjusted data show an extraordinary relation, as is shown in the solid line in Figure 1–B. Despite the serious conditions brought about by the Japan's war-escalation from the Manchurian Incident to the China Incident and on to World War II, it is difficult to believe that per capita real consumption expenditures should have followed a decreasing trend with the increase in per capita real income. I cannot believe that except for their absolute level our estimates, which were carried out by compiling the flows of individual goods and services to consumers, should be incorrect as regards their general trend. As for their level itself it might perhaps give rise to a controversy: some people may doubt whether our estimates of consumption are not too high estimates in that they nearly coincide with official disposable income. However, at the same time there is a question as to whether the official data are too low or not.

Table 15. Comparisons of Deflators

| Year | Cost of living index | | | Aggregate consumer price index (1934–36 =100) | | Morita's effective retail price index |
	Asahi Newspaper (July, 1914 =100)	Cabinet Bureau of Statistics		Shinohara's	Official estimate	
1935	181(100.0)			100.7	101	
1936	185(102.0)(100.0)			102.9(100.0)	104(100.0)	100.0
1937	193(106.6)(104.3)	100.0(July)		111.2(108.1)	111(106.7)	108.6
1938	207(114.4)(111.9)	110.1		122.9(119.4)	122(117.3)	120.3
1939	221(122.1)(119.5)	121.2		131.8(128.1)	152(146.2)	134.8
1940	247(136.5)(133.5)	143.4		149.7(145.5)	197(189.4)	175.0

Note: Morita's index is based on *Estimates of National Income of 1940–1944 Fiscal Years*, by Ministry of Finance, March, 1947. It is computed by dividing the cash turnover index (the bank-notes circulation index multiplied by the velocity of circulation index) by the volume of commodity transaction index.

Employing our implicit deflator for official consumption and disposable income, we are given the dotted line as shown in Figure 1-B, which seems more moderate compared with the solid line, although it still does not show any reasonable curve for the period 1930–1938.

Results here depend so much upon the deflator used. Thus in Table 15 some deflators are checked against each other. The reason why I feel the official data strange and unreasonable is that the officially empolyed deflator (1936=100) shows an index number of 189.4 in 1940, when, at the same point, the lower figure of 175.0 is to be measured even by Mr. Morita's index which is constructed as an "effective retail price index" considering war-time black-market prices. Still more, the wartime black-market prices are considered not to have as widely prevailed in 1940 as Morita's high index suggests. Here I should like to call the reader's attention to our implicit deflator standing between Mr. Morita's index and the Asahi's cost-of-living index.

Following the numerical comparisons with the data estimated in the past, we shall have to look further into their estimating procedures. The estimating procedure for the official series of personal consumption expendirtues are as follows: They are computed by the family budget survey method with all families grouped into farmers, non-farmers living in urban areas, and non-farmers in rural areas. The results from this are then summed up. For farmers the expenditure per household with respect to owners, owner-tenants, and tenants, and also with respect to subdivisions within those classifications, using the data in the *Nôka Keizai Chôsa* (Farm Household Economy Survey), are derived and then multiplied by the numbers of farm households obtained from the *"Nôgyô Dôtai Chôsa"* (Survey of Agricultural Dynamics). Sampling errors for the number of persons per household are corrected before the above-mentioned procedures are applied. For non-farmers in urban areas, calculation is made through the multiplication of household expenditures per family found in the *Kakei Chôsa Hôkoku*

(Family Income and Expenditure Survey) by the Cabinet Bureau of Statistics by the number of non-farm households in cities obtained from the *Census of Population*. Of course, in this case too, the correction of sampling errors is made concerning the number of persons per household. Lastly, expenditures of non-farmers in rural areas are estimated through using various adjustments on the basis of the average of the two foregoing cases. For the period after 1940, an extrapolation is made on the basis of consumption expenditures in officially controlled prices submitted to the Commission of the U.S. Strategic Bombing Survey, after converting them to the effective price terms.

Next, the following problems are to be examined with regard to the estimates for 1930–1940. The prewar *Family Income and Expenditure Survey* conducted by the Cabinet Bureau of Statistics, on which the estimation of urban expenditures per household is based, is a survey carried out almost exclusively on families who rent rather than own their housing with a monthly income of ¥50–100. Therefore, the estimation partly depending on these data will apparently minimize the actual growth rate of personal consumption expenditures during 1930–1940; even though the actual average household expenditures may have risen, the survey shows a smaller increase since they are restricted to incomes less than ¥100 a month.

Although such surveys made during the war attempted to sample more families with an income over ¥100 than before, the above defect seems to have remained in the data. The samples of families with over ¥100 in monthly income rose from 24.6% in 1931–1932 to 71.3% in 1939–1940. Samples in four income classes under ¥70–79, totalling 39.46% in 1931–1932, made a sharp drop to 5.9% in 1940. This indicates that due to the general increase in income it became difficult to find appropriate subjects for the survey among low-income classes. In the *Family Income and Expenditure Survey* the average real income of all households is reported to have increased from ¥86.47 to ¥115.42, that is, an increase of 33.5%, during the period between

1931–1932 and 1939–1940. Corresponding to this, the real
income wage index of the Bank of Japan (1926=100, average of
men and women workers in private factories in Japan) rose from
88.1 (1932) to 134.8 (1940), i. e., an increase of 53.0%. During
the same period the wage per working hour increased from 11.82
sen[2] to 19.62 sen, i.e., a rise of 66.0%, according to the *Factory
Statistics* by the Ministry of Commerce and Industry. It may
already be obvious that the *Family Income and Expenditure Survey*
underestimated the growth rate of real income, hence minimized
the rate of increase for household expenditures based on it.

A major problem arises when the estimates of consumption
expenditures for 1930–1940 computed through the family budget
survey method are extended to the years 1940–1944 utilizing
the retail valuation and commodity flow methods.

Table 16 compares the estimates of consumption expenditures
by the Commission of the U.S. Strategic Bombing Survey with
the official estimates given by the Economic Planning Agency.
The table shows a marked difference of 39% for 1940. However, the difference tends to be reduced thereafter, the U.S.
Commission's data being higher by 18.5% over the Economic
Planning Agency data in 1944. The reason for the narrowing
of the gap in percentages is that in the case of the extrapolation

Table 16. Comparisons in Consumption Expenditure Between
U.S.S.B.S. Estimates and Official Estimates

unit: million yen

	1940	1941	1942	1943	1944
U.S.S.B.S. estimates (Fiscal year)	26,707	27,342	28,488	30,504	31,478
Economic Planning Agency estimates (Calendar year)	19,155	20,701	28,734	26,001	26,554

Sources: Financial Bureau of Ministry of Finance, *Estimates of National
Income of 1940–1944 Fiscal Years*; Economic Planning Agency, *Report on
National Income*, 1963.

2) 100 sen=1 yen

for 1940–1944 by the Economic Planning Agency adjustments are made between effective prices and official prices, while the U.S. Commission's data which is the basis of the above extrapolation are valued in terms of only official prices. Therefore, the difficulty lies in the fact that in the beginning year of 1940 the U.S. Commission's estimate shows a figure no less than 39% over the result calculated through the family budget survey method. When the retail valuation and commodity flow methods are employed, some expenditures which have to be regarded as costs or non-family expenses may possibly be included, thus creating over-estimations. On the other hand, in the family budget survey method, expenses for second-hand goods are included which would act similarly. However, the results of the U. S. Commission's data are shown in official prices. Considering these matters, we can safely admit that the difference of 39% for 1940 between the two estimates is due to a deficiency (i.e., it is not representative) in the *Family Income and Expenditure Survey* by the Cabinet Bureau of Statistics, on which the official estimates are based. The cause of the strange income-consumption relationship shown in Figure 1–B must be found not in the critical conditions of the war-time economy but rather in a defect in the source statistics.

Incidentally, according to the U. S. Commission's survey the estimates for food expenditures for 1940 amount to an enormous sum of ¥14,658 million, far over our estimated value of ¥9,955 million which is 21.6% above the official figure. Furthermore, the sum is much more than ¥ 11,027 million (about 33% above), the figure which we derived before we eliminated the food expenditures for the army and navy and a uniform cut of 5% on every item. The reason may be that, compared with the U. S. Commission's data, we estimated more expenditures on processed goods, feeds, fertilizer, etc., which should be subtracted. The percentage of food expenditures in total consumption is 54.9% according to the data submitted to the Commission of U. S. Strategic Bombing Survey. It is astonishingly higher than our estimate of 48.9%, despite the fact that both used the same estimating technique.

4. Comparisons with Family Budget Surveys

Our estimates of consumption expenditures should desirably be collated as closely as possible with the outcomes of family budget surveys. However, we must warn ourselves against too much confidence in these surveys. We ought to look into their authenticity as criteria for checks.

For the Meiji era we have no family budget survey worthy of the name except some data in the *Kahei Seido Chôsakai Hôkoku* (Report of the Monetary System Investigation Committee), for which the survey method remains unknown. Figures in Tables 17 and 18 are quoted from this report. Since the survey on Gumma prefecture indicates the annual expenditures of *a middle-class family of five members*, the figure shown divided by 5 gives average personal expenditures for six periods, e.g., ¥14, ¥20, ¥24, ¥30, ¥36, and ¥36. Our personal expenditures corresponding to these six periods are derived from Table 9 except for the first period and the beginning year of the second period (1873); the results are ¥13 for 1874–1877, ¥20.8 for the third period, and ¥19, ¥23.8, and ¥27 for the other three. These are considerably below the figures in the survey of Gumma prefecture. This may be partly because the middle class which the survey dealt with may have been actually closer to an upper middle-class than the national average and partly because Gumma prefecture may have had a higher consumption levels than the other prefectures. However, there is not much difference between the two growth rates; in Gumma prefecture it rose by 80% from 1873–1877 to 1893 while our estimates become double during the same years. We can, therefore, say that our results have been checked with regard to the increase rate of expenditures for this period. The lower class may be thought of as having stood perhaps closer to the national average than

Table 17. Surveys of Family Expenses in the Early Period of Meiji (I)

unit: yen

Year	Gumma prefecture survey (Annual values of middle-class family of 5)	Year	Tochigi prefecture survey (Annual per capita values)								
			Agriculture			Industry			Trade		
			Up. Class	Mid. Class	Low. Class	Up. Class	Mid. Class	Low. Class	Up. Class	Mid. Class	Low. Class
1868~1872	70	1868~1872	42.42	31.18	19.84	45.00	33.72	25.07	55.72	39.56	25.54
1873~1877	100	1873~1877	44.38	31.45	20.09	46.80	34.41	25.28	57.85	39.67	25.98
1878~1882	120	1878~1882	55.27	39.29	24.19	58.20	42.98	32.94	80.31	51.73	33.96
1883~1887	150	1883~1887	47.10	33.65	20.18	47.99	36.62	26.85	64.96	41.17	26.47
1888~1892	180	1888~1890	51.80	35.87	22.19	51.81	37.59	29.82	72.04	45.93	30.78
1893	180	1891~1893	54.21	37.55	23.17	53.37	39.59	31.57	75.28	48.61	32.43

Source: Kahei Seido Chōsakai, *Kahei Seido Chōsakai Hōkoku* (Report of the Monetary System Investigation Committee), 1895, pp. 372ff.

Table 18. Surveys of Family Expenses in the Early Period of Meiji (II)
——Shizuoka Prefecture Survey in Annual Per Capita Values——

unit: yen

	Year	Food	Clothing	Miscellaneous expenses	Total
Upper Class	1868	32.120(47.0)	7.700(11.3)	28.600(41.7)	68.420(100.0)
	1872	32.120(43.5)	8.800(11.9)	33.000(44.6)	73.920(100.0)
	1877	44.165(47.7)	9.900(10.7)	38.500(41.6)	92.565(100.0)
	1882	48.180(43.5)	13.200(11.9)	49.500(44.6)	110.880(100.0)
	1887	40.150(42.7)	9.900(10.5)	44.000(46.8)	94.050(100.0)
	1892	40.150(37.8)	11.000(10.4)	55.000(51.8)	106.150(100.0)
Middle Class	1868	20.075(47.7)	4.400(10.5)	17.600(41.8)	42.075(100.0)
	1872	20.075(43.2)	4.400(9.5)	22.000(47.3)	46.475(100.0)
	1877	32.120(51.1)	4.400(7.0)	26.400(41.9)	62.920(100.0)
	1882	40.150(48.3)	9.900(11.9)	33.000(39.8)	83.050(100.0)
	1887	24.090(42.2)	5.500(9.6)	27.500(48.2)	94.050(100.0)
	1892	28.105(41.5)	6.600(9.8)	33.000(48.7)	106.150(100.0)
Lower Class	1868	16.060(64.6)	2.200(8.9)	6.600(26.5)	24.860(100.0)
	1872	16.060(57.0)	2.200(7.8)	9.900(35.2)	28.160(100.0)
	1877	24.090(60.2)	2.750(6.9)	13.200(32.9)	40.040(100.0)
	1882	28.105(51.6)	4.400(8.1)	22.000(40.3)	54.505(100.0)
	1887	18.062(53.1)	2.750(8.1)	13.200(38.8)	34.012(100.0)
	1892	20.075(50.3)	3.300(8.3)	16.500(41.4)	39.875(100.0)

Note: Dates approximate.
Source: Same as Table 17.

264

the middle class surveyed at a period when agriculture played an important role.

Direct comparison is possible with the survey of Tochigi prefecture, for this survey shows annual values of per capita personal consumption expenditures. Strangely enough, it reports a very low rate of increase during the years from 1868–1872 to 1891–1893. Agriculture (lower class) rose only by 16.8% and trade (lower class) by 27.0%. Considering our implicit deflator indicating no less than a 49.1% rise for the period from 1874–1877 to 1891–1893, we may well regard the survey of Tochigi prefecture as disqualified for a time-series analysis. We shall confine our comparison only to the last period covered by the survey, 1891–1893. At that time, agriculture (lower class) averaged ¥23.17, differing only a little from the ¥26 which is the per capita personal consumption expenditures according to our estimates for the same period. If we take the simple arithmetic mean of trade (lower class) and agriculture (lower class), we arrive at ¥27.8 and the difference is considerably reduced. Even the average of lower class and middle class in agriculture comes to ¥30 and reveals no great difference from our estimates.

In the survey on Shizuoka prefecture, as in Gumma prefecture, the per capita consumption estimates are still higher than our estimates, even for the lower class. Although the figures for the middle and lower classes fluctuate irregularly around 1882, there is a small degree of increase seen in the period as a whole. However, a rise such as that seen from 1877–1892 is so small that we have doubts with regard to the time trend.

Only the percentages for food and clothing expenditures are heplful to us. In the case of the lower-class percentage of food expenditures lies between 50.3% and 64.6%, that of clothing between 6.9% and 8.9%, both of which are close to our estimates. Even though the average is assumed to be represented by the middle class, its food proportion would be roughly equal to ours, provided that food expenditures involved in miscellaneous expenses (for gifts and ceremonial purposes) were transferred

Table 19. G. Yokoyama's *Lower Classes in Japan*

	Case 1	Case 2	Case 3	Case 4	Case 5	Case 6
Date of surveys	Feb. 1898	Feb. 1889	Nov. 1898	Nov. 1898	Nov. 1898	Nov. 1898
Occupation	rikisha man	artisan	lathe turner	finisher	worker in gun mfg.	lathe turner
Number of family members	3	3	3	5	3	4
Living expenses	45.9 sen* (Daily)	33.3 sen (Daily)	20.54 yen (Monthly)	19.60 yen (Monthly)	17.60 yen (Monthly)	29.04 yen (Monthly)
Food expenses	35.6 sen	25.7 sen	13.20 yen	14.75 yen	10.90 yen	19.10 yen
Proportion for food	77.6%	77.2%	64.3%	75.3%	61.9%	65.8%
Annual per capita consumption	33.5 yen	40.5 yen	82.2 yen	47.0 yen	70.4 yen	87.1 yen
Pages	42	44	227	228–229	229–230	230–231

Source: Gennosuke Yokoyama, *Nihon no Kasô-shakai* (Lower Classes in Japan), Iwanami Bunko Series, Tokyo, Iwanamishoten, 1949.
* Including several miscellaneous expenses.

Table 20. Consumption Expenditures in the *Farm Household Economy Survey*, by Mankichi Saitō

unit: yen

	Year	Food & beverages	Cloth-ing	House repair-ing	Furni-ture & utensils	Fire-wood, charcoal & oils	Educa-tion	Interest payment & others	Total	Food propor-tion (%)	Clothing propor-tion (%)
Owner	1890	119.00	18.00	10.00	5.00	10.00	3.00	31.00	196.00	60.7	9.2
	1899	181.00	27.00	20.00	8.00	15.00	9.00	46.00	306.00	59.2	8.8
	1908	278.00	40.00	16.00	13.00	22.00	19.00	72.00	406.00	59.2	8.7
	1911	334.00	50.00	27.00	18.00	26.00	19.00	81.00	555.00	60.2	9.0
	1912	391.00	54.00	24.00	20.00	27.00	24.00	94.00	634.00	61.7	8.8
	1920	679.57	161.17	43.95	20.37	47.71	30.17	243.80	1,226.74	55.4	13.1
Tenant	1890	67.00	8.00	3.00	—	6.00	—	4.00	107.00	71.0	11.3
	1899	124.00	17.00	4.00	—	9.00	—	26.00	180.00	68.9	9.4
	1908	178.00	17.00	7.00	—	13.00	—	38.00	253.00	70.4	5.5
	1911	218.00	23.00	9.00	—	15.70	—	46.00	311.00	70.1	6.4
	1912	256.00	24.00	10.00	—	17.00	—	50.00	357.00	71.7	6.7
	1920	427.01	53.91	16.16	—	28.32	—	119.98	645.38	66.2	8.4

Note: The number of household members for 6 years is 6, 7, 7, 7, 7, and 6, as to owners and 5, 6, 6, 6, 6, and 6, as to tenants.

Source: Taizō Inaba ed., *Fukkokuban Nōka Keizaichōsa Hōkoku—Chōsa-hōhō no Hensen to Ruinen Seiseki* (Reprinted Edition of the Report of the Farm Household Economy Survey—Changes in Survey Method and Annual Results), Oct., 1952.

267

STRUCTURAL CHANGES IN JAPAN'S ECONOMIC DEVELOPMENT

to the sum of food expenditures. Next we shall consult *Nihon no Kasô-shakai* (Lower Classes in Japan) by Gennosuke Yoko-yama.[3] This book offers a great deal of materials on the lives of the lower classes in the Meiji period. (Table 19)

Viewed generally, all the families shown above appropriated 60–70% for living expenditures for food. Our consumption estimates gave a per capita value of 48 yen (naturally including farm families) and food expenditures of 64.8% for 1898. However, Cases 2 and 4 show food expenditure percentages to be 77.2% and 75.3% though both fall within 40–50 yen in annual per capita consumption. The cases showing percentages of 60–70% have respective values of 82.2 yen (Case 3), 70.4 yen (Case 5), and 87.1 yen (Case 6). Is our estimate of food expenditures (64.8% in 1898), therefore, too conservative?

In order to answer this question we shall have to turn to an analysis of the *Farm Household Economy Survey*. We shall here take up the famous survey by Mankichi Saitô and sort out the expenditure on food and beverages, clothing, house repairs, furniture and utensils, fire-wood, charcoal, oils, education, interest payments and miscellaneous, assuming that the sum of them equals total consumption expenditures. We shall thereupon look into the absolute values and the percentages for food and clothing expenditures classified by owners and tenants.

Table 20 shows the following:

(1) The simple arithmetic means of per capita consumption expenditures of owner and tenant households are represented as follows:

Unit: yen

	1890	1899	1908	1911	1912	1920
Saitô's survey	27.04	36.86	53.94	65.56	75.04	156.01
Per capita consumption by Shinohara (National)	25.12	47.12	68.26	74.17	80.78	211.45

The difference between the average nation-wide per capita consumption and those of farm households is seen to have in-

268

creased as time went on although it was almost imperceptible in 1890. This can be explained partly by the fact that the proportional share of the number of inhabitants in urban areas or non-farm households increased.

(2) The average percentages of food expenditure by owners and tenants are as follows:

						(%)
	1890	1899	1908	1911	1912	1920
Saitô's survey	65.9	64.1	64.8	65.2	66.7	60.8
Food percentages by Shinohara (National)	66.3	62.4	64.2	62.9	64.2	61.8

Both are unexpectedly close to each other in levels. Therefore, even though the percentage of food expenditure for urban worker's households may show 70–79% on an average, the average nation-wide percentage for both farmers and non-farmers is supposed to be in the 60–69% range.

(3) The average percentages of clothing expenditures by owners and tenants are as follows:

						(%)
	1890	1899	1908	1911	1912	1920
Saitô's survey	10.3	9.1	7.1	7.7	7.8	10.8
Clothing percentages by Shinohara (National)	7.2	10.3	8.1	9.2	8.3	12.5

Although one does not always vary in the same direction as the other, as for 6 years' average (8.8%, 9.5%), one differs little from the other.

We shall next go into the family budget surveys on urban workers. We refer here to four surveys. The first of them is a survey carried out from June 1921 to May 1922 by the *Kyôchôkai* (Cooperation Association) and shown in the *Hôkyû Seikatsu-sha Shokkô Seikei Chôsa Hôkoku* (Survey Report on Livelihoods of

Salaried and Manual Workers), published in March, 1925. The second is an investigation ranging from September, 1926 to August, 1927, shown in the *Family Income and Expenditure Survey* by the Cabinet Bureau of Statistics. The third and the fourth were made by the same Bureau for the period September, 1931 to August, 1932, and from September, 1935 to August, 1936.

(1) Survey of June, 1921–May, 1922

Consumption expenditures of 651 households of salaried and manual workers averaged ¥103.96 (taxes, duties, etc. not included). The annual value, ¥1,247.52, divided by the average number of household members, 4.17, gives the average annual per capita consumption expenditures, ¥299.

(2) Survey of September, 1926–August, 1927

The survey reported ¥101.42 in expenditures per household, of which the annual value, ¥1,217.04, divided by the average number of household members, 4.2, gives the average annual per capita consumption expenditures, ¥290.

(3) Survey of September, 1931–August, 1932

Consumption expenditures per household amounted to ¥75.73. The annual value, ¥908.76, divided by the average number of family members, 40.7, gives the average annual per capita consumption expenditures, ¥223.

(4) Survey of September, 1935–August, 1936

Expenditures amounted to ¥79.55 per household. The annual value, ¥954.60, divided by the average number of household members, 4.12, gives the average annual per capita consumption expenditures, ¥232.

All four surveys show larger values for the average annual per capita consumption expenditures (¥299, ¥290, ¥223, ¥232) than our estimates (¥216 [average of 1921, 1922], ¥207 [1927], ¥154 [1932], and ¥197 [1936]). However, if they are averaged with the lower expenditures of farmers, they may approach

Table 21. Consumption Expenditures by the *Farm Household Economy Survey* (Annual Values)

Year	Consumption expenditures			Weight			Weighted average of consumption expenditures of the whole farmers (yen)	Per capita consumption expenditures (A Family of 6 supposed) (yen)
	Owner (yen)	Owner-tenant (yen)	Tenant (yen)	Owner	Owner-tenant	Tenant		
1922	1,176.450	997.406	719.990	30.56	41.10	28.34	973.502	162.24
1923	1,177.865	1,082.557	775.135	30.60	41.17	28.23	1,024.837	170.81
1924	1,339.117	1,261.941	806.123	30.63	41.40	27.97	1,158.089	193.01
1925	1,471.026	1,233.868	866.017	30.54	41.68	27.78	1,204.107	200.68
1926	1,324.951	1,094.518	909.663	30.64	41.92	27.44	1,114.399	185.73
1927	1,278.566	1,052.096	860.996	30.68	42.14	27.18	1,069.636	178.27
1928	1,246.203	1,001.781	829.404	30.79	42.33	26.88	1,086.126	181.02
1929	1,238.124	967.333	860.220	30.60	42.61	26.79	1,021.500	170.25
1930	897.181	749.528	650.327	30.55	42.63	26.82	768.031	128.00
1931	615.550	536.190	463.870	30.61	42.58	26.81	541.090	90.18
1932	617.370	548.310	480.100	30.53	42.64	26.83	546.830	91.14
1933	678.490	587.300	519.110	30.49	42.55	26.96	596.720	99.45
1934	664.110	661.500	553.690	30.41	42.46	27.13	633.050	105.50
1935	778.500	683.900	619.130	30.30	42.35	27.35	694.840	115.81
1936	824.460	760.010	667.370	30.36	42.25	27.39	754.200	125.70
1937	878.540	759.990	687.460	30.53	42.26	27.21	776.450	129.41
1938	924.260	856.960	760.660	30.17	43.06	26.77	851.490	141.91
1939	1,167.870	1,082.350	933.640	30.37	42.76	26.87	1,068.360	178.06
1940	1,385.640	1,363.250	1,128.350	30.53	42.42	27.05	1,306.550	217.76

Source: Same as Table 19.

Table 22. Consumption Expenditures by the *Family Income and Expenditure Survey* of Cabinet Bureau of Statistics

		1926.9–1927.8	1931.9–1932.8	1932.9–1933.8
Total consumption	(in yen)	101.42	75.73	76.78
expenditures		100.00	100.00	100.00
Food & beverages		37.21	34.33	34.58
Housing		16.96	18.09	18.07
Fuel & lighting		4.59	4.72	4.68
Clothing		13.43	13.03	12.63
Health & personal care		6.36	7.67	7.48
Child care		1.54	0.83	0.81
Education		1.42	1.26	1.33
Transportation expenses		1.46	1.55	1.42
Communication & carriage		0.30	0.38	0.36
Stationery		0.16	0.17	0.17
Social expenses		7.61	8.98	9.10
Gifts		5.65	5.74	5.83
Others		1.96	3.24	3.27
Culture & recreation		4.11	5.20	5.40
Travelling expenses		1.06	1.08	1.12
Wages for employees		0.19		
Others		2.90	2.54	2.64
Expenses of ceremonial occasions			0.71	0.98
Others			1.82	1.67
Inappropriate entry		0.70	0.17	0.21

our estimates. For example, our estimate (¥210) lies between ¥156, the annual per capita expenditures of farmers for 1920, and though a year later, ¥299, annual per capita expenditures of urban residents above for 1921.

It is not very significant to make detailed weighted averages concerning farmers' and urban workers' per capita expenditures, for there may be deviations in the objectives surveyed and biases in the samples. We must satisfy ourselves with the result of general checks in which our nation-wide estimates of consumption expenditures do not diverge greatly from the outcomes of family budget surveys.

(Average of Salaried and Manual Workers, Monthly Values)

(%)

1933.9–1934.8	1934.9–1935.8	1935.9–1936.8	1936.9–1937.8	1937.9–1938.8	1938.9–1939.8	1939.9–1940.8	1940.9–1941.8
78.29	79.43	79.55	81.59	83.05	86.22	96.22	103.21
100.00	100.00	100.00	100.00	100.00	100.00	100.00	100.00
34.40	36.49	37.91	37.85	39.11	39.93	43.15	43.53
17.56	17.03	16.95	16.30	16.35	15.55	13.95	13.67
4.91	4.92	5.02	4.84	5.19	5.44	5.36	5.68
12.45	12.11	11.43	11.39	10.86	9.96	9.63	10.10
7.32	6.94	6.89	7.10	7.10	7.47	7.02	7.16
0.84	0.78	0.75	0.83	0.87	0.89	0.80	0.92
1.47	1.64	1.70	1.84	1.87	1.97	1.90	1.79
1.50	1.51	1.55	1.53	1.52	1.61	1.59	1.64
0.37	0.36	0.36	0.38	0.35	0.32	0.29	0.27
0.20	0.15	0.15	0.28	0.12	0.13	0.14	0.35
9.03	8.38	8.13	8.40	8.32	8.16	7.89	7.47
5.72	5.35	5.09	5.34	5.44	5.32	5.05	4.80
3.31	3.03	3.04	3.05	2.88	2.84	2.84	2.67
5.68	5.38	5.18	5.18	4.94	4.85	4.57	4.49
1.11	1.06	0.97	0.99	0.85	0.99	1.08	0.91
2.94	3.05	2.80	2.87	2.35	2.53	2.40	1.83
1.01	1.00	0.85	0.97	0.63	0.72	0.86	0.48
1.93	2.05	1.95	1.90	1.72	1.81	1.54	1.35
0.22	0.20	0.21	0.22	0.20	0.20	0.23	0.19

Next we shall check our estimates by family budget surveys on workers as well as on farmers from the Taishô era to World War II. Table 21 shows changes in annual per capita values of farmers' consumption expenditures computed from annual household values (classified by owners, owner-tenants and tenants) of the *Farm Household Economy Survey*, the number of households in each class being used as a weight and each household being supposed to consist of 6 members. Although violent changes are noticed in the table and it is not impossible to think that the farmers under survey may have undergone considerable

Table 23. Comparisons in Per Capita Annual Values of Consumption Expenditures

unit: yen

Year	Farm Household Economy Survey (A Family of 6 supposed)	Family Income and Expenditure Survey of Cabinet Bureau of Statistics	Shinohara's estimates (Nation-wide average)
1922	162.24	—	212.83
1923	170.81	—	214.26
1924	193.01	—	217.38
1925	200.68	—	224.34
1926	185.73	—	214.04
1927	178.17	289.80	207.23
1928	181.02	—	205.32
1929	170.25	—	195.43
1930	128.00	—	177.31
1931	90.18	—	157.21
1932	91.14	223.32	154.11
1933	99.45	223.68	167.88
1934	105.51	229.20	184.88
1935	115.81	231.96	190.52
1936	125.70	231.72	197.18
1937	129.41	237.60	222.49
1938	141.91	241.92	247.21
1939	178.06	252.36	252.84
1940	217.76	280.92	285.11

changes in their scale of farm operation during the period, we shall tentatively accept the results as shown.

For salaried and manual workers we shall again consult the *Family Income and Expenditure Survey* conducted by the Cabinet Bureau of Statistics (Table 22). We shall compute annual per capita expenditures by dividing the annual totals of given monthly expenditures by the average number of household members for the year. These are shown in Table 23 for comparison with the results of the *Farm Household Economy Survey* and our estimates. At first sight our estimates seem to be consistent on the whole with the other surveys for total sums

Table 24. Percentacge Compositions of Farmer's Expenditures by the *Farm Household Economy Survey*

(%)

Year	Food & beverages	Clothing	Housing	Fuel & lighting	Medical & personal care	Social expenses	Education & recreation	Expenses for ceremonial occasions	Others	Total
1922	53.2	10.1	5.7	4.8	4.2	6.7	3.4	6.9	5.0	100.0
1923	51.6	10.3	5.8	5.0	4.1	6.9	4.0	6.4	5.9	100.0
1924	50.3	10.0	5.6	6.3	4.4	7.1	4.0	6.3	6.0	100.0
1925	48.6	9.6	5.7	5.7	5.4	6.7	4.0	8.2	6.1	100.0
1926	50.1	9.9	5.5	6.1	4.3	7.2	4.1	6.0	6.8	100.0
1927	50.7	8.9	5.5	6.9	5.4	7.6	3.4	5.8	5.8	100.0
1928	47.9	9.4	5.6	6.8	4.7	7.5	4.4	6.8	6.9	100.0
1929	46.7	8.7	5.5	6.1	5.4	7.9	3.9	6.4	9.4	100.0
1930	49.4	7.4	5.1	6.4	5.1	7.7	4.1	7.1	7.7	100.0
1931	48.4	8.0	6.4	6.1	5.7	8.6	3.5	6.8	6.5	100.0
1932	51.7	8.2	6.4	5.8	4.6	8.4	3.6	4.6	6.7	100.0
1933	49.4	9.4	6.2	5.7	5.4	8.4	3.8	5.8	5.9	100.0
1934	51.2	8.6	5.9	5.1	6.0	7.9	3.5	6.4	5.4	100.0
1935	51.8	9.4	6.2	4.8	4.3	7.7	3.6	7.1	5.1	100.0
1936	51.3	9.7	6.5	4.5	4.7	8.1	3.6	6.7	4.9	100.0
1937	52.8	9.2	5.7	4.4	5.3	8.4	3.6	5.7	4.9	100.0
1938	52.0	10.1	5.6	4.8	5.4	8.1	4.0	5.0	5.0	100.0
1939	50.6	11.3	5.2	4.6	5.1	8.3	4.0	6.3	4.6	100.0
1940	49.6	11.6	5.9	4.6	5.1	8.0	4.5	5.7	5.0	100.0

Note: Computed by the family-number-weighted average of the classfied percentage compositions by owners, owner-tenants, and tenants.

275

of per capita consumption expenditures, since they stand between the results of the farmer's survey and those of workers as far as the period up to 1936 is concerned. However, from 1937 on our results become similar to those of the Cabinet Bureau of Statistics and from 1938 on our estimates are a bit higher than the results of the official surveys. If the results of the *Family Income and Expenditure Survey* with regard to workers were undeniably correct, our estimates would be implausible for the World War II period. But, as I fully explained before, the survey extremely underestimated the rate of increase of consumption expenditures of workers' households during the period concerned. As is shown in Table 22, expenditures of workers rose by only 25.7% from 1932 to 1940, while expenditures of farmers achieved an increase of 2.39 times. As this is obviously impossible, the *Family Income and Expenditure Survey* on workers cannot be used as a criterion for the evaluation of our estimates.

Table 24 gives the percentage composition of each expenditure, based on the *Farm Household Economy Survey* for 1922–1940. The number of households of owners, owner-tenants and tenants was used as a weight, in deriving the proportion of each expenditure for "all" farmers. In the table the percentage of food expenditures (including tobacco and alcoholic drinks) is approximately 50%, which is close to our percentages shown in Table 2. Although the percentage of food expenditures in the *Farm Household Economy Survey* conforms with our estimates, that of workers' households, which stands between 34.33–43.53% as seen in Table 22, is far less than our estimates. However, if such food expenditures for child-care, gifts, travelling, and ceremonial purposes are included in the total, total food expenditures are expected to rise to 39–48%. Moreover, as the number of salaried and manual workers increased in the process of industrialization, some portion of food expenditures may not have been covered by the survey due to husband's dining out, most frequently in cities. Further, the purchases of food and beverages on company expense accounts may have tended to increase relatively from about 1920, although I have no appropriate data to rely upon. We should remember that our estimates through the commodity flow and other methods cover food expenditures on company expense accounts and some other expenses likely to be omitted by the surveys. Above all, as analyses for the postwar period have revealed, tobacco and alcoholic drinks have too often not appeared enough on urban family budget surveys. Another no less important issue is that the *Farm Household Economy Surveys* carried out before the war are generally said to have chosen as their objectives farm households with a relatively higher income than the average. If so, the food percentages shown in Table 24 may be concluded to stand rather lower than the average of all farmers (I am indebted to Professor Kazushi Ohkawa for this suggestion). The question concerning this point is how to bridge the Engel's Coefficient gap between our estimates and the results of the *Family Income and Expenditure Survey* by the Cabinet Bureau of Statistics. In any case, the appearance of the disproportionately higher food expenditure percentages in our estimates in comparison with the outcome of the urban family income and expenditure survey do not necessarily invalidate our series. In the percentage of clothing expenditures there is no great difference, instead a strange conformity between our estimates, the family budget and expenditure surveys of urban workers households and the farm household economy surveys. However, we should mention the important finding that the percentages of clothing expenditures in our estimates more changed volatilely than they are believed to have done till now. Clothing expenditures, of which the annual figures and percentages are omitted in this paper, increase steadily from 9.7% to 13.7% during 1930–1936, but in 1937 and 1938 they increase suddenly to 15.9%, 17.7%, and then in 1939 and 1940 show a precipitous fall to 10.7% and 11.0%. This fact is conjectured to be due to the omission of an adjustment of stock changes in production and distribution processes when we estimated clothing expenditures through the commodity flow method. Estimated expenditures of clothing are subject to violent business fluctuations and indicated noticeably sharp drops during the Matsukata Deflation, after World War I and during World War II. It is not impossible to correct this phenomenon, for instance, by smoothing the basic data by three year moving averages, though we did not attempt to do so in making these estimates.

As is made clear above, our estimated results can be said to be consistent on the whole with the family budget surveys carried out in the past. If we bear in mind the nature of the family budget surveys as well as their limitations and take into consideration the characteristics of our estimates, it will not be very difficult for us to fill the gap between them.

CHAPTER 7

INDUSTRIAL GROWTH, 1874–1940: LONG SWINGS AND STRUCTURAL CHANGES

1. Problems in Estimating Procedure

The industrial product ɔn index of the Nagoya College of Commerce has long been in use, as an indicator of the long-term movement in Japan's industrial production. However, Yasukichi Yasuba and Yûichi Shionoya have recently compiled industrial production indices for the periods 1905–1935 and 1874–1940 respectively, and have strongly emphasized the large upward bias present in the industrial growth rate of the Nagoya index.[1] On the other hand, we are presently engaged in compiling separate set of estimates for gross industrial output (in current as well as 1934–36 constant prices) to be published in the volume, *Mining and Manufacturing* (Vol. X of *Estimates of Long-term Economic Statistics of Japan since 1868*, edited by K. Ohkawa, M. Shinohara and M. Umemura). As regards our estimation procedure and the detailed results, the readers are advised to see the forthcoming

---

1) The Nagoya College of Commerce, Industrial Research Section, "Hompô Seisan Sûryô Shisû (Meiji Gannen naishi Showa 11 nen)", (Japan's Production Index, 1868–1936), *Shôgyô Keizai Ronsô*, November 1938; Yasukichi Yasuba, "Nihon no Kôgyôseisan Shisû, 1905–1935 nen," (Japan's Industrial Production Index, 1905–1935) in K. Inada and T. Uchida ed., *Keizaiseichô no Riron to Keisoku* (Theory and Measurement of Economic Growth) Iwanami-shoten, 1966; Yûichi Shionoya, "Nihon no Kôgyôseisan Shisû, 1874–1940 nen" (Japan's Industrial Production, 1874–1940), the addendum of M. Shinohara's *Sangyô Kôzô Ron* (Industrial Structure), Chikuma-shobô, 1966.

volume. However, in this chapter we shall first briefly deal with the basic features of these new estimates and problems encountered in their estimation; and then pass on to a detailed examination of long swings and structural changes in industrial production, in the latter part of this chapter.

The Shionoya and Yasuba indices do not indicate any marked differences in their overlapping years, and as Table 1 shows we cannot also find considerable differences between Shionoya's index and ours for the whole period, as far as the manufacturing index as a whole is concerned.

Table 1. Comparison with the Shionoya's Production Index for Manufacturing

	Shionoya's index (1935=100)	Shinohara's index (1934–36=100)	
		(a)	(b)
1874	4.27	4.76	4.72
1880	5.47	6.30	6.21
1890	8.15	9.20	9.08
1900	14.74	14.46	14.35
1905	16.92	14.86	14.78
1910	19.34	20.65	
1915	26.90	29.26	
1920	35.89	39.77	
1925	47.25	47.78	
1930	62.45	62.77	
1935	100.00	102.22	
1940	151.14	136.89	

Note: The difference of (a) and (b) in Shinohara's index is due to the fact that I have computed two indices for metal and machinery industries, in view of the too great differences in output between the *1874 Census of Production* (Bussanhyô) and the extrapolated result from 1920's and 1930's data as based on the official output statistics. In the metal and machinery industries, the former is considerably higher than the latter in the earlier period.

Thus, there exist virtually no differences between the two indices for manufacturing as a whole, but when broken into subsectors of manufacturing we find remarkable dissimilarities particularly for the earlier periods.

Taking for example the lumber and wood products industry, the value of production in the Shionoya's data is extremely high in comparison with that of ours. For the same industry, Shionoya's index is about 200% higher than ours for the period 1874–90. This is due to the fact that Shionoya wholly depended upon Minoru Kumano's industrial wood estimates[2] from forestry output for 1879–1958, but it seems to be a general consequence that the lumber and wood products output in manufacturing industry is always far lower than the round wood production (or consumption) used as industrial wood. In this sense, we did not use the absolute value of Kumano's estimate, but extropolated to the Meiji period the value of lumber and wood products production, from the benchmark of the Factory Statistics of the 1920's and 1930's, using Kumano's estimates as an index.

In the case of our estimate, we tried first to consolidate the value of gross output (including the output of private and public enterprises) on the basis of *Nôshômu Tôkeihyô* (the Statistical Yearbook of the Ministry of Agriculture and Forestry) as well as *Kôjô Tôkeihyô* (Factory Statistics), for the 1920's and 30's period. We then interpolated between the *Census of Production* (Bussanhyô) in 1874 and the above estimate for 1920's and 1930's by means of the time series of "major" commodity output, broken down into each industry categories. However, in the case of Shionoya's estimate, he used the Nagoya production index in the interpolation of the Meiji period. Even though Shionoya made some improvement in the computation process of the Nagoya index, it is to be noted that the latter may be unreliable since it is a product of unexplained statistical sources and obscure computational procedure. Consequently, we have decided to reject completely the Nagoya index even as an interpolator, and followed a difficult process of determining the time

---

2) M. Umemura and others, *Nôringyô* (Agriculture and Forestry), pp. 232–233, and pp. 238–240, (the 9th volume in *Estimates of Long-term Economic Statistics of Japan since 1868*, ed. by K. Ohkawa, M. Shinohara and M. Umemura), Oriental Economist, 1966.

series of the values and volumes of output of "major" commodity items by each industry for the Meiji period.

Of course, this does not give us the total of gross output in each sector of manufacturing, but by utilizing it as an interpolator, we believe that a much more reliable interpolation can be obtained between the output of the *1874 Census of Production* and our estimate of the output for 1920's and 1930's. Before deriving the index of volume of production, we have computed the value of output in 1934–36 constant prices (Laspeyres) for each subsector of manufacturing.

In the determination of each commodity output, we have depended as a rule on the *Statistical Yearbook of the Ministry of Agriculture and Commerce* and also the *Statistical Yearbook of the Ministry of Commerce and Industry*, for the years when they are available.[3] (We will hereafter quote these sources in the following abbreviated forms: SMAC and SMCI). However, it has been generally accepted that the statistical coverage of SMAC is narrower than that of the *Factory Statistics*, for the former's survey objective is said to be the establishments with 10 manual workers and more, while the latter is those with 5 manual workers and more. This is correct in the statistics of the number of workers, but it become now clear after our careful checks that as far as the value and volume of output are concerned all the establishments were surveyed as a principle. Actually, we find that mostly the output of each commodity item in SMAC is greater than that in the *Factory Statistics*, while the number of workers in the former is smaller than that of the latter.

Therefore, the output of SMAC is adopted as a rule, but for the years when the SMAC data become unavailable, we used the output data from the *Factory Statistics*. In this case, we

---

3) In the Statistical Yearbook of the Ministry of Commerce and Industry (*Shôkô-shô Tôkeihyô*), the figures which link directly with those in the Statistical Yearbook of the Ministry of Agriculture and Commerce (*Nôshômu Tôkeihyo*) are available, except a few cases when the figures of the *Factory Statistics* are requoted.

adjusted it upward by including the establishment with 4 workers and less, public enterprises, and also the receipts for contract works.

In this procedure, we used Keiko Akasaka's work "Estimate of Employees in Manufacturing, 1919–1942", Rockefeller Project, Material C15, Inst. of Economic Research, Hitotsubashi University. By adjusting this employee estimate (which is divided into different categories depending upon the scale of establishments and also private and public enterprises) on the basis of assumed productivity of each category, we get the value of output in the establishments with 4 workers and less as well as the output of public enterprises. Consequently, the proportion of output in public enterprises and establishments with 4 workers and less, varies year by year, and this may account for some differences, although not great, which exist between the Shionoya's and our estimate for the Taishô and Shôwa periods.

Considerable difficulty was encountered in the determination of the values and volumes of output of major commodity items particularly for the early Meiji period. For instance, according to scattered data available, sulphuric acid and cement came to be produced since early Meiji, while the according to official statistics these products came into being only in the later period.[4] We tried to collect scattered data extensively from various sources, in order to make possible the determination of the long-term industrial output series, without depending on the obscure Nagoya index of industrial production.

---

4) For instance, the figures of sulphuric acid were derived from SMAC for 1905–1921 and from the *Factory Statistics* for 1922–1940, but for the years before 1904, we estimated it by *Nihon Soda Kôgyôshi* (History of Japan's Soda Industry), 1938. As for cement, the figures are available from SMAC after 1905, but before 1904, we used the prefectural statistics and Seiji Fujitsu's collected data based on the newspaper reports of the earlier period. S. Fujitsu, "The History before the Promotion of the Onoda Cement Co., Ltd. (in Japanese), in *Business Review* (ed. by the Inst. of Business Research, Hitotsubashi University, Vol. 14, No. 3, 1966.)

2. *Long Swings in Industrial Growth*

We have divided the 1874–1940 period into thirteen over-lapping decades, and explored first the annual growth rate of manufacturing output (in 1934–36 prices) in relation to its total and subsectors, from decade to decade. Table 2 and 3 are the average value of manufacturing production (in current and 1934–36 prices), for each decade, and Table 4 presents a computation of annual growth rate from decade to decade, based on the data of Table 3. Table 5 computes the annual growth rate for the two periods, 1874–1900 and 1900–1940, by fitting natural logarithm lines upon the basic annual series. The results being: the growth rate of manufacturing production (in 1934–36 prices) is 4.6% in 1874–1900 and 5.9% in 1900–1940, which are very close to that of Shionoya's result.

In our estimate, the metal industry is divided into iron and steel and nonferrous metals, and this division gives us some insight into the emergence of the Yawata Iron and Steel Mill in 1901 and its impact upon the extremely rapid expansion of production of iron and steel around that year. In other words, the value of output of iron and steel (in 1934–36 prices) increased by 9.7 times (in the A estimate) or 13.4 times (in B estimate), from 1892–1901 to 1902–1911. This manifests very vividly the manner in which a public enterprise such as the Yawata Mill, financed by Sino-Japanese War reparations (1894–95) could contribute to the tremendous expansion of the Japanese iron and steel industry. This could be termed a "big-push" in the sense that under active state intervention, the first capital-intensive industry came into being in a labor abundant economy.

The next problem is the analysis of long swings in industrial growth rate during the course of Japan's industrialization. Fig. 1 depicts such long swings movements using the three year, seven year and ten year moving averages of the annual industrial growth rate. Fig. 1(A) depicts the growth cycle (the Kuznets

Fig. 1. Long Swing of Industrial Growth Rate

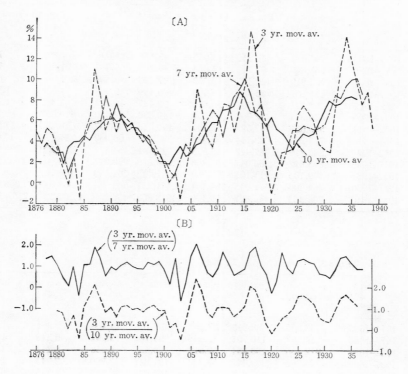

cycle) which is obtained by smoothing out the movements in the above 3 cycles of industrial growth rate. Fig. 1(B) shows the ratio of the three year moving averages to the seven and ten year moving averages. This could be construed of as a shorter cycle (a Juglar cycle) of 7 to 10 year durations.

By observing the ten year moving average of the annual growth rate, the existence of long swings in the rate of industrial growth can be confirmed. The dulations of growth cycles are; 20 years

Table 2. Gross Output (in Current Prices) in Manufacturing

		Food processing	Textiles	Lumber & wood prod.	Chemicals	Ceramics	Iron and steel	
							A	B
I	1874–1883	92,032	68,310	13,065	45,145	5,698	1,870	708
II	1877–1886	107,640	82,716	14,088	47,218	5,805	1,826	738
III	1882–1891	132,319	122,107	12,960	47,726	6,500	1,662	823
IV	1887–1896	175,207	225,464	15,309	66,499	9,969	1,825	1,065
V	1892–1901	299,321	358,397	30,375	99,437	16,222	2,351	1,702
VI	1897–1906	438,234	432,807	46,251	140,658	24,459	10,857	9,797
VII	1902–1911	593,031	547,593	55,281	194,913	38,997	28,332	27,611
VIII	1907–1916	775,299	823,114	65,924	282,146	60,930	77,677	77,677
IX	1912–1921	1,383,714	2,087,978	143,523	627,141	154,423	299,549	299,549
X	1917–1926	2,215,322	3,380,047	253,296	938,873	269,845	433,968	433,968
XI	1922–1931	2,449,185	3,411,101	292,260	1,051,442	284,046	458,767	458,767
XII	1927–1936	2,362,606	3,571,945	334,101	1,481,231	303,964	863,049	863,049
XIII	1931–1940	2,784,383	4,440,627	605,172	2,813,368	436,359	2,201,534	2,201,534

Table 3. Gross Output (in 1934–36 prices) in Manufacturing

		Food processing	Textiles	Lumber & wood prod.	Chemicals	Ceramics	Iron and steel	
							A	B
I	1874–1883	503,306	88,345	52,002	87,769	15,400	2,961	1,132
II	1877–1886	529,587	110,701	52,856	94,703	13,692	3,226	1,321
III	1882–1891	612,486	198,434	52,519	103,522	14,856	3,242	1,603
IV	1887–1896	746,862	362,447	55,389	131,942	22,790	3,243	1,884
V	1892–1901	917,880	491,328	71,164	165,674	29,589	3,175	2,257
VI	1897–1906	995,907	526,436	87,482	198,842	35,447	11,091	9,948
VII	1902–1911	1,063,757	626,052	93,125	247,039	51,500	30,938	30,200
VIII	1907–1916	1,249,286	912,025	101,690	326,512	73,245	61,430	61,430
IX	1912–1921	1,538,912	1,334,783	121,724	453,954	102,044	116,462	116,462
X	1917–1926	1,947,464	1,792,588	150,802	590,253	153,936	227,911	227,911
XI	1922–1931	2,238,034	2,359,983	206,528	847,147	210,094	430,811	430,811
XII	1927–1936	2,326,555	3,360,198	314,122	1,463,093	289,486	901,902	901,902
XIII	1931–1940	2,475,992	4,061,589	422,587	2,357,413	390,907	1,530,603	1,530,603

unit: thous. yen

nferrous metals		Machinery		Printing & publishing	Others	Total	
A	B	A	B			A	B
7,683	3,932	6,901	4,785	726	14,541	255,970	248,940
9,516	5,066	7,576	5,398	991	16,501	293,876	286,161
3,315	7,801	8,304	6,341	1,328	19,648	365,868	357,552
8,705	12,117	12,422	10,236	1,870	27,974	555,242	545,709
0,293	22,179	26,934	23,858	4,181	42,491	910,003	898,163
9,507	41,000	55,705	52,597	9,175	57,853	1,265,507	1,252,831
8,162	63,643	100,091	98,856	17,167	78,107	1,721,675	1,715,199
5,699	165,055	213,735	213,735	32,067	103,868	2,600,460	2,599,815
8,276	358,276	816,883	816,883	79,085	204,430	6,155,001	6,055,001
1,889	331,889	1,056,515	1,056,515	153,603	312,376	9,345,734	9,245,734
7,324	217,324	850,136	850,136	229,687	322,973	9,566,919	9,566,919
2,384	302,384	1,340,518	1,340,518	293,900	371,249	11,224,946	11,224,946
7,511	557,511	3,402,707	3,402,707	377,401	630,416	18,249,476	18,249,476

unit: thous. yen

nferrous metals		Machinery		Printing & publishing	Others	Total	
A	B	A	B			A	B
0,711	5,449	11,910	8,285	2,085	70,870	845,360	834,643
4,456	7,724	14,688	10,509	2,804	80,678	917,482	904,665
3,290	13,723	16,935	12,927	4,992	104,091	1,134,366	1,119,151
2,241	20,774	24,095	19,832	8,061	137,068	1,524,137	1,507,048
7,036	26,642	44,077	38,882	15,033	149,658	1,924,613	1,908,106
6,350	38,065	80,303	75,653	28,263	156,461	2,166,582	2,152,505
4,751	80,375	139,759	137,976	46,032	180,545	2,563,497	2,556,100
7,351	206,565	261,581	261,581	78,944	209,834	3,481,896	3,481,110
2,416	382,416	611,226	611,226	128,958	239,229	5,029,707	5,029,707
9,488	359,488	776,823	776,823	184,475	246,994	6,430,735	6,430,735
9,620	289,620	831,279	831,279	241,191	267,408	7,922,095	7,922,095
6,708	366,708	1,388,876	1,388,876	299,591	368,793	11,079,324	11,079,324
1,761	511,761	2,636,410	2,636,410	362,772	490,013	15,240,048	15,240,043

Table 4. Inter-Decade Industrial Growth Rate (in 1934–36 Prices)

	Food processing	Textiles	Lumber & wood prod.	Chemicals	Ceramics	Iron and Steel A	B
I~II	1.74	8.44	0.55	2.63	−3.70	2.98	5.56
II~III	3.13	15.85	−0.13	1.86	1.70	0.10	4.27
III~IV	4.39	16.53	1.09	5.49	10.68	0.01	3.51
IV~V	4.58	7.11	5.70	5.11	5.97	−0.42	3.96
V~VI	1.70	1.43	4.59	4.00	3.96	49.86	68.17
VI~VII	1.36	3.78	1.29	4.85	9.06	35.79	40.71
VII~VIII	3.49	9.14	1.84	6.43	8.44	19.71	20.68
VIII~IX	4.64	9.27	3.94	7.81	7.86	17.92	17.92
IX~X	5.31	6.86	4.78	6.00	10.17	19.14	19.14
X~XI	2.98	6.33	7.39	8.70	7.30	17.81	17.81
XI~XII	0.79	8.48	10.42	14.54	7.56	21.87	21.87
XII~XIII	1.61	5.22	8.63	15.28	8.76	17.43	17.43

Table 5. Annual Growth Rate of Industrial Production
——in terms of 1934–36 prices——

	1874–1900	1900–1940
Manufacturing (A)	4.55%	5.85%
(B)	4.57	5.87
Food processing	3.31	2.94
Textiles	9.87	6.26
Lumber and wood products	1.60	4.84
Chemicals	3.44	7.25
Ceramics	3.26	7.08
Iron and steel (A)	0.87	14.43
(B)	4.37	14.74
Non-ferrous metals (A)	7.30	6.11
(B)	9.24	6.51
Machinery (A)	8.02	9.65
(B)	9.35	9.77
Printing and Publishing	11.45	7.33
Others	4.03	3.17

Nonferrous metals		Machinery		Printing & publishing	Others	(% per annum) Total	
A	B	A	B			A	B
11.65	13.92	7.78	8.95	11.50	4.66	2.84	2.80
12.22	15.53	3.06	4.60	15.61	5.78	4.73	4.74
7.69	10.28	8.46	10.68	12.30	6.43	6.87	6.93
2.97	5.65	16.59	19.21	17.30	1.84	5.26	5.32
5.03	8.57	16.44	18.91	17.60	0.91	2.51	2.56
16.57	22.23	14.81	16.48	12.57	3.08	3.66	3.75
28.93	31.40	17.43	17.92	14.30	3.24	7.17	7.23
16.89	17.03	26.73	26.73	12.67	2.80	8.89	8.90
−1.20	−1.20	5.42	5.42	8.61	0.65	5.57	5.57
−3.89	−3.89	1.40	1.40	6.15	1.65	4.64	4.64
5.32	5.32	13.42	13.42	4.84	7.58	7.97	7.97
9.89	9.89	22.46	22.46	5.27	8.22	9.37	9.39

from 1881 (trough) to 1901 (trough), 23 years from 1901 to 1924 (trough), 23 years from 1891 (peak)to 1914 (peak), and 21 years from 1914 (peak) to 1935 (peak). Thus Kuznets cycle of about twenty year duration can be observed in the prewar industrial growth. We adopted the ten year moving average because the duration of the Juglar cycle is said to be about ten years and also by using the ten year moving average, we could eliminate shorter cycles of less than ten year duration. Consequently the waves which emerge after this smoothing process portray a cycle longer than those of ten year duration.

However, Shôzaburô Fujino once pointed out that the average duration of the Juglar cycle in the prewar period of Japan was about 7.5 years.[5] We do not intend here to test his findings, but, under the assumption that the Juglar cycle lasted for about seven years, the seven year moving average of the growth rate

5) Shôzaburô Fujino, *Nihon no Keiki Junkan* (Business Cycles in Japan), Keisô Shobô, 1965, p. 20.

is also depicted in Fig. 1(A). Although some difference can be observed in the year of peak and trough between the two smoothed series, the both moving averages give us similar 20 year cycles.

We will not discuss here as to which of the two cycles is more reliable. However, there is one point to be noticed, namely the growth cycle in Fig. 1 gives us an upswing beginning from about 1900 and ending in 1914–15 (1917 in the case of three year moving average). It is of great interest to note that, even before 1914 when World War I broke out, the upswing of the long swing had already been under operation. It goes without saying that the outbreak of the War played an important part in accelerating the upswing of the long swing, as suggested from the three year moving average, but the chart also indicates that the War was not the sole predominant factor for the 1900–1924 Kuznets cycle of Japan's industrial growth rate.

Another aspect which may attract our attention is that the trough of the long swing after World War I occurred in 1922 or 1924, and not in 1930–31 when the impact of the Great Depression came to be strongly felt all around the world. Consequently, one can interpret the 1931 trough as more due to downward trend in the operation of the Juglar cycle.

Fig. 1(B), on the other hand, gives us shorter Juglar cycles as contrasted with the long swing. Take for instance the curve depicting the ratio of the three year to the ten year moving average, and we see a repetition of almost ten year cycles for the post–1903 period assuming that 1911 is a trough year and we neglect the brief peak between 1909 and 1913. Then the troughs of the Juglar cycle become 1903–1911–1921–1931, which leaves us with a cycle of about ten year durations. If we adopt the seven year moving average as a criteria of reference, we come up with an additional peak in 1922, while a more detailed observation may allow us yet another interpretation, namely that the four, six, or seven year cycles had also coexisted.

Therefore, from above analysis it may not be possible to determine whether the seven or ten year cycle strongly prevailed.

However, if we look at the three year moving average, placing particular emphasis upon the severity of oscillation as a criteria of our judgment, then the series of troughs become 1903–1911–1920–1931, suggesting a duration of 8–11 years Juglar waves. (Here we also retain the assumption that 1911 was a trough year).

Fig. 1(B) gives us no clear indication of the 10 year cycle before 1900, and this may be due to the weakness or biases underlying our estimate in the earlier period attributable to scarcity of data or to the strong "take-off" trend which may have reduced the regularity of ten year oscillations.

Fig. 1(B) also suggests a following point: In the ratio of the three year moving average to the seven or ten year moving average, it is interesting to see that years 1884, 1903 or 1920, which form the troughs of the Kuznets cycle, the severity of recession of the 10 year cycle is also conspicuous. In addition, the trough in 1931 seems to be relatively intense, probably owing to the effect of the World Depression.

Figs. 2~4 depict the behavior of a few selected industries (textiles, food, and machinery) which fall under the category of manufacturing. We observe that the patterns of the growth cycle which prevailed in textile and food-processing industries had a decided influence upon the behavior of the growth cycle in manufacturing as a whole, in the former half of the observed period. However, since 1900, a different situation prevailed. On the one hand, the trough in 1920's is not so evident in the textile industry, in spite of the clear emergence of the trough for manufacturing as a whole during 1922–24. In the food industry, on the other hand, we find a considerable lag in the occurrence of a trough (1928–29), when compared to that of manufacturing as a whole (1922–24). A decline in the share of textiles and food in total output and the lagged occurrence of trough in these industries may also explain the reduced influence upon the over-all manufacturing cycle.

In the case of machinery industry, as depicted in Fig. 4, the conformity of cycles in the same industry with those in the manu-

Fig. 2. Growth Cycle in Textile Industry

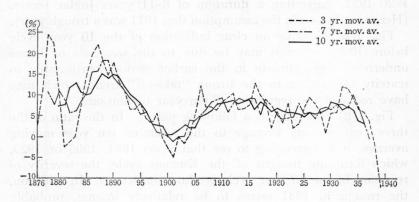

Fig. 3. Growth Cycle in Food Processing Industry

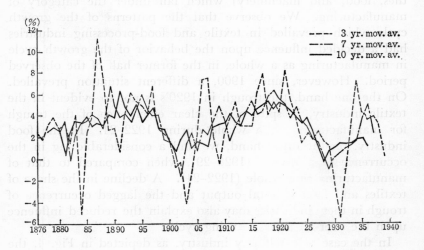

Fig. 4. Growth Cycle in Machinery Industry

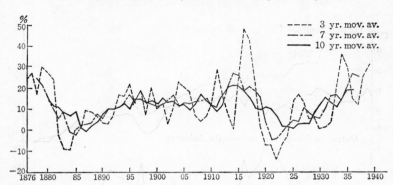

facturing as a whole is not so clear for the pre-1900 period. On the one hand, the first trough due to the Matuskata's deflation beginning from 1881 was considerably delayed as compared with that of manufacturing, while the trough around 1900 is quite obscure. However, in the post-1900 period, we find a fairly similar behavior in the occurrence of peaks and troughs between manufacturing and machinery industry. Thus, we are in a position to generalize that influence of cycles in neavy industry, particularly machinery industry, were considerably high in the post-1900 period than in the pre-1900 and this stands in clear contrast with the case of light industry.

3. Changes in Industrial and Price Structures

The relative composition of gross output in subsectors of manufacturing is computed in Table 6 and 7 (in both current prices and 1934–36 prices respectively). Due to considerations of space, Tables 6 and 7 indicate the output composition only in terms of the A estimate. For a brief definition of A and B estimates refer to the footnote of Table 1.

293

Fig. 5. Output Compositions in Food and Textile Industries

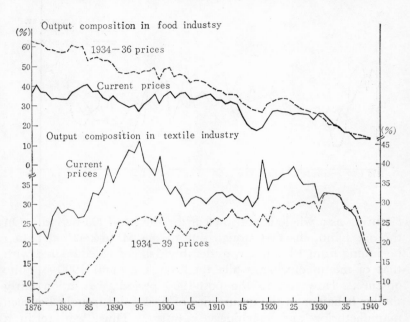

The long-term changes of industrial structure in terms of decade are shown in Table 6 and 7, and the annual changes of the output proportions of food-processing and textile industries, are depicted in Fig. 5, in order to pinpoint the divergent movement of output proportions when plotted in terms of current prices and 1934–36 prices. Fig. 5 indicates a huge discrepancy in the output proportions of food industry when estimated in terms of current prices and constant prices, particularly for the early years of our observed period. In the early few years we found that the output proportion in terms of current prices was about 36%, while that in terms of 1934–36 prices was over 60%, indicating thereby that the former proportion was extremely lower

294

Table 6. Manufacturing Output Composition in Terms of Current Prices

—— Based on the A Estimate —— (%)

	Food processing	Textiles	Lumber & wood prod.	Chemicals	Ceramics	Iron and steel	Nonferrous metals	Machinery	Printing & publishing	Others
1874—1883	36.29	26.06	5.01	18.03	2.22	0.74	2.95	2.63	0.27	5.81
1877—1886	36.65	27.81	4.77	16.31	1.98	0.63	3.27	2.57	0.34	5.69
1882—1891	36.68	32.56	3.69	13.14	1.77	0.46	3.62	2.29	9.37	5.43
1887—1896	32.17	39.70	2.77	12.14	1.82	0.35	3.45	2.20	0.33	5.08
1892—1901	32.27	40.19	3.18	11.09	1.88	0.26	3.29	2.78	0.43	4.75
1897—1906	34.66	34.57	3.68	11.08	1.91	0.59	3.83	4.23	0.70	4.57
1902—1911	34.57	31.79	3.30	11.37	2.23	1.38	3.99	5.66	0.96	4.57
1907—1916	31.13	31.65	2.66	10.97	2.36	2.65	5.59	7.70	1.20	4.10
1912—1921	24.58	32.87	2.34	10.38	2.43	4.46	6.39	12.02	1.30	3.45
1917—1926	23.64	35.84	2.69	10.00	2.87	4.74	3.72	11.52	1.63	3.33
1922—1931	25.64	35.57	3.06	10.96	2.97	4.77	2.28	8.91	2.41	3.38
1927—1936	21.82	32.16	3.01	13.00	2.72	7.26	2.77	11.38	2.69	3.30
1931—1940	17.06	26.96	3.19	14.81	2.49	10.66	3.01	16.11	2.33	3.40

Table 7. Manufacturing Output Composition in Terms of 1934–36 Prices

—— Based on the A Estimate ——

(%)

	Food processing	Textiles	Lumber of wood prod.	Chemicals	Ceramics	Iron & steel	Nonferrous metals	Machinery	Printing & publishing	Others
1874—1883	59.68	10.29	6.21	10.37	1.86	0.34	1.25	1.36	0.24	8.40
1877—1886	57.76	11.96	5.80	10.36	1.51	0.35	1.57	1.59	0.30	8.81
1882—1891	54.55	16.73	4.76	9.25	1.31	0.29	2.01	1.51	0.42	9.16
1887—1896	49.39	23.29	4.09	8.67	1.48	0.22	2.13	1.55	0.52	9.05
1892—1901	47.73	25.57	3.66	8.62	1.54	0.17	1.93	2.23	0.76	7.02
1897—1906	46.04	24.34	4.04	9.16	1.63	0.50	2.13	3.66	1.29	7.21
1902—1911	41.87	24.28	3.70	9.67	1.98	1.15	3.18	5.32	1.77	7.10
1907—1916	36.63	26.03	2.99	9.41	2.12	1.72	5.50	7.25	2.21	6.13
1912—1921	31.17	26.61	2.47	9.07	2.04	2.26	7.43	11.52	2.54	4.89
1917—1926	30.25	27.76	2.34	9.15	2.36	3.45	5.75	12.24	2.85	3.86
1922—1931	28.73	29.71	2.58	10.52	2.66	5.26	3.68	10.42	3.05	3.39
1927—1936	21.92	30.46	2.83	12.89	2.61	7.74	3.39	12.07	2.78	3.33
1931—1940	16.98	27.08	2.82	15.10	2.56	9.64	3.39	16.01	2.46	3.26

than the latter. The discrepancy in the two proportions is naturally due to an increasing trend of relative prices of food.

In the textile industry, on the other hand, an opposite tendency is observed, due to a decreasing trend in the relative prices of textiles. In the early Meiji period, the output proportion in terms of current prices was around 26%, but it fell to less than 10% in terms of 1934–36 prices. Barring the extraordinary war time period (the latter half of the 1930's) when the proportion of textiles showed a drastic decline, we can observe its steadily increasing trend in terms of 1934–36 prices. In particular, textile proportion for 1874–1891 (in terms of constant prices) rose from less than 10% up to about 25%. For the next thirty years (1891–1920), this ratio was stable at around 25%, but in the 1920's it approached the level of 30%.

It goes without saying that the divergent movement of the two proportions in the textile industry is due to the sustained decline in the relative prices of textiles, in contrast with the sustained increase in relative prices of the food processing industry for long period. The textile industry, with this background, became one of the staple export industry, and contributed to the sustained high rate of growth of Japan's exports and domestic production. It is worthy of notice that Japan's textile industry, which had been extending its powerful influence in the world market and possessing a strong comparative advantage in the domestic industry, was endowed with the long-term declining trend of its relative price structure.

Regarding the proportion of metals, machinery and chemicals, following trends are observed:

	Metals and Machinery		Chemicals	
	(current prices)	(1934–36 prices)	(current prices)	(1934–36 prices)
1874–1883	6.32%	2.95%	18.03%	10.37%
1897–1906	8.65	6.29	11.08	9.16
1927–1936	21.41	23.20	13.00	12.89

Although the prewar Japanese economy was predominantly oriented to the light industry, we see, nevertheless, a long-term trend towards heavy industrialization and a secular reduction of their relative prices. Particularly, in the metal and machinery industry, this trend was conspicuous. In the chemical industry, the output proportion in terms of current prices tended to decrease, and only began to increase in the 1930's. However, as is often the case with many countries, its relative price tended to decline, without exception, particularly since the emergence of modern chemical industries. This caused a divergence of the two proportions in terms of current and constant prices.

Thus, it may be of great interest to directly analyze the trends of relative prices in different industries. Table 8 (based on implicit deflators for different industries) is constructed with this in mind. In Fig. 6, some industries are taken up, but in Table 8 we can see the relative price trends in all industries. We see conspicuous declines in relative prices of textiles, iron and steel, non-ferrous metals, machinery and chemicals, but steady rise in relative prices of food-processing, lumber and wood products, and other industries. In printing and publishing, the relative price declines in the former-half, and rises in the latter-half of the period.

The interesting problem is how these changes of price structure relate to those of industrial structure. Utilizing the output data in constant prices by industry, we first derive the annual average rate of growth between 1897–1906 and 1934–1936. We compared this with changes in the relative prices by industry within the same period in Fig. 7. Except for printing and publishing, and nonferrous metals, a fairly consistent inverse relationship can be obtained between them. In short, industries with higher growth rate saw a more conspicuous relative price decline.

The logical background for this result may be explained as follows: In industries with higher output growth rate, the productivity growth rate may also be higher due to the mass

Table 8. Relative Prices by Industry

Manuf. = 100; 1934-36 = 100

	Food processing	Textiles	Lumber & wood prod.	Chemicals	Ceramics	Iron & steel	Nonferrous metals	Machinery	Printing & publishing	Others
1874—1883	60.6	253.0	85.2	170.7	132.0	220.8	235.6	206.0	110.7	68.7
1877—1886	61.6	227.2	82.0	151.0	131.8	168.3	205.2	157.8	106.4	63.0
1882—1891	69.4	209.2	79.6	147.3	120.8	161.3	191.1	156.0	87.8	61.7
1887—1896	64.9	170.3	75.9	139.6	122.4	157.3	161.2	142.5	64.2	56.6
1892—1901	68.3	155.5	87.5	128.0	116.3	154.3	172.5	125.6	57.1	61.6
1897—1906	75.7	141.2	90.6	110.7	117.2	156.2	180.3	116.7	54.1	63.2
1902—1911	83.1	130.8	89.2	117.8	112.9	140.3	134.4	107.1	54.9	64.6
1907—1916	84.2	121.6	87.9	117.8	112.0	153.9	99.9	105.9	54.5	66.9
1912—1921	75.5	126.7	98.5	114.3	122.7	204.0	76.0	102.6	51.1	74.7
1917—1926	77.6	130.1	109.8	110.1	123.6	158.3	60.1	91.6	56.8	88.9
1922—1931	88.8	121.4	121.1	105.3	113.0	92.7	62.1	85.0	76.7	100.1
1927—1936	99.4	106.5	107.8	101.6	103.8	93.2	80.0	93.3	96.3	99.7
1931—1940	97.8	122.3	117.5	98.2	95.3	112.0	90.7	101.1	90.5	107.0

Fig. 6. Changes of Price Structure by Industry

(A) Implicit deflators of some industry

(B) **Relative Prices** by Industry

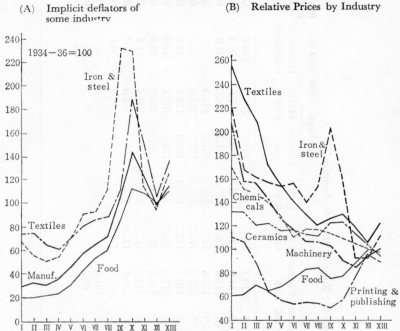

production effect, and therefore the unit cost may decline considerably. Consequently, in industries with higher output growth rate, the relative price may decline. However, this is a long-term effect, and in the short run, the relative price may increase due to excess demand, e.g., in the war period or in the investment boom. In Fig. 6, the sharp increase of the iron and steel relative price during World War I is one such example. But in Fig. 7, wherein about thirty-five year period is covered, changes in price structure are largely due to the supply-side factors rather than the demand-side factors, and in particular, the inter-industry differences in the productivity increase and the unit cost may have a decisive influence upon them.

Fig. 7. Growth Rates and Changes in Relative Prices by Industry[6]

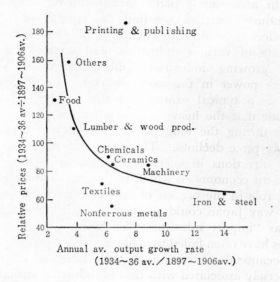

The two exceptions to the above inference are printing and publishing, and nonferrous metals (Fig. 7). Regarding the dispersion of nonferrous metals, our analysis of this industry for the postwar period can be found elsewhere (see the end of Chapter 8). The prices of nonferrous metals always follow an erratic, instable changes, which may account for some dispersion from the downward sloping curve. On the other hand, the excessive upward deviation of printing and publishing may be due to the fact that in the former-half period its relative price declined considerably, and in the latter-half period (in which the period

---

6) Shôzaburô Fujino and Yûichi Shionoya once made similar chart, based on the Shionoya's data respectively at about the same time. S. Fujino, *Analysis of Cyclical Fluctuations and Development in Machinery Industry, II*, (in Japanese), Economic Research Institute of *Kikai Shinkô Kyôkai*, April 1967 and Y. Shionoya, "Long-Term Analysis of Prices of Manufactured Commodities" (in Japanese), *Keizaigaku Kenkyû* (Studies in Economics), Hitotsubashi University, 1967.

from 1897–1906 to 1934–1936 is almost included), it rose as a reaction against the movement in the former-half period.

Thus, in analysing Japan's manufacturing structure in the prewar industrialization, we find that the inverse changes of relative prices were associated with the differences in the relative growth rate of various industries, and consequently that the relatively growing industries could strengthen their export competitive power in the world market. Textile industry can be cited as a typical example of this pattern. It should be pointed out that the heavy industrialization process which also continued during the long prewar period was associated with the relative price declines. This may be assumed as one of the favorable directions in variation in industrial structure, particularly in an economy in which the exports have always played a leading role in the process of economic development.

In this way Japan could accomplish both "export promotion" as well as "import substitution". Many presently developing economies have often failed to achieve such a "export promotion", mainly because the variation of price structure may not have been inversely associated with that of industrial structure.

CHAPTER 8

FORMATION AND TRANSITION OF
THE DUAL ECONOMY

1. Problems

The Japanese economy of the 1960's is, in a sense, in a period
of transition because the wide interscale wage differential of firms
has begun to be greatly narrowed and the characteristic feature
of the past century (except during wars) of surplus labor is now
being replaced by a labor-shortage situation. Although labor
markets for small industries and agriculture have long retained
some pre-modern elements, they are now forced to transform
themselves because of this labor shortage—which was initiated
by the super-boom of 1955–61. This process of transformation
is destined to be further intensified in the future due to the declining tendency in the rate of increase in the labor force. Therefore, various aspects of the so-called dual economy are expected
to disappear within the coming ten years, although this process
will create tremendous friction in every field of the economy
such as: the rapid rise of consumer prices; the difficulties
confronting small enterprises due to occupational changes; the
shortage of labor in agriculture due to the exodus of youth from
villages; the difficulties of expanding farming scale due to the
lack of efficient labor; and the juxtaposition of the strenghened
position of labor unions and the increasing desire of the entrepreneurs to change drastically the present employment and wage
systems (the "life-time commitment" as well as the strong seniority
system in wage-payments), etc.

I shall first be concerned with the causes or background which account for the dual structure of the Japanese economy in the past, as well as historical explanation why some symptoms of the dual economy, e.g., interscale wage differentials, were intensified in the manufacturing sector in the 1920's and have continued until the present. Secondly, we shall explore various aspects of the dual economy in the labor market, small industry, and the capital market. Thirdly, we shall take up the current phenomena namely, the rapid transition taking place in the dual economy, as labor shortage becomes more and more intensified and the level of the Japanese economy approaches those of the Western countries. Before going into the above, however, we shall analyze the present state of the employment and wage structures in the Japanese economy; then, we shall proceed to set up a hypothesis which will explain the historical process as well as the present status of the dual economy.

2. Structures of Employment and Wages

Although the term dual economy has been understood so far to mean the coexistence of modern big firms and the traditional or less modernized smaller firms, including agriculture, the focus has been directed in Japan more and more upon the dualistic or multi-layer employment and wage structures of the manu-facturing sector. We shall return later to the problem concerning the relationship between agriculture and smaller enterprises in the non-agricultural sectors, but in this section, we shall con-centrate on the quantitative aspects in the non-agricultural sectors, particularly in manufacturing.

Table 1 shows the proportion of individual proprietors and family workers, who belong to the non-agricultural category of the total employed labor force, based on the data on *Census of Population* or the *Labor Force Survey* in various countries. We may assume that, in this table, the higher this ratio, the less modernized is the employment structure. Although the above-

Table 1. Ratio of Individual Proprietors and Family Workers to Total Employed Labor Force in the Non-agricultural Sectors

Thailand	(1960)	45.2%
Philippines	(1961)	36.8
Turkey	(1960)	31.0
Greece	(1961)	30.6
Venezuela	(1961)	23.8
Mexico	(1960)	23.2
Israel	(1961)	22.6
Japan	(1955)	26.5
Japan	(1965)	21.6
Portugal	(1960)	22.4
Italy	(1962)	21.5
Argentina	(1947)	20.2
Puerto-Rico	(1963)	17.4
Netherlands	(1960)	14.1
Austria	(1961)	13.1
West Germany	(1961)	12.8
Australia	(1954)	11.8
Norway	(1960)	10.3
Canada	(1962)	10.0
U.S.A.	(1962)	9.9
Ireland	(1960)	9.8
Sweden	(1960)	9.0
U.K.	(1951)	6.2

Sources: ILO, *Yearbook of Labour Statistics*, 1963 and, for Japan, *the Census of Population*.

mentioned ratio for Japan is 26.5% for 1955, 22.6% for 1960 21.6% for 1965 and is lower than the ratios given for Thailand (45.2%), the Philippines (36.8%), Turkey (31%), Greece (30.6%), etc., it is very close to the ratios given for Venezuela, Mexico, Israel, and Portugal (22–23%)—countries which can be considered even less developed than Japan, industrially. In this respect, we find this conspicuous feature that Japan, which is regarded as a highly industrialized nation, still preserves pre-modern traits or so it seems, at least, from the quantitative measures indicated in Table 1.

In Table 2, we see the employment structure as revealed by the size of establishments in manufacturing of six selected countries: the United States, Japan, Denmark, West Germany, the United Kingdom, and Norway. According to this table, the proportion of the size "less than one hundred employees" of the total number of employees is 27% in the United States, 20.3% in the United Kingdom, and 36.1% in West Germany, but it is 52.8% in Japan, indicating that Japan has an employment pattern more strongly biased in the lower-size establishments than do the other advanced countries. The same ratio was 58.8% in 1956. However, it is not impossible to find similar cases even among western countries, for the ratio is 53.2% in Norway and 47.2% in Denmark, which figures fall between Japan, on the one hand, and the United States, the United Kingdom, and West Germany, on the other. Thus, the concentration of employment in the lower-size establishments is not peculiar only to Japan. In this sense, the phenomenon of dual economy has not come to stay for ever as is felt by some Japanese Marxist economists. Such a phenomenon can be improved as the economy grows, although the improvement process will be accompanied by some frictions. It follows from this observation, that in countries such as Greece, Spain and Portugal, the interscale employment structure in manufacturing might be equally or more biased toward the lower-size establishments than it is in Japan. Taking into account also that in some underdeveloped countries like India, Ceylon, and the Philippines, such a tendency is much more conspicuous than in others, it may not be deniable that, in general, as the economy grows the interscale employment structure will tend to move towards the pattern existing in advanced countries.

Another quantitative feature of the labor market in Japan, particularly with reference to manufacturing, is found in the wage differential by size of establishment. As Table 3 indicates, the wage differential in manufacturing (if we take the ratio of the size "4–9 employees" to that of "1,000 employees and over") was 42.3% in 1951, which widened to 37.8% in 1958, but nar-

Table 2. Employment Structure in Manufacturing in Six Countries

Size of establishment	U.S.A. (1958)		Japan (1964)		Denmark (1955)		West Germany (1961)		U.K. (1958)		Norway (1958)	
	thousand	%	thousand	%	thousand	%	thousand	%	thousand	%	thousand	%
1-49 Employees	2,645.3	(17.2)	4,108	(41.5)	106.1	(33.6)	2,757.6	(29.0)	897	(11.7)	132.4	(40.7)
50-99	1,512.8	(9.8)	1,115	(11.3)	42.9	(13.6)	676.8	(7.1)	658	(8.6)	40.6	(12.5)
100-499	4,647.3	(30.2)	2,183	(22.0)	96.2	(30.4)	2,260.2	(23.8)	2,428	(31.6)	90.2	(27.7)
500-999	1,893.3	(12.3)	808	(8.2)	29.9	(9.4)	1,007.0	(10.6)	1,043	(14.6)		
1,000 and over	4,695.1	(30.5)	1,687	(17.0)	41.3	(13.0)	2,806.0	(29.5)	2,654	(34.5)	62.1	(19.1)
Total	15,393.8	(100.0)	9,901	(100.0)	316.3	(100.0)	9,507.6	(100.0)	7,680	(100.0)	325.3	(100.0)

Sources: U.S.A., *Census of Manufactures*, 1958; Japan, *Kōgyō Tōkeihyō* (Census of Manufactures), 1964; Denmark, *Statistiske Efterretninger*, 2 Juli, 1959; West Germany, *Statistisches Jahrbuch für Bundesrepublik Deutschland*, 1963; U.K., *Census of Production*, 1958; Norway, *Norges Industri, Produksjonsstatistikk 1958, 1960*.

Note: In the size "1-49" in West Germany, those who engaged in Handwerk (handicraft) amounting to 1,884,300 men are included. If it is excluded, the proportional percentages become, from the lowest size, 11.5%, 8.8%, 29.6%, 13.2% and 36.8%, respectively.

Table 3. Wage Differential by Size of Establishment in Manufacturing Japan

Size of establishment	1951	1958	1961	1962	1965
1,000 employees over	100.0	100.0	100.0	100.0	100.0
500–999	91.4	75.1	78.8	82.8	84.4
200–499	79.2	65.8	71.3	74.9	78.1
100–199	67.8	55.6	61.9	64.7	70.0
50– 99	59.8	50.4	58.6	63.3	66.3
30– 49	54.3	46.7	55.7	61.0	63.8
20– 29	50.5	44.1	52.7	57.9	—
10– 19	46.6	41.5	47.3	54.8	—
4– 9	42.3	37.8	44.9	50.2	—

Source: Ministry of International Trade and Industry, *Kôgyô Tôkeihyô* (Census of Manufactures). The computation is based on the average wages which is derived by dividing the wages and salaries by the monthly average of regular employees. The 1965 figures are based on the short summary announced in advance, and in the computation of average wages, the number of employees at the end of 1965 is used.

Table 4. Wage Differential in Manufacturing in Four Advanced Countries

	U.K. (1954)	Japan (1960)	U.S.A. (1958)	W. Germany (1954)
1,000 and over	100.0	100.0	100.0	100.0
500–999	89.3	78.7	85.0	} 91.6
300–499	86.0 }	} 64.4	} 77.9	
200–299	83.0			
100–199	82.0			
50– 99	80.9	55.0	74.4	} 87.8
25– 49	80.3 }	} 48.5	} 71.1	
10– 24	79.3			
4– 9	—	41.2	} 64.0	} 81.7
1– 3	—	—		

Sources: Japan, *Kôgyô Tôkeihyô* (Census of Manufactures), 1960; U.K. *Census of Production*, 1954; U.S.A., *Census of Manufactures*, 1958; W. Germany *Statistisches Jahrbuch fur Bundesrepublik Deutschland*, 1960.

rowed again to 44.9% in 1961, and to 50.2% in 1962 owing to an increasing shortage of labor from around 1959. This wage differential is evidently greater than those in the United Kingdom or the United States wherein the relative difference between the highest size and the lowest remains within the margin of 20 per cent. Table 4 illustrates the wage differentials in Japan, the United States, the United Kingdom, and West Germany. The differential is wider in West Germany than in the United States, but the differential of the latter is a bit wider than the United Kingdom's. Japan's differential is relatively wider than the other three nations.

Although the interscale wage differential in underdeveloped countries, such as the Philippines, India, Ceylon, etc., is almost equally as wide as it was in Japan during the postwar period, it is not clear as to what the situations are in medium-industrialized countries. In this respect, the data for Danish manufacturing indicated in Table 5 are very suggestive. According to this data, in Denmark, the ratio between the highest and the lowest of average wages per employee is 100 to 66.7. Since, on the other hand, the differential in Japan was 100 vs. 37.8% in 1958, and 100 vs. 44.9% in 1961, the interscale wage differential is clearly greater in Japan than in Denmark, but the difference is not so large. In this sense, the Danish wage differential falls between Japan and West Germany.

As already indicated, the interscale employment structure in Denmark is also of a pattern concentrating in lower-size establishments. It should be noted that in Denmark the proportion of "less than 100 employees" size is 47.2%, while it is 52~58% in Japan, and this should be understood in close correspondence with the fact that the wage differentials in the two countries are relatively close. It may be possible that, in the short run, the interscale employment structure may change inversely with the interscale wage differential but both may be expected to move *pari-passu* in the long run.

Table 5. Wage Differential in Danish Manufacturing (1955)

unit: krone

Size of firms	Wages and salaries per employee	Corporations			Other firms		
		Earnings per man	Salaries per man	Wages per man	Earnings per man	Salaries per man	Wages per man
0–10 employees	7,602 (66.7)	9,574 (84.2)	11,574 (65.6)	8,333 (81.3)	7,097 (61.9)	5,045 (31.6)	7,927 (76.3)
10–25	8,959 (78.7)	10,131 (89.1)	13,746 (77.9)	8,623 (84.2)	8,346 (72.8)	8,454 (53.0)	8,316 (80.1)
25–50	9,483 (83.3)	10,052 (88.4)	14,164 (80.3)	8,695 (84.9)	8,904 (77.6)	11,162 (69.9)	8,319 (80.1)
50–100	9,923 (87.1)	10,185 (89.6)	14,809 (84.0)	8,837 (86.2)	9,501 (82.8)	12,815 (80.3)	8,648 (83.3)
100–200	10,300 (90.4)	10,475 (92.1)	16,321 (92.6)	8,893 (86.8)	9,765 (85.1)	13,890 (87.0)	8,841 (85.1)
200–500	10,236 (89.9)	10,425 (91.7)	16,288 (92.4)	9,091 (88.7)	9,251 (80.7)	13,745 (86.1)	8,213 (79.1)
500–1,000	11,083 (97.3)	11,007 (96.8)	17,395 (98.6)	9,335 (91.1)	11,421 (99.6)	15,351 (96.2)	10,679 (102.8)
1,000 employees and over	11,391 (100.0)	11,371 (100.0)	17,635 (100.0)	10,246 (100.0)	11,471 (100.0)	15,960 (100.0)	10,387 (100.0)

Source: *Statistiske Efterretninger*, udgived af det Statistiske Department, 51, Argang Nr. 32, 2 Juli 1959.

Table 6. Interscale Wage Structure in Prewar Manufacturing

A. Wages of Total and Male Workers in the Manufacturing Firms in Japan, 1909 and 1914

unit: sen. (100 sen = 1 yen)

Average daily wage	Size of establishment by number of employees						
	5–9	10–29	30–49	50–99	100–499	500–999	1,000 and above
1909–All	34.2	33.2	31.7	32.5	34.0	32.5	34.4
Male	43.0	46.0	47.7	49.4	50.5	49.5	53.5
1914–All	39.5	37.0	34.6	35.4	35.9	39.3	43.4
Male	47.2	50.2	51.3	53.8	55.5	57.0	65.5

Source: Estimates by M. Umemura and A. Nakamura based on data in Nōshōmushō, *Kōjōkeisahyō* (Summary of Factory Statistics); also available in Shōwadōjinkai, ed., *Wagakuni Chinginkōzō no Shitekikōsatsu* (Historical Analysis of Japanese Wage Structure), p. 471.

B. Wages of all Workers in Manufacturing Firms in Tokyo and Yokohama, 1932

unit: yen

Average annual earnings	Size of firm by amount of invested capital (yen)									
	1–99	100–499	500–999	1,000–1,999	2,000–4,999	5,000–9,999	10,000–49,999	50,000–99,999	100,000–499,999	500,000 and above
Tokyo	178.7	185.8	206.4	232.8	281.2	352.1	486.6	570.6	624.6	793.9
Yokohama	121.1	158.5	178.4	241.3	297.3	373.5	445.4	560.7	671.7	771.5

Source: Estimates by A. Nakamura based on data in *Kōgyō Chōsahyō* (Survey of Manufactures), 1932; also available in Shōwa Dōjinkai, ed., *op. cit.*

An example of Danish data again seems to illustrate that the interscale wage differential in Japan will not be so peculiar a phenomenon as we usually feel. The fact that a wage differential which has a similarity with that of Japan prevails in the present underdeveloped countries will also strengthen this impression.

However, one point should be borne in mind. Even if a sharp interscale wage differential exists in the manufacturing sector in the present day underdeveloped countries, it was not evident in Japan before World War I. Japan's wage differential expanded tremendously only from around World War I onward as is shown in Table 6. If we take this into account, we may find that the formation of a sharp interscale wage differential in the present-day underdeveloped countries is only a postwar phenomenon, accelerated by the introduction of foreign aids and technology, and that before World War II such countries probably may not have had such a sharp wage differential.

In this sense, it is of immense interest that the steep interscale wage differential expanded in Japan even in the prewar period when foreign aid was almost negligible. If so, it would be our next step to explain the endogenous factors responsible for the emergence of such a conspicuous pattern of interscale wage differential.

3. Hypothesis Relating to the Labor Market

We shall focus our attention here on why the interscale wage differential, which steeply tilted from the highest to the lowest size of establishments, has emerged in the manufacturing sector. Since this is a phenomenon noted in the labor market, the easiest way is to analyze only the characteristics of the labor market. Some peculiarities or imperfection of labor market, if any, seem to be directly responsible for the above phenomenon, so the labor economists in Japan mostly analyse the problem from this aspect. However, actually in the price-formation of a commodity, for example, not only the demand-and-supply relations of the commodity in question, but also the situations in the markets of various other commodities are involved. In the same way, it seems to me that not only the labor market, but also the product and the capital markets may be relevant in the process of formation of the wage structure, although the degree of their influences will differ. We may resort to the partial analysis approach to solve the above problem, by concentrating our attention on the labor market alone, or else we may adhere to a more general analysis by setting up a hypothesis explaining the interscale wage differential, which not only involves an analysis of the labor market, but also that of product and capital markets in a systematic way. Professor Tokutarô Yamanaka once complained that studies on small industries in Japan were apt to adopt a "truncated approach" rather than a "comprehensive approach," so to speak, forgetting in the process that the so-called small-industry problem should be analyzed as a facet and an integral part of the structure of the national economy as a whole. It is necessary to emphasize this point, for, although we shall take up each market fairly in detail in what follows, we would like eventually to combine them into what Yamanaka calls the "comprehensive appoach." As in the theory of prices, we have a general equilibrium theory as well as a partial equilibrium theory, so in the analysis of wage differential too, we attempt to follow a general approach, although our model is descriptive rather than mathematical.

When the interscale wage differential is discussed in the analysis of the labor market, the "life-time commitment" and "seniority wage-payment system" become pertinent. Once a person is employed in a big corporation, as a rule, he will continue to remain employed until his retirement. During that period, his wage or salary is destined to increase as a function of the length of his service. Wage will automatically increase in the fashion of an escalator, according to the worker's age, and not necessarily due to any improvement in his skill or his contribution towards production. The "life-time commitment" and the

313

"seniority wage-payment system" explained above are adopted mainly in the large enterprises, and not in the small-medium enterprises.

Moreover, generally, the large enterprises and the small-medium enterprises are separated in their relation to labor market. This fact is made clear by the *Report on the Survey of the Tokyo-Yokohama Industrial District* conducted in 1951–52 by Kanagawa Prefecture under the guidance of Professors K. Ôkouchi, S. Ujihara, and others. As Table 7 shows, in large factories, those workers who have experiences of working only in large factories amount to a very high ratio of 78%; in small factories, those who have experiences of working only in small factories amount to 47.7%. Therefore, roughly about half of the small-medium factory workers are closed within their labor market. If the β ratio in the table below (21.4%)—for those who moved from small to large factories but again came back to small factories—is added to the above, it becomes almost 80%. In such a way, the large and small factory labor markets are mutually separated, and the labor migration is restricted within each labor market. In addition, the labor mobility among small-medium factories is generally very high, but that among large factories, very low.

In the field of large enterprises, the recruitment of new personnel is dependent much more upon the new graduates than it is in the field of small enterprises, because workers who seek employ-

Table 7. Labor Migration between Large and Small Factories
I. A Case of Large Factories

	A	B	C	Total
Metal industry	78.4	5.3	16.3	100.0%
Chemical industry	82.0	5.1	12.9	100.0
Machinery industry	75.0	6.2	18.9	100.0
Total of industries	78.0	5.6	16.4	100.0

A. Those who have experiences of working only in large factories.
B. Those who had moved from large to small factories, and moved back to large factories.
C. Those who have moved from small to large factories.

FORMATION AND TRANSITION OF THE DUAL ECONOMY

II. A Case of Small Factories

	α	β	γ	Total
Metal industry	60.7	11.3	27.8	100.0%
Chemical industry	48.0	9.2	42.8	100.0
Machinery industry	42.0	32.0	26.0	100.0
Total of industries	47.7	21.4	30.9	100.0

α. Those who have experiences of working only in small factories.
β. Those who had moved from small to large factories, and then moved back to small factories.
γ. Those who have moved from large to small factories.
Source: Kanagawa Prefecture, *Kehin-kôgyô-chitai Chôsa-hôkokushyo,—Sangyô-rôdô-hen Kakuron* (Report on the Survey of the Tokyo-Yokohama Industrial District,—Further Descriptions on Industrial Labor), March, 1954.
Note: Large and small factories are defined as those with more than, or less than, one hundred employees, respectively.

ment in small enterprises get it through the personal help of relatives or friends. Taking these into account, Fig. 1 describes the labor market of large and small-medium enterprises. Although it may be too simplistic it seems to explain the structure of the Japanese labor market clearly. Once the large firm employs new graduates and the latter enter the large firm, the practice of so-called "life-time commitment" is enforced on them, and their wages increase, like a sliding scale, in accordance with an increase in the length of their services. Of course, the so-called "Rinjiko" (temporarily employed) come in and out from the backdoor of large firms, and their wages are, in most cases, tremendously low, say, half of the regular worker's wage. Moreover, they are employed under the contract that they can be laid off at any time whenever the employer so desires. In the past, the "Rinjiko" increased with the upswing of the business cycle and decreased sharply with the downswing of the business cycle, and as a tendency it is decreasing in accordance with the recent intensification of labor shortage. However, such a mobility of the "Rinjiko" between the small-medium enterprise and the large enterprise labor markets has never played an equilibrating function of wages in the two labor markets. In addition,

315

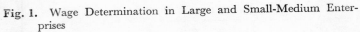

Fig. 1. Wage Determination in Large and Small-Medium Enterprises

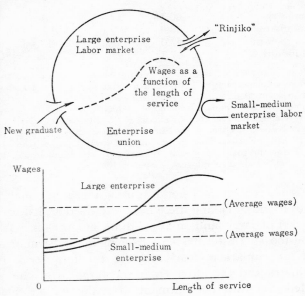

strong "enterprise unions" (enterprise-based, not organized along craft or occupational lines)have acted as ramparts between the two labor markets, consequently this possible route for wage equalization is also canceled out.

In the lower part of Fig. 1, it is shown that the difference in the starting wages between large and small-medium firms is very small, because of the keen competition for new graduates. However, the wage curve as a function of the length of service is much steeper in large firms, while in the labor market for small-medium enterprises, the slope of the wage curve is much more moderate, owing to the pressure of surplus labor and high labor mobility among small-medium enterprises. Therefore, we have a conspicuous differential between the two average wages which

316

are computed respectively as an average of the large enterprise wage curve, on the one hand, and as an average of the small-medium enterprise wage curve, on the other. In this sense, the "life-time commitment" and the "Nenkô-Joretsu" (length of service) wage system have played important roles in explaining the steep interscale wage differential when viewed from the standpoint of Japanese labor market.

In large firms, such systems almost emerged in the Taishô period (1912–1925), but had been absent in the Meiji period (1868–1911). Kazuo Ôkouchi, one of the famous labor economists in Japan, explains as follows: The labor mobility in the Meiji period was actually realized through the medium or agency of senior skilled workers or technicians in the particular firms or regions ... And, the firm did not perform any labor management and planning under its own responsibility but merely manipulated senior ranking bosses or big shots, from behind the curtain, making them a puppet of the firm. Senior ranking bosses pulled out members from other firms or mustered a number of members entrusted by the company to mobilize through the help of their relatives or friends. .... Furthermore, it was up to these senior ranking bosses to decide the criterion and the method of calculation of wage payments among workers as these jobs were almost entrusted to them by the company. In other words, it was this kind of worker-bosses who performed in a very naive way the wage management, which at present is conducted by the enterprisers; and the same kind of worker-bosses also carried out the job of discharging employees, once the company decided to do so.[1]

However, from the end of the Taishô period, big corporations were obliged to rationalize their business management in a scientific way by themselves, and to establish the organs which functioned effectively, such as the labor management section, the personnel section, the wage section, the welfare section, etc.

---

1) Kazuo Ôkouchi, ed., *Nihon no Keiei to Rôdô*, I (Management and Labor in Japan), (Tokyo, Yûhikaku, 1961), pp. 12–13.

The rational and scientific method of labor management had to prevail in place of the traditional labor management based on paternalism or the status hierarchy.[2] According to Ôkouchi, the practice of having a long apprenticeship training, given by labor bosses to employees, began to retreat, and in its place, training programs to produce skilled workers and technicians ca ne to the fore in various corporations for graduates from all three levels of school — primary, middle, and high schools. Thus, the problem of how to foster technicians and skilled workers, the shortage of which was intensified by the development of modern enterprises, was coped by the systems of "life-time commitment" and the "length of service" wage payment.

Some raised a somewhat different view to the emergence of the above employment and wage-payment systems. Takafusa Nakamura,[3] for instance, laid emphasis on the rise of heavy industry from around World War I. As a result, he argued that, each corporation in heavy industry felt an urgent need for skilled labor, which accelerated the adoption of the "life-time commitment" system together with the wage-payment policy based on the principle of "length of service." Each corporation did this in order to ensure itself a steady supply of skilled labor. Since there was a relative surplus of unskilled labor — typical example being the female workers in the cotton spinning industry — wages for unskilled labor tended to decline during the long recession in the years 1920–1931. During this time, even whole-sale prices fell by one half, but the wages for skilled labor showed an extraordinary rigidity due to the adoption of the new systems mentioned above. Consequently, we see a widening tendency of skill differential in wages, and this was reflected not only in the interscale wage differential but also in the wage difference between heavy and light industries. Although Nakamura's speculation seems to be interesting and seems to have some

---

2) *Op. cit.*, p. 14.

3) M. Shinohara and N. Funabashi, ed., *Nihongata Chingin-Kôzô no Kenkyû* (Studies in the Japanese Pattern Wage Structure), (Tokyo, Rôdôhôgaku Kenkyûsho), p. 52.

validity, his hypothesis might not be able to explain why the interscale wage differential was enlarged even within light industry (typically, textiles) too.

At any rate, the labor market approach for explaining the emergence of the sharp wage differential seems to be very effective and important, and we cannot neglect this point here.

Although the following is a digression, it may be of interest here. It concerns the very famous hypothesis of Alexander Gerschenkron[4] that a relatively underdeveloped country could develop rapidly if it could import foreign technology from advanced countries. In this case, the foreign technology inclines to be capital-intensive, so at first sight it does not seem to be profitable for an underdeveloped country to adopt it, because it is more advantageous to have the utilization of cheap labor and the labor-intensive production than to have the capital-intensive production which entails an immense capital cost. However, Gerschenkron noticed a difficulty in forming modern industrial labor which would rather see its relative wages raised. Therefore, he maintains that even if an under-developed country is characterized by its surplus labor, the combination of having a relatively high wage system for industrial labor and of having the capital intensive technique introduced as a "big push" will be useful in enhancing the level of an underdeveloped economy and in accelerating the industrialization of such an economy.

Gerschenkron's hypothesis concerning the utilization of imported technology is very persuasive. However, his another hypothesis concerning the high wage cost for industrial labor does not seem to be applicable to Japanese case. Therefore, Henry Rosovsky[5] put forth his hypothesis. Rosovsky argued, that the labor management of the Japanese pattern pertaining to the "life-time commitment" and the "length of service" wage-

---

4) Alexander Gerschenkron, *Economic Backwardness in Historical Perspective*, (Harvard University Press, 1962), Chapter 1.

5) Henry Rosovsky, *Capital Formation in Japan*, 1868–1940, (Glenco, 1961), Chapter 4.

payment systems was a very smart device, because it enabled to form modern industrial labor inexpensively. In this respect, we can observe in Rosovsky's viewpoint a peculiarly Japanese-type responsiveness, which is quite different from the formulation made by Gerschenkron.

Rosovsky's evaluation and interpretation stop here. However, if his evaluation, that the "life-time commitment" and the "length of service" wage-payment systems are very low-priced and inge-nious devices, is correct, we can further assume that the inex-pensive industrial labor is tied up with imported technology through the establishment of such a peculiar pattern of labor management. The combination of inexpensive industrial labor and imported technology of high level has brought about two consequences: 1) It has made it possible to produce relatively inexpensive commodities as compared with other countries and has accelerated the expansion of the export industry, particularly, light industry in the prewar period. 2) The introduction of imported technology and the capital-intensive production method tended to create the polarization of large and small-medium firms in the domestic economy. Naturally, industrial labor in large enterprises could be brought forth more cheaply than in other underdeveloped countries. However, the productivity and, hence, wage levels in large firms were obliged to be raised far in excess of those in small-medium firms, which necessitated the formation of the dual economy. If this line of explanation is correct, the "life-time commitment" and the "length of service" wage-payment systems have not only enlarged the interscale differential of wages — by carrying in effect the steeper wage curve of large firms than that of small firms — but it has also contributed in some degree towards the combination of high-level technology and low wages, thus, creating the dual structure in manufacturing sector.

We now move on to the analysis of another hypothesis in relation to capital market.

320

4. Capital Concentration Hypothesis

If the introduction of capital-intensive technology in less-developed economies has brought about a dualistic or multi-layer differential in wages in the manufacturing sector, then the capital-concentration hypothesis to be discussed here seems to become very important. This is particularly important, when we take into account the fact that the sharp interscale wage differential came about only after World War I — it had not existed before in Japan — and also the fact that we have similarly tilting wage differentials in underdeveloped countries only, probably, in the postwar period, when the injection of foreign aids brought about large enterprises in the domestic economies.

The implication of the capital-concentration hypothesis become clear when we pursue the following line of logic: Steep interscale wage differential may come into effect by the interscale differential of value added per employee and the latter will, in turn, depend upon the fact that the capital intensity (capital-labor ratio) becomes progressively higher from the small-size up to the large-size establishments. As a simple explanation of production function any textbook of economics tells us, that if the output is a function of capital and labor, then the output per man would be a function of the capital-labor ratio. Therefore, from the interscale differences of productivity, we may infer that the slopes of capital-labor ratio varies among scales of establishments. Thus the steeply sloped capital intensity among different-size establishments may be one of the important causes explaining the interscale productivity differential.

The problem is that, if the interscale productivity differential in Japan is far steeply sloped than it is in advanced countries, we may expect that the same relationship will also hold true as regards differences in capital-labor ratio among scales of establishments. If this is correct, we may also guess that the interscale capital-intensity differential which is more steeply tilted, is

321

probably much more dependent upon the allocation of capital, which is mostly concentrated in large establishments. The capital-concentration hypothesis comes to the fore through such a line of reasoning. It is true that the Japanese interscale value added per employee is more steeply sloped than it is in advanced countries, but an international comparison of capital-labor ratio is difficult, because the statistics on capital is book-valued, and the basis of valuation may differ from country to country. In postwar Japan, it is well known that the revaluation of fixed assets was done three times, in 1950, 1951, and 1953, but although large enterprises revalued their assets up to the limit, many of the small-medium enterprises failed either to do so or left their assets undervalued. However, we may safely speculate that capital concentration in relatively larger firms can be expected to be at the top in the following chain of causations: capital concentration → differential in capital intensity → productivity difference → wage differential.

In a country such as Japan, which started late in the arena of industrialization but has attempted to catch up with the level of advanced countries, it would be unavoidable to some extent to have, in one extreme of the economy, a big business sector highly modernized by the introduction of top-level technique of production, and, in another extreme, a vast number of medium and small enterprises which have also expanded, so far, but with considerable lag and delay. Moreover, since the potential for a high rate of growth in Japan is tremendous, we have always had a situation in which there was an abundance of labor force but a capital shortage. If the big business sector tries to introduce new techniques and raise the level of investment rapidly, it is quite natural that the investment concentrates in one sector of the economy while there arises a capital shortage in other sectors. Consequently the tilting of capital intensity between big business and small-medium enterprises in Japan would be sharper than it would be in other advanced economies. The affiliation of city banks and big business, the priority allocation of state funds

322

to big business, etc., have enhanced this tendency. Such is the background of the capital-concentration hypothesis which helps us in the interpretation of the Japanese dual economy, and the Gerschenkron's hypothesis discussed earlier can be quite interestingly synthesized in our exposition on the historical formation of the dualistic economic structure of Japan even in the manufacturing sector.

The labor-market hypothesis was applied very deftly in the historical explanation of the sharp wage differential — which emerged and was enlarged in the 1920's — and succeeded in explaining why the wage differential widened. How about the historical applicability and validity of the capital-concentration hypothesis? In the 1920's there seemed to have been no positive concentration of capital conjunct with the rapid investment expansion, because the period was just a long, continued process of depression, accompanied time and again by financial crises. Moreover, during this period, a lot of local banks or small financial institutions were bankrupt. The total number of city banks in Japan fell to one-third, from 2069 in 1919 to 663 in 1932, owing to their bankruptcy or amalgamation with larger banks. Since local banks or small financial institutions were, by and large, specialized in financing small-medium enterprises, their bankruptcy meant a terrible blow to the small-medium enterprises. In this sense, on the one hand, the fund directed towards small-medium enterprises was greatly reduced not only in its absolute magnitude but also in its relative proportion. On the other hand, in the 1920's, the amalgamation of industrial corporations began. The rationalization went, by laying off surplus employment and introducing new equipments, and cartelization of firms proceeded. Since there was a great reduction in loans made by small financial institutions to small-medium firms, funds tended to concentrate to big banks, and this probably contributed much towards accelerating the *relative* concentration of investment in larger enterprises. This is an aspect of the formation of the dual economic structure of the manufacturing

323

sector in the 1920's, from the viewpoint of capital concentration, which accounts in some degree for the widening of wage differential in this period.

The term dual economy means: the coexistence of modern large enterprises, which are equipped with high-level techniques, and smaller enterprises, including handicrafts, little business, small and medium size enterprises. The latter are a mixture of a variety of firms — the traditional and the less modernized, the small and the medium, those "to be disorganized" and those "to be developed into larger size," etc. The problem is that if the big-enterprise sector still occupies a very small share in the national economy as a whole, then the term, "dual economy," may not be adequate. However, once the big-enterprise sector comes to share a considerably high proportion, we see the establishment of two extremes, the big and small enterprises, and their polarization. In this case, since each of both sectors occupies a high proportion, the word "dual" economy will be worth while using in its true sense. In an economy which is dominated by the small enterprise sector and in which the big enterprises constitute only a small island in the ocean, so to say, the use of the word "dual economy" may not be permitted. The Japanese economy, which is at present polarized to the two extremes, each proportion being very high, belongs to the very few of such economies worthy of the title, "dual economy." If the big-and-small enterprise sectors are polarized, we may naturally have intermediate-size firms, which are distributed continually between the biggest and the smallest firms. One may call this the "differential employment structure," as Professor K. Ohkawa did,[6] or the "multi-layer structure," but we shall use the term "dual structure" here, since this particular concept is always used as the ideal type, and the word "dual economy" is useful in depicting such a polarization each of which has a high proportion.

---

6) Kazushi Ohkawa, "The Differential Employment Structure in Japan," *Annals of the Hitotsubashi Academy*, April, 1959.

We have Table 8 as an illustration of wages, productivity, capital intensity, etc., classified by the size of firms. This is based on the detailed statistics of the small-medium enterprises which were surveyed in 1957, on the firm-basis (not the establishment-basis); the *Comprehensive Basic Survey of the Small-Medium Enterprises*, 1957 (Small-Medium Enterprises Agency). The valuation of assets was standardized in terms of the valuation used for tax purposes. This is not a book-value, and also, not a replacement cost. However, it shows, in a satisfactory way, the rising tendency of capital intensity and capital coefficient, as

Table 8. Capital Intensity, Capital Coefficient, Share of Wages and Salaries in Value Added by Size of Manufacturing Firms ——1957——

Size of firms (employees)	Number of firms	Value added per man	Capital intensity	Capital-value added ratio	Wages per man	Wages and salaries value added
		1,000 yen	1,000 yen		1,000 yen	%
1–9	300,374	186	69	0.371	114	34.6
10–29	77,644	289	78	0.270	136	44.5
30–49	13,332	348	91	0.261	146	42.1
50–99	8,460	420	120	0.285	157	38.1
100–199	3,146	492	166	0.337	172	35.7
200–299	981	564	209	0.371	187	33.6
300–499	645	696	309	0.445	205	29.9
500–999	441	780	408	0.523	230	29.6
1,000–1,999	222	922	589	0.639	259	28.7
2,000–4,999	135	1,078	687	0.669	301	28.3
5,000–9,999	46	866	558	0.729	287	37.8
10,000 and over	28	897	651	0.727	329	37.1
Total	405,424	516	289	0.560	194	34.4

Source: Recompiled from the original data of the *Chûshô-kigyô Sôgô Kihon-Chôsa* (Comprehensive Basic Survey of Small-Medium Enterprises), 1957. Quoted from Economic Planning Agency, Economic Research Institute, *Shihonkôzô to Kigyô-kan Kakusa* (Capital Structure and Interfirm Differential), Tokyo, Ministry of Finance, Printing Office, Study Series 6, 1960, p. 71. Incidentally, Kenichi Miyazawa headed the project of completing this book.

the scale of firms increases, and the wage differential which is positively correlated with the capital intensity. The following numerical relationships were obtained:

$$O/L = 746.8 \log K/L - 1,150, \qquad R = 0.987,$$
$$W/L = 0.2885 \, K/L + 115, \qquad R = 0.976,$$

O/L denotes the valued-added per man, W/L the wages and salaries per man, and K/L the capital per man (capital intensity).

A similar result regarding prewar manufacturing and commerce was obtained by Mataji Umemura.[7] Utilizing the *Kôgyô Chôsa-hyô* (Survey of Manufactures) of Tokyo city, Yokohama city, Nagoya city, Kobe city, Osaka city, and Osaka prefecture in 1932, he made clear the sharp differentials which have been existing in the wages, the value added per man, the capital intensity, and the capital coefficient. In view of the fact that in 1909 and 1914 we saw no such clear interscale differential in productivity and wages, the downward-sloping curve of capital intensity seems to have been intensified in the 1920's.

5. Hypothesis Relating to the Product Market

Since we have explained the roles of the labor and capital markets in the formation of the striking wage differential, we have to move on to discuss another important factor of the wage differential, the product market. Actually, we would like to take up in this section the following two problems which are related to each other. 1) The prices of commodities produced by large enterprises are apt to be relatively more rigid than those produced by small enterprises. In general, this is due to the fact that oligopoly prices have a higher rigidity while competitive prices are more flexible. In the long price-fall process in the 1920's, the prices of commodities produced by small enterprises were much more downward-flexible than those

---

7) Mataji Umemura, *Chigin Koyô-Nôgyô*, (Wages, Employment and Agriculture), (Tokyo, Taimeidô, 1961), p. 209.

produced by large enterprises, and the price dispersion between them could be expected to have increased. This widening price dispersion would naturally have been absorbed in the increasing wage differential between large and small firms. Of course, we do not have enough statistical data to explain the changes in the price relationship, classified by large and small enterprises in this period, but in such a long continued depression, in which the wholesale prices fell 50% for ten years, we may expect the occurrence of the widening price dispersion and the consequent aggravation of the wage differential. 2) The second problem is closely related to the first. From postwar experiences, we may easily infer that in recessions the processing fee for the subcontracting of small-medium enterprises always tends to decline very sharply, e.g., the processing fee for fountain pens dropped to almost one-half in 1957–58, and the processing fee in acetate and nylon wearing plants, which were subcontracted to a big textile corporation, declined almost to one-third of its earlier fee in January, 1957–April, 1958, as is indicated in Tables 9 and 10. Since we had such events even in the postwar period, we may be safe in assuming that it prevailed also in the prewar period, particularly in the 1920's.

The so-called "small-medium industry problem" came to the fore in the 1920's for two reasons. First, in the Meiji period, people were only conscious of the confrontation of large enterprises implanted from abroad with small enterprises which were mostly of indigenous character, but in the Taishô period and thereafter not only small enterprises but also medium-size enterprises which had evolved from small enterprises became objectives of exploitation by large enterprises through the development of subcontracting. Thus, in the Taishô period, the new concept of the "small-medium" industry emerged, as different from the "small industry" of the Meiji period.

Since the core of the so-called "small-medium industry problem" was the exploitation by large corporations through the subcontracting system which became an object of heated discussion

Table 9. Examples of the Declining Processing Fees in Weaving Subcontractors

		Processing fees of weaving	Price of thread	Price of woven fabrics
Acetate	1957, Jan. 1	2,000 yen	5,000 yen	7,000 yen
woven fabrics	1957, July 1	1,200	4,500	5,700
(50 yards, 1 unit)	1958, April 1	700	4,500	5,200
Nylon	1957, Jan. 1	3,000	5,000	8,000
woven fabrics	1957, July 1	1,500	4,500	6,000
(50 yards, 1 unit)	1958, April 1	1,000	4,500	5,500

Note: This is an example of a small weaving factory with about 50 employees in Fukui Prefecture under the subcontract of a big enterprise, which was surveyed by the writer himself. Quoted from M. Shinohara, ed., *Sangyô Kôzô* (Industrial Structure), (Tokyo, Shunjûsha, 1959), p. 113.

Table 10. Two Examples of Processing Fees for Fountain Pens for Exports and Mufflers

A. Fountain pens for exports			B. Processing fees for mufflers		
	1957	1958		Ordinary mufflers	Figured mufflers
Cost of parts	255 yen	155 yen	1949	35 yen	55 yen
Processing fees	125	65	1951	18	23
Appurtenances &	145	115	1952	16	20
overhead costs			1955	14	17
Total	525	295	1958	12	15
Around Osaka			Kiryû district		

Sources: A. Chûshô-kigyô Chôsakai, (Japan Small Busisnes Research Institute), *Chûshô-kigyô Kenkyû* (Studies of Small-Medium Enterprises), Vol. IV, *Yushutsu Chûshô-kigyô no Keizaikôzô* (Economic Structure of Small-Medium Export Industries) (Tokyo, Oriental Economist, 1962), p. 161.

B. M. Kajinishi, H. Iwao, Y. Kobayashi and T. Itô, ed., *Kôza Chûshô-kigyô* (Courses: Small-Medium Enterprises), Vol. II, *Dokusen Shihon to Chûsho-kigyô* (Monopoly Capital and Small-Medium Enterprises), (Tokyo, Yûhikaku, 1960), p. 190.

just in the midst of the 1920's we may guess how conspicuous the exploitation of large corporations was in this period. We have a lot of economists devoting themselves to a study of small-medium industry in Japan, but almost all of them assume that the exploitation was the core of the small-medium industry problem.

Such being the case, the behavior of the product market, particularly its price dispersion can be assumed to have played a great role in enlarging the interscale wage differential from the end of World War I to the Great Depression of the 1930's.

Thus, the labor economists were mostly interested in the institutional peculiarity of labor market, and the small-business economists, by and large, paid great attention to the factor of exploitation through the subcontracting system. Both aspects are true, and cannot be neglected in understanding the formation of Japan's extraordinary wage differential, as compared with advanced countries, but we have raised here an additive complementary hypothesis on the capital concentration to larger firms. It is our assertion that the three pillars — the labor market, the product market, and the capital market — are all indispensable in the full understanding of the dualistic aspect of the Japanese economy. However, we are tempted to lay a slightly greater emphasis on the hypothesis of capital concentration, because without this we cannot have in mind the polarization of the large and the small enterprise sectors, each with predominant proportion in the national economy as a whole. And, without relying on this hypothesis, we may not be able to see how the dualistic structure had to come about as an inevitable consequence of the catching-up process of a rapidly developing economy.

6. Criticism and Rejoinders

Our analysis has merits in that it is realistic and comprehensive but from a theoretical viewpoint it is subject to a few criticisms.

Although in our capital-concentration hypothesis the logic of causation starts from capital concentration to larger firms, and the establishment of the sloping capital intensity by size of firms through the productivity differential down to the wage differential, a person with a textbook knowledge in the micro-economics may raise a fundamental doubt with respect to such a reasoning. What is decided or given in the market first is the wage rate, interest rate and prices of products, and after that the entrepreneur is supposed to try to maximize his profit by choosing the best combination of capital and labor. Therefore, in the static theory, the direction of causation does not begin from capital concentration or tilting of capital-labor ratios among different size firms, but it is completely reversed. If this is correct, one may be naturally skeptical about our hypothesis.

If we assume that the entrepreneur will behave perfectly in a passive way to a set of commodity and factor prices determined in the markets, this doubt is absolutely right. However, the question is whether or not the actual entrepreneur behaves along the textbook formulation described in a very static world. Although in the price theory, it is often assumed that the choice of technique or the combination of factors of production is dependent, passively, upon the relative prices of factors *at a point of time*, actually the purchased machinery or structures will continue to be employed over a period of time, e.g., ten or fifteen years. Consequently, what should be taken into account is not the present factor-price structure, but the present as well as the future rates of interest and the expected real average wage rates for the coming, say, fifteen years. In such a dynamic economy as Japan, the real wage rate can easily double during the same period. We do not deny the validity of the static theory within the confines of many assumptions and regard it as a good excise of economic logic and also as a useful pedagogic device. However, in the actual world, the entrepreneur must choose a set of techinques, taking into consideration, of course, the real wage rate expected to prevail fifteen years hence. In this sense, the prevalent empirical derivations of the so-called CES production function, which is essentially based upon the static assumptions of profit maximization, seem very often neglectful of the gap existing between the static theory and the dynamic real world. The CES function is outside the scope of our present discussion, but if one sets up an empirical function where the output per man is a linear function of the real wage rate at the present time, this also involves the same misapplication of the static tools of analysis to the real world. The fixed investment of large enterprises in a highly dynamic economy makes due allowances for the future increase in real wages, the expansion of domestic and foreign mearkts, and the strategy for enlarging their market shares. Therefore, the usual assumption of the passive choice of technique, dependent on the present prices, wage rate, and interest rate is in reverse order of the actual causation. In the dynamic world, the entrepreneur is inclined towards introducing top-level technology or equipment, sometimes disregarding the present factor prices. In this sense, he would even try to introduce the first-class technology, if he has adequate provision of funds. Top-level technique is, first, given from outside. Once this is given, it is beyond doubt that the capital intensity in large enterprises will indicate a marked difference as compared with that in smaller enterprises.

The second criticism was raised by Mitsuharu Itô.[8] Let us summarize the essence of his argument.

Let us assume that the production functions for three industries (treating them as if they were integrated in one firm respectively) are of shapes $(f_1 f_1, f_2 f_2,$ and $f_3 f_3)$ as indicated in Fig. 2. In this case, the production function is designated by the following formula

$$Y/N = f(K/N)$$

8) Mitsuharu Itô, "Nijûkôzô-ron no Tembô to Hansei" (Review and Retrospection of Theories of the Dual Structure), in Kawaguchi, Shinohara, Nagasu, Miyazawa and Itô, *Nihon Keizai no Kisokôzô* (Underlying Structure of the Japanese Economy), Symposium, (Tokyo, Shunjûsha, 1962).

Fig. 2. Production Function and Wages

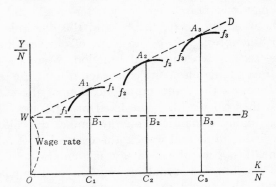

where Y/N (the value added per man) is a function of K/N (the capital-labor ratio or the capital intensity). Each industry will try to choose a technique or capital intensity which will yield the maximum rate of profit, by the adaptation to the wage rate wO given in common to each industry. The chosen points, A_1, A_2, and A_3, are given by the tangent points between the curves ff's of the production functions and the given straight line wD drawn from the point of the wage rate w; therefore, OC_1, OC_2, and OC_3, are the selected capital intensities for the three industries. For instance, in the industry 1, the capital intensity OC_1 is employed, but, since the wage rate is B_1C_1 and the value added per man is A_1C_1, A_1B_1 stands for the profit per man. If the profit per man (A_1B_1) is divided by the capital per man (wB_1), we have the profit rate which is represented in Fig. 2 by the slope of wA_1 itself.

However, in Fig. 1, the wage rates as well as the profit rates are equalized among the three industries. In other words, the wage rate wO is common to each of the three industries, and wD is tangential to any of the production functions, f_1f_1, f_2f_2, and f_3f_3. Nevertheless, there are considerable differences in the capital intensity, and $OC_1 < OC_2 < OC_3$ prevails. We see differences among different-size firms not only in the capital intensity, but also in the value added per man. Moreover, despite the marked difference in the value added per man (A_1C_1, A_2C_2, and A_3C_3), we see that this difference is not reflected in the wage differential. This prevails even under the assumption of the equalized profit rate among industries. Itô presumes that this model can be a decisive material as a criticism for the capital-concentration hypothesis, for even if the sharp interscale differential emerges in the caital intensity and productivity through capital concentration to big business, the above model illustrates that it will not necessarily be reflected in the wage differential. Furthermore, this relation holds true even as an equilibrium point.

His second point of criticism is as follows. Although productivity has been measured so far in terms of value added, what we are concerned with is the physical productivity, because the production function denotes essentially a technological relationship. Let us assume that in the x industry technological progress occurs and the production function is shifted to $f_x f_x$, as indicated in Fig. 3. In this case, the industry may have a higher profit rate and wage rate owing to its higher productivity. However, the price of x commodity may fall just in an inverse proportion with the rise of the physical productivity in the competitive economy, so as to bring about a situation in which the wage rate as well as the profit rate are equalized among industries. If such a classical price adjustment works, a temporary rise in the physical productivity due to an increase in the capital intensity in the x industry will be eventually removed by price decline of equal magnitude. In other words, its value-added per man will be lowered, until the profit rates are equalized among industries. If $f_x f_x$ fell to $f_x'' f_x''$, then we have an identical chart as Fig. 2.

Itô, therefore lays great stress on the role of the product market, because his theoretical model seems to demonstrate very cogently that the oligopolistic price rigidity which prevents the full working

Fig. 3. Productivity, Prices and Production Functions

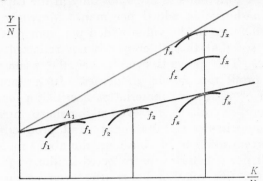

of the classical price adjustment plays an indispensable role in widening the wage differential very abnormally. If we neglect the oligopolistic factor in the product market, the causal chain of the interscale differentials in capital intensity, physical productivity, and wage rate cannot help but be cut off midway, and the capital-concentration hypothesis will cease to operate.

Itô's criticism of laying greater stress on the role of oligopolistic pricing in the dual economy does not stop here and goes into few other points. However, since the above two seem to be most important, we shall not take up the rest of his criticisms here. His important contribution lies in pointing out that the relation between physical-productivity difference and wage differential is not as directly connected as it appears to be, and his assertion was that the role of the product market is more important than those of the capital and labor markets.

We are now in a position to answer each of his criticisms. We will start from his second critisicm. Itô emphasizes the role of the big firms' oligopolistic pricing and the price rigidity. However, even when the physical-productivity differential is passed on completely to the net value productivity differential through price rigidity, it does not necessarily happen that the latter will automatically induce a spread also of the wage differential. Just in the same way as Itô stresses in the product market, if perfect competition and high labor mobility prevail in the labor market, the wage rates will be equalized among industries, notwithstanding the existence of oligopolistic pricing in the product market. This is the reason why Naomichi Funabashi,[9] insisted that what is really responsible for the wage differential by size of firms is the imperfection of the labor market, and neither the capital concentration nor the oligopolistic pricing by big corporations is responsible for this. Itô, however, exaggerates the importance of the oligopolistic pricing, anticipating, although unconsciously, the unconditional transmission of the value-added-per-man difference to the wage differential. However, it is logically feasible that there is no wage differential despite the tilting differential of value-added-per-man caused by the inflexible oligopolistic prices. In such a case of competitive labor market, even Itô's point loses its validity.

Consequently, even when competitive equilibrium prices are assumed to be established in the product market, the widening gap in the physical-productivity differential will not be a sufficient condition for the prevalence of the wage differential. And, once the perfect competition and high labor mobility are assumed in the labor market, however large the value-added-per-man differential might be, it cannot be transmitted down to the wage differential. However, only if we assume the imperfection of the product market as well as labor market, the sharp differential in the physical productivity can be reflected in the corresponding wage differential. If this point is stressed too much as Itô does, the labor economists would say that they are also entitled to emphasize, in a strategic and independent way, the imperfection of labor market. Labor economists would maintain that what is only relevant is an imperfection in the labor market.

9) M. Shinohara and N. Funabashi, ed., *Nihongata Chingin-kôzô no Kenkyû* (Studies in the Japanese Pattern Wage Structure), (Tokyo, Rôdôhôgaku Kenkyûsho), pp. 47–51

But this point, when emphasized, will be damaging to Itô's hypothesis mentioned above.

However, we are not going to dodge the main question by changing the subject. What was made clear was that if we become overly worried about the perfection or imperfection of the individual market, the broad comprehensive analysis of the dual structure from a nation-wide angle will retreat to the background, and instead a partial or "truncated way" approach will again come to the fore. As Professor Tokutarô Yamanaka has once pointed out in relation to the studies of small-medium industry in Japan, we should not be biased toward an overly "truncated" approach. To go back to it is nothing but a retreat to a poor, partial analysis.

If so, can we find a proper way to prevent any retreat toward a partial analysis, and at the same time still maintain an exact formal logic? Probably, when Itô gives prominence to the co-existence of oligopolistic and competitive prices in the product market, he might or should anticipate the existence of some imperfection in the labor market. And only when this idea is postulated can we say that the enlarged physical-productivity differential is reflected upon the greater wage differential. In a similar way, if the imperfection in the product market can be assumed to be given, as it is in the real world, the capital concentration in bigger corporations and the consequent extension of capital-intensity differential will be able to be embodied in the enlarged interscale difference in the value added per man. Consequently, if we can assume, as given, both the imperfection of the product and labor markets at a level which prevails in the actual world, then we can easily say that the more the capital is concentrated in bigger firms, the more the wage differential will be enlarged as a necessary consequence of a causal process set forth already. The partial, static analysis seems to be correct at first sight, but it may run a risk of being involved in a narrow "truncated" approach, in spite of the fact that the problem of the dual economy is essentially of a nation-wide, inter-related

Fig. 4. Capital Concentration and Interscale Wage Differential

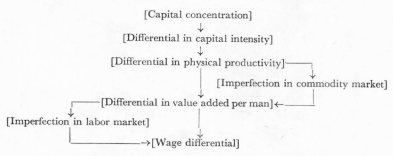

nature. Once the imperfection of the product and labor markets are assumed as given, the polarization of investment will have a strong influence upon the widening wage structure. If we assume that the degree of imperfection of the product and labor markets is the same in countries *A* and *B*, then *A*'s wage differential will be more steeply sloped than *B*'s, when investment is much more concentrated in bigger enterprises in *A* than it is in *B*.

If we stick to the static, partial approach which limits our scope of observation to a particular market and which only presumes entrepreneurial behaviors of a very passive nature, we may not be able to grasp their highly dynamic activities and the consequential divergence of productivities and wages between the larger and the smaller enterprise sectors. Actually, their activities are never adaptations to the existing interest rate, wage rates, and commodity prices.

We shall now move on to Itô's first criticism, in which he has theoretically pointed out that some perennial differences in the capital intensity and the value-added-per-man among different-size firms can coexist with the profit rate and the wage rate both of which are perfectly equalized among different firms. From such a theorizing, he went on to say that the capital-intensity differential and the consequent value-added-per-man

337

Fig. 5. An Alternative Case with Wage Differential

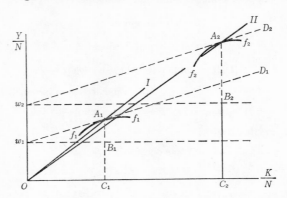

differential due to capital concentration will not necessarily bring about the differential in wage rates.

Insofar as we discuss this problem within his theoretical framework, he is absolutely correct. However, we can set up another model in which the capital intensity and the value-added-per-man differentials differ among different-size firms, having, however, the profit rate equalized, and the wage rate higher in the firm of higher capital intensity and productivity. Fig. 4 illustrates this case.

In Fig. 5, the profit rate is the same in industry 1 and 2, because w_1D_1 and w_2D_2 are mutually parallel, and $\dfrac{A_1B_1}{w_1B_1}$ and $\dfrac{A_2B_2}{w_2B_2}$ are equal. However, since $OC_2 > OC_1$, the capital intensity in industry 2 is higher. Since $A_2C_2 > A_1C_1$, the value added per man is also higher in industry 2. The capital-output ratio is measured by $\dfrac{K}{N} \Big/ \dfrac{Y}{N}$, so the steeper slope of I than II means a lower capital-output ratio. In this sense, industry 2 has a higher capital-output ratio. The wage rate is higher in industry 2, for w_2O is higher than w_1O. In this model, we need not worry about a possibility that a higher capital intensity will not entail a higher wage rate. Therefore, Itô seems to point out only one possibility and does not give any proof that in equilibrium a higher capital intensity will always coexist with the same wage rate as in other industries which have a lower capital intensity. We may formally prefer either Fig. 2 or Fig. 5. However, we cannot but imagine that the case of Fig. 5 is much closer to the reality.

Returning again to Itô's second criticism, we have to make further additions. If Itô presumes that, in order to do away with an abnormal wage differential, a sufficient decline in the relative prices of the commodities must occur in the industry in which the comparative physical productivity manifested a marked increase, something very unrealistic seems to be implied in the policy recommendation stemming from his hypothesis. He seems to have set up unconsciously a reference criterion that a relative price decline in an inverse direction with the relative physical-productivity increase is required in order to evade the occurrence of the sharp wage differential, or that if the sharp wage differential already prevails, an important remedy for it would be to have a relative price decline in the oligopolistic industry, which is large enough to eliminate the wage differential. However, this criterion is valid only in a closed system. Actually, in an open economy, the price decline cannot be so exorbitant as compared with the prices in advanced industrial countries. Therefore, if we take into account the international price relationship, there would be limit in the relative price decline which will eliminate the wage differential. In other words, Itô's point seems to put too much weight upon a factor which is rather commonly found in most countries and which does not vary greatly from country to country. It would not be smart thing to introduce such a factor common to most countries in order to explain a unique phenomenon, like the wage differential in Japan. If the relative price decline is set up as a policy for eliminating the wage differential this is expecting too much, and it is a rather unrealistic policy.

7. *Agriculture and Labor Market*

As long as the topic we are concerned with is dual economy, we should not miss the problem of agriculture, because Japanese agriculture has long been assumed as a pool of disguised unemployment and a basis of "cheap labor" in general. If so, its analysis is indispensable to the understanding of the dual economy in Japan. Although we have so far discussed the problem of dual economy, it is very evident that a dual economy will not exist in a labor-shortage situation. Japan is now in transition from the labor-surplus to the labor-shortage situation which means Japan is undergoing a fundamental change in her basic structure. In this sense, the question as to whether or not the economy is in the stage of surplus labor becomes a crucial factor for the persistence of the dual structure.

In the process of economic growth, agriculture seems to have played a great role. In such a country, like the United Kingdom, where the proportion of agriculture is extremely reduced, agriculture cannot supply enough labor with relatively low wages for the demand from manufacturing and service industries. Sometimes, this becomes one of the bottlenecks to her economic growth. However, in the economies, endowed with surplus labor, high growth rate is sometimes realized if it has a sufficient propensity to invest and introduce innovation.

In Japan, agriculture has long been considered as an "exploited," and "sacrificed" industry. Of course, it is a relatively declining industry in the sense that its proportion in terms of labor force or output is decreasing, but it has also been recognized as the "sacrificed" industry in the sense that its relative income has long been suppressed and the cheap labor coming forth from agriculture has played an important role in the development of the non-agricultural sectors. It is only due to their low wages that the high growth rate in the manufacturing sector was thought to have become feasible through its high rate of capital accumulation. In this sense, Japan's agriculture has had the characteristics of being exploited by, sacrificed for, and instrumental to the development of the non-agricultural sectors. Whether or not this is true can be a subject of a heated debate, but what is important is to have in mind that such a typical Japanese notion of agriculture was held by many, even by non-Marxian economists, although to a foreigner who is accustomed to the high efficiency of big-scale farming, such a view may appear strange.

At any rate, the proportion of the net supply of labor force from agriculture in the total increase of employment in the non-agricultural sectors in the Meiji and Taishô periods was extremely high. According to the estimate of Mataji Umemura,[10] the ratio was 91.8% in 1875-80, 81.7% in 1895-1900, and 72.5% in 1910-1915. This indicates that agriculture played a very important role as a source of labor supply to the non-agricultural sectors, insofar as the Meiji and Taishô periods are concerned. His estimate has also made clear that the ratio was still 53.4% in 1930-1935. We are not sure about the postwar figure. Since the increase in the labor force employed in the non-agricultural sectors for 1955-1960 was 5.66 million, while the decline in agriculture (including forestry and fishery) was 1.77 million, the ratio of the latter to the former was 31%. However, even when the employed labor force in agriculture does not decrease, the outflow of labor force will still exist. If we can estimate this portion, the proportion of labor supply from the agricultural sector can be expected to be very high even in the postwar period.

In this sense, the labor market in the non-agricultural sectors has been strongly supported by the labor migration from farm villages. Recently, we see an increasing number or proportion of side-work farmers and commuters from farm households. Such a high dependency of the labor market upon agriculture

---

10) Mataji Umemura, "Meiji-nenkan niokeru Jusshitsu Chingin to Rôdô no Kenkyû" (Real Wages and Labor Supply in the Meiji Period), *Shakaikeizaishigaku*, April, 1961.

cannot be ignored in the analysis of Japan's labor market and particularly in the construction of some hypotheses or theories in relation to it. In this sense, we shall take up the famous "Dekasegi-gata Chinrôdô-ron" (a thesis of the household-supplementing type labor migration), presented by Professor Kazuo Ôkouchi.[11]

Ôkouchi suggested that as petty peasants who had been under serfdom, so to say, in the feudal age were thrown into the exchange economy since the Meiji Restoration, they could not but send out household members as factory or mine workers in order to supplement the fall in their farm incomes. If wage labor in Japan was essentially of the "household-supplementing type," then the wages paid to them would, by its very nature, be very low. In the prewar period, the proportion of labor of the textile industry was predominantly large and its female composition of labor, very high. So we can generally presume that the female workers supplied from rural districts were typically of the "household-supplementing type" receiving low wages. This was due to the fact that the supply price for their labor was very low, for the incomes they earned did not have to cover all expenses of farm households and were only supplementary. He did not restrict the concept of the "household-supplementing type" labor only to female labor in the textile industry. Although female labor was dominant in the prewar period, the huge exodus of second and third sons to non-agricultural sectors in conjunction with the development of heavy industries from the 1910's to the 1930's is also included in his concept. Moreover, from 1937 — when the Sino-Japanese Incident occurred — to the present, we had a lot of "semi-farm and semi-manufacturing worker" type farm households, which did not go through the process of emigration. All these are recognized by Ôkouchi as those elements which constitute the "household-supplementing type" labor,

---

11) E.g., Kazuo Ôkouchi, "Nihonteki Rôshikankei no Tokushitsu to sono Hensen", (Peculiarities of the Japanese Employer-Employee Relation and Its Changes), *Nihon Rôdô Kyôkai Zasshi*, April, 1959.

the character of which is, according to him, peculiar to the Japanese economy.

Ôkouchi goes on to discuss that, in a period of depression, the workers return to the farm and in prosperity they go out for work in the factories. Therefore, the farm villages were, so to say, a pool of the disguised unemployment which swelled during depressions and decreased during prosperity. His theory assumes the persistent existence of the reserve army in farm villages, and ignores a possibility that an exodus of farm labor might result in the disintegration of farm villages. In this sense, his theory is in line with the so-called "Kôzaha" Marxian thinking. In other words, the relics of semi-seigniorial relations in rural villages and government regulations for maintaining the pre-capitalistic landownership prevented the complete disintegration of the peasant. Consequently, in Ôkouchi's theoretical framework, he could not but set up a kind of relief valve, the "household-supplementing type" labor, which goes out to other industries during prosperous periods and returns during periods of depression, whereby the rigidity of the institutional structure of villages is maintained and a complete exodus of the farm peasants is prevented. This way of thinking was confronted by another stream of Japanese Marxists, the so-called "Rônôha," which has viewed the disintegration of the peasants and their exodus from their farms as necessary consequences of the permeation of the money economy.

Ôkouchi's thesis is very prominent at least as an expository hypothesis of the prewar Japanese labor market. It is true that the Japanese economy has gradually become heavy industry-oriented, which is why the proportion of the "household-supplementing type" labor, the core of which was the female labor in textile industry, has become gradually reduced as well. However, Ôkouchi's thesis has presented the typical Japanese notion of agriculture and the clear-cut and distinct ideal type of the relationship between the rural village and the labor market in a very interesting and excellent way. Masakichi Namiki[12] raised a point of criticism against Ôkouchi's hypothesis and indicated empirically that there was no cyclical movement in the net supply of labor from agriculture and that the net labor supply from agriculture was relatively constant regardless of the booms and slumps of the business cycle. This entailed some debates between him, and Ryôshin Minami = Akira Ono.[13] But, leaving aside the cyclical variation, it cannot be denied that the prewar farm village had been a constant source of plentiful labor supply needed by the manufacturing industry, etc.

Even in the postwar period, the same phenomenon held true to some extent. In this connection, the *Report on the Survey of the Tokyo-Yokohama Industrial District,* based on a survey conducted in 1951–52 by Kanagawa Prefecture under the guidance of Ôkouchi, Ujihara, and others, is to be noted. From this survey, various interesting conclusions emerge, but we will restrict ourselves to an exposition of only a few points: 1) The proportion of male laborers whose parents' occupation was agriculture was 43.3% in the factories with 5–29 employees, 36.4% in those with 30–99 employees, 38.5% in those with 100–499 employees, and 48.2% in those with 500 employees and over. 2) The summary result of the occupational experiences of male laborers in this district indicates that about half of them had no experience of working in fields other than factories, and a majority of another half had engaged in agriculture. 3) Among factory laborers, there were many from the "semi-farm and semi-manufacturing worker" type households, who had not abandoned agriculture, but who commuted from such households to the factory. 4) Quite a few of the laborers of farm origin still continued to have economic relations with their parents' farm households. 5) Once urban workers were dismissed, retired or taken ill, many of them returned to their parents' farm households.

---

12) See footnote (15)
13) See footnote (17).

Another comprehensive survey was conducted in March, 1953, by Ôkouchi, Ujihara, and others, on the factors governing admission to higher schools and employment opportunities open for new graduates from middle schools in Kanagawa Prefecture.[14] This covered big and medium, commercial and industrial cities and their adjacent rural villages. According to this survey, middle school graduates prefer to go to the manufacturing industry, particularly to big factories. Since the demand for labor in big factories is mainly satisfied by the new graduates in the same districts, the local labor force which flows into the Tokyo-Yokohama district is necessarily absorbed by small factories. In this district, wages at the outset, are relatively high, and their coefficient of variation among factories is low, reflecting the acute demand for labor in the same area. Thus, laborers of farm origin in local areas cannot but be observed into the lowest stratum in any occupation.

Even after the proportion of heavy industry had risen, there still existed a close relation between the rural districts and non-agricultural development with respect to the source of the latter's labor force. However, it may be naturally expected that the role of agriculture in supplying labor would have diminished in a long course of time, particularly during 1955–60 when the extraordinarily rapid economic expansion occurred. The proportion of laborers whose parents belong to agriculture is probably still high, but if we restrict laborers from agriculture to only those who changed their occupations, excluding new graduates, etc., then the proportion would not be so high, as indicated in Table 11. There would be only very few who would have returned to the village in a depression in the postwar period. Rather, it is plausible that they would more likely have changed their jobs from one small factory to another small factory or to small commercial stores when they were dismissed, in view of the higher rates of accession to and separation from jobs in

14) K. Ôkouchi and S. Ujihara, *Rôdôshijô no Kenkyû* (Analysis of the Labor Market), (Tokyo, Tokyo University Press), 1955.

Table 11. The Proportion of Laborers Whose Previous Occupation was Agriculture
——in relation to the already employed——

	Total	Male
1956	8.7%	11.6%
1957	8.2	10.7
1958	5.1	7.0
1959	6.4	8.2
1960	6.7	8.6
1961	7.6	9.7
1962	7.1	8.5
1963	6.8	8.1
1964	3.8	—

Source: Ministry of Labor, *Rôdô Idô Chôsa* (Survey of Occupational Changes of Laboers.)

lower-size establishments. Therefore, it seems to be important to analyze whether or not the new net migration of labor from agriculture has shown a higher amplitude than that from, say, the service industry. If the service industry played a higher role as a cushion for absorbing unemployment than did agriculture, then the Ôkouchi hypothesis of the "household-supplementing type" wage labor should be modified to that extent. However, we lack such an analysis so far.

Although Table 11 indicates the proportion of the "already-employed" (this excludes new graduates) whose previous occupation was agriculture, another statistical source, the Ministry of Education's, *The Basic Survey of Schools*, makes clear the proportion of the new graduates (middle and high schools) who remained and worked in agriculture, as indicated in Table 12. This ratio was 48.5% as concerns the middle school graduates in 1952, but it decreased to 7.4% in 1965. The same ratio for high school graduates declined from 21.3% to 3.6% in the same period.

The concept of the so called "Hojûritsu" (the replenishment ratio) for the male occupancy in agriculture was initiated and computed by Masakichi Namiki.[15] Mataji Umemura, however, computed the same by making use of the aforementioned Ministry of Educations's data (Namiki's data are different) under the assumption that thirty years constitute one generation.[16] His formula was,

$$\begin{bmatrix} \text{Replenishment} \\ \text{ratio} \end{bmatrix} = \begin{bmatrix} \text{New male graduates employed} \\ \text{in agriculture} \end{bmatrix} \div \frac{6 \text{ million households}}{30 \text{ years}}$$

The replenishment ratio, thus computed, declined from 81% in 1953 to 50% in 1959 and down again to 21% in 1965, although it increased to 29% in 1963 temporarily. The replenishment ratio stands for the ratio of *actually* replenished male labor year by year to the *required* number of labor in order to maintain the level of the pool of agricultural labor force constant. In Umemera's case, it was computed in such a way that the denominator signifies the number of *male* labor force to be replenished annually, in order to make feasible the simple reproduction of the normal core of labor force of six million farm households.

If the replenishment ratio is equal to unity, the agricultural labor force can be maintained at a constant level. However, it decreased to 21% in 1965. Once, Namiki pointed out, in view of the decreasing replenishment ratio, that now the land slide is taking place, so to say, in the farm villages, emphasizing that the fundamental transfiguration of agriculture is anticipated to be inevitable. The discussion on this ratio by Namiki is interesting, for this ratio decreases when the growth rate is high and increases when the growth rate is low. Therefore, if the economy grows at a faster rate than before, the replenishment

---

15) Masakichi Namiki, "Sangyô Rôdôsha no Keisei to Nôka-jinkô" (Formation of Industrial Laborers and the Farm Population) in *Nihon Shihonshugi to Nôgyô* (Capitalism and Agriculture in Japan) ed., by S. Tôbata and K. Uno, (Tokyo, Iwanami-shoten, 1959).

16) Mataji Umemura, *Sengo Nihon no Rôdôryoku* (Labor Force in Postwar Japan), (Tokyo, Iwanamishoten, 1964).

Table 12. New Graduates and Agriculture

	New graduates from middle schools employed in			New graduates from high schools employed in		
	Total	Agriculture and fishery	Manu-facturing	Total	Agriculture and fishery	Manu-facturing
	thousand			thousand		
1952	798	48.5%	28.2%	281	21.3%	15.3%
1953	729	36.1	38.1	288	15.5	17.2
1954	613	33.1	41.0	330	15.4	18.6
1955	693	31.9	37.8	341	18.1	21.0
1956	797	26.6	43.3	390	15.9	23.5
1957	865	21.9	50.1	427	12.5	23.7
1958	775	20.0	47.1	447	11.0	24.9
1959	786	17.0	50.4	496	10.1	25.0
1960	684	13.7	59.6	573	8.0	23.8
1961	501	9.9	65.5	612	5.9	23.1
1962	652	9.7	64.4	649	4.6	22.7
1963	764	9.8	60.5	626	4.6	25.1
1964	698	8.4	61.7	557	3.7	36.2
1965	625	7.4	61.9	700	3.6	36.4

Source: Ministry of Education, *Gakkô Kihon Chôsa* (The Basic Survey of Schools).

Note: This table refers to new graduates of *male* as well as *female* pupils employed in two industries, but in the computation of the replenishment ratio made by Umemura, only the number of male pupils are used.

ratio declines rapidly, and the proportion of agricultural labor force will naturally decline. This process of causation reflects mostly the "pull effect" of economic growth in the non-agricultural sectors, and not necessarily the "push effect" from inside agriculture through the innovation of Japanese agriculture.

So far, agriculture has not undergone any fundamental change in the sense of pushing out labor by increasing its productivity through drastic innovation (e.g., the expansion of unit of operation) owing to the still existing abundant labor. However, since labor shortage in the national economy as a whole will be intensified in the future, the mere "pull effect" from outside agriculture will probably be replaced by the "push effect" from within agriculture itself. When such changes occur, the characteristic of the present agriculture as a pool of cheap labor will begin to disappear, and the long, continued dual structure will cease to exist.

If we can speculate in this way, the Japanese notion of agriculture as a sacrificed or exploited industry seems to have been dependent basically upon the labor-surplus situation. If the situation changes to that of labor shortage, the per capita productivity gap between agriculture and non-agricultural sector should naturally be narrowed, and the dualistic gulf between the two sectors would be considerably normalized as we see it in advanced countries. Therefore, although the thesis of the "household-supplementing type" labor emigration may involve somewhat a sweeping generalization, it emphasises essentially the role of agriculture in a labor-surplus economy. In this sense, agriculture plays a very important role in a dualistic economy, not only because it provides a tremendous amount of labor supply for the non-agricultural sectors, but also because it does so with a very low wage rate. Thus, the base wage rate in the wage differential in manufacturing may have a close bearing on the income earned in agriculture, particularly when agriculture is in a labor-surplus condition, and it presents the basis of the dual structure in the national economy as a whole.

8. Service Industry and Labor Market

Professor Ôkouchi's household-supplementing type labor theory involves, as already explained, the hypothesis that the level of the pool of agrarian surplus labor will be reduced in prosperity and raised during depression. Masakichi Namiki presented a criticism that the net outflow of agrarian labor force for 1920–25, 1925–35, and 1935–40 had been almost constant, despite the ups and downs of the business cycle. Ryôshin Minami and Akira

Ono,[17] however, found some waves in the above when they estimated the annual (instead of five-year) figures. But, what is much more important is not the existence or non-existence of the emigration cycles, but, the pertinent question as to which of the amplitudes is larger in terms of the absolute magnitude as concerns the net emigration of agriculture and that of service industry. My guess is, first, that in view of the debate between Namiki, and Minami = Ono, we shall certainly see cycles in each of the outflow and inflow of rural labor force, if we can estimate each of the above figures. Secondly, it seems to be certain that the service industry has also a characteristic of accumulating a surplus labor force during a period of depression, but pours it out in the prosperity phase of the business cycles.

Table 13 indicates changes in the labor force employed within selected industries among the census years and gives us a im-

Table 13. Changes in Labor Force Employed by Industry

——unit: thousand men——

	Increases or decreases				
	1920–30	1930–40	1950–55	1955–60	1960–65
Employed labor force, total	+2,375	+2,890	+3,635	+4,430	+3,938
Agriculture, forestry and fishery	+ 48	− 297	−1,097	−1,875	−2,490
Manufacturing and construction industries	+ 524	+2,144	+1,464	+3,542	+2,632
Wholesale and retail trades	+1,463	− 30	+1,510	+1,447	+1,665
Service industry	+ 527	+ 428	+1,151	+ 754	+1,108

Source: *Census of Population.*
Note: The last, "service industry" is used in a narrower sense, and corresponds to tertiary industry other than wholesale and retail trades, financial institution and real estate trade, transportation, communication, and other public utillities, and public service.

17) R. Minami and A. Ono "Nôkajinkô Idô to Keikihendô tono Kankei nitsuiteno Oboegaki" (A Comment on the Relation of Farm Population Movement and Business Fluctuations) and M. Namiki's, Rejoinder, *Rironkeizaigaku*, September, 1963.

pression of the role of service industry as being a cushion for the business cycle. On the one hand, for the period 1920–30, when prices were falling almost continually af.er World War I, the increase in the labor force employed in the manufacturing and construction industries was only 524 thousands (only 22% of that in all industries). Among them about half were absorbed by the construction activity which was very active even during the long period of depression. Therefore, the increase in labor force employed in manufacturing was only 11% of the total increase. On the other hand, the number of increase in labor force employed in the wholesale and retail trades amounted to 1,464 thousands (62% of the total increase), and the same in the service industry was 527 thousands (22%), so the increase in the wholesale and retail trades plus the service industry occupies 84% of the total increase. This means that the two tertiary industries could absorb 84% of the total increase in employed labor force! This is extremely important and worthy of consideration in that even during the long depression years of the 1920's, more than 80% of the total increase in employed labor force was absorbed by the tertiary industry. Naturally, as a trend in economic growth, the proportion of labor force working in the tertiary industry tends to increase. However, the tendency in the 1920's was much more of a cyclical phenomenon, and its scale is strikingly impressive.

When examing in detail the breakdowns of the increase in employed labor force, we see quite a number of occupations which could easily absorb the unemployed persons. The rate of increase in male employed labor force for 1920–30 was 52% for green-groceries, 47% for fish dealers, 80% for meat dealers, 12% for soft drink and alcoholic beverage sellers, 202% for confectioneries and bakeries, 54% for tea dealers, 66% for china-and glass-ware sellers, 93% for leather and its product sellers, 17% for woven fabrics and other textiles sellers, etc. It is thus evident clearly that the surplus labor was absorbed in large magnitudes by these service industries.

On the other hand, it is also impressive that the employed labor force indicated only 0.1% increase in agriculture. From this, we may infer at least that we did not have a large amount of inflow of labor force from the non-agricultural sectors into the agricultural sectors during this depression. While the increase in labor force employed in manufacturing was only 5.9%, that of the wholesale and retail trades amounted to 55.2%. The fact that about 2.3 millions of the increasing labor force were absorbed by the tertiary industry, however, is not a normal long-run process which accompanies the economic growth, but rather a highly characteristic aspect of a depression phase.

According to Table 13, we have a contrary situation in 1930–40 as compared with 1920–30, for the increase in the labor force employed in the manufacturing and construction industries then occupied 74% of the total increase. In the wholesale and retail trades, we see an absolute decrease. Moreover, though probably the development of the war economy may also have had some influence, this decrease reflects the cyclical tendency to a great extent, that, in general, the labor force in the service industry tends to swell during a depression and tends to decrease during a prosperous period. This seems to suggest that the service industry has played a much greater role as a pool of surplus labor than has agriculture. Although the above is an exposition only of a cyclical aspect of the service industry, it can be expected that it also has a secular aspect. In view of the tremendous amount of a small unit of the wholesale and retail trades, the service industry seems to have taken the role also of a reservoir for the secular, disguised unemployment. Consequently, as we come down to the later period, it can be presumed that the role of the service industry as the pool of the reserve army will become larger and larger as compared with that of agriculture.

The postwar data also tend to substantiate somewhat a similar conclusion. The growth rate of a real *GNP* was 7–8% for 1950–55. When the economy moved from this phase to the next, 1955–60, as the growth rate increased up to 9–10%, we see drastic changes in the incremental composition of labor force employed among industries. An increasing outflow of labor from the agricultural sectors has proceeded at a phenomenal scale and with an accelerated speed between 1950–55 and 1960–65. On the one hand, the incremental proportion of labor force employed in the manufacturing and construction industries in the 1950–55 period was 40%, but it increased up to 80% in the 1955–60 period. On the other hand, the same incremental proportion of the wholesale and retail trades and the service industry (in a narrow sense) decreased from 73% (in the former period) to 50% (in the later period). After World War II, we have had no such long, continued depression as we had experienced in the prewar period, but it is worthy of notice that in the two phases of economic growth, both having conspicuous different growth rates respectively, we see a considerable difference in the incremental proportion of employed labor force absorbed by the tertiary industry.

In the 1960–65 period, which was characterized as an investment stagnation phase, the incremental proportion of employed labor force in the manufacturing and construction industries decreased to 67% from 80% of the 1955–60 period. On the other hand, the corresponding ratio increased from 50% to 70% in the wholesale and retail trades and service industry. These facts, derived from Table 13, again make clear the cyclical nature of the tertiary industry already explained.

Mataji Umemura[18] called the former period the "process of the accumulation of the reserve army of the labor force," although here the word "the reserve army" is used differently from the sense in which Karl Marx used. At any rate, he explained that in the former period the annual rate of increase in labor force amounted to a surprising magnitude 3–3.5%, while the natural increase in non-farm labor force as well as the inflow of labor force from farms — which once emigrated from urban to rural

18)   Mataji Umemura, *op, cit.*

districts during the postwar food-shortage period — were almost absorbed by the tertiary industry. According to Umemura, however, the rate of increase in labor force in the latter period fell to 1.5%, and now the "pull-down" or the use of the labor in reserve — which has been accumulating since the former period in the tertiary industry — began to take place. Therefore, the increase rate of labor force employed in the service industry in the latter period was not so conspicuous as it was in the former period. In the transition from the "employment-increase pattern" to the "capital intensity or productivity-increase pattern" growth, and in the shift from the service-industry-oriented pattern increase of employed labor force to the manufacturing-industry-oriented one, we can see the medium-term cycle expressed in the behavior of the employment structure.

9.   Transition of Labor Market

The Japanese economy is now departing from the long, continued labor-surplus phase and is entering into the labor-shortage phase. Such a change will be the first of its kind for the Japanese economy except for the wartime periods, and it will entail a tremendous transformation of the Japanese economy in future.

The so-called baby boom which occurred in the immediate postwar years brought about the natural increase in population up to slightly more than 1.7 million, but, thereafter, rapid decrease in population, as indicated in Fig. 6, and the average of the natural increase in population for 1956–62 fell to about 920 thousands. Naturally, we may expect a wave of an increase in the working-age population after an adequate time span from that of the natural increase in population. As working-age populations, we have selected two magnitudes; those falling in 15–59 age group and those within 15–64 age group. Compared with the peak of the natural increase in population (1948), the peak of the increase in the working-age population (1964) indicates a time lag of sixteen years. Just around the time when the peak of the "high rate of growth" of 1960–61 was reached, the rate of increase in the working-age population fell drastically. This merely reflects a conspicuous decline in the birth rate during World War II with a particular time lag, but it became an important background for an intensified labor shortage coexisting with the rapidly increasing demand for labor due to the "high rate of growth."

The peak of the increase in the working-age population occurred in 1964, which thereafter is expected to decline very steeply. According to the prediction of the "Institute of Research on Population Problems," it is expected that in 1970 the annual increase of the working-age population will fall to about the same level as 1961. As a matter of course, the labor participation ratio (the proportion of labor force in the population who are 15 years old and over) declined from 70.8% in 1955 to 66.1% in 1964 as a result of the increasing percentage in school attendance. Therefore, the long-run declining tendency of the increase in labor force is destined to accelerate the shortage of labor.

The second point which should be taken into account is that the hitherto tremendous exodus of agrarian labor force to non-agricultural sectors may not continue in the future with the present tempo. This is suggested by Table 14. Due to the large outflow of young labor force, which is concentrated around those who are less than thirty years old, the drastic decline of the employed labor force in 1950–60 gives us a striking impression insofar as the younger age group is concerned. Probably, after ten years from now, the labor force pyramid in the primary industry will be predominantly occupied by the older age groups, and then the declining tendency of the number of farm households will necessarily ensue. This will bring about a shortage of labor even in the farm villages, and labor shortage will be extended into every segment of the economy. Moreover, since the non-agricultural sectors have been highly dependent upon the inflow of labor from agriculture, the decline of agriculture as a source of labor force will also intensify the phenomenon of

355

Fig. 6. Waves of Increases in the Total Population and Working-Age Population

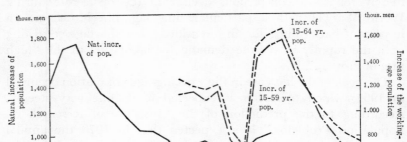

Source: Statistics Bureau of the Prime Minister's Office, *Nihon Tôkei Nenkan* (Statistical Yearbook of Japan); Institute of Research of Population Problems, Ministry of Welfare, "Estimate of Future Population Classified by Sex and Age" (the July 1, 1964 estimate).

labor shortage in the non-agricultural sectors. Such is the reason why we predict that, in the long-run, labor shortage will be accelerated, say, in the next ten or twenty years.

The third point to be made is that, as a long-run trend, the proportion of the tertiary industry in the total labor force will tend to increase. Measuring the above proportion on the vertical axis and the proportion of the primary industry on the horizontal axis, we get Fig. 7. This takes up ten countries and makes clear that, not only as a time series but also as a cross-section, the proportion of the tertiary industry tends to increase as the level of the economy rises, reducing the proportional share of the primary industry in terms of labor force.

If the proportional composition of the tertiary industry has an inclination to expand in terms of labor force, this will play another part in intensifying the shortage of labor in the future. Some will be apt to argue that even if the labor shortage becomes more intense, mechanization and consequently the increase in

Fig. 7. Proportional Composition of Labor Force in the Tertiary Industry in International Comparison

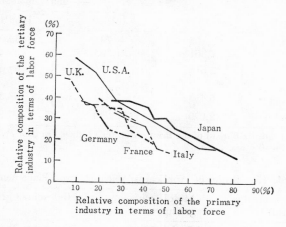

Source: Simon Kuznets, "Quantitative Aspects of the Economic Growth of Nations, II," *Economic Development and Cultural Change*, Supplement to Vol. V, No. 4, July 1957; P. Deane and W.A. Cole, British Economic Growth 1886–1959; K. Ohkawa and others, *The Growth Rate of the Japanese Economy 1878*, 1957; The *Censuses of Population* in Japan; and OECD data.

Note: Great Britain—1801, 1851, 1881, 1891, 1901, 1911, 1938, 1964. (1964=U.K.)
U.S.A.—1820, 1850, 1870, 1900, 1940, 1963
Japan —1878–82, 1898–1902, 1908–12, 1920, 1930, 1940, 1955, 1960, 1965
France—1866, 1901, 1921, 1931, 1964
Italy —1871, 1881, 1936, 1960, 1964

productivity will be a cure for it. But it is almost beyond doubt that in the tertiary industry the increase in productivity tends to be far behind that of the secondary industry, except in the areas of transportation and communication. The extent to which the increase in productivity in the tertiary industry is possible is limited within a narrow range, and the increasing share of the tertiary industry in the labor force will be an additional factor accelerating the labor shortage. Of course, we do not deny that in many sectors of manufacturing, the pheno-

357

Table 14. Labor Force Employed in the Primary Industry by Age Groups

——unit: thousand——

Age groups	1950	1960	1960/1950
15–19 years	2,403	793*	33.0%
20–24	2,361	1,303	55.2
25–29	} 4,919	1,617	} 97.9
30–39		3,300	
40–49	} 5,454	2,672	} 93.3
50–59		2,419	
60 years and over	2,079	2,243	107.9

Source: Statistics Bureau of the Prime Minister's Office, *Census of Population.*
Note: *14–19 years.

Table 15. Ratios of Applicants, Vacancies and Placements

	Labor exchange (general)		Middle school graduates		High school graduates	
	Ratio of vacancies to applicants	Ratio of placements to vacancies	Ratio of vacancies to applicants	Ratio of placements to vacancies	Ratio of vacancies to applicants	Ratio of placements to vacancies
1958	0.32	41.9%	1.2	60.8%	1.1	55.7%
59	0.43	34.8	1.2	63.5	1.1	54.2
60	0.59	29.2	1.9	43.7	1.5	47.2
61	0.71	23.3	2.7	31.4	2.0	37.2
62	0.67	22.0	2.9	29.6	2.7	30.1
63	0.71	18.3	2.6	32.9	2.7	30.3
64	0.72	15.7	3.6	25.3	4.0	21.7
65	0.63	18.6	3.7	24.7	3.5	24.9
66	0.73	16.7	2.9	31.8	2.6	34.0
67	1.00	13.0	3.4	26.7	3.1	28.4

Source: Ministry of Labor, "Shokugyô Antei Gyômu Tôkei" (Statistics on the Public Employment Security Service).

menon of productivity increase will continue to exist, but we must take into account the fact that the most growing industry, the machinery industry, in a wider sense, is essentially more labor-intensive when compared with other segments of the manufacturing sector. The Japanese economy is thus destined to run into the phase of labor shortage, due to the interplay of the above three factors, and her growth rate of *GNP* is likely to be reduced owing not only to the direct effect of the labor shortage, but also due to the indirect effect of the rise in prices, particularly those of commodities which is more labor-intensive. The latter effect, if dominant, will reduce the growth rate of exports, and also the domestic growth rate by suppressing the balance-of-payments ceiling.

The labor shortage which was already beginning from around 1959 has deeply influenced the wage differential, the consumer prices, etc. Let us, for the time being, check these phenomena, attendant upon the increasing shortage of labor. Table 15 indicates the increasing shortage of labor by two indicators. The ratio of job vacancies to job applicants (it is termed as the "job vacancy ratio") is increasing from 0.32 in 1958 to 0.63 in 1965 according to the general statistics of the labor exchange, although the extent of increase must be discounted in view of the revised statistics given in 1962. In relation not only to middle school but also to high school graduates, we see a rapid increase in this ratio, reflecting the intensification of the shortage of labor. The "fill-up" ratio (the placements divided by the job vacancies), on the other hand, indicates a decreasing trend in statistics denoted in Table 15, showing thereby an increasing tendency of a failure for employers to satisfy their demand for labor due to the shortage in job positions. In such a situation, the number of the actually unemployed decreased from 650 thousands in 1959 to 400 thousands in 1963.

The interscale wage differential in manufacturing has been reduced in the new phase. This has already been shown in Table 3. The ratio of average wages in 4–9 employee compared with 1,000 employees and over was 42.3% in 1951, and expanded to 37.8% in 1958, but in 1962 it began to be reduced to 50.2%.

Fig. 8 depicts annual changes of average wages by size of establishment according to the *Census of Manufactures*. In 1952

359

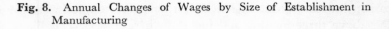

Fig. 8. Annual Changes of Wages by Size of Establishment in Manufacturing

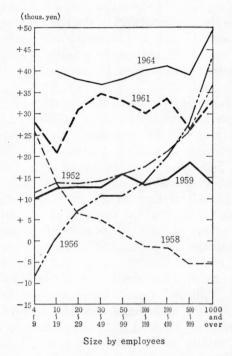

and 1956, the curves slope upward to the right, indicating that the higher the size of establishment, the higher the increase in average wages. Although the 1953–54 curves are omitted here, their shapes are similar. And, the slope became steepest in 1956 during the so-called "Jimmu" boom. However, in the 1958 recession, a perfectly opposite slope (rising to the left) appeared. This may be due to the fact that quite a few establishments reduced their scales, and therefore, the average wages went up relatively due to their downward shift in scales. Further, it is expected that the reduction of bonus payment was higher,

Table 16. Interscale Differential of Starting Wages for New Graduates (Male, Manufacturing)

——over 500 employees = 100——

	Middle school graduates		High school graduates	
	100–499 employees	15–99 employees	100–499 employees	15–99 employees
1957	84.6	78.6	86.9	81.9
58	90.7	83.5	88.0	82.3
59	91.8	87.3	85.9	83.4
60	94.9	91.6	90.1	86.3
61	100.1	97.9	91.4	85.7
62	100.2	100.3	95.3	94.3
63	100.0	101.2	94.6	96.7
64	103.8	106.7	96.7	94.2
65	101.4	101.7	97.9	96.6
66	102.0	103.2	96.7	96.2
67	99.1	99.7	93.9	92.4

Source: Ministry of Labor, *Shinki Gakusotsusha Shoninkyū-Chōsa* (Survey of the Starting Wages for New Graduates). Quoted from the *Rôdô Hakusho* (White paper on the Labor Economy), 1964,

as we view the larger establishments. The curves remain with an upward slope (to the right) until 1956 but tend to become horizontal in shape from 1959 onwards. Since the increase of wages in absolute amount made no systematic difference, this means that the percentage rate of increase of wages became higher in the lower-size establishments. In this sense, the change in the shape of wage curves coincided with the intensification of labor shortage in the labor market.

The narrowing tendency of wage differential so far analyzed may naturally be due to labor shortage. Particularly, most conspicuous was the reduction of starting wage differential. Table 16 gives us the interscale differential in starting wages in relation to the middle school graduates as well as the high school graduates, with the establishments of over 500 employees = 100. From this, we can conclude that as far as the starting wages are concerned, the interscale differential has almost disappeared, with no conspicuous differences in recent time.

Table 17 explains the interscale wage differential, with particular emphasis on the difference of wages by age group. This is the relative wage differential in the size of 30–99 employees, compared with that of 1,000 employees and over. This shows that as far as the age groups of less than 30 years are concerned, the interscale wage differentials completely disappeared. Since the labor mobility of medium and old age workers will be accelerated when labor shortage becomes more intense in the future, we can expect an equalizing tendency even for the groups over 30 years old. However, insofar as the statistics before 1962 on the age groups over 30 years old are concerned, the interscale differential in wages has indicated no tendency of any reduction. However, the relative wages for the 30–34 age group began to increase from 74.8% in 1962 to 87.3% in 1964, and to 91.7% in 1967.

But in order that the equalization of wages should proceed even for the medium age groups and over, the transfiguration of wage and employment systems should take place. This would not take place without tremendous frictions. As long as the "life-time commitment" employment system and the "length of service" wage payment system prevail in the large enterprise sector, the wage equalization between large enterprises and small-medium enterprises will be extremely difficult. However, the strenuous pressure of labor shortage should at last break through the institutional rigidity. It will be necessary that the high "capacity to transform"— which has been displayed during the period of "high rate of growth" — should be also exhibited in this sphere in the coming several years.

Our labor market with cheap, abundant labor has so far supported the high rate of growth, while the increasing labor shortage, as a recent tendency, may be a bottleneck to the rapid growth of the economy in the near future. The small-medium enterprises will face a more and more difficult situation in that

FORMATION AND TRANSITION OF THE DUAL ECONOMY

Table 17. Interscale Regular Wage Differential Further
Classified by Age

(Male manual worker in Manufacturing, the ratio of 30–99 employees to
1,000 employees and over)

Age groups	1954	1958	1961	1962	1963	1964	1965	1967
Leass thn								
18 years	82.6	91.4	110.7	106.0	111.0	114.0	109.6	102.9
18–19	84.4	86.6	96.4	101.0	104.8	108.1	105.8	100.8
20–24	81.7	92.9	98.2	100.2	104.2	108.4	108.1	103.2
25–29	75.7	80.3	91.0	92.8	101.5	104.2	103.5	101.3
30–34	72.8	73.2	76.1	74.8	86.4	87.3	90.3	91.7
35–39	67.7	70.3	71.8	69.6	72.6	77.0	77.7	79.2
40–49	62.4	61.9	63.3	64.6	67.1	71.0	70.8	70.3

Source: Ministry of Labor, *Kojin Chingin Chôsa* (Survey on Personal Wages)
1954; *Chingin-kôzô Kihon Chôsa* (Basic Survey on Wage Structure) 1958;
Chingin Jittai Sôgô Chôsa (Comprehensive Survey of the Actual Situation
of Wages) 1961; and *Tokutei-jôken Chingin Chôsa* (Survey of Wages under
Specific Conditions), 1962 and 1963; and *Chingin-kozô Kihon Tôkei Chôsa*
(Basic Statistical Survey on Wage Structure) 1964, 1965 and 1967.

their required labor cannot be provided with from sources within
the prefecture, because the larger enterprises absorb such sources
within the prefecture. Moreover, another problem is that
there is insufficient regional mobility of labor.   Thus, the enforcement of government policy for the mobilization of labor will
become more and more important.   In a labor-shortage situation,
when the locations of industries are set up, the difficulty or
easiness of recruiting labor in relation to the locations themselves
should be taken into account. In such a phase, the modernization of small-medium enterprises, with higher capital intensity,
will become increasingly urgent, coupled with their financing.
Policies concerning the acceleration of the following measures —
regional labor mobility, the structural improvement of agriculture, the housing construction, the location of enterprises, the
financing of small-medium business for their modernization, the
fostering of the skilled and the technicians in shortage, etc. —
will become more and more important, although they will not
be so effective when independently followed.

363

In the event that these policies turn out to be ineffective, we may have a menace of cost inflation, i.e., the money-wage increase surpassing the physical-productivity increase. This is a most serious problem which may eventually affect the speed of economic growth. Japan may in the near future go into a world in which not only the "commodity gap" (the excess demand for products) but also the "factor gap" (the excess demand for factors) will tend to bring about inflation. Since causes of inflation will become multifarious, the policy should also be based on such policies, and not be restricted to a fiscal and monetary policies alone.

Thus, whereas a highly expansive policy might have been valid where labor is still abundant, in a labor-shortage situation, the policy should be oriented much more toward stability, because even if the price stability deters the growth to some extent in the short run, its reasonable stability will be a basis for keeping the economic growth steady and continually high in the long run. "The higher, the better" type growth policy would be good in a labor-surplus situation, but it will tend, in the long run, to accelerate inflation in a labor-shortage economy. Japan is moving from the former to the latter phase. Since the wages will tend to increase in parallel with physical-productivity increase in large enterprises, the wages will be apt to surpass the physical-productivity increase in smaller factories as well as in service industries where physical productivities cannot but remain far behind. Such being the case, the labor market involves troublesome problems, when it is viewed from the policy aspect toward the future.

10. Interindustry Productivity Differentials and Prices

Once the pressures to raise wages is strengthened due to labor shortage, and the leading industries experiencing the rise in physical productivity allow money ways to rise pari passu with their productivity, then the general price level will naturally rise, for in the industries which experience comparative decline in physical productivity levels the wage cost and the prices should inevitably increase. In postwar Japan, the prices of manufacturing goods were relatively stable, but the prices of agricultural products tended to rise particularly from around 1960. Actually, the prices of commodities produced by big enterprises declined slightly but those in small enterprises in general showed an upward trend from the years when labor shortage began to be intensified. These tendencies seems to be important in the light of expectations that the oligopolistic price rigidity will be strengthened in various industries and at the same time that labor shortage will be more and more intense in future.

From this point of view, some statistical analysis can be presented. Taking seven industries, i.e., (1) agriculture, forestry and fishery, (2) mining, (3) manufacturing, (4) construction, (5) public utilities, incl. electricity, gas, transportation and communication, (6) wholesale and retail trades, and (7) services, the relationship between interindustry movements of productivities and prices is explored in Table 18 and Fig. 9.

From Fig. 9 [A] which is derived from Table 18, we see an inverse relationship between interindustry labor productivity changes and price movements for the ten years; 1955–1965. In other words, the prices in manufacturing and mining were roughly constant, due to the higher productivity increases in comparison to the other industries. However, in agriculture, construction, services, etc., which experienced smaller increase in productivity considerable price increases occurred. One point to be remembered is that in manufacturing and mining which showed the highest productivity increases, the prices did not decline. Therefore, the overall price level was forced to rise, due to the stability of manufacturing prices.

The similar reciprocal movement of productivities and prices suggests itself for the period, 1955–1960 [B], but in 1960–1965 a different pattern emerges [C]. In services, construction and

Table 18. Output Prices and Labor Productivities by Industry

	Output price index			Real net product per capita of employed labor force (1,000 yen)		
	1955	1960	1965	1955	1960	1965
Agriculture, forestry and fishery	93.9	100.0	145.5	106.5	132.4	169.9
Mining	97.7	100.0	101.1	249.3	386.0	686.3
Manufacturing	99.9	100.0	99.1	222.6	381.1	598.9
Construction	80.9	100.0	128.9	214.7	260.4	405.6
Public utilities	89.9	100.0	114.5	337.4	476.2	605.4
Wholesale and retail trades	91.3	100.0	138.8	229.9	309.8	355.1
Services	82.9	100.0	147.6	220.3	240.7	339.5

Sources: Output price index data from the appendix of the Economic White Paper of 1967. The ouptut price index of electricity and gas, on the one hand, and that of transportation and communication, on the other, are combined with the weight of their output (24.7:75.3), and are assumed for public utilities in general. Real net output per employed labor force (in 1960 constant prices) are derived as based on factor incomes by industry (*Annual Report on National Income Statistics*, 1967), the output price indices in the above table, and the employed persons by industry in the population census.

agriculture, whose levels of per capita net output were relatively lower so far, experienced a sudden shift to the upper curve, probably due to the pressure of labor shortage. Two curves declining downward thus emerge.

Almost similar analysis can be conducted for industries belonging to manufacturing sector. Using the *Census of Manufactures* data for 1955, 1960, and 1965 and also the output prices in the statistical appendix of the 1967 Economic White Paper and the Bank of Japan's wholesale price data, we can compare the real shipment per employees and output prices in terms of rates of change for 1955–60 and 1960–65. We used the shipment figures of various subsectors including every scale of establishments.

In Fig. 10, we find that for 1955–60 two free hand lines needs to be fitted, but that for 1960–65 one free hand curve is enough

Fig. 9.   Reciprocal Changes of Productivities and Prices

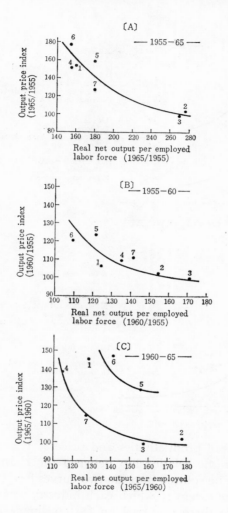

[A]
— 1955—65 —

Output price index (1965/1955)

Real net output per employed labor force (1965/1955)

1. Agriculture
2. Mining
3. Manufacturing
4. Wholesale & retail trades
5. Construction
6. Services
7. Public utilities

[B] — 1955—60 —

Output price index (1960/1955)

Real net output per employed labor force (1960/1955)

[C] — 1960—65 —

Output price index (1965/1960)

Real net output per employed labor force (1965/1960)

Fig. 10. Productivities and Prices among Subsectors of Manufacturing

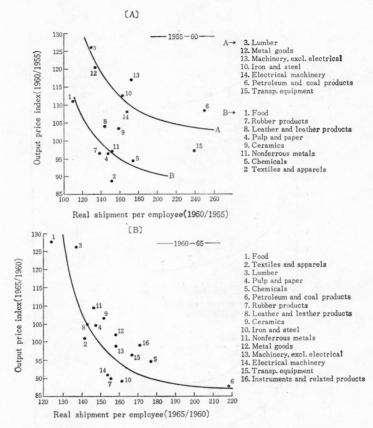

to explain the changes of productivities and prices. It seems to us that the reason for the relationship between the changes in the two magnitudes to be splitted into the two curves for 1955–60 lies in differences of the extent to which each industry was under excess demand. Since there occurred an extraordinary investment boom during this period, it may be imagined that metal

368

and engineering industries experienced a higher excess demand but that in light industries the extent of excess demand was not so high. This fact may be a probable reason why the two curves are needed to show the relationship between the two magnitudes. However, in 1960–65, we get a single downward sloping curve. This is probably due to the fact that from 1962 to 1965 the Japanese economy was in a phase in which the private fixed investment as a ratio of GNP showed a downward trend, i.e., she shifted from the capacity shortage to the capacity excess phase. Since almost all of industries were not in excess demand (this situation was generally understood by such phrases as "prosperity without profit", or "expansion without boom feeling"), it is natural that a single curve can be derived, and in such industries, as food-processing and lumber, whose productivities did not increase so much, output prices rose relatively and in such industries, as petroleum and coal products, whose productivity increased tremendously, prices declined.

Thus, the existance of inverse relationship between changes in output prices and relative changes of productivities in various subsectors of manufacturing, becomes quite evident. We get a relatively clear picture on the relationship of productivities and prices, not only by a broader classification of industries, like agriculture and manufacturing, but also in a detailed breakdown of manufacturing industry itself. Probably, our analysis is not complete, because we employed the labor productivity, and not the total productivity, in the sense of output divided by total input, inclusive of labor and capital. However, according to the Economic Planning Agency's study, the fixed capital output ratio tended to decline more in relatively growing industries (automobile, chemicals, etc.) and declined less or even increased in relatively stagnant industries (textiles, food-processing, etc.). In other words, the capital productivity seems to tend to rise hand in hand with the labor productivity, as far as the postwar interindustry data on the capital output ratio is concerned. Therefore, our approach based on labor productivity may not

369

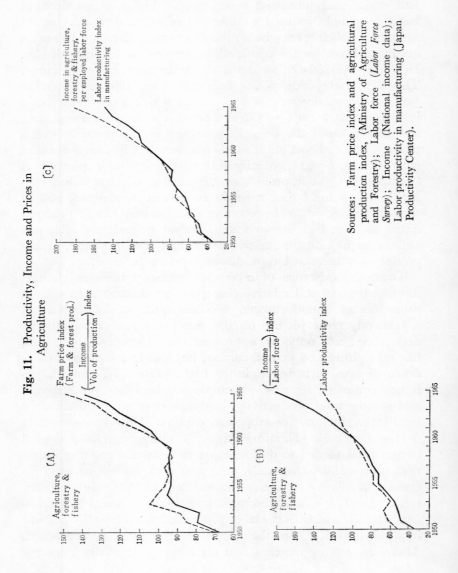

Fig. 11. Productivity, Income and Prices in Agriculture

Sources: Farm price index and agricultural production index, (Ministry of Agriculture and Forestry); Labor force (*Labor Force Survey*); Income (National income data); Labor productivity in manufacturing (Japan Productivity Center).

be complete, but probably suggests the important relationship between productivities and prices.

In the postwar period, the prices in manufacturing were relatively stable. However, from around 1960, the prices of farm products began to increase sharply. As manifested in Fig. 11, the labor productivity indices in agriculture and manufacturing ran almost parallel until 1960, but from then on manufacturing productivity increased more than that of agriculture (Compare [B] with [C]). Therefore, the rice price together with the prices of other farm products, has been continuously increased in order to prevent the widening income gap between agriculture and non-agricultural sector. This brought about the higher increase of the "income/labor force" index in agriculture than that of the labor productivity index of agriculture [B]. Thus, as indicated in [A], farm prices as well as the "income/volume of production" index in agriculture showed almost parallel movement.

It now becomes evident that the rise of food prices has contributed 40–50% of the rise of the consumer price index from about 1960 onwards. Therefore, if an increase in food prices continues at the present speed, one may ʜless that the rise in consumer price index will still continue unabated in future.

Agriculture is an important example, but the prices of products in labor intensive small enterprises are also destined to rise. Thus, the existing productivity gap among higher and lower productivity sectors will not only entail the changes in relative prices, but also in the general price level, provided that the prices in industries with relatively higher productivity increase are stable or do not decrease enough. Naturally, these tendencies will not go on if the monetary authorities do not allow money supply or effective demand to increase, in accordance with the pressure of the rising costs. However, it is to be noticed that the tendencies of rising prices in the lower productivity sectors, have played a role in narrowing the dual structure among industries.

In so far as the rapid productivity increase will continue in the modern big business sector, leaving behind a wide productivity gap for the low productivity sectors, inevitable course for the Japanese economy will be an upward adjustment of prices of the latter sectors. Consequently, in order to maintain the stability of general price level, the relative decline in the price of the products of the big business sector is necessary. However, if the big business sector is already highly competitive in the world market, any further decline in the export prices of these products in the future may not be expected, despite the relative productivity rise in heavy industrial products, e.g., in steel. If so, the Japanese economy has an additional heavy burden in the future, i.e, the possibility of price rise due to the narrowing of dual structure.

The increasing labor shortage and narrowing interscale wage differential will, on the one hand, necessitate the increasing capital intensity or mechanization in the smaller enterprises, thus bringing about the convergence of the inter-enterprise productivity gap in real terms. However, since the Japanese economy has displayed an unbalanced rapid growth and it will still proceed, the above process may not be sufficient. Therefore, there seems to be a possibility that to some extent the relative price rise of products in lower productivity sector will be inevitable in future for the disappearance of the interindustry dual structure.

CHAPTER 9

INDUSTRIAL GROWTH, REGIONAL STRUC-
TURE AND DIFFERENTIALS

1. *Regional Differentials—Causes and Remedies—*

The rapid postwar economic growth, particularly the 1955–61 boom, has brought forth various problems in the national economy such as the widening of regional income and productivity differentials, the excessive concentration of population in the big cities, the distorted accumulation of productive capacity in particular industrial districts, the shortage of industrial water and consequent sinking of the ground, the emergence of smog in the big cities, aggravated traffic congestion, and the rise in consumer prices. Consequently, the regional economy problems as well as the development of less developed areas, have increasingly attracted the attention of the public. This was really an unprecedented phenomenon never experienced before the war. Although the development of less developed areas (e.g., Hokkaidô) before 1950 aimed mostly at an increase in the production of foods or the development of natural resources, after the Korean War this emphasis has gradually shifted toward different objectives. Although the Plan for the Industrial Belt along the Pacific Ocean in the Income-Doubling Plan strongly aimed at the rational location of factories, it also emphasized a new target, namely, the elimination of excessive concentration. Thus, as the economic growth proceeded rapidly, different kinds of targets have come to be more seriously considered such as the reduction of regional productivity or income differentials, the elimination of public nuisances accompanied by the excessive expansion of cities, and the enhancement of the welfare of local inhabitants. The enforcement of various acts such as the Act for Accelerating the Development of Industries in Local Undeveloped Areas of 1961, the Act for the Nationwide Comprehansive Development and the Act for Accelerating the Construction of New Industrial Cities in 1962 emphasize the importance of the strategic development of local key points and the urgency with which the nation-wide systematic plan should be established.

From around 1966, the problem of "excessive sparsification" of population in rural remote villages has been the object of heated debate together with the "excessive concentration" of population in big cities. Owing to the extraordinary exodus of population, it became increasingly difficult to maintain the basic services in regional societies such as fire departments, educational institutions or medical facilities. Moreover, the radical decrease of population density and the higher age composition of population in the villages has extremely reduced the productive capability of the remaining population. These were brought about by the so-called "excessive concentration" of the young population in the big cities or industrial districts caused by the "high-pitch economic growth" which has still continued to operate in the 1960's.

In the prewar period these problems did not attract great attention. Of coure, there were some policies for the destitute condition of the Tôhoku region before the war or the the national land planning policies (Kokudo Keikaku) adopted mostly for military purposes during the war. Nevertheless, the importance of regional problems in the economy as a whole was never so generally recognized as in the postwar period. In 1961, the per capita income of Tôkyô was ¥274,692 but that of Kagoshima Prefecture was ¥78,316 (28.5% of Tôkyô). In addition to the existence of such a wide gap in prefectural incomes, it is generally held that the regional discrepancy of the prefectural incomes has tended to expand under "high-pitched growth".

Whether this is true or not should be tested carefully, but even if it is not so, we cannot deny that the regional income differential is already tremendously aggravated.

In this analysis, we shall focus our attention on the regional income or productivity differentials, on the regional differences of industrial structure which is generally supposed to be attendant upon the high-pitched growth and on heavy industrialization of recent years.

In contrast to inter-industry or inter-scale differentials, the regional differential, in terms of per capita income or productivity, is relatively unlikely to disappear. If there occurs a phenomenal increase in physical productivity in some industry, we shall have an adjustment process whereby the relative price of its commodity will decline so as to interrupt the rise of the relative wages in that industry. However, even if physical productivity increases fantastically in one region, it may be quite unlikely that commodity prices in that region become permanently cheaper because, in an economy in which the transportation is highly developed, prices for the same commodity tend to equalize. Therefore, it is impossible for us to have changes in the regional price structure in inverse proportion to changes in regional physical productivity. If cheaper commodities permeate other regions and prove more competitive, the decline of relative per capita income in other regions seems to be inevitable. In this sense the regional differential of physical productivity will not be absorbed in the regional price structure and is likely to result in the regional differences of wages and per capita incomes. This is the fundamental reason why the regional differential is more apt to be aggravated than the inter-industry or inter-sacle differential.

It is true that the regional differential of incomes will be reduced if we have sufficiently flexible mobility of labor. However, in this case one may have instead an excessive migration of labor to the big cities to aggravate the overcrowded traffic, the shortage of residences, the increasing land prices, and other public nuisances.

375

Moreover, the location of industry has a common attribute of regional concentration, particularly if various types of "combinations" are set up, and different factories are connected by pipes transmitting various intermediate products to each other. Such an inherent tendency toward regional concentration will also manifest a rather cumulative trend in accordance with the rapid progress of heavy industrialization. And this is not restricted to the petro-chemical industry alone. In the neighborhood of big automobile factories too, such as Toyota or Nissan, we have an innumerable number of parts makers getting together. In these big automobile factories, they adopt the so-called "supermarket system," according to which the parts produced by a lot of parts makers flow in at each stage of the production process without time lag. In order for this system to work effectively, it is of course necessary for parts makers to locate themselves very closely to the big factories. Thus, the so-called "industrial estate" sometimes is inevitably built up.

The industrial development will inevitably result in regional specialization, taking into account of the closeness of the product market, the distance to the raw material supplying area, the supply of labor force, the existence or non-existence of complementary industries, and the supply of industrial water.

If so, the concentration of investment in the particular industrial districts will bring about a strong regional concentration of industrial capacity and serve to enlarge productivity differentials between prefectures. But since this will not be absorbed in the regional price structure, the per capita income differential will be necessarily widened. The migration of population which tends to equalize the differential will stimulate, on the one hand, the population concentration in the big cities and make inevitable the occurrence of public nuisances. If we intend to evade this excessive concentration then the regional differential of per capita incomes cannot but be accelerated. The speedier the tempo of industrial development the more we are destined to be plagued by this dilemma. The fact that the adjustment via the regional price structure and the regional migration of labor force is decidedly limited will be an ultimate cause explaining the inevitable occurrence of regional differentials.

Thus, the objective of removing the regional differentials cannot be achieved only by the acceleration of regional labor force mobility. By pushing forth a comprehensive, systematic plan for the development of local undeveloped areas, concentrating particularly on the strategic development of local key points, the need for public investment in the social-overhead capital and for the decentralization of the location of industries has begun to be recognized. On the one hand, the pursuit of the business-profit motive (private rational behavior) will necessarily entail regional concentration. On the other hand, the objective to decentralize industries is socially rational. Thus, there is an urgent need at the present to reconcile the private and social rationalities and to set up a long-term, comprehensive regional plan in order to minimize the problems thus far explained. In view of the above, social-overhead investment in the construction of roads, harbors, and rivers, even in areas where no factories will intend to locate themselves, is desirable under a consistent and effective regional plan to build up new industrial districts in under-developed areas.

2. Is the Regional Differential Aggravated?

It is a generally accepted view that since the regional income or productivity differential has been widened between advanced and less advanced areas, the politics to eliminate such differentials are urgently necessary. It is true that we have a wide dispersion of per capita incomes and productivities among regions, but is it equally true that these differentials have been widened in the course of postwar economic development? There may be several statistical methods used to estimate the degree of the regional differential. One may simply examine the difference of two extremes, the highest and the lowest, but since we have 46 prefectures, this is very unsatisfactory. Hence, we have preferred to use here a statistical technique, the computation of the well-known coefficient of variation (the standard deviation divided by the mean value). If we would like to know some indicator on the degree of absolute dispersion among 46 prefectures as concerns the variable X, then the standard deviation will be derived by using the formula, $\sqrt{(X-M)^2/N}$, where M is the simple average of the X's in 46 prefectures and N is the number of prefectures.

If we take up M_w, the average of X's weighted by the population of each prefecture, instead of M, then the formula becomes

$$\sqrt{\frac{\sum_1^{46} f(X-M_w)^2}{\sum_1^{46} f}}$$

where f stands for the weight of population in each prefecture.

However, in this formula we may encounter the following problem. Since there may be a migration of population from low-income to high-income prefectures, the figures for the f's may change yearly, and the weighted average of X's $(= M_w)$ can change only due to the population migration among prefectures, even when there were no change in each value of the X's. This is illustrated by a simple example. Let us assume that in Japan we have only two prefectures, α and β, and that the per capita incomes were unchanged from last year to this year and that α is higher than β in the per capita income level. If we have a population movement from β to α in this case, the weighted average of prefectural per capita incomes M_w cannot but rise to some extent, even when per capita income in α and β are invariant. The relative income of α and β, compared with M_w, will both decline despite the constancy of incomes in the two prefectures.

This strange result can be evaded, if we use a "fixed" weight every year instead of the "variable" weight, e.g., the weight of 1955 population in each prefecture. In this case, even if there were any migration among prefectures, the weighted average of incomes would be constant, in so far as the per capita incomes in α and β are invariable. Denoting as f_{55}, the fixed weight given by the population in 1955 in each prefecture and $M_{\bar{w}}$ as the consequent weighted average, we will find that the standard deviation will then be,

$$\sqrt{\frac{\Sigma f_{55}(X - M_{\bar{w}})^2}{\Sigma f_{55}}}$$

In looking for an indicator of regional differentials, it is necessary that we use the "fixed" weight instead of the "variable" weight. The simplest standard deviation based on the simple average $\sqrt{\Sigma(X - M)^2/N}$ is a special case of the "fixed" weight standard deviation in which each prefecture is given the same weight. We shall therefore use the standard deviations based on the simple average M, as well as the weighted average $M_{\bar{w}}$, with 1955 populations as the fixed weight.

In Table 1, we have computed the standard deviation and the coefficient of variation of per capita incomes as well as the value-added per employee in manufacturing (further broken down into heavy and light industries) among 46 prefectures. Since the standard deviation (an indicator of the *absolute* differential) increased hand in hand with an increase of the average per capita income for 1955–61, the coefficient of variation, — the ratio of the two, will present us an indicator of the *relative* regional differential.

As Table 1 and Fig. 1 indicate, the coefficient of variation of prefectural per capita incomes indicates cyclical changes in accordance with the actual business cycle, except for an abnormally high coefficient of 1950. From these indicators, it is noticed that we cannot observe any clear evidence of a widening regional income differential. Although a slight upward trend (except for 1950) can be discerned it is expected that from 1962 to 1965 the coefficient of variation would have declined owing to the cessation of the rapidly increasing tempo of fixed invest-

Table 1. Regional Differential Indicators of Per Capita Incomes and Productivities

	Standard deviation					Coefficient of variation (%)				
	Per capita income		Gross value-added per employee			Per capita income		Gross value-added per employee		
	A	B	Manu-facturing	Heavy ind.	Light ind.	A	B	Manu-facturing	Heavy ind.	Light ind.
1950	12089	18850	52265	75127	48000	35.84	46.56	30.5	47.2	33.1
1951	10910	14445	81811	144083	73157	25.64	29.92	32.1	43.6	37.2
1952	12138	16065	78224	133124	61782	24.18	28.38	29.6	40.0	29.2
1953	14130	19405	93632	134213	66184	25.24	30.63	29.3	32.3	27.6
1954	13256	18617	104485	159135	81621	21.53	27.19	30.0	35.2	29.9
1955	14836	22252	109211	165928	76577	21.72	29.15	29.2	34.5	26.4
1956	18550	27742	113080	152076	79177	24.70	32.52	28.3	28.9	26.1
1957	21545	31168	114586	190074	84042	25.97	32.82	27.8	35.4	26.9
1958	20863	29971	130258	167126	81364	24.42	30.90	29.8	29.4	25.2
1959	23826	34813	149673	206235	88803	24.90	32.03	30.3	31.4	25.3
1960	29406	42577	184050	251921	103583	26.46	33.60	32.7	33.3	26.7
1961	30604	52114	203117	278029	119476	27.56	34.78	32.0	33.1	27.1

Source: Income: Economic Planning Agency, *Kenminshotoku Suikei* (Estimate of Prefectural Incomes), 1963, and *Shōwa 37 nendo-ban, Kokuminshotoku Hakusho* (National Income Report, 1962); Gross value-added per employee: Ministry of International Trade and Industry, *Kōgyō Tōkeihyō* (Census of Manufactures).

Notes: 1) Heavy industry (in this chapter) includes iron and steel, nonferrous metals, metal goods, machinery, electrical machinery, transportation equipment, optical, scientific and other machineries, chemicals, pertoleum and coal products, pulp and papers, ceramics and weapons. Light industry includes others.

2) *A* is the standard deviation and the coefficient of variation based on the simple average *M* and *B* is based on the weighted average $M_{\bar{w}}$ with 1955 population fixed.

Fig. 1. Coeffcient of Variation of Per Capita Incomes Among Prefectures

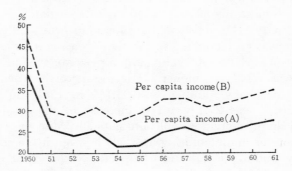

ment. Therefore, it is safe to assume that there is no upward trend in regional income differential following 1951.

However, one may be skeptical of the reliability of the prefectural income statistics. Therefore, we have also computed the coefficient of variation of the value-added per employee in heavy and light industries as well as manufacturing industry based on the *Census of Manufactures* data. We note here three observations: 1) There is no tendency for the coefficient of variation for this period. 2) The year-to-year fluctuations of the coefficient of variation are very irregular. 3) Most noteworthy is the fact that, although the coefficient of variation for manufacturing as a whole is almost level, the coefficients for heavy and light industries both tend to decline for this period. This apparent discrepancy in trends between the total coefficient and the partial coefficients may throw some doubt upon the computational accuracy, but this has been double checked and no error was found.

The discrepancy is merely superficial and can be reconciled. When heavy and light industries are taken up separately, regional productivity differentials in each should have been reduced, for not only have new big factories extended their locations beyond the existing industrial districts, but new industrial districts have emerged also. Since the difference of productivities at the large enterprise level will not be so large, the extension of industrial districts will naturally have reduced the inter-regional differential in productivity. However, in the process of heavy industrialization, there was an increasing proportion of heavy industry, whose coefficient of variation for value-added per employee among prefectures was relatively higher. For instance, the coefficient of variation for heavy industry was 33.1% in 1961, but that for light industry was 27.1%. The increase of the former's proportional share, therefore, will automatically raise the coefficient of variation for manufacturing as a whole, even if the coefficients for heavy and light industries respectively are assumed to be constant. This latter effect can be called the "shift" effect accompanied by heavy industrialization. The reason why the coefficient of variation for manufacturing as a whole levels off can be explained by the the declining tendency of the coefficients of variation for heavy and light industries has been offset by the purely "independent" effect due to heavy industrialization. In the earlier phase of this period, the coefficient of variation for manufacturing as a whole resembled that of light industry while in the later period the former coefficient tends to approach more closely to that of heavy industry. If we total the differences between the coefficients of variation for heavy and manufacturing industries, we have 52.3 points for 1950–55, but only 10.6 points for 1956–61. This substantiates cogently the above relationship.

Although the above may suggest conclusions contrary to generally held notions concerning the interregional differentials the economist must be faithful to his analytical result, because we cannot deny the reliability of the *Census of Manufactures*, even if one may be skeptical toward some of prefectural income statistics. Be that as it may, we can derive the interesting conclusion that heavy industrialization, by itself, will enlarge the interregional productivity differential through the shift-effect if other factors are equal. Therefore, we may infer that if the speed of heavy industrialization slows down in the future, we may even see a declining coefficient of variation for the interregional value-added per man in manufacturing. This seems to be a point no one has been aware of so far.

It should be noted, however, that the conclusion that the regional differentials in terms of per capita income or value-added per employee have not so far been widened relates to the 46 prefectures as a whole, while we may have an increasing differential among some prefectures and a reducing differential among other prefectures.

If we use the inter-prefectural coefficient of variation of per capita incomes (B indicator), the average of 1950–55 is 31.97, but that of 1956–61 is 32.78. This shows a slight increase of the indicator of the regional per capita income differential as far as the observation of all 46 prefectures is concerned. But, in some prefectures, the differential may have been smaller, while in others, it may have been made larger. Table 2 and Fig. 2 were prepared in order to make clear changing relative incomes of various prefectures from 1950–55 to 1956–61. On the horizontal axis of Fig. 2, the relative incomes of prefectures in the former period (1950–55) i.e.,

$$\frac{\text{Per capita income in each prefecture}}{\left(\begin{array}{l}\text{Per capita average income of all} \\ \text{prefectures standardized each year} \\ \text{with prefectural populations of} \\ \text{1955 as the fixed weight}\end{array}\right)} \quad \text{(1950–55 av.)}$$

are measured, and on the vertical axis the magnitudes of their changes from the former period (1950–55) to the latter (1956–61).

A casual look at the chart gives us a feeling that there is no clear-cut relationship. However, around the downward sloping curve (drawn in free hand) in the third quadrant, the figures for sixteen prefectures merge, except for Kagoshima and Ehime which are slightly deviated from the line. In so far as these sixteen prefectures are concerned there was a tendency, on the one hand, that those prefectures in which the relative incomes in 1950–55 were relatively higher, show larger declines in their

Table 2. Changes of Relative Incomes of Various Prefectures

Prefecture	Per capita incomes in various prefectures *divided by* standardized average of incomes of all prefectures			Prefecture	Per capita inocmes in various prefectures *divided by* standardized average of incomes of all prefectures		
	1950–55 Av.	1956–61 Av.	Increase of decrease		1950–55 Av.	1956–61 Av.	Increase or decrease
Hokkaidô	1.0087	0.9321	−0.0766	Miye	0.8099	0.8432	0.0333
Aomori	0.7293	0.7051	−0.0242	Shiga	0.8595	0.8948	0.0353
Iwate	0.6915	0.6708	−0.0207	Kyôto	1.1339	1.0979	−0.0360
Miyagi	0.7765	0.7876	0.0111	Ôsaka	1.4806	1.5205	0.0399
Akita	0.7730	0.7145	−0.0585	Hyôgo	1.2714	1.2303	−0.0411
Yamagata	0.7677	0.7616	−0.0061	Nara	0.8658	0.8827	0.0169
Fukushima	0.7237	0.7387	0.0150	Wakayama	0.9612	0.8611	−0.1001
Ibaragi	0.6034	0.7545	0.1511	Tottori	0.8078	0.7261	−0.0817
Tochigi	0.7468	0.8034	0.0566	Shimane	0.7541	0.7279	−0.0262
Gunma	0.7413	0.7657	0.0244	Okayama	0.8973	0.8420	−0.0553
Saitama	0.9461	0.8615	−0.0846	Hiroshima	0.8448	0.8956	0.0508
Chiba	0.7999	0.8326	0.0327	Yamaguchi	0.9477	0.8744	−0.0733
Tôkyô	1.7304	1.7673	0.0369	Tokushima	0.6484	0.7315	0.0831
Kanagawa	1.3198	1.3201	0.0003	Kagawa	0.8753	0.8357	−0.0096
Niigata	0.8676	0.8491	−0.0185	Ehime	0.8942	0.8019	−0.0923
Toyama	0.9023	0.9604	0.0581	Kôchi	0.7551	0.7570	0.0019
Ishikawa	0.8632	0.9261	0.0629	Fukuoka	1.0820	1.0557	−0.0263
Fukui	0.8420	0.8549	0.0129	Saga	0.7708	0.7192	−0.0516
Yamanashi	0.6743	0.7931	0.1188	Nagasaki	0.8252	0.7576	−0.0676
Nagano	0.7966	0.8266	0.0300	Kumamoto	0.7429	0.6799	−0.0630
Gifu	0.8190	0.8249	0.0059	Ôita	0.7857	0.7172	−0.0685
Shizuoka	0.9531	0.9895	0.0364	Miyazaki	0.6564	0.6511	−0.0053
Aichi	1.1444	1.2378	0.0934	Kagoshima	0.5860	0.5513	−0.0347

relative incomes from 1950—55 to 1956–61. On the other hand, those prefectures of lower relative incomes in 1950–55 show smaller declines in the relative income from 1950–55 to 1956–61. In other words, we find that among the sixteen prefectures, there was a equalizing tendency of per capita incomes. This is the first noticeable relationship we find in Fig. 2, and we can include the following sixteen prefectures in this group: Miyazaki, Iwate, Kôchi, Yamagata, Shimane, Aomori, Saga, Tottori, Kumamoto, Akita, Ôita, Nagasaki, Okayama, Wakayama, Yamaguchi and Hokkaidô.

Although we see an intra-group equalization in the above group, we must note that the prefectures belonging to this group are almost those whose relative incomes were less than unity in 1950—55 and tended to decline further in the latter period. Thus, we can say that the relative downward deviation of income as a group became larger compared with the national average. Therefore, the group of these prefectures manifests an intra-group equalization, but a wide inter-group dispersion in their relative incomes. It is of immense interest to see that in this group a lot of undeveloped prefectures in Kyûshû and Tôhoku are included.

Second, we can draw another free-hand downward sloping line through the second and fourth quadrants. There are twenty-two prefectures closely scattered along this line excluding the value for Ishikawa, Toyama and Shizuoka whose deviations are considerable: Ibaragi, Yamanashi, Tokushima, Tochigi, Hiroshima*, Nagano, Fukui, Shiga, Chiba*, Miye*, Nara, Gunma, Fukushima, Miyagi, Gifu*, Kagawa, Niigata, Saitama, Kyôto*, Fukuoka*, Kanagawa* and Hyôgo* (*here indicates a relatively high degree of industrialization).

We find again an equalizing tendency of their relative incomes among twenty-two prefectures, but some involved in this group are relatively industrialized prefectures, such as Hiroshima, Chiba, Miye, Gifu, Kanagawa, and Hyôgo. Within this group, it is evident that the per capita income equalization has proceeded, but between this group and the aforementioned group, mostly

Fig. 2. Direction of Changes in Relative Per Capita Incomes of Various Prefectures

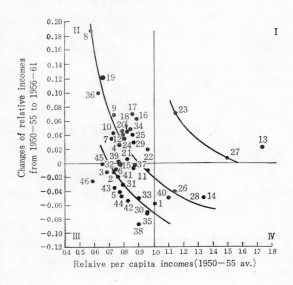

I	13.	Tôkyô	23.	Aichi	27.	Ôsaka
II	4.	Miyagi	7.	Fukushima	8.	Ibaragi
	9.	Tochigi	10.	Gunma	12.	Chiba
	16.	Toyama	17.	Ishikawa	18.	Fukui
	19.	Yamanashi| 20.	Nagano	21.	Gifu
	22.	Shizuoka	24.	Miye	25.	Shiga
	29.	Nara	34.	Hiroshima	36.	Tokushima
	39.	Kôchi	45.	Miyazaki		
III	2.	Aomori	3.	Iwate	5.	Akita
	6.	Yamagata	11.	Saitama	15.	Niigata
	30.	Wakayama	31.	Tottori	32.	Shimane
	33.	Okayama	35.	Yamaguchi	37.	Kagawa
	38.	Ehime	41.	Saga	42.	Nagasaki
	43.	Kumamoto	44.	Ôita	46.	Kagoshima
IV	1.	Hokkaidô	14.	Kanagawa	26.	Kyôto
	28.	Hyôgo	40.	Fukuoka		

consisting of prefectures in Tôhoku and Kyûshu, we see a widening gap in their relative incomes. Without overstating the case, it can be said that within relatively industrialized prefectures, as well as within less industrialized prefecture, we see an equalizing trend in relative incomes, but that between the above two groups the per capita income differential tends to have increased. Although accompanied by some exceptions, this seems to be the essential pattern, and the apparent stability of the coefficient of variation of prefectural per capita incomes can be presumed of to be the result of the offsetting effect of the above tendencies.

Third, Tôkyô, Ôsaka and Aichi are prefectures whose relative incomes are among the top. In Fig. 2, their relative incomes increased for this period. This is because we used the average of 1956–61 as the latter period, but if we take up the average of 1955–59, Tôkyô's relative income will indicate a slight decline.

We can present a similar analysis in relation to the regional differential of the gross value-added per employee in manufacturing. Table 3 is based upon the gross value-added per employee and computes changes of the relative value-added per employee of various prefectures from 1950–55 to 1956–61. The denominator in the relative productivity is the average of productivities in all prefectures standardized each year with manufacturing employees of 1955 as the fixed weight. With respect to the "relative" gross value-added per employee, we have derived the 1950–55 average and the 1956–61 average and observed changes between the two period.

Fig. 3, drawn from the data of Table 3, gives us again interesting results. We find in the same way as in Fig. 2, relatively less industrialized (or lighter industry) prefectures scattered around the downward sloping line A consisting of following 32 prefectures: Miyazaki, Akita, Iwate, Ôita, Aomori, Kagawa, Miyagi, Nara, Gifu, Kôchi, Saga, Tokushima, Tochigi, Yamagata, Tottori, Nagano, Ishikawa, Fukui, Gunma, Yamanashi, Shimane, Fukushima and Ibaragi. The downward sloping line demonstrates very clearly that there was a tendency for

Table 3. Gross Value-Added Per Employee in Each Prefecture Relative to the Standardized Average of All Prefectures

Prefecture	1950–55 Av.	1956–61 Av.	Increase or decrease	Prefecture	1950–55 Av.	1956–61 Av.	Increase or Decrease (Manufacturing)
Hokkaidô	1.2121	1.1045	−0.1076	Miye	1.0950	1.0774	−0.0176
Aomori	0.8877	0.7054	−0.1823	Shiga	0.9615	0.8772	−0.0843
Iwate	1.0542	0.8567	−0.1975	Kyôto	0.9334	0.9184	−0.0150
Miyagi	0.7966	0.6902	−0.1064	Ôsaka	1.0986	1.1317	0.0331
Akita	1.0792	0.8504	−0.2288	Hyôgo	1.1548	1.2274	0.0726
Yamagata	0.5627	0.5302	−0.0325	Nara	0.7746	0.6744	−0.1002
Fukushima	0.7408	0.7518	0.0110	Wakayama	1.1127	1.0130	−0.0997
Ibaragi	0.8274	0.7982	−0.0382	Tottori	0.6335	0.6188	−0.0147
Tochigi	0.7198	0.6911	−0.0287	Shimane	0.7132	0.7298	0.0166
Gunma	0.5763	0.6090	0.0327	Okayama	0.8178	0.8112	−0.0066
Saitama	0.7785	0.8088	0.0303	Hiroshima	0.9073	0.9502	0.0429
Chiba	0.8022	0.9187	0.1165	Yamaguchi	1.5749	1.5789	0.0040
Tôkyô	1.1555	1.0838	−0.0717	Tokushima	0.7139	0.6285	−0.0854
Kanagawa	1.4576	1.5754	0.1178	Kagawa	0.8652	0.6589	−0.2063
Niigata	0.7509	0.7910	0.0401	Ehime	0.9756	1.0010	0.0254
Toyama	1.0512	0.9832	−0.0680	Kôchi	0.7188	0.6490	−0.0698
Ishikawa	0.6107	0.6197	0.0090	Fukuoka	1.3109	1.3741	0.0632
Fukui	0.5439	0.5608	0.0169	Saga	0.7232	0.6537	−0.0695
Yamanashi	0.4629	0.4961	0.0332	Nagasaki	0.7122	0.8796	0.1677
Nagano	0.6096	0.6096	0	Kumamoto	0.9522	0.9321	−0.0201
Gifu	0.7671	0.7002	−0.0669	Ôita	1.0816	0.9282	−0.1534
Shizuoka	0.9712	0.9873	0.0161	Miyazaki	1.2027	0.9193	−0.2834
Aichi	0.8700	0.9380	0.0680	Kagoshima	0.4966	0.4751	−0.0215

Fig. 3. Direction of Changes in Relative Value-Added Per Employee of Various Prefectures

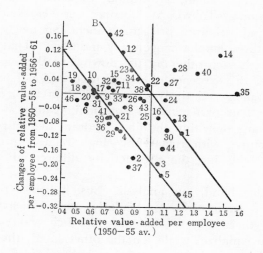

1.	Hokkaidô	17.	Ishikawa	32.	Shimane
2.	Aomori	18.	Fukui	33.	Okayama
3.	Iwate	19.	Yamanashi	34.	Hiroshima
4.	Miyagi	20.	Nagano	35.	Yamaguchi
5.	Akita	21.	Gifu	36.	Tokushima
6.	Yamagata	22.	Shizuoka	37.	Kagawa
7.	Fukushima	23.	Aichi	38.	Ehime
8.	Ibaragi	24.	Miye	39.	Kôchi
9.	Tochigi	25.	Shiga	40.	Fukuoka
10.	Gunma	26.	Kyôto	41.	Saga
11.	Saitama	27.	Ôsaka	42.	Nagasaki
12.	Chiba	28.	Hyôgo	43.	Kumamoto
13.	Tôkyô	29.	Nara	44.	Ôita
14.	Kanagawa	30.	Wakayama	45.	Miyazaki
15.	Niigata	31.	Tottori	46.	Kagoshima
16.	Toyama				

the value-added per employee of these twenty-three prefectures to equalize from 1950–55 to 1956–61.

Prefectures surrounding the upper line B, include the following: Nagasaki, Chiba, Aichi, Hiroshima, Shizuoka, Ehime, Miye, Ôsaka, Toyama, Tôkyô, Wakayama and Hokkaidô. These are mostly industrialized prefectures including newly industrialized prefectures emphasizing heavy industry. That these are connected with each other by the downward sloping curve will again suggest the existence of a narrowed regional productivity differential among relatively industrialized prefectures.

The other four prefectures, Yamaguchi, Kanagawa, Fukuoka and Hyôgo are all within the first quadrant demonstrating that these prefectures with remarkably high relative productivities are further widening the productivity differential with other prefectures.

On the one hand, our analysis, thus, indicates that among industrialized prefectures, particularly among heavy industry prefectures, there was a tendency for their value-added per employee to equalize, while, on the other hand, there was the same equalizing tendency among less industrialized prefectures. Offsetting these equalizing tendencies *within* each group, we have an widening productivity gap between the industrialized and the less industrialized group. The two opposing tendencies are mutually cancelled out and in the end we get a constancy of the coefficient of variation of value-added per employee among the forty-six prefectures.

It is exceedingly interesting that the apparent constancy of the overall indicator of the regional productivity differential has concealed the two opposite tendencies: the equalization as well as the aggravation of the regional differentials. Taking into account that the relatively industrialized prefectures in Fig. 3 are mostly the heavy-industry prefectures, our thesis that heavy industrialization plays a "differential-aggravating" role, other thing being equal, seems to be further strengthened.

REGIONAL STRUCTURE AND DIFFERENTIALS

Table 4. Time-series Elasticity of Employment for 1950–59
——log $N = a + b$ log V——

Prefecture	b	R^2	Prefecture	b	R^2
Hokkaidô	0.269	0.774	Miye	0.229	0.905
Aomori	0.329	0.816	Shiga	0.223	0.867
Iwate	0.351	0.903	Kyôto	0.383	0.946
Miyagi	0.444	0.921	Ôsaka	0.386	0.961
Akita	0.340	0.835	Hyôgo	0.274	0.905
Yamagata	0.326	0.889	Nara	0.263	0.646
Fukushima	0.257	0.862	Wakayama	0.329	0.864
Ibaragi	0.365	0.831	Tottori	0.271	0.877
Tochigi	0.352	0.869	Shimane	0.250	0.968
Gunma	0.316	0.902	Okayama	0.272	0.884
Saitama	0.363	0.960	Hiroshima	0.314	0.929
Chiba	0.353	0.956	Yamaguchi	0.211	0.745
Tôkyô	0.500	0.972	Tokushima	0.242	0.599
Kanagawa	0.365	0.923	Kagawa	0.301	0.820
Niigata	0.273	0.926	Ehime	0.183	0.785
Toyama	0.227	0.688	Kôchi	0.188	0.849
Ishikawa	0.285	0.884	Fukuoka	0.168	0.703
Fukui	0.191	0.685	Saga	0.268	0.810
Yamanashi	0.208	0.925	Nagasaki	0.102	0.451
Nagano	0.294	0.847	Kumamoto	0.177	0.857
Gifu	0.353	0.842	Ôita	0.214	0.885
Shizuoka	0.371	0.963	Miyazaki	0.164	0.720
Aichi	0.368	0.976	Kagoshima	0.352	0.977

Source: Based on the *Census of Manufactures*.
Note: The gross value-added based on the *Census of Manufactures* for 1950–59 was deflated by the wholesale price index for manufacturing commodities.

In order to check the above consequences, we shall present here a different type of analysis based on the computation of the elasticity of employment with respect to the gross value-added in manufacturing.

Here we get the following cross-section results fitted among forty-six prefectures as to the three years with respect to the number of employees N and the gross value-added V in manufacturing for the years 1951, 1955 and 1959.

1951 $\log N = - 0.00320 + 0.723 \log V, \quad R^2 = 0.800$
1955 $\log N = - 0.00481 + 0.814 \log V, \quad R^2 = 0.940$
1959 $\log N = - 0.00557 + 0.807 \log V, \quad R^2 = 0.949$

In other words, the cross-section elasticity of employment with respect to the value-added is about 0.7–0.8. However, if we compute the time-series elasticity of employment for 1950–59, we get a different result as shown in Table 4.

The implications to be derived from Table 4 can be summarized as follows:

1) The cross-section elasticity of employment is about 0.7–0.8, while the time-series elasticity is very low from 0.1 to 0.5. If we compute it for the former period (1950–55) and the latter (1956–61), then the elasticity will be naturally higher in the latter period in view of the trends in employment. Nevertheless, we have no reason to doubt the fact that the time-series elasticity is far lower. This may be due to the extraodinarily rapid expansion of productivity in fitted for manufacturing for 1950–59 and to the fact that the slope the employees and gross value-added for 1950–59 is much steeper than that fitted among prefectures.

2) The elasticity for Miyagi is 0.444, the highest in the Tôhoku district, that for Tôkyô is 0.500, the highest in the Kantô district, and those for Shizuoka and Aichi are 0.371 and 0.368 respectively, belonging to the highest in the Chûbu district. Furthermore, in Kansai district, Ôsaka is 0.386, the highest. These demonstrate that the center of each district has a very high employment elasticity, and one of the reasons for this may be due to the concentration of the small-medium enterprises with highly labor-intensive technique under the subcontract of large enterprises towards the central city of the district. This entails high absorption of employment increasing the elasticity of employment, particularly in machinery industry.

3) In Tôhoku, the time-series elasticity of employment is more than 0.3 in almost every prefecture, but the number

of prefectures in Kyûshû and Shikoku, the elasticity of which is in the range of 0.1×0.2, amounts to six. This constitutes a tremendous difference which we shall check by the changes of relative productivities in these prefectures from 1950–55 to 1956–61 based on the data mentioned in Table 3.

$\begin{bmatrix}\text{Tôhoku}\\\text{district}\end{bmatrix}$		$\begin{bmatrix}\text{Shikoku}\\\text{district}\end{bmatrix}$		$\begin{bmatrix}\text{Kyûshû}\\\text{district}\end{bmatrix}$	
Aomori	−0.1823	Tokushima	−0.0854	Fukuoka	0.0632
Iwate	−0.1975	Kagawa	−0.2063	Saga	−0.0695
Miyagi	−0.1064	Kôchi	−0.0698	Nagasaki	0.1677
Akita	−0.2288	Ehime	0.0254	Kumamoto	−0.0201
Yamagata	−0.0325			Ôita	−0.1534
Fukushima	0.0110			Miyazaki	−0.2834
				Kagoshima	−0.0215

The decline of relative productivities seems to be larger in the Tôhoku district than in the Kyûshû and Shikoku districts which explains why the elasticities of employment are higher in the Tôhoku district. The connection between the two sets of data cannot be made clear perfectly without going into an industry breakdown which will not be attempted here.

4)   The fact that the cross-section elasticity of employment is relatively stable at 0.7 to 0.8 suggests that the regional differential of value-added per employee in manufacturing has not indicated any conspicuous change for the past ten years and coincides very closely with the relative constancy of the coefficient of variation of value-added per employee computed among the forty-six prefectures.

3.   Cyclical Changes of Indicators for the Regional Differential and Concentration

As indicated in Fig. 1 the coefficient of variation of per capita incomes, as an indicator of regional differential, moves concomitantly with the actual business cycle, but the same coefficient of the value-added per employee (not only in manufacturing as a whole but also in heavy and light industries) does not necessarily correspond to the business cycle.

Therefore, we depict the increase or decrease of the standard deviation of per capita income and value-added per employee in Fig. 4. Although the increment of the standard deviation of per capita incomes fluctuates very clearly together with actual business cycle, that of value-added per employee moves in an irregular way.

Consequently, we have proceeded further to check the standard deviations of population, prefectural income, employees, and gross value-added, respectively. Since the per capita income and the value-added per employee are the ratios of two magnitudes, the increment of their standard deviations may not reflect the business cycle movements, even when the standard deviations of their numerator and denominator reflect them.

According to Table 5, both the standard deviations and the coefficients of variation of those magnitudes indicate a rising trend for 1950–61. The fact that the coefficient of variation is rising indicates an increasing regional concentration in terms of these variables. Taking the year-by-year increments of these standard deviations, Figs. 5~7 are constructed. In Fig. 5 it is interesting to see, on the one hand, that the increment of the standard deviation of population between prefectures is decreasing until 1955 when it begins to rise. This turing point, 1955, exactly coincides with the time of the jump in the *GNP* growth rate from about 8% for 1950–55 to 10% for 1956–61. Thus, the transition to the phase o higher growth rate seems to affect the incremental behavior of the regional population distribution very vividly. On the other hand, the increment of the standard deviation of the prefectural incomes is in perfect agreement with actual business fluctuations. As to why changes in the standard deviation of per capita incomes are cyclical may be due to the fact that those of prefectural incomes are cyclical

Fig. 4. Incremental Fluctuations in the Standard Deviations of Per Capita Incomes and Productivities in Manufacturing Among Prefectures

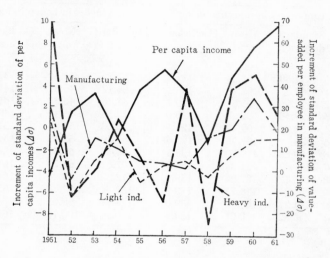

Fig. 5. Changes in the Standard Deviations of Populations and Incomes Among Prefectures

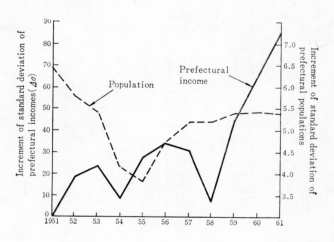

Table 5. Indicators of Regional Concentration of Population, Value-Added and Income

	Employees in manufacturing			Employees in heavy industry		
	Standard deviation	Mean	Coefficient of variation	Standard deviation	Mean	Coefficient of variation
	$\times 10^3$	$\times 10^3$	%	$\times 10^3$	$\times 10^3$	%
1950	94.58	83.93	112.7	57.34	41.58	137.9
1951	107.26	92.12	116.4	64.12	45.37	141.3
1952	112.95	93.61	120.7	67.20	46.35	145.0
1953	127.56	101.26	126.0	75.36	50.49	149.3
1954	130.89	102.98	127.1	76.00	50.22	151.3
1955	139.72	107.78	129.6	80.79	52.33	154.4
1956	159.63	119.70	133.4	94.56	59.66	158.5
1957	179.02	131.35	136.3	107.61	66.73	161.3
1958	185.12	132.86	139.3	112.26	68.28	164.4
1959	205.27	146.75	139.9	128.51	77.78	165.2
1960	231.21	165.26	139.9	148.11	90.02	164.5
1961	246.22	178.01	138.3	160.96	100.10	160.8

	Gross value-added in manufacturing			Gross value-added in heavy industry		
	Standard deviation	Mean	Coefficient of variation	Standard deriation	Mean	Coefficient of variation
	$\times 10^9$	$\times 10^9$	%	$\times 10^9$	$\times 10^9$	%
1950	20.67	15.88	130.1	13.18	9.10	144.8
1951	33.66	25.62	131.4	22.19	15.57	142.5
1952	40.29	28.42	141.7	25.77	16.92	152.3
1953	52.27	36.63	142.7	34.50	22.67	151.3
1954	60.86	41.19	147.8	38.30	24.58	155.8
1955	66.53	45.31	146.8	41.55	26.75	155.3
1956	83.83	55.26	151.7	54.56	34.18	159.6
1957	101.10	63.77	158.5	68.08	40.52	168.0
1958	110.04	68.86	159.8	74.78	44.49	168.1
1959	130.40	83.59	156.0	91.64	55.59	164.8
1960	171.52	109.45	156.7	122.79	74.80	164.2
1961	212.31	134.56	157.8	152.98	93.23	164.1

Employees in light industry			Population		
Standard deviation	Mean	Coefficient of variation	Standard deviation	Mean	Coefficient of variation
$\times 10^3$	$\times 10^3$	%	$\times 10^4$	$\times 10^4$	%
40.32	42.32	95.3	108.16	180.87	59.8
46.63	46.71	99.8	114.59	183.78	62.4
49.23	47.20	104.3	120.39	186.54	64.5
55.80	50.73	110.0	125.82	189.09	66.5
58.29	52.70	110.6	130.02	191.82	67.8
62.34	55.40	112.5	133.87	194.08	69.0
68.80	59.99	114.7	138.61	196.02	70.7
75.50	64.54	117.0	143.80	197.66	72.8
76.70	64.49	118.9	149.01	199.48	74.7
81.29	68.88	118.0	154.40	214.42	76.7
88.09	75.24	117.1	159.83	203.08	78.7
90.38	77.92	116.0	165.97	204.97	80.6

unit: yeu

Gross value-added in light industry			Income		
Standard deviation	Mean	Coefficient of variation	Standard deviation	Mean	Coefficient of variation
$\times 10^9$	$\times 10^9$	%	$\times 10^9$	$\times 10^9$	%
8.23	6.79	121.3	87.69	71.06	123.4
12.55	10.05	124.9	87.57	85.59	100.0
15.47	11.50	134.6	105.73	104.76	100.9
19.55	13.96	140.0	129.36	119.36	108.3
23.89	16.61	143.8	138.35	131.11	105.6
26.60	18.56	143.4	166.31	148.13	112.3
30.99	21.08	147.0	220.70	167.88	119.5
34.46	23.25	148.2	231.69	189.38	122.3
37.34	24.37	153.2	239.42	195.85	122.2
40.96	28.00	146.3	283.94	222.70	127.5
51.58	34.64	148.9	347.76	263.43	132.0
63.22	41.33	153.0	432.83	316.27	136.9

397

Fig. 6. Changes in the Standard Deviation of Employees in Manufacturing Among Prefectures

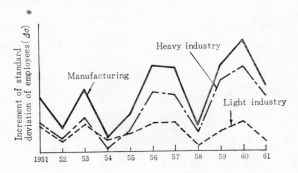

Fig. 7. Changes in the Standard Deviation of Gross Value-Added in Manufacturing Among Prefectures

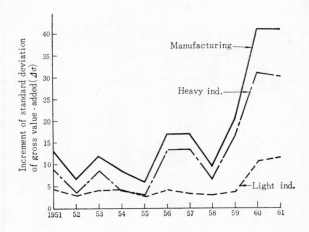

but those of prefectural populations are free from the influence of short-run cycles.

In Fig. 6 and 7, we have depicted the increments of the standard deviation of employees and the gross value-added in manufacturing, as well as heavy and light industries. Although we could not see any regular cycles in the increment of the standard deviation of value-added per employee in Fig. 4, we now find markedly regular cycles in the increments of the standard deviations of the value-added and employees themselves in Fig. 6 and 7, particularly as concerns heavy industry. Consequently, the lack of a regular cycle in the increment of the value-added per employee may be due to the mutual cancellation of cycles in its numerator and denominator.

4. Regional Differences in Industrial Structure

In the international comparison of the industrial structure of various countries we can find some empirical law in the relationship between the per capita national income and the industrial structure of each country. In the same way, we may find some empirical relationship between the per capita prefectural income and the industrial structure of each prefecture; for example, the proportion of primary industry in Kagoshima is much higher than in Tôkyô.

Fig. 8 shows that the proportion of the primary industry in terms of prefectural "income produced" tends to decline as we move to higher per capita incomes. Fig. 9, to the contrary, makes clear that the same proportion of the secondary industry has an increasing tendency. However, very interesting is the fact that the income proportion of secondary industry is rising up to Kanagawa prefecture, and then turns down in Ôsaka and Tôkyô. This is a point to be noticed in the interregional comparison of industrial structure because Tôkyô or Ôsaka, with excessive population concentrations, may develop as big cities focussing much more on tertiary industry than on secondary

Fig. 8. Per Capita Prefectural Incomes and the Income Proportions of the Primary Industry, 1960

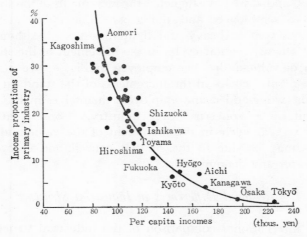

Fig. 9. Per Capita Prefectural Incomes and the Income Proportions of the Secondary Industry, 1960

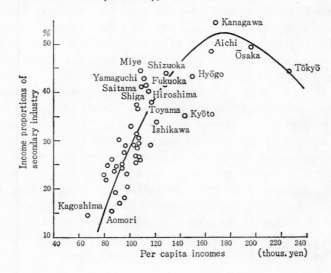

industry. Except for these two, we may say in general that the prefecture with a higher per capita income is more industrialized and vice versa, and the proportion of the primary industry declines in inverse proportion to the degree of industrialization. From this point of view, the policy which makes possible the regional dispersion of industry will be a first step toward the improvement of regional differentials.

Moving to Fig. 10, it is also interesting to see that there is no systematic relation between the income proportion of the tertiary industry and the per capita prefectural income. However, in Fig. 11 in which the labor force proportion of the tertiary industry is correlated with the per capita income, some systematic relations can be derived: the share rises as the per capita income increases. Also interesting is the fact that tourist resorts like Kyôto, Nara, Nagasaki, Kumamoto, etc., are rather upward of the free-hand line.

As is well known, the same relation can be derived also from international comparison as well as the long-term analysis. If we denote the income proportion of tertiary industry as Y_3/Y, and the labor force proportion of it as L_3/L, then the ratio of the two will indicate the comparative productivity of the tertiary industry, for the relation will identically hold true.

$$Y_3/Y \div L_3/L \equiv \frac{Y_3}{L_3} \Big/ \frac{Y}{L}$$

As Y_3/Y merely scatters, quite arbitrarily, with respect to the increase of per capita income, while L_3/L rises fairly systematically as is indicated in Fig. 11, the comparative productivity ($Y_3/Y \div L_3/L$) will necessarily tend to decline as per capita income rises. Fig. 12 shows this relationship for 1960. The split into two curves is worth noticing for, along the lower curve, we see a scatter of heavy-industry prefectures such as Kanagawa, Fukuoka, Shizuoka, Yamaguchi, Wakayama and Miye. Most interesting is the fact that we have only one declining curve connecting the comparative productivity and the per capita income in 1955, yet in 1960, after the unprecedented investment boom, the

401

Fig. 10. Per Capita Prefectural Incomes and the Income Proportions of the Tertiary Industry, 1960

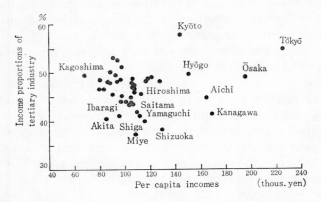

Fig. 11. Per Capita Prefectural Incomes and the Labor Force Proportions of the Tertiary Industry, 1960

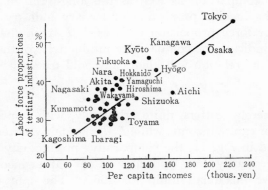

curve is decomposed into two parts. In view of the scatter along the lower curve of the heavy-industry prefectures, this split is seen as a consequence of rapid heavy industrialization. As the per capita income is lower, the comparative productivity of tertiary industry will be higher. This is quite in common with

402

Fig. 12. Declining Tendency of Comparative Productivity of the Tertiary Industry, 1960

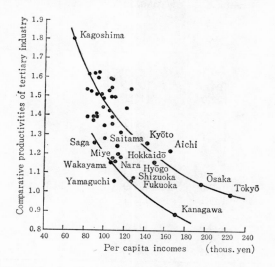

the results of international or long-term analyses. However, the above split into two curves is unique, reflecting an unprecedented, rapid heavy industrialization over 1955–61.

Of course, the declining tendency of comparative productivity in the tertiary industry, as per capita income rises, is subject to considerable deviation. Therefore, the fifteen prefectures are selected in Table 6, laying an emphasis on the three groups consisting typically of 1) high per capita income prefectures, 2) newly industrialized, medium per capita income prefectures and 3) underdeveloped prefectures. Among the fifteen prefectures in Table 6, the comparative productivity of the tertiary industry to all industries tends to increase as we move to the lower-productivity prefectures, although the association is not strong. However, if the comparative productivity of the tertiary industry as a ratio to the secondary industry is computed (column 2),

Table 6. Some Aspects of Comparative Productivities, 1960

	Tertiary ind. / All ind.	Tertiary ind. / Second. ind.	Primary ind. / Second. ind.	Incomes per employed labor force in all ind.
	(1)	(2)	(3)	(4)
				thous. yen
Tôkyô	99.4%	95.9%	43.0%	484
Ôsaka	104.5	102.7	33.9	448
Aichi	122.0	112.2	33.3	328
Kanagawa	88.5	69.5	30.8	437
Hyôgo	115.6	98.5	30.2	320
Hiroshima	120.1	86.3	29.4*	253
Yamaguchi	105.8	62.7	26.8*	283
Miye	117.5	69.4	25.7*	252
Kagawa	149.9	125.3	40.2	228
Fukushima	163.0	122.9	39.3	219
Tottori	139.1	135.1	67.8	192
Ôita	136.8	93.6	39.6	203
Aomori	153.3	111.9	46.4	193
Kumamoto	139.2	89.1	36.9	199
Kagoshima	177.4	145.4	48.7	145

Note: The comparative productivities (primary ind./second. ind.) in 1955 of the three prefectures with* were 34.0%, 32.4%, and 22.0% respectively, so it can be presumed that especially in Hiroshima and Yamaguchi the widening of the differential between the secondary and the primary industries was conspicuous in the high-pitched growth period of 1955–60.

we cannot find so obvious a tendency as can be seen in the column 1 of Table 6 for the comparative productivities (as compared with all industries); the 136.8 of Ôita and the 139.2 of Kumamoto are reduced to 93.6 and 89.1 (as compared with the secondary industry). It is to be emphasized that in such a heavy-industry prefecture, as Kanagawa, Yamaguchi and Miye, the comparative productivity of the tertiary industry in the column 2 definition is extremely low.

There is another notable point in Table 6. In Hiroshima, Yamaguchi and Miye, the incomes per capita of labor force in all industries are in the range of 250–280 thousand yen, locating themselves in the medium position in all prefectures. However, these prefectures have been in transition toward becoming the new industrial districts, centering on heavy industry. It is very striking to see that as a consequence, the productivity differential between agriculture and industry has been much more aggravated in these prefectures. In these three prefectures with *in column 3 the above productivity differential (the primary vs. the secndary) is in the range of 25–29%, and the lowest among the selected fifteen prefectures.

According to an international comparison, the proportion of the secondary industry in terms of employed labor force is not closely correlated with the per capita income. Therefore, although Y_2/Y is higher in the country of higher per capita income, L_2/L is indefinite with respect to an increase of per capita income (a bit flat tendency on the graph, although dispersed widely). Consequently, the comparative productivity of the secondary industry tends to increase as the per capita income becomes higher. However, when the counterpart relation is drawn of Fig. 13 as to the inter-regional data, we are struck with a new fact. The chart for the proportion of the secondary industry in terms of employed labor force seems to have a rather higher correlation than that in terms of income, with a steeply rising curve to the left. Fig. 13 shows an excellent fit beyond our expectation, with forty-five prefectures closely clustered around a curve, but with an only exception as concerns Tôkyô. Why we can derive an opposite conclusion to the international or time-series analyses from the cross-section analysis among prefectures is hard to make clear. Tentatively, we feel that since the productivity-dispersion between its highest and lowest prefectures is not so wide as in the long-term or international analysis, the regional dispersion of productivity will not offset the regional distribution of employment. There seems to remain much to be discussed in this problem, but we shall not go into detail.

With respect to secondary industry, we have to explore the problem of the heavy-industry ratio. Fig. 14 elucidates the

Fig. 13. Per Capita Prefectural Incomes and the Labor Force Proportion of the Secondary Industry, 1960

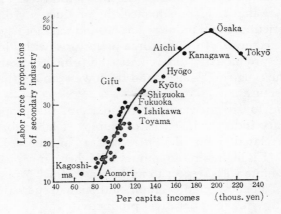

Fig. 14. Value-Added Productivities in Manufacturing and the Heavy-Industry Ratio, 1960

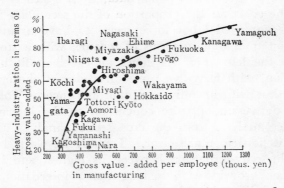

relation between the heavy-industry ratio in terms of the gross value-added and the gross value-added per employee. We have a positive correlation between the two, but in relation to prefectures whose value-added per employee is in the range of 400–600 thousand yen, the dispersion from the fitted line seems to be so high. However, the productivity of heavy industry is higher without exception than that of light industry in any prefecture, and this seems to be one of the causes why we have positive correlation between the two.

How is the ranking of prefectures in terms of the manufacturing gross value-added per employee or the heavy-industry ratio connected with the ranking in terms of the per capita income level? It is noteworthy that Yamaguchi prefecture, which is the highest in Japan in terms of the gross value-added per employee ranks only twentieth in her per capita income level in 1959. In general, the productivity in manufacturing is higher in prefectures located in the industrial districts surrounding big cities like Chiba, Kanagawa, Wakayama and Yamaguchi. This is in terms of productivity and not in terms of shipment or value-added.

The apparent difference between productivity and per capita income in the ranking will be, of course, due to the fact that in the determination of per capita income level, the productivities in the primary and tertiary industries also are important. However, there is a very important point which has been long ignored. Table 7 is the result of computation in 1959 of the ratio of manufacturing income (based on the prefectural income statistics) to gross value-added (based on the *Census of Manufactures*). This means that (1) the gross value-added includes depreciation charges, but the manufacturing income does not, (2) in the former the overhead cost, such as advertisement cost, rent, freight, reception expenses, and insurance premiums (i.e., the outflow to the tertiary industry) is included, but from the latter they are excluded. (3) gross value-added is based on the *Census of Manufactures*, covering only the establishments with four employees and over, but the manufacturing income covers all establishments. Although the third factor makes the manufacturing income larger than the gross value-added, the first and second factors serve to reduce the level of manufacturing income relative to the gross value-added. Income consists of

Table 7.   Income/Gross Value-Added Ratio in 1959

Yamaguchi	57.5%	Saga	82.9%
Toyama	60.3	Akita	83.3
Nagano	62.8	Iwate	85.1
Wakayama	63.5	Kôchi	85.5
Miyazaki	65.5	Kagoshima	86.4
Hiroshima	66.7	Ibaragi	89.5
Chiba	66.9	Shiga	90.7
Kanagawa	67.5	Tokushima	92.5
Shizuoka	67.9	Ôita	92.7
Aichi	68.7	Tottori	97.8
		Miyagi	100.5
Kumamoto	80.8	Nara	102.3
Okayama	80.9	Yamagata	109.7
Nagasaki	81.6	Yamanashi	116.9
Aomori	81.9	Kagawa	119.3

Note: We have omitted prefectures which are between Aichi (68.7%) and Kumamoto (80.8%).

wages and salaries plus profit and interest, but the gross value-added includes the depreciation and the above overhead costs in addition to the manufacturing income.

From Table 7, we know that the income/gross value-added ratio in manufacturing is very low in the new heavy-industry prefectures. In 1959, it is 57.5% in Yamaguchi, 60.3% in Toyama, 62.8% in Nagano, 63.5% in Wakayama, 65.5% in Miyazaki, 66.7% in Hiroshima, 66.9% in Chiba, and 67.5% in Kanagawa. Naturally, the rank of this ratio may change from year to year, but Table 7 will inform us of the broad outline of the situation.   It is almost an unrecognized fact that some of the gross value-added created inside the prefecture flows to the head office of the corporations or other industries outside the prefecture, not belonging to the same prefecture. This demonstrates that the dispersion of industries by the development of regional key points or the formation of new industrial districts will not be a sufficient condition for the improvement of the regional income differential.   If a part of the profit of the factories is sent out to the head office in Ôsaka or Tôkyô, it does not belong to the prefecture in which the factories are located. Of course, this point should not be overemphasized, and any attempt to industrialize the local district ought not to be assumed as meaningless. However, it must not be overlooked that, in such a highly capital-intensive industry as petro-chemicals, the proportion of wage and salary bills is very small, and the depreciation, interest and profit, amounting to an enormous portion, flow out of the prefecture. Probably, it is necessary that the location of big factories will entail a simultaneous emergence of complementary industries consisting of, say, parts makers, and the like in order to bring industrialization to the local district. It is very difficult to satisfy such a requirement in some prefectures, but in order for the local industrialization to contribute to the improvement of the regional income differential, the construction of a capital-intensive industry alone as mentioned above will not be sufficient. The conjunctive development of complementary industries in an organic manner will be necessary to distribute the benefits of development more within the prefecture.

The regional differential in terms of income per employed labor force in all industries can be decomposed into two parts. One is the differences in productivity due to the differences of industrial structure; in those prefectures whose proportion of the secondary industry is high, the overall productivity will be higher owing to the relatively higher productivity of secondary industry. Another is a residual part which still remains, even if the differences of industrial structure were assumed as zero. In Fig. 15, this is presented based on the prefectural income statistics and the *Census of Population*. Since the data is limited, we have to be satisfied with the decomposition into the industrial-structure factor and other.

In Fig. 15, we have first computed the standardized income per capita of the employed labor force, assuming that every prefecture has the same inter-industry employment structure as that of all prefectures This was then deducted from the "actual"

409

Fig. 15. Prefectural Incomes Per Capita of Employed Labor Force and the "Industrial-Structure Factor", 1960

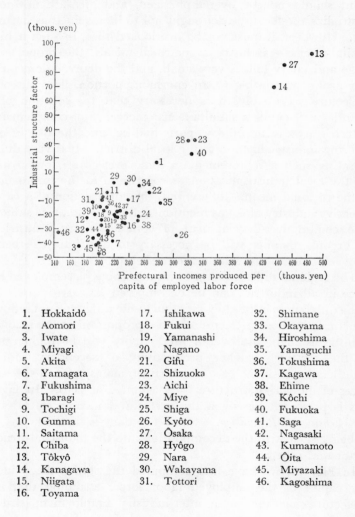

(thous. yen)

Prefectural incomes produced per capita of employed labor force (thous. yen)

1. Hokkaidô	17. Ishikawa	32. Shimane
2. Aomori	18. Fukui	33. Okayama
3. Iwate	19. Yamanashi	34. Hiroshima
4. Miyagi	20. Nagano	35. Yamaguchi
5. Akita	21. Gifu	36. Tokushima
6. Yamagata	22. Shizuoka	37. Kagawa
7. Fukushima	23. Aichi	38. Ehime
8. Ibaragi	24. Miye	39. Kôchi
9. Tochigi	25. Shiga	40. Fukuoka
10. Gunma	26. Kyôto	41. Saga
11. Saitama	27. Ôsaka	42. Nagasaki
12. Chiba	28. Hyôgo	43. Kumamoto
13. Tôkyô	29. Nara	44. Ôita
14. Kanagawa	30. Wakayama	45. Miyazaki
15. Niigata	31. Tottori	46. Kagoshima
16. Toyama		

income per capita of employed labor force; the difference was measured along the vertical axis of Fig. 15. Since the dispersion of the actual income per employed labor force among prefectures along the horizontal line amounts to about 360 thousand yen and that of the industrial-structure factor to about 150 thousand yen, we may roughly guess that about 42% of per labor force income differential among prefectures is accounted for by the industrial-structure factor and 58% by other factors.

As an example of the above the income per employed labor force in the secondary industry is not the same in every prefecture. In 1960, that of Tôkyô was 501,954 yen, and that of Kagoshima was 176,963 yen, still showing a tremendous gap. In the tertiary industry, Tôkyô is 481,485 yen and Kagoshima is 257,284 yen, and in the primary industry Tôkyô is 210,734 yen and Kagoshima is 86,257 yen. Thus, even in the same industry we have an enormous differential in productivity. More than that, the proportion of primary industry is far higher in Kagoshima, so the actual productivity measured in terms of income exhibits a wider difference between the two prefectures than in each industry.

However, the above analysis may be illusory, because it is based on the three-industry division, and if we have a further detailed breadkown, we may have a higher industrial-structure factor. Moreover, if we have data on the scale of establishment, we can also explore another factor, the size-of-establishment factor. We shall attempt such a type of analysis in section 6.

5. By-Industry and By-Size Characteristics of Regional Concentration and Differential

In the following we attempt to examine the differential or dispersion of selected variables among prefecture with respect to subgroups of manufacturing and also to size-groups of each industry. We shall continue to use the coefficient of variation, but it measures the regional differential when applied to the value-added per employee, and the degree of concentration or dispersion when applied to the employees or the value-added. In the latter case, analyses will be made as to how the number of employees or the value-added is regionally concentrated or dispersed by subgroups of manufacturing or by size-groups of each industry. The following points will be relevant.

First, the data to be used here is the *1958 Census of Manufactures* but in the detailed breakdowns of prefectural data, further classified into each industry and scale of establishment, we find a lot of concealed figures denoted by x, included in the adjacent figures or total, when in one category only one establishment exists and its figures need to be concealed. Therefore, in our analysis, we have filled up the x's by other supplementary scattered data.

Second, we have to bear in mind that 1958 is a recession year. Owing to the recession in some scale of some industries in some prefectures, we have a minus figure of net value-added, particularly in higher-size establishments. This may introduce some distortion to our analysis.

Third, we have used the net value-added instead of the gross value-added in this section. In the preceding analysis for 1950–61, we have converted the net value-added from 1957 on to gross terms, connecting them to the gross value-added for 1950–56. However, in this section, the net value-added is used as it is.

Fourth, the industrial classification available to us is not detailed. The two-digits classification may not be sufficient for our purposes. The classification of the size of establishments into three divisions is also not satisfactory. The lowest classification, "4–29 employees" will still be rough, because even if its proportion is the same between two prefectures, in terms of employees, one may have a higher proportion of very small establishments, and another may have a higher proportion of relatively large-size establishments. However, the data classified into subgroups of manufacturing, by prefecture as well as size of establishment, are only available in 1957 and 1958.

Taking into account the above limitations of the statistical data, we have computed the coefficient of variation among prefectures in relation to the total size (more than 4 employees), the size of 4–29 employees, the size of 30–299 employees, and the size of more than 300 employees. Table 8 indicates the coefficient of variation of the value-added per employee in the above classifications. This is derived by dividing the standard deviation (from the simple average of net value-added per employee) by that simple average.

Checking the rank of the coefficient of variation in all the sizes, we get the following arrangement. Industries in the higher rank have a larger regional differential in the value-added per employee compared with those in the lower rank. In the lower rank industries, the regional differential of value-added per employee is smaller.

1.	Rubber products	11.	Others
2.	Petroleum and coal products	12.	Chemicals
3.	Nonferrous metals	13.	Publishing and printing
4.	Pulp and paper	14.	Metal products
5.	Electrical machinery	15.	Textiles
6.	Leather and leather products	16.	Apparel
7.	Iron and steel	17.	Food products
8.	Ceramics	18.	Machinery
9.	Transportation equipment	19.	Furniture and fixture
10.	Instruments and related products	20.	Lumber and wood products

In general, there are many factors operating on the regional productivity differentials. But, the industry with a higher average value-added per employee may have a higher capital intensity, so some regional capital concentration will inevitably take place. Speculating in this way, we have computed the coefficient of

413

rank correlation between the rank of industry in the coefficient of variation of value-added per employee among prefectures in Table 8 and the average net value-added per employee in all prefectures and got 43.9%. On the other hand, the coefficient of rank correlation between the rank of industry in the coefficient of variation of productivity and the rank of industry in the net value-added per establishment in all prefectures is 58.3%. We compute, further, the proportion of the size of 4–29 employees in the total employees (excluding the size of 1–3 employees) and get a coefficient of rank correlation of 61.7%, between this and the coefficient of variation in Table 8. However, if we exclude chemicals and leathers from the twenty industries, the coefficient of rank correlation is raised to 77.4%. From these tentative computations, we have a feeling that the inter-industry differences of the coefficient of variation of the value-added per employee are to a great extent influenced by the proportion of small-medium enterprises in each industry.

The above is the pattern for establishments of all sizes, but by each size, we observe the following. There is a tendency in every industry that, as the size of establishment becomes larger, the coefficient of variation of the net value-added per employee among prefectures becomes higher indicating a greater regional productivity differential in the higher size. In the case of 300 employees and more, there are no establishments at all in some industries of some prefectures. Incidentally, the figures in brackets in Table 8 and 9 are computed, leaving out the empty part which sometimes appears in establishments of the highest size. In other words, when we have figures for only twenty prefectures in the total forty-six prefectures, the bracketed figure is the coefficient of variation among the twenty prefectures as based on the simple arithmetical average of net value-added per employee of the twenty prefectures. On the other hand, the figures without brackets are computed on the assumption that the productivity of prefectures without figures is zero, but is included in the computation of the coefficient of variation.

Therefore, in the latter computation, the larger the number of the empty box in the statistical table, the higher the coefficient of regional productivity differential tends to be. One of the reasons why the coefficient of variation in the latter concept becomes higher can be traced to this computation.

Those industries, in which the coefficients of variation among prefectures of the net value-added per employee in the size of 300 employees and more are extremely high, are not always the industries centered about the big enterprises. As is indicated in Table 8, industries, such as furniture and fixture, lumber and wood products, apparel, and leather are of a small-enterprise type. Yet, they indicate a considerably high coefficient of variation in the highest size, despite the fact that the big enterprise is the exception in these industries. If there are a fair number of prefectures with zero employee and net value-added except for some prefectures, the high coefficient of variation will necessarily result from the latter calculation.

Table 9 computes the coefficient of variation among prefectures in relation to the number of employees. In the case of the net value-added per employee, it represents an indicator of the regional differential, but in the case of the number of employees, it stands for an indicator of regional concentration or dispersion.

We may not always have a close correlation between the two coefficients of variation of the net value-added per employee, on the one hand, and the number of employees, on the other. Fig. 16, however, presents the interesting case when both coefficients of variation are correlated as to all sizes excluding the size of 1–3 employees. The two lines (H and L) are split, and heavy industries of the capital-intensive type cluster around the H line while light and heavy industries of the relatively labor-intensive type closely scatter around the L line. In the former there are rubber products, petroleum and coal products, iron and steel, nonferrous metals, paper and pulp, transportation equipment, ceramics and chemicals. In the latter, we have food products, lumber and wood products, furniture and fixture,

415

Table 8. Coefficient of Variation of Net Value-Added Per Employee Among Prefectures in Subgroups of Manufacturing, Cross-classified by Size of Establishment, 1958

	All sizes (excl. 1–3 employees)	4–29 employees	30–299 employees	300 employees and more
Food products	0.2725	0.1348	0.3447	1.2516(0.7116)
Textiles	0.3051	0.3279	0.3560	0.5490(0.4653)
Apparel	0.2879	0.3547(0.3184)	0.4832(0.3912)	2.1757(0.4965)
Lumber	0.1903	0.1541	0.3153	2.3685(0.3867)
Furniture and fixture	0.2238	0.2093	1.1440(1.0996)	3.5212(1.1534)
Pulp and paper	0.5913	0.3208	0.6867(0.6380)	1.0806(0.7128)
Publishing and printing	0.3787	0.2537	0.2899	1.1623(0.3526)
Chemicals	0.4243	0.3414	0.6065(0.5553)	0.8124(0.5128)
Petroleum and coal products	0.8193	0.5398(0.5132)	1.0110(0.7335)	2.8092(0.9659)
Rubber products	0.8826(0.6852)	0.8921(0.4586)	0.8923(0.4589)	1.7178(0.7949)
Leather and leather products	0.5793(0.4685)	0.6239(0.5182)	1.0570(0.4440)	3.6176(0.4744)
Ceramics	0.5306	0.3060	0.4133	0.8712(0.5479)
Iron and steel	0.5738	0.3639	0.5947(0.5694)	1.1659(0.5672)
Nonferrous metals	0.5999(0.5208)	0.6239(0.3843)	0.8276(0.5310)	1.0988(0.6630)
Metal goods	0.3407	0.1884	0.3909	1.9309(0.8029)
Machinery, exc. electrical	0.2687	0.1838	0.3499	0.6948(0.3098)
Electrical machinery	0.5892(0.5372)	0.4724(0.3787)	0.6096(0.4037)	0.9966(0.4618)
Transp. equipment	0.5074	0.2356	0.4022	1.1216(0.4766)
Instruments and related products	0.4842(0.4252)	0.3913(0.3209)	1.7790(1.5032)	2.0135(0.3142)
Others	0.4305	0.3001	0.5566(0.5029)	1.7225(0.5418)

Source: Ministry of International Trade and Industry, *Census of Manufactures*, 1958. Figures for the concealed x's were estimated by the writer.

Notes: 1) "Total" excludes "1–3 employees".

2) In some industries, the establishment is non-existent in the upper size. In such a case, the coefficient of variation was computed under the assumption that the productivity is zero, and in the computation of the average it was also included as a sample. The figures in brackets are the results, excluding these values.

3) The weapons industry is omitted, for the sample size is extremely small.

Table 9. Coefficient of Variation of the Number of Employees Among Prefectures in Sub-groups of Manufacturing, Cross-Classified by Size of Establishment, 1958

	All sizes (excl. 1–3 employees)	4–29 employees	30–299 employees	300 employees and more
Food products	0.8777	0.6641	1.0590	1.7972(1.2179)
Textiles	1.5388	1.5841	1.5262	1.6805(1.6046)
Apparel	1.6729	1.8491(1.8235)	1.5100(1.4381)	2.7669(0.9452)
Lumber and wood products	0.7489	0.5723	1.0700	3.1064(0.9261)
Furniture and fixture	1.3714	1.2687	1.6983(1.6491)	2.3250(0.3693)
Pulp and paper	1.5295	1.7158	1.6585(1.6087)	1.6327(1.2452)
Publishing and printing	2.7047	2.1301	2.7349	3.5860(2.3728)
Chemicals	1.3109	1.6526	1.8881(1.8352)	1.2462(0.9710)
Petroleum and coal products	1.6325	1.6648(1.6839)	1.8463(1.5417)	2.4052(0.6925)
Rubber products	2.0301(1.7977)	3.1619(2.5271)	2.5863(2.0456)	2.0251(1.0528)
Leather and leather products	3.5179(3.3492)	3.5850(3.4138)	3.1683(2.2916)	4.7082(1.0113)
Ceramics	1.4022	1.3308	1.5863	1.5763(1.2561)
Iron and steel	1.7239	1.8580	2.0486(2.0214)	2.1728(1.4946)
Nonferrous metals	1.5332(1.4603)	2.7171(2.4381)	2.5703(2.1891)	1.1690(0.7375)
Metal products	2.4170	2.5680	2.3434	2.3733(1.1444)
Machinery	1.7732	1.9424	1.9329	1.5900(1.2683)
Electricla machinery	2.3981(2.3361)	3.4189(3.2956)	2.9369(2.6761)	2.1904(1.5904)
Transp. equipment	1.7352	2.1804	1.9020	1.8769(1.2076)
Instruments and related products	3.6881(3.6012)	3.3874(3.3080)	3.3369(2.9154)	4.3341(1.8173)
Others	2.0629	1.9310	2.2492(2.1899)	2.3826(1.0865)

Fig. 16. Coefficients of Variation of Net Productivites and Employees Among Prefectures, 1958

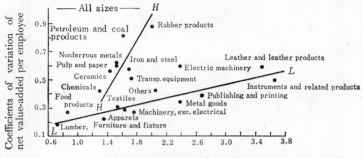

Coefficients of variation of employees

textiles, apparel, leathers, printing and publishing and other light industry, plus the metal goods, machinery, instruments and related products. The electrical machinery industry is located between the two lines. From these observations, we derive the important conclusion that the regional concentration of employees in relatively capital-intensive industries will bring about a much larger regional differential in net productivity between prefectures than in the case of the regional concentration of relatively labor-intensive industries. However, on the basis of the size of establishment, this will be less obvious as shown in Fig. 17 where the 300 employees and over size is presented as well as the 4–29 employees size. In the size of 300 employees and over, the sixteen industries are clustered around the free-hand line except for furniture and fixture, petroleum and coal products and instruments and related products. However, in the 4–29 employees size, the dispersion becomes very irregualr.

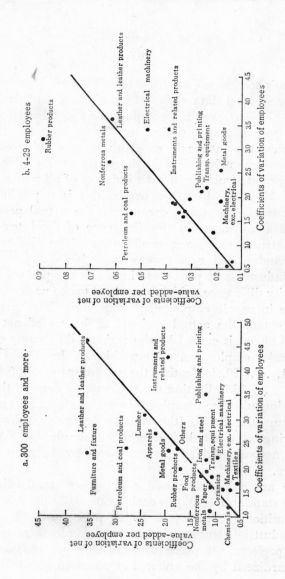

Fig. 17. Coefficients of Variation of Net Productivities and Employees Among Prefectures, by Size of Establishment, 1958

6. *Factors Affecting the Regional Differential of Net Productivity in Manufacturing*

In this section we shall use the *Census of Manufactures* of 1958 (the prefectural data classified by industry and size) for another purpose. First, we shall compute the "standardized" net value-added per employee derived on the assumption that in every prefecture the interscale composition of employees in each industry of manufacturing is the same as the interscale average employment structure in each industry of all prefectures (including Hokkaidô). In other words, this is a productivity which has abstracted or taken away from the actual productivity the influences arising from the difference of the interscale employment structures among prefectures. The difference between this standardized productivity and the actual productivity in each industry and prefecture indicates the part of regional productivity difference, which is ascribed to the prefectural difference of the interscale employment structures, thereby explaining to what extent the actual regional differnces of net value-added per employee is caused by the regional differences of the relative interscale employment composition. In the following, $\bar{Y}_{ij}$ ($i = 1, \ldots, 20$, indicating the subgroups of manufacturing and $j = 1, \ldots, 46$ indicating the prefectures) denotes the *standardized* net value-added per employee in various industries and in various prefectures, and Y_{ij} (the value-added per employee in manufacturing as a whole is designated simply by Y_i) denotes the *actual* net value-added per employee by industry and by prefecture.

We are going to consider a further standardization of the above standardized $\bar{Y}_{ij}$ in each industry by the relative industrial composition of employees in all prefectures. In other words, the industrial structure in terms of employment actually differs from prefecture to prefecture, but what we are going to do is to standardize it by the uniform or common industrial structure in

420

46 prefectures as a whole in terms of employees. Denoting by $\overline{W}_i$ the relative industrial composition of employees in all prefectures and by W_{ij} the actual relative industrial composition of employees in each prefecture, we find that the net value-added per employee in manufacturing industry as a whole, which is standardized only for the interscale employment structure of each prefecture, is

$$\sum_{i=1}^{20} W_{ij} \overline{Y}_{ij}$$

and the net value-added per employee which is standardized for both the interscale and the "industrial" employment structures, is

$$\sum_{i=1}^{20} \overline{W}_i \overline{Y}_{ij}.$$

Simplifying the notion,

$$\overline{Y}_j = \sum_{i=1}^{20} W_{ij} \overline{Y}_{ij}; \quad \overline{\overline{Y}}_j = \sum_{i=1}^{20} \overline{W}_i \overline{Y}_{ij}$$

we have two kinds of standardized net productivities. From the combination of the two and the actual productivity we can derive the "industrial-structure factor" as $(\overline{Y}_j - \overline{\overline{Y}}_j)$ and the "size-structure factor" as $(Y_j - \overline{Y}_j)$.

$\overline{\overline{Y}}_j$ is already standardized not only in the differences of the interscale structure but also of the industrial structure in terms of employment, so the prefectural differences of $\overline{\overline{Y}}_j$ are attributed neither to the "industrial-structure factor" nor to the "size-structure factor." Tentatively, we consider it here as being due to the "residual-regional factor" which may be highly dependent on the "external economy" benefit accompanied by regional industrialization or the enhancement of regional industrial level.

However, we must add hastily that the above procedure will not elucidate what part of the "level" of the productivity in the "specific" prefecture should be attributed to the "industrial-structure factor", the "size-structure factor" and the "residual-regional factor". For instance, some industries in some prefecture were assumed to have the same interscale employment structure

421

as in all prefectures. Then $Y_{ij} = \overline{Y}_{ij}$ would prevail, and the "size-structure factor" would be zero in our calculation. But this does not point toward the non-existence of the "size-structure factor" in that prefecture. It merely indicates what percentage of the regional "differential" in some industries among prefectures is dependent on the difference of industrial structure, size structure, and so on. What we are concerned with here is the analysis of factors relating to the absolute "differences" of productivity among prefectures, not to the absolute "magnitude" of productivity in each prefecture.

Therefore, we shall use simple regression analysis in order to make clear the causes of the regional "differences" of productivity. For each industry, we have fitted a linear function between the computed "size-structure factor" in each prefecture and the actual value-added per employee as follows:

$$(Y_{ij} - \overline{Y}_{ij}) = a + b(Y_{ij}).$$

In some cases this was computed after excluding extremely scattered prefectures. The year 1958 was a year of recession, and in some sizes of establishments, industries and prefectures, the value-added becomes negative. Therefore, we have decided to omit some of the unusual values from our regression analysis.

The coefficient of determination is not always high in Table 10. However, the regression coefficient is almost always 20–40%, if we omit equations in which the coefficient of determination is extremely low (less than 0.2). Moreover, the regression coefficient "b" is always positive, and the intercept "a" is unanimously negative. It is thus clear that the "size-structure factor" makes a positive contribution to the regional differences of productivity to the extent that the regression coefficients are 0.2–0.4.

In manufacturing as a whole, the coefficient of the "size-structure factor" is 0.2072–0.2468 and that of the "industrial-structure factor" is 0.3266–0.4682. Consequently, the total of the two is 0.5338–0.7150, and the "residual-regional factor" will be 0.4662–0.2850. However, it is erroneous to give these

Table 10. Size-Structure Factor and Industrial-Structure Factor, 1958

(thous. yen)

Equations explaining the "size-structure factor"	Manufacturing (excl. Chiba)	$y = -80.23 + 0.2072x$	$R^2 = 0.5239$
	" (excl. Chiba, Tōkyō, Ōsaka, Kyōto)	$y = -91.94 + 0.2468x$	$R^2 = 0.6933$
	Food products (excl. Kyōto, Miye, Kumamoto)	$y = -97.71 + 0.2136x$	$R^2 = 0.3465$
	Textiles (excl. Kyōto, Akita, Kagoshima)	$y = -48.26 + 0.2134x$	$R^2 = 0.3102$
	Lumber and wood products (excl. Miye, Nara)	$y = -41.71 + 0.1388x$	$R^2 = 0.1294$
	Furniture and fixture (excl. Tōkyō, Hyōgo, Fukushima)	$y = -21.93 + 0.0860x$	$R^2 = 0.0825$
	Pulp and paper (all prefectures)	$y = -210.37 + 0.5160x$	$R^2 = 0.6174$
	Publishing and Printing (all prefectures)	$y = -202.47 + 0.3836x$	$R^2 = 0.4804$
	Chemicals (excl. Saitama, Saga, Tokushima)	$y = -127.52 + 0.1418x$	$R^2 = 0.1188$
	Rubber products (excl. Chiba and Niigata)	$y = -83.88 + 0.1893x$	$R^2 = 0.3291$
	Leather and leather products (excl. Hiroshima)	$y = -18.49 + 0.0309x$	$R^2 = 0.0131$
	Ceramics (excl. Hokkaidō)	$y = -158.09 + 0.3876x$	$R^2 = 0.5628$
	Iron and Steel (excl. Miyazaki, Aonori, Ōita, Shiga)	$y = -180.61 + 0.3287x$	$R^2 = 0.3895$
	Nonferrous metals (all prefectures)	$y = -169.60 + 0.2820x$	$R^2 = 0.2413$
	Machinery (all prefectures)	$y = -142.84 + 0.3518x$	$R^2 = 0.5173$
	Electr. machinery (excl. Nara, Wakayama, Kōchi, Kumamoto)	$y = -180.04 + 0.3513x$	$R^2 = 0.4450$
	Transp. exuipments (excl. Shizuoka, Ōita, Ehime, Shiga, Nara)	$y = -218.13 + 0.3918x$	$R^2 = 0.5137$
Equations explaining the "industrial-structure factor"	Manufacturing (all prefectures)	$y = -130.59 + 0.3266x$	$R^2 = 0.4976$
	" (Kanagawa, Fukuoka, Hyōgo, Tōkyō, Ōsaka, Hokkaidō, Miye, Shizuoka, Kyōto, Ōita, Wakayama, Kagawa, Kōchi, Gifu, Ishikawa, Fukui, Nara, Shiga, Saitama, Aichi)	$y = -197.67 + 0.4111x$	$R^2 = 0.8341$
	" (other prefectures)	$y = -157.18 + 0.4682x$	$R^2 = 0.7735$

coefficients an absolute meaning. The size classification is only of three breakdowns, and the number of industries is only twenty. Therefore, the total of the two factors should far exceed 0.5–0.7.

Nevertheless, these computations can be suggestive. In Fig. 18, which explains the "industrial-structure factor" as compared with the net value-added per employee we have, along the lower line, the big city areas, the industrialized regions, and the prefectures in which they have established already important light industries. As such, we can mention Tôkyô, Ôsaka, Kanagawa, Hyôgo, Miye, Shizuoka, Kyôto, Wakayama, Aichi, Fukui, etc. On the other hand, along the upper line in Fig. 18, the underdeveloped prefectures cluster together in the region of lower value-added per employee, although some newly developed heavy-industry prefectures are involved. This probably can be taken to mean that the prefectures belonging to the lower line are supposed to have a higher "residual-regional factor" for in Fig. 19, which explains the "size-structure factor", almost all prefectures except for Tôkyô, Ôsaka, Kyôto and Chiba, are along one line. Therefore the residual part should be necessarily higher in the prefectures on the lower line. If so, those prefectures along the lower line should logically have higher external economies provided by the development of complementary industries and the expansion of the consumer's as well as producer's market. This is so provided that the major part of the "residual-regional factor" will consist of the benefit from the external economy.

The above is an analysis developed only in relation to the recession year, 1958, so it should be accepted only after similar analyses are conducted for other years. However, this analysis here is only intended as a first step to explore the factors causing the regional productivity differential.

In order to add a more detailed concrete analysis we shall take up next the textile industry. In this industry, there are only three prefectures, Aomori, Akita, and Nagasaki, which have no establishment in the size of over 300 employees. There-

424

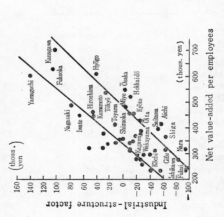

Fig. 18. Regional Differential of Net Value-Added Per Employee in Manufacturing and the Industrial-Structure Factor, 1958

Fig. 19. Regional Differential of Net Value-Added Per Employee in Manufacturing and the Size-Structure Factor, 1958

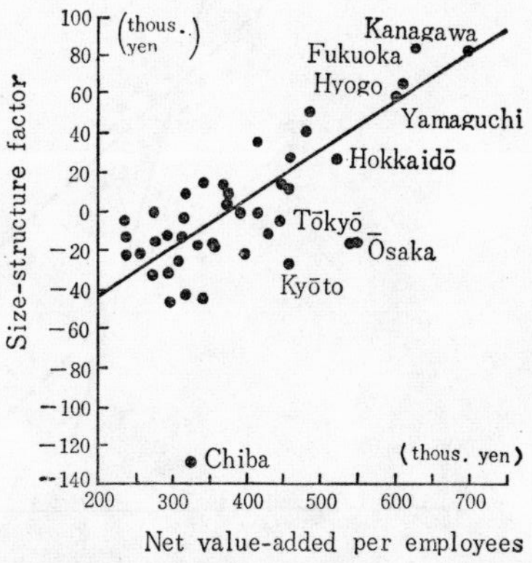

Fig. 20. Prefectural Differences of the Size-Structure Factor in Textile Industry, 1958

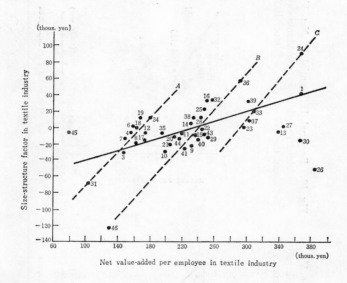

1. Hokkaidô	18. Fukui	32. Shimane
3. Iwate	19. Yamanashi	33. Okayama
4. Miyagi	20. Nagano	34. Hiroshima
6. Yamagata	21. Gifu	35. Yamaguchi
7. Fukushima	22. Shizuoka	36. Tokushima
8. Ibaragi	23. Aichi	37. Kagawa
9. Tochigi	24. Miye	38. Ehime
10. Gunma	25. Shiga	39. Kôchi
11. Saitama	26. Kyôto	40. Fukuoka
12. Chiba	27. Ôsaka	41. Saga
13. Tôkyô	28. Hyôgo	43. Kumamoto
14. Kanagawa	29. Nara	44. Ôita
15. Niigata	30. Wakayama	45. Miyazaki
16. Toyama	31. Tottori	46. Kagoshima
17. Ishikawa		

fore, we are trying to conduct a special-type analysis as to the "size-structure factor" in relation to the remaining 43 prefectures. Measuring on the vertical axis the "size-structure factor", and on the horizontal axis, the net value-added per employee, we have constructed Fig. 20. A casual glance at the chart will give us an impression of poor correlation. But a free-hand line drawn for all the scattered points will suggest that the "size-structure factor" contributed by about 20–30% to the regional dispersion of the net value-added per employee among prefectures (this free-hand line is different from the regression derived from an equation in Table 10, for the latters' coefficient of determination of 0.3102 does not permit any confidence that the one way fitting from x to y is worthier than the free hand). However, a careful observation will elucidate the following interesting points. All the scattered points can be divided, by and large, into three subgroups: A, B, and C. Each of these subgroups can be further examined in Table 11. Pattern A mainly consists of prefectures in which the silk-reeling industry occupies a major part in the textile industry. Within pattern A, pattern A-1 has a predominant proportion of silk-reeling industry in the shipments of the textile industry. However, even in pattern A-2, the proportion of silk-reeling is fairly high. Therefore, among eleven prefectures, the seven prefectures have a very close connection with the silk-reeling industry.

The peculiarity of pattern B lies in the high proportion of the yarn-and-thread industry. Patterns B-1 and B-2 are particularly so, and among the twenty-one prefectures belonging to B, we can say fourteen prefectures perfectly conform to the yarn-and-thread industry pattern.

On the other hand, the prefectures Aichi, Miye and Okayama have a particularly high absolute amount of shipments of the yarn-and-thread industry. In pattern A-2 we have prefectures in which the proportion of the yarn-and-thread industry is very high, but their absolute amount of shipments is low. Pattern C, however, involves prefectures in which the absolute amount

Table 11. Analysis of Fig. 20

Pattern A

1. Centered on the silk-reeling industry
   Iwate (45.1%), Miyagi (49.9%), Ibaragi (59.7%), Yamanashi (41.5%) Fukushima (41.6%)
2. Others
   Yamagata (silk-reeling 26.4%, weaving 55.8%), Chiba (yarn and thread 68.5%), Ishikawa (weaving 41.1%, yarn and thread 38.5%), Fukui (weaving 61.8%, dyeing 17.3%), Tottori (yarn and thread 67.2%, silk-reeling 29.3%), Hiroshima (yarn and thread 37.0%, weaving 32.3%).

Pattern B

1. Centered on the yarn and thread industry
   Kanagawa (42.5%), Toyama (69.6%), Gifu (73.5%), Shizuoka (44.8%), Shiga (46.6%), Hyôgo (54.8%), Shimane (55.7%), Tokushima (44.3%), Ôita (64.5%).
2. Yarn and thread mixed with others
   Tochigi (yarn and thread 23.1%, weaving 33.2%), Saitama (yarn and thread 23.5%, weaving 32.7%), Nagano (yarn and thread 33.6%, silk-reeling 56.5%), Ehime (yarn and thread 38.0%, weaving 48.8%), Kumamoto (yarn and thread 45.7%, silk-reeling 43.4%).
3. Yarn and thread, but with small proportions
   Gunma (yarn and thread 14.7%, weaving 40.2%, silk-reeling 31.3%), Niigata (yarn and thread 12.9%, w aving 48.4%, knitted fabrics 14.8%), Nara (yarn and thread 28.7%, knitted fabrics 48.6%), Yamaguchi (yarn and thread 2.4%, rope and net 56.1%), Saga (obscured by concealment, *x*), Fukuoka (yarn and thread 19.7%, weaving 37.6%, other textiles 27.7%), Kagoshima (yarn and thread 10.8%, weaving 33.7%, silk-reeling 20.4%).

Pattern C and Others

1. Shipments of yarn and thread high, by and large, with high proportions (Pattern C)
   Aichi (yarn and thread 39.1%, weaving 39.2%), Miye (85.2%), Okayama (59.2%), [Kagawa (58.7%), Kôchi (58.5%)—shipments are small]
2. Dispersed pattern
   Hokkaidô (yarn and thread 27.5%, rope and net 40.6%), Miyazaki (silk-reeling 69.9%), Kyôto (weaving 33.5%, dyeing 31.7%)
3. Diversification of products pattern (high in shipments too)
   Tôkyô (knitted fabrics 38.8%, yarn and thread 17.1%, weaving 15.8%, dyeing 15.3%), Ôsaka (yarn and thread 40.6%, weaving 22.4%, dyeing 18.5%, knitted fabrics 12.5%), Wakayama (dyeing 33.8%, knitted fabrics 29.1%, yarn and thread 18.2% weaving 15.8%).

---

of these shipments of them is also particularly high. To the dispersed pattern belong Miyazaki, in which the proportion of the silk-reeling occupies about 70% (the highest), and Kyôto, which is very famous for the Nishijin weaving industry (which produces the highest quality in woven fabrics and whose value-added per employee is the highest). The former scatters to the extreme left and the latter scatters to the extreme right. Hokkaidô also scatters far from any of the three subgroups, but it is characterized by the shipments of nets and ropes amounting to about 40%.

The most interesting are Tôkyô, Ôsaka, and Wakayama, and they are characterized by an enormous amount of shipments as well as by the extremely diversified production of various textiles.

When the straight lines are fitted to each of the patterns, A, B and C, it is notable that within each particular subgroup the size-structure factor" plays about a 100% role in the rise of the net value-added per employee. Thus, the more the industry is broken down in detail, the higher the role of the "size-structure factor" would be as an explanatory variable of the regional productivity differential.

Another special analysis will be conducted in Fig. 21 with respect to the machinery industry (in narrower sense, excluding electrical machinery, transportation equipments, etc.), by a graphical procedure. In Fig. 21, marked with sign " $\times$ " are the prefectures in which there are no establishments with over 300 employees. Therefore, we have estimated a "potential" net value-added per employee in that size by making it proportional to the inter-scale slope of the average net value-added per employee of the same industry in all prefectures. After this is done, a standardized productivity was computed in that prefecture by applying the inter-scale employment composition in all prefectures. The difference between the actual and the standardized productivities thus computed is the "size-structure factor" we have already referred to. Therefore, the "size-structure factor" in the prefectures

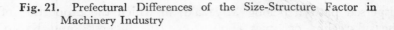

Fig. 21. Prefectural Differences of the Size-Structure Factor in Machinery Industry

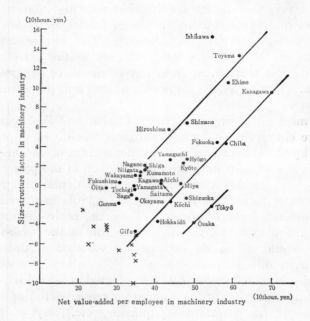

with sign " × " may involve some errors, and we have not mentioned names of those prefectures in the Fig. 21.

The derived observations are as follows: Drawing the three rightward rising lines in free-hand, we find that Tôkyô and Ôsaka are along the lowest line. In other words, compared with productivity, the "size-structure factor" is relatively low. This may be due to two reasons. 1) As far as the machinery industry is concerned, the proportion of the lower sizes is unexpectedly high in Tôkyô and Ôsaka, and this reduces the "size-structure factor". 2) However, when the productivities of the same size are compared, Tôkyô and Ôsaka are relatively higher in the lower sizes.

Table 12. Inter-Prefectural Comparison of Employment Structure and Productivity in Machinery Industry, 1958

	By-size employment composition (%)				By-size net value-added per employee (thousand yen)			
	Total	4–29 employees	30–299 employees	300 employees and more	Total	4–29 employees	30–299 employees	300 employees and more
Tôkyô	100	32.6	46.1	21.2	552	381	565	785
Ōsaka	100	31.2	55.5	13.3	501	344	522	784
Kanagawa	100	17.4	31.9	50.7	700	340	610	880
Aichi	100	29.3	39.5	31.2	416	282	412	547
Chiba	100	31.7	32.9	35.4	587	260	450	1008
Hyôgo	100	19.7	38.5	41.8	488	317	488	569
Yamaguchi	100	22.5	43.3	34.2	439	287	352	649
Hiroshima	100	23.5	32.8	43.7	441	224	334	638
Shimane	100	27.8	37.1	35.1	484	175	246	981
Ehime	100	22.9	37.3	39.7	592	221	305	1077
Toyama	100	21.8	32.2	46.0	619	233	348	992
Ishikawa	100	17.2	24.4	58.4	560	232	310	762
Kagoshima	100	59.4	40.6	0	227	195	271	—

Table 12 makes this point clear. Among thirteen prefectures, the proportion of employees in the size of 4–29 employees is 32.6% in Tôkyô and 31.2% in Ôsaka, surpassing those of other industrial prefectures. However, the net value-added per employee in the size of 4–29 employees is 381 thousand yen in Tôkyô and 344 thousand yen in Ôsaka, far exceeding that of Aichi, Chiba, Yamaguchi, Hiroshima, Toyama and Ishikawa, which is in the range of 230–280 thousand yen. They have productivities twice as high as the 195 thousand yen value of Kagoshima. The fact we have so wide a differential in the same size and in the same industry may be partly due to the higher composition of the upper part in the intrastructure of the size of 4–29 employees in Tôkyô and Ôsaka. But it may be further dependent upon the greater benefit from the external economy compared with other prefectures. Those small enterprises, which act as parts makers and are located in the neighborhood of a big assembly factory, will benefit more than those in other prefectures in increasing their shipments and production by specializing themselves in small number of products and by increasing their productivities through mass production. Tôkyô and Ôsaka occupied 36.2% of the total employees and 39.9% of the total shipments of machinery industry in the country as a whole in 1958. It is to be noted that, even if the productive activity is highly concentrated in big cities, the proportion of small-medium enterprises is much higher than that of large enterprises in big cities. The number of employees in Tôkyô and Ôsaka in the size of over 300 employees is 23.7% of the entire country, but it is 40.7% in both of the sizes of 4–29 and 30–299 employees.

In Fig. 21, Ishikawa is located in the highest place, and this may be due to the existence of the Komatsu Seisakusho (Komatsu Manufacturing Co. Ltd.,) which has one of the biggest factories of the construction machinery there. In Ishikawa prefecture, the proportion of construction and mining machineries in the shipments of the general machineries amounted to 39.7% in 1958. Further, the composition of employees in the size of over

300 employees in the same prefecture is 58.4%, the top in Japan. Toyama is also scattered near Ishikawa in Fig. 21, and this may be due to the existence of the Fujikoshi Kôzai Kôgyo (Fujikoshi Steel Industry Co. Ltd.), which is devoted to the production of bearing and machine tools. In Toyama prefecture, the proportion of shipments of the "other machineries and parts" amounts to 73.5%, owing to Fujikoshi's existence. In such a way, a big factory in a local prefecture will strongly affect the "size-structure factor" and the productivity there. On the other hand, in the big cities the small-medium enterprises of machinery industry grow in clusters in the close network of organic and hierarchical subcontracting systems. These contrasts in the local and central machinery factories are noticeable in the location of machinery industry.

In Fig. 21, if we take out Ishikawa, Tôkyô and Ôsaka and prefectures with signs × (none in the size of over 300 employees), we may have the two lines fitted by free-hand. Scattered along the lower line we find are early-industrialized prefectures (Kanagawa, Hyôgo, Fukuoka, Kyôto, etc.) or thier adjacent industrial prefectures (Chiba, Miye, Shizuoka, Gifu, etc.). We find, round the upper line, however, Ishikawa, Toyama, Ehime, Shimane, Hiroshima, Nagano, Niigata, Fukushima, etc. Some of these are late-industrialized prefectures, and others are non-industrial ones. It is interesting to see the existence of a rather inverse relation in the machinery industry between the "size-structure factor" and the economic levels of various prefectures.

7. Regional Differential and Concentration in Prewar Period

The emphasis in our analysis so far has been placed mostly upon the postwar movements of regional income or productivity differential and employment concentration, but it may be of some interest to explore how these indicators behaved in the *prewar* period and to what extent their levels differed from those of the postwar years. In this section we cannot present a detailed analysis, but can hopefully make the following clear.

In the prewar period, we have no prefectural income statistics, so what we can only measure the regional differential of gross value of product per manual worker, and the regional concentration of employment and gross output in manufacturing. The basic statistical source from which we are computing these measures is the *Kôjô-tôkeihyô* (Factory Statistics). The figures broken down into 46 prefectures and Okinawa, are restricted to *private* manufacturing establishments of five or more employees.

A few observations follow from the computations of Table 13. (1) When the 1955 postwar coefficients of variation are compared with these counterpart prewar figures, we are struck by the fact that there are no great differences between the prewar and postwar coefficients. There appear no conspicuous discontinuities.

(2) In relation to the coefficient of variation of gross output per worker, the general trends for manufacturing, heavy industry and light industry are declining, particularly for heavy industry (94.85% in 1914, 79.04% in 1930, 47.08% in 1940, and 41.56% in 1955). In manufacturing as a whole the coefficient of variation was relatively stable in the prewar period, but, in heavy as well as light industry, it tends to decline and their differing behaviors in the prewar period perfectly correspond to those in the postwar period.

(3) The coefficient for heavy industry is higher than those for light as well as manufacturing industry. This indicates that the regional concentration of output and employment was higher in heavy industry than in light industry, and also that the regional productivity differential was greater in heavy than in light industry.

(4) Compared with the results of Table 5 (an upward trend in the coefficients of variation of employment and gross value-added for 1950–58 and levelling-off for 1958–61) the results of Table 13 seem to show us the relative stability of the coefficient

434

Table 13. Coefficients of Variation of Gross Productivities, Gross Output and Manual Workers Among Prefectures in the Prewar Period

	Gross value of product	Manual workers	Gross output per manual worker
Manufacturing			%
1914	171.10	132.96	37.39
1920	161.94	130.31	47.43
1930	156.13	125.01	44.03
1935	164.20	138.04	45.70
1940	169.07	153.17	35.67
1955	141.32	129.6*	26.09**(29.2***)
Heavy industry			%
1914	232.68	194.17	94.85
1920	210.20	190.99	51.85
1930	212.53	198.45	79.04
1935	208.10	197.14	65.29
1940	203.77	196.64	47.08
1955	159.86	154.4*	41.56**(34.5***)
Light industry			%
1914	153.25	127.03	38.35
1920	142.77	119.89	54.03
1930	131.08	112.56	43.67
1935	137.05	113.53	35.70
1940	119.70	105.51	25.65
1955	129.59	112.5*	26.13**(26.4***)

Notes: *   Employees incl. non-manual workers.
 ** Gross output per employee.
 *** Gross value-added per employee.

of variation of output and employment in manufacturing for the long period from 1914 to 1961. However, we cannot but find that the coefficients of variation in heavy industry are much lower in the postwar period than in the prewar period, even though those coefficients in heavy industry increased in the postwar-period.

8. Conclusion

The major conclusions derived from our analysis can be summarized as follows.

1) Although it is generally argued that the regional differentials of per capita income and productivity have widened in the process of rapid economic growth, we cannot substantiate this view statistically.

2) When dividing the entire country into two parts, the industrialized and the non-industrialized prefectures, the regional differential has widened between the two groups, but within each group, we see a tendency for the differential to be reduced. The two counter-vailing tendencies of aggravation and equalization having been offset, the overall indicator shows a flat trend.

3) Although the indicator for the productivity differential in manufacturing tends to level off, it tends to decrease when we take up heavy and light industries separately. This is because the increasing regional differential due to the rise of the proportion of heavy industry with a higher differential might have offset the differential-reducing tendency in each of the heavy and light industries. In this sense, heavy industrialization has been differential-accelerating by itself, when the trend of the productivity differential of light and heavy industries is separately presented. Therefore, it might be said that the future of the regional productivity differential is highly dependent on the pace of heavy industrialization.

4) When all industries are broken down into the primary, secondary, and tertiary industries and their proportions — be they in terms of labor force or income— are correlated with per capita income levels, the pattern which emerges from the prefectural analysis conforms with that usually derived from international comparison. This holds true not only in the industrial composition but also in the comparative productivities of the

three industries. What is different from the case of international comparison is that the labor force proportion of the secondary industry is higher in the higher per capita income prefectures. This correlation is very strong, despite the inconclusive case derived from international comparison. We have also a positive correlation between the manufacturing value-added per employee and the heavy-industry ratio.

5) In industrial prefectures located in the neighborhood of big cities or in newly developed heavy-industrial prefectures the proportion of income, which will belong to their prefectures in the total value-added by manufactures is sometimes very low. In the prefectures in which the income/gross value-added ratio is very low, the profit is sent to the head office in Tôkyô or Ôsaka and the interest or other overhead charges tend to flow outside the prefecture. This seems to be a blind spot in the current argument for regional development.

6) The regional productivity differential may emerge not only from the productivity differential in each industry but also from the regional differences of industrial structure. Based on the prefectural income statistics and the *Census of Population*, we have tried to analyze the "industrial-structure factor" in the latter sense. Furthermore, we have analyzed the "industrial-structure factor", the "size-structure factor" and the "residual-regional factor" by applying the standardization method, based upon the *Census of Manufactures*. Our results will be subject to the statistical limitations, but about 40% of the prefectural productivity differential is explained by the "industrial-structure factor" and about 25% by the "size-structure factor" and the residual can be judged as accruing from the benefit of external economies. In general, the "residual-regional factor" seems to occupy a relatively higher proportion in such places as Tôkyô, Ôsaka, Kyôto, Aichi and Kanagawa around which (or inside which) the complementary industries and the wide consumer or producer market develop to the full, benefitting from advantages of the external economies.

7)   As concerns the "size-structure factor" in the textile and machinery industries, more detailed analyses were conducted specifically, and some regional peculiarities of them were derived from them.

8)   The coefficient of variation of value-added per employee among the prefectures can be an indicator of regional differential, but that of employees an indicator of regional concentration or dispersion. Computing them by industry, cross-classified by size of establishment, we find that heavy industry, rather than the light industry, and a higher size, rather than a lower size of establishment, have higher indicators of regional differential and concentration.

1. Hokkaidō	21. Gifu	36. Tokushima
2. Aomori	22. Shizuoka	37. Kagawa
3. Iwate	23. Aichi	38. Ehime
4. Miyagi	24. Miye	39. Kōchi
5. Akita	25. Shiga	40. Fukuoka
6. Yamagata	26. Kyōto	41. Saga
7. Fukushima	27. Ōsaka	42. Nagasaki
8. Ibaragi	28. Hyōgo	43. Kumamoto
9. Tochigi	29. Nara	44. Ōita
10. Gunma	30. Wakayama	45. Miyazaki
11. Saitama	31. Tottori	46. Kagoshima
12. Chiba	32. Shimane	
13. Tōkyō	33. Okayama	
14. Kanagawa	34. Hiroshima	
15. Niigata	35. Yamaguchi	
16. Toyama		
17. Ishikawa		
18. Fukui		
19. Yamanashi		
20. Nagano		

Map of Japan

439

INDEX

INDEX

Social security benefits   58
Sophisticated goods   218
Starting wages   316, 361
Stock of crude steel   37
Stock prices   132
Subcontracting   27, 328
Surplus labor   340–349, 351
System for various reserve   18

T

Tachi, R.   164
Take-off   32, 291
Taxation   17–19
Tax System Research Council   17–19
Technological progress (innovation)
   11–13, 216
Tertiary industry   15, 357, 402
Textile industry   205–214, 292, 294,
   426–428
Transitory income ratio   72, 94
Truncated approach   313, 336
Tsuru, S.   110

U

Uchida, T.   279
Ujihara, S.   314, 344–345
Umemura, M.   14, 279, 311, 326, 341,
   347, 353
Unbalanced growth   114
Undervaluation of exchange rate
   160–165
U.S. Aid Counterpart Fund   11, 16, 23

Used equipment   26

V

Value added   172, 179, 182, 196–197
Value added per employee   172, 179,
   182
Value added ratio   194–200
Value added weights   150

W

Wage composition   59
Wage determination   316
Wage differential   24–25, 310–311,
   337–338, 359–364
Wages in big and small enterprises   65
Weber, Max   31
Working-age population   356
World Depression   290–291

Y

Yamada, R.   38
Yamada, S.   253–264
Yamanaka, T.   313, 336
Yasuba, Y.   279
Yawata Iron and Steel Mill   284
Yen   160, 163
Yokoyama, G.   266–267
Yuize, Y.   80, 84

Z

Zaibatsu   12, 32,